Reading and Writing the *Ambiente*

Reading and Writing the *Ambiente*

Queer Sexualities in Latino,
Latin American, and Spanish Culture

Edited by

Susana Chávez-Silverman
and
Librada Hernández

THE UNIVERSITY OF WISCONSIN PRESS

The University of Wisconsin Press
2537 Daniels Street
Madison, Wisconsin 53718

3 Henrietta Street
London WC2E 8LU, England

Library of Congress Cataloging-in-Publication Data
Reading and writing the ambiente: queer sexualities in Latino, Latin American,
   and Spanish culture / edited by Susana Chávez-Silverman & Librada Hernández.
      344 pp.   cm.
Includes bibliographical references and index.
   ISBN 0-299-16780-1 (cloth: alk. paper)
   ISBN 0-299-16784-4 (pbk.: alk. paper)
   1. Spanish literature—History and criticism.   2. Spanish American literature—
History and criticism.   3. Homosexuality and literature.   4. Homosexuality in
literature.   5. Literature and society—Spain.   6. Literature and society—Latin
America.   I. Chávez-Silverman, Susana.   II. Hernández, Librada.   III. Title.
PQ6041.R43   2000
860.9'353—dc21   00-008919

Contents

Preface   vii
Acknowledgments   viii

Introduction   3
Robert Richmond Ellis

Part 1. Reading Slant: Daring to Name

1. María de Zayas and Lesbian Desire in Early
   Modern Spain   21
   Sherry M. Velasco

2. Concealing Pleasures: Cross-dressers, Tribades, and
   Sodomites in Lope de Vega's *El rufián Castrucho*   43
   Harry Vélez Quiñones

3. Queer Reader/Queer Muse: Romantic Friendships,
   Sexual Identity, and Sapphic Representations in Gómez
   de Avellaneda's Poetry   62
   Librada Hernández

Part 2. Si(gh)ting the *Armario:* Restoring Visibility

4. "Para objetos solamente": The Silencing of a Voice   93
   Carmen Tisnado

5. As Invisible as He Is: The Queer Enigma of
   Xavier Villaurrutia   114
   Robert McKee Irwin

6. Alternative Identities of Gabriel(a) Mistral, 1906–1920   147
   Elizabeth Rosa Horan

Part 3. *Loca*ting Queer(s)

7. Chicanas in Love: Sandra Cisneros Talking Back and
   Alicia Gaspar de Alba "Giving Back the Wor[l]d"   181
   Susana Chávez-Silverman

8. Traveling Transgressions: *Cubanidad* in Performances
   by Carmelita Tropicana and Marga Gómez   200
   Yvonne Yarbro-Bejarano

9. Evita Perón, Juan José Sebreli, and Gender   218
   David William Foster

10. Queer Cortázar and the *Lectora Macho*   239
    Rosemary Geisdorfer Feal

Part 4. Living/Writing Queer: An Open Book

11. Looking Queer in the Autobiography of Terenci Moix   257
    Robert Richmond Ellis

12. Lesbianism, Female Homosociality, and the Maternal
    Imaginary in Montserrat Roig's *L'hora violeta*   275
    Emilie L. Bergmann

13. Arenas's *Antes que anochezca:* Autobiography of a Gay
    Cuban Dissident   299
    Emilio Bejel

Contributors   319
Index   323

Preface

Reading and Writing the Ambiente: *Queer Sexualities in Latino, Latin American and Spanish Culture* is a collection of works in which various paradigms of queer theory are applied to U.S. Latino, Latin American, and Spanish literary and cultural texts. It contains an introduction posing the problems and possibilities entailed in the juxtaposition of queer theorization and Latino and Hispanic texts, followed by a presentation of the chapters. These are divided into four sections: "Reading Slant: Daring to Name"; "Si(gh)ting the *Armario:* Restoring Visibility"; "*Loca*ting Queer(s)"; and "Living/Writing Queer: An Open Book." The authors in "Reading Slant: Daring to Name" attempt to read same-sex desire and its expression in texts produced before the late nineteenth-century construction of homosexual identity. Those in "Si(gh)ting the *Armario:* Restoring Visibility" interrogate modern texts in which lesbian/gay sexuality has been closeted, either within the texts themselves or through the workings of a heteronormative critical establishment. The contributors in "*Loca*ting Queer(s)," in contrast, highlight explicit literary and cultural representations of the queer. Finally, "Living/Writing Queer: An Open Book" addresses issues of lesbian and gay self-representation and the intersection of gay discourse and the discourses of AIDS.

Acknowledgments

Susana Chávez-Silverman would like to thank family, friends, and colleagues who have contributed to the making of this book: I am grateful to my research assistants at Pomona college—Elizabeth Vogel, Amy K. Wood, and Annie Mascorro. For their skill and alacrity with proofreading, I thank Anna Moore and my partner Pierre T. Rainville, who offered his support throughout the entire project. For their inspired and deligent sleuthing and other help with the cover-image search, I thank Adam Teicholz, Jean Franco, Diana Palaversich, Coco Fusco, Luis Cárcamo, David W. Foster, and most especially Paul Allotson. For his enthusiastic support from the beginning, I am most grateful to Robert Richmond Ellis. I am also very grateful to Fred Grieman, associate dean of Pomona College, for financial support of this book during the crucial final stretch.

Librada Hernández would like to do the same: I am most grateful to Robert Richmond Ellis for his continued support, for his advice, and for his contribution to the book. María Elena Francés-Benítez, I thank for her *apoyo moral* and for being a true friend. For his always wise guidance and trust in me, and for being a wonderful human being, I wish to thank Rubén Benítez. My colleagues Paul Harper and Carmen Salazar at Los Angeles Valley College were very supportive in the final stages of the project. Most valuable was the support I have received from my partner Mary Power. For his judicious reading and reviewing of the manuscript, I thank Anthony P. Espósito. Finally I want to remember four very dear friends who are no longer with me, but whose memory has inspired me to keep working on the subject—Fintan Power, Robert Granberg, Vicente García Márquez, and Santos Torres Rosado.

Both editors would like to thank those working at or under the auspices of the University of Wisconsin Press: we are most grateful to Raphael Kadushin for his early and continued editorial enthusiasm. We also thank Robin Whitaker for her skilled editorial assistance.

Reading and Writing the *Ambiente*

Introduction

Robert Richmond Ellis

Since the late 1980s, queer theory has been applied extensively to Anglo-American writing and culture, but until recently only several major attempts have been undertaken to read Latino, Latin American, and Spanish texts from a queer, or lesbian/gay, perspective.[1] Not only have queer voices from these various traditions been silenced by mainstream national and academic criticism, but also queer theory has been constrained by its focus on Anglo-American and European paradigms of gender and sexuality. The juxtaposition of queer theory and Latino and Hispanic writing and culture is for this reason a heuristic enterprise, charting sites of difference while making possible a reconceptualization of sexuality and the ways in which sexuality can be known and represented. This is precisely the aim of the contributors to *Reading and writing the* Ambiente: *Queer Sexualities in Latino, Latin American, and Spanish Culture ("En el ambiente"* is an expression of lesbian and gay self-affirmation meaning "in the environment"): to bring queer theory to the Latino/Hispanic lesbian and gay *ambiente* and to engage queer theory from the vantage point of the *ambiente* itself. This latter proposal in fact entails an epistemological shift, for whereas Anglo-American conceptions of sex and gender derive largely from an ontology of individual identity, the *ambiente* is a common space arising through a reciprocity of praxes. Although in the Anglo-American setting the mutual recognition of lesbian and gay sexuality can lead to the constitution of a community, one is, strictly speaking, lesbian or gay regardless of whether one is positioned inside the closet or out. The *ambiente,* in contrast, can be experienced only collectively, even if this collectivity is initially private. Reading the *ambiente* is hence less an act of "outing" than of "joining" in a process of generating a social space and infusing it with a sexuality of inclusiveness. Such a reading shares affinities with lesbian/gay and queer criticisms as these have been typically conceived, but is not wholly reducible to either mode.

Lesbian/gay criticism aims to make visible a sexual identity that has been closeted within the text or through the workings of a heteronormative critical establishment complicitous with the erasure of lesbian and gay sexuality. It "outs" the text, and at times the author as well, and in so doing replicates the coming-out metanarrative of modern lesbian and gay discourse. Lesbian/gay critique thus presupposes the existence of a potential but nonetheless real essence of sexual identity, the meaning of which is manifested through the teleological structure of an "orientation." Queer critique differs from lesbian/gay critique, not only because of its emphasis on the constructedness of sexuality, but also because it examines the mechanisms through which sexuality can be discerned and known at all. It turns first from heteroconfigurations to those marked "queer" or different and turns subsequently to the queerness or difference within all sexualities. Ultimately, however, it turns on itself, questioning the very epistemological structure implied by an ontology of identity. Lesbian/gay critique struggles to intervene in and change an oppressive social system; queer critique, with its underpinnings in postmodernist social theory and poststructuralist literary theory, seeks to expose this system in its entirety as a system (Bredbeck). But queer critique is also an engaged, activist practice that was developed, at least in part, as a response to the AIDS crisis. As Lauren Berlant and Michael Warner remark:

AIDS made those of us who confronted it realize the deadly stakes of discourse; it made us realize the public and private unvoiceability of so much that mattered, about anger, mourning, and desire; it made us realize that different frames of reference—science, news, religion, ordinary homophobia—compete and that their disjunction is lethal. (345)

The all too frequent charge of lesbian/gay essentialism is of course problematic, since it homogenizes the multiple positions and aims of lesbian and gay-male praxes. Nevertheless, both lesbian/gay and queer modes of analysis can pose problems for readers of Latino, Latin American, and Spanish writing. The lesbian/gay approach, on the one hand, tends to operate within a gay/straight binary opposition, in which the homosexual term has been suppressed by the heterosexual. Yet in a number of Latino and Hispanic texts, the overdetermining sexual binary is not gay/straight but feminine/masculine. Reinaldo Arenas, for example, sees the "gay" male as inherently feminine and rejects the Anglo-American equation of orientation with identity as ill-conceived and unauthentic. An uninformed gay reading of his life-writing might thereby obscure its "truth" and subsume it within a North American sexual (and, by extension, political) hegemony. Queer theory might seem better suited to the task of reading Latino and Hispanic writing, since its fundamental interrogation of sexual identity in principle decenters Anglo-European configurations of sexuality. But as an avatar of postmodernism, queer theory also occupies an uneasy position vis-á-vis Latin America. Some Latin American(ist)s regard postmodernism as an accessory of Anglo-European dominance, maintaining that it undermines the foundation necessary for the production of an oppositional subjectivity and an oppositional politics (see García-Moreno 66). And though Latin Americans, and even the Spanish for that matter, do not share a common ethnic or cultural identity or engage in a single, overarching historical project, the pairing of Latin America and postmodernism is difficult given the region's uneven and incomplete modernity.

Others have actually suggested that Latin America is postmodern *avant la lettre,* since its "modern" history begins, through the process of *mestizaje* (miscegenation), with a disruption of the fundamental binary oppositions (same/different, metropolitan/peripheral, European/indigenous, etc.) through which modernity is constructed (see García-Moreno 68, n. 7). The same could also be said of Spain, where modern national identity, forged through centuries of reconquest, is itself a kind of hybrid. A postmodern interrogation, again *avant la lettre,* might thus be detected in the culturally Semiticized writers of the late medieval and early modern periods. Such notions, nevertheless, dehistoricize the postmodern, and in fact the "Latin American postmodern" is split between what Nelly Richard calls a rhetoric of difference and a politics of difference (456), each of which depends on the provenance ("foreign" or "indigenous") of the postmodernist model in question.

This split between the rhetorical and the political is less apparent in lesbian and gay Latino and Hispanic writers to the extent that they tend to situate same-sex desire in terms of concrete material conditions. In Arenas's *Arturo, la estrella más brillante* (published in English as *The Brightest Star*), for instance, the Cuban gay male not only occupies the lowest rung in the hierarchy of power but is also relegated to a forced-labor camp and made to work as a virtual slave, harvesting sugarcane and thereby producing the primary commodity on which the national economy is founded. The *ambiente* of this camp is characterized by scarcity (of adequate food, water, medicine, and shelter) and by violence. In his "free" time Arturo is encouraged to cultivate stereotypically feminine behavior and to submit to the sexual demands of a hypermasculinized soldier-guard. Sex in this context is thus a means of further atomizing a class of unpaid workers and rendering them more passive.

Sexual difference in Latino and Hispanic writing is also often inflected by race and ethnicity. This is, in fact, the case in the first extended representation of gay-male sexuality in Latin American literary history, *Bom-crioulo,* by Brazilian novelist Adolfo Caminha. More recent Spanish representations of lesbian and gay sexuality are frequently marked by ethnic alterity, especially in the Catalan-identified writers at the forefront of Spain's contemporary lesbian- and gay-rights movement. In the writing of Juan Goytisolo, sexual dissidence is explicitly conjoined with a political and cultural subversion which is originally intended to sabotage the power of the Francoist state but which ultimately leads to the articulation of a complex border site of sexual, linguistic, cultural, and ethnic difference. This space is even more thoroughly delineated by recent Chicana writers, including Gloria Anzaldúa, Sandra Cisneros, Cherríe Moraga, and Alicia Gaspar de Alba.

As numerous commentators have observed, Latino and Hispanic writing typically highlights the performative rather than the identity aspects of lesbian and gay sexuality. In the conventional scheme of Latino-male sexual relations, which José Piedra reads in the context of the discourse of colonization, the so-called *activo* enacts a masculinity irreducible to homosexuality. The *pasivo,* in contrast, through his perceived passivity, is endowed with the essence of the feminine and, when such vocabulary is employed, with the identity of homosexuality. In this way male homoeroticism is subsumed within gender. Yet homoeroticism also reveals, despite the rigor with which the masculine/feminine binary is enforced, the very constructedness of gender and how gender can be dissociated from the seeming fixity of biological sex. What is more, though the male assumption of femininity is stereotypically regarded as a *surrender* of power, male femininity is frequently asserted, in texts such as Manuel Puig's *El beso de la mujer araña* (published in English as *Kiss of the Spider Woman*), as a *subversion* of power. The inversion of gender roles depicted in female relations is nevertheless of even greater consequence, given the virtual invisibility of female sexuality in traditional Spanish and Latin American writing. In nineteenth-century Spain, for example, lesbian sexuality becomes discernable when writers such as Gertrudis Gómez de Avellaneda adopt a male-gendered poetic voice in addressing their female friends. This "transvoicing," as Librada Hernández puts it, leads not only to an elucidation of a lesbian discourse but also to a de-essentialization of the feminine gender role, which has historically worked to oppress both lesbian and straight women as well as feminized gay men.

Lesbian and gay sexuality emerged in Spanish and Latin American writing long before the invention of modern homosexuality in the late nineteenth century. As Sherry Velasco reminds us in "María de Zayas and Lesbian Desire in Early Modern Spain," the term "lesbian" is not new, having appeared in various written documents of the early modern period. Although defined as a "silent sin" (the *peccatum mutum*), lesbian sexuality was, according to Velasco, more vocal and more visible than traditional Golden Age criticism would have us believe. To a certain degree, Zayas reiterates the prevailing sexual ideology of her day, exposing and condemning sex between men, as she does in *La burlada Aminta* (Aminta deceived), while withholding lesbian sex from view, as well as from possible censure. Yet as Velasco demonstrates, Zayas frequently insinuates lesbian desire into her writing through the medium of female transvestism. Velasco further argues not only that lesbian sexuality is implicit in much of the female cross-dressing of Golden Age writing and theater but also that readers and spectators of the time were aware of the queer subtexts and were actually aroused by them. The stories of Zayas are, in fact, remarkable as much for the expression of lesbian desire as for the positive response this desire elicits within the texts—from other women (both Laurela in *Amar sólo por vencer* [Love for the sake of conquest] and Aminta in *La burlada Aminta*); from the family and society (through the figures of the father and the maids in *La burlada Aminta*); and from the icons of the religion itself. These challenges to patriarchal society are not unique to Zayas, and as Velasco points out, a model of her *mujer varonil,* or "manly woman" (a term often applied to Zayas by her own contemporaries), is perhaps Catalina de Erauso, whose "autobiography" contains some of the most forthright representations of lesbian desire in early modern Spain. At the conclusion of the *Desengaños amorosos* (published in English as *The Disenchantments of Love*), Zayas affirms a utopian space for women, which Velasco reads as a lesbian utopia. In so doing Velasco reveals the queer ambiguities and possibilities of a text that even recent feminist criticism of Zayas has chosen to overlook or instead to reduce to a mere rescription of Neoplatonism.

Though the cross-dressers in most Golden Age texts are female, their drag at times functions to make visible lesbian as well as male homoerotic desire. In "Concealing Pleasures: Cross-dressers, Tribades, and Sodomites in Lope de Vega's *El rufián Castrucho*" (Castrucho the pimp), Harry Vélez Quiñones shows how in certain instances Golden Age theater comes remarkably close to unraveling heterosexual patriarchy. Almost the entire cast of *El rufián Castrucho* is composed of sexually ambiguous characters.

The pimp, Castrucho, is defined as "medio mujer" (half a woman), while the prostitute Fortuna, whom he eventually marries, dons the drag of a soldier and pursues another woman who is dressed as a man. Because Fortuna is a prostitute, she is presumed to be syphilitic, and it is feared that through a bodily excretion she might contaminate her borrowed garb. As in the age of AIDS, then, sexual nonconformity in the early modern period is similarly conflated with disease and posited as a threat to the health of the body politic, symbolized in the Lope play by the quintessential masculine garment, the military uniform. Whereas lesbian desire is insinuated through Fortuna, male homoeroticism is evoked when Castrucho has two women who are dressed as men and are perceived as such then "re-dress" as women and engage in sex with two soldiers. The soldiers are subsequently informed that their sex partners are "men," which surprises them but leads to no condemnation of what, from their perspective and that of Castrucho, amounts to an act of sodomy. For this reason *El rufián Castrucho* can be read as a quasi affirmation of male homoeroticism. Nonetheless, it is also implicated in patriarchy to the extent that Castrucho exploits both the female prostitute and the women that he employs as male hustlers. As Vélez Quiñones explains, the Golden Age representation of cross-dressing works to "mend" heterosexual patriarchy and contain its underlying instabilities. But through its twisted layering of clothing and its refabrication of gender and sex, it also discloses the unsettled and unsettling cultural tensions of the period and provides at least a glimmer of male and female homoerotic desire.

These Golden Age texts reveal an *ambiente* imbued with queer desires that move between and across gender lines but that have not yet coalesced into distinct sexual orientations. On the one hand, this sexual fluidity suggests a certain social tolerance for difference, especially in instances of cross-dressing and the ostensible performance of gender. But tolerance in the early modern period is the counterpart of a refusal to recognize the reality of same-sex desire, and as Velasco clarifies with regard to lesbian sexuality, homoeroticism can be voiced only insofar as it is emptied of meaning. In keeping with the rigorous phallocentric ideology in force, it acquires the status of the real only when expressed through penetration (of a man by a man or a woman by a woman) but it is then radically derealized as a sin such that it cannot even be named. Ultimately, same-sex penetration is seen as a gratuitous act of evil unrelated to homosexual motivation. As Rafael Carrasco indicates in his study of the persecution of sodomites under the Spanish Inquisition, inquisitors, as recorded in the annals of the Valencia tribunals, never once interrogated the accused about their sexual preferences or questioned if their sexual practices were exclusively homoerotic (134). During the nineteenth century, this theological conception of sex was gradually supplanted by biological and psychological discourses of deviance, and the apparatus was set in motion for what was to become a far more thorough policing of homoerotic activity. From the outset, however, those who came to be known as homosexuals were also agents of their identity.

In "Queer Reader/Queer Muse: Romantic Friendships, Sexual Identity, and Sapphic Representations in Gómez de Avellaneda's Poetry," Hernández locates in the nineteenth-century poems of Avellaneda not only a representation of lesbian desire but the very genesis of modern homosexual identity in Hispanic writing. Like traditional Zayas critics, those of nineteenth-century Spanish letters have been disinclined to read the passionate friendships recorded by women of the period as lesbian. Hernández, in contrast, by analyzing the Sapphic intertexts in the poetry of Avellaneda, is able to demonstrate how the poet achieves authorial power and, more important, how she asserts a lesbian identity by (re)investing the figure of Sappho with a lesbian sexuality erased by contemporary male writers bent on portraying her as a tragic heterosexual lover. According to Hernández, Sappho's suicidal leap is reconfigured in the poetry of Avellaneda as a rejection of heterosexual love for the love of women. Although the trajectory of this discursive gesture is fraught with textual aporias and ends in a coda of silence, the poetic narrator manages to utter the name of Sappho as she bestows a kiss on her loved one. This, then, is a love that dares for the first time in Spanish literature to speak its name. The poetry of Avellaneda is significant, nevertheless, in the history of both same-sex desire and gender, for just as it inscribes a protolesbian identity, so too does it reinscribe women as agents of their own sexuality. While this reinscription might be read as a masculinization of the feminine (like Zayas, Avellaneda was herself labeled a *mujer varonil*), it also shows how all sexual and gender identities exist solely to the extent that they are enacted, despite the efforts of a repressive ideology to reify and control them.

In modern heterosexual writing and criticism, homosexuality is conceived of antithetically, not as a fully integrated being, but as the negative contrary through which heterosexuality and its attendant powers are affirmed. As a consequence, lesbian and gay-male lives are often inscribed as invisible and silent. The aim of the chapter by Carmen Tisnado, "'Para objetos solamente': The Silencing of a Voice," is to examine this process of inscription. She takes as her case study the short story "Para objetos solamente" (For objects only) of Uruguayan writer Mario Benedetti. Here the narrator, in keeping with the rhetorical distinctions established by Gerard Genette, simply "shows" the action, while the reader is left to "tell" it and enunciate its meaning. In and of themselves the various objects enumerated in the text signify nothing. But by piecing them together, and in particular by juxtaposing the two fragments of a torn letter, the reader begins to articulate the suicide of a gay man. The tear in the letter can in fact be taken as the rupture of a "normal" sexuality, wrought through the character's "deviant" desire but reintegrated as the reader constitutes his body as both homosexual and feminine (through the encoding of his clothing) and in the end as dead. This equation of homosexuality with death will have tremendous repercussions in later generations of writers confronted with the contingencies of AIDS. Benedetti, who frequently assumes the voice of the silenced, exposes the persecution of gays through what amounts to a murder in which the victim is his own executioner. Yet Benedetti unwittingly reiterates the silencing discourse of gay oppression, both by depriving the gay subject of a voice of his own and by obliging the reader, through a subtle rhetorical game, to adopt what Tisnado, following Foucault, denotes as a panoptical, heterosexual gaze. As a result, we are made to erase the gay *ambiente* without ever even clearly perceiving it. The queer reading of Tisnado hence urges us to question our position as readers vis-à-vis the text while providing us with the means to formulate a story different from those produced by the ostensibly impartial but nonetheless heteronormative representations of the world.

Gay sexuality is silenced not only by the author, as occurs in the writing of Benedetti, but also by what Robert McKee Irwin, on the basis of his reading of Sylvia Molloy, identifies as the "homosexual panic" of the critic. This panic, he maintains, is more apparent in critics of Latin American and third-world writing than in those of Anglo-American literature. In his chapter, "As Invisible as He Is: The Queer Enigma of Xavier Villaurrutia," he calls on professional readers, and by extension all those engaged in Latin American and postcolonial studies, to recognize their own complicity in the enforcement of heteronormativity and their concomitant blindness to the very real sexual diversity of Latin American cultures. His primary aim is to disclose and interrogate the homoerotic meanings of Villaurrutia's poetry. To do this, he invokes Eve Kosofsky Sedgwick's model of the closet as a binary structure through which one can be both "in" and "out" and shows how Villaurrutia's homosexuality is at once visible and invisible, knowable and unknowable. Homosexuality is the logic of Villaurrutia's writing, but it is a logic that resists textual incarnation. Thus, as Irwin notes, Villaurrutia fills his poems with body parts (lips, fingers, shoulders, thighs) but never with an organic whole, much less a unity of ego. Moreover, though homosexuality is ever present in his work, it is neither a defining principle nor an instrument of totalization. The thrust of Villaurrutia's writing is suggestive of the process of homographesis elucidated by Lee Edelman. Yet, whereas homographesis involves an inscription/description of homosexual identity, what Villaurrutia ostensibly inscribes is silence. To the extent that this silence is "described," a sexuality unspeakable within his cultural milieu fleetingly enters our ken. This sexuality, as Irwin explains through his analysis of the poem "Nocturno de la estatua" (Nocturn of the statue), is neither wholly masculine nor wholly feminine but, for lack of a better word, "queer." For those "in the know," Villaurrutia's poetry has always been gay. But by juxtaposing it with queer theory, Irwin reveals the sexuality of Villaurrutia from the outside, and in so doing "outs" the not-so-hidden homophobia of traditional critical practice.

According to Elizabeth Rosa Horan in "Alternative Identities of Gabriel(a) Mistral, 1906–1920," the life and writing of Gabriela Mistral has been similarly co-opted by a masculinist and heteronormative critical establishment. Horan detects in the poetry of Mistral a queer desire, rendered visible through the disembodied imagery of her particular discourse of *modernismo* as well as through her incorporation of the gender-bending *ambiente* of the theosophy movement. Horan nevertheless chooses not to identify Mistral herself as lesbian but instead reads her representation of maternity as a female eroticism independent of male desire and as such as a quasi-lesbian poetics. Mistral was unable in her social and cultural milieu to make explicit a lesbian identity or sexuality, yet according to Horan, her depiction of the mother (in relation to the child rather than the male) functions to disengage the female body from patriarchy and thereby invokes the lesbian as the "nonwoman" in the sense of Monique Wittig, for whom woman is a body already thoroughly colonized by man. For Horan, then, Mistral's writing is in fact a significant moment in the construction of Latin American lesbianism.

The maternal figure of Mistral is asserted in opposition to both masculinity and femininity as interlocking binaries. This imagined mother occupies an intermediate zone, often highlighted by Chicana writers in an attempt to subvert oppressive lines of demarcation and identity and to generate a polysemous border region of hybridity and difference. According to Susana Chávez-Silverman in her chapter, "Chicanas in Love: Sandra Cisneros Talking Back and Alicia Gaspar de Alba 'Giving Back the Wor[l]d,'" lesbian Chicana writers are particularly inclined to situate themselves within a border space. In the heterosexual poetry of Cisneros, Chávez-Silverman discerns an act of "self-tropicalization" that gives expression to Chicana sexuality by reversing the valency of such traditional binary oppositions as virgin/whore. Yet because Cisneros fails to recognize the problem of the underpinning structure of these binaries, her poetry ends by reinscribing Chicana sexuality in the limiting roles in which it has conventionally been cast in both Latino and Anglo cultures. Chávez-Silverman thus questions the conclusion of the poetic voice of the poem

"Loose Woman," which confidently proclaims: "I break things." The lesbian poetry of Gaspar de Alba, in contrast, differs not only from Cisneros's but also from much Anglo-lesbian writing in that it traces a trajectory not in the direction of a lesbian utopia but back to the border. Gaspar de Alba envisions this border as a porous geosexual region, neither "in" nor "out," as Anglo-American identity politics would have it, but "*en el umbral*," or on the threshold. The *ambiente* of the border, which Chávez-Silverman characterizes in terms of a "*fronterótica*," or "borderotics," is represented by Gaspar de Alba in the poem "Giving Back the World" through the open and connective image of the Río Grande. Here the river is not a sign of separation demanding a choice of "either/or" but a locus of inclusivity and the possibility of the freer and more generous stance of "both/and."

The border space examined by Yvonne Yarbro-Bejarano in "Traveling Transgressions: *Cubanidad* in Performances by Carmelita Tropicana and Marga Gómez" mediates both Cuban and Anglo cultural and racial identities as well as the dichotomization of *cubanidad* (Cubanness) by rightist and leftist political ideologies, which are themselves rigorously defined in terms of heteronormativity. In the performances of Marga Gómez and Carmelita Tropicana a trajectory is delineated between (and beyond) hardened sexual, cultural, and racial polarities. As a result, essentialist and constructionist notions of identity begin to blur, as when Gómez and Carmelita Tropicana enact their fathers and in so doing affirm biological bonds of ethnicity and simultaneously subvert their gender status as women. These performances are not ideal expressions of the self, since they actually produce the cultural norms they aim to challenge. But like camp, they are ambivalent gestures that permit, according to Yarbro-Bejarano, alternative imaginings of identity, and indeed of aesthetics itself, for as the title of the Carmelita Tropicana film makes eminently clear, "Your *Kunst* is your *Waffen*" (Your art is your weapon).

In "Evita Perón, Juan José Sebreli, and Gender," David William Foster applies contemporary performance theory to a rereading of the quintessential symbol of modern Argentine culture, Eva Perón, as well as to the ways she has been interpreted in literary and theoretical writing, including the existentialist-Marxist analysis of Juan José Sebreli. Foster is intrigued by how the surpluses generated by public figures like Evita lend themselves to multiple appropriations, such as that of the guerrilla movement of the 1970s ("Si Evita viviera, sería montonera" [If Evita were alive, she would be a guerrilla fighter]), and in particular that of Argentina's fledgling lesbian and gay movement of the late 1980s, as its rallying point ("Si Evita viviera, sería tortillera" [If Evita were alive, she would be a dyke]). Though no evidence exists to suggest that Evita was a lesbian, she has been portrayed throughout the decades since her death as a woman capable of defying a macho-dominated society. Her persona, moreover, as that of a parvenu, has been regarded as an obvious construction, always in excess, and for Foster a form of display coterminous with drag. The writer Copi thus depicts her, Foster says, as the drag queen's "unholy icon," and Sebreli, while attempting to read her life through the theoretical apparatus propounded by Sartre in the *Critique of Dialectical Reason,* endows her with the dimensions of an operatic heroine. Foster is therefore able to establish a connection between Evita and a certain gay sensibility and, more important, her connection with the emerging sexual dissidence of contemporary Argentine society. He furthermore reveals a need for queer theory to engage more thoroughly not only written texts but also a wide range of products of Latin American popular and political culture.

Evita might seem an obvious site of queerness, but queer dynamics often operate in the most unqueer-seeming places, such as the ostensibly sadistic, sexist, and misogynistic texts of Julio Cortázar. In "Queer Cortázar and the *lectora macho*," Rosemary Geisdorfer Feal avoids what she sees as reductionist characterizations of Cortázar's writing and shows how in fact he represents various marginalized sexualities while undoing the master dichotomies of gay/straight, perverse/normal, and pain/pleasure. Furthermore, she identifies in his writing a rhetorical duality between a sadistic and masculinized narrator and a masochistic and feminized reader, whom she cleverly repositions as an active-feminine reader—the *lectora macho.* As a result, the reader ceases to be the object of Cortázar's writing game and transforms herself from "battered reader" into "battering reader." Through her critique, Feal thus queers not merely the text but the reader as well, and in so doing empowers her as an agent of gender and sexuality.

Whereas Feal reconceptualizes the role of the reader, I, in "Looking Queer in the Autobiography of Terenci Moix," examine how a queer gaze can rework ostensibly unqueer expressions of popular culture and in particular Hollywood cinema. In *El beso de Peter Pan* (The kiss of Peter Pan), the Catalan Moix describes his childhood persona as "la perfecta imagen del jovencito colonizado" (299) [the perfect image of the colonized little lad]. This cinematic colonization preceded his birth (his mother supposedly went into labor during a screening of *Gaslight*), fixing the parameters of his alienation as a gay youth and simultaneously fomenting the context for his eventual act of defiance as an openly gay writer and autobiographer. For the young Moix, however, cinema was not an instrument of social control (or "mass culture" as propounded by the Frankfurt School), but rather, as Michael Denning writes with regard to the term "popular culture," "a contested terrain" (253). During his formative years Moix in fact both passively internalized and, through the prism of his burgeoning homoerotic desire, actively refocused the heterosexual (and heterosexist) lens of Hollywood cinema. As Frances Wyers writes of the collaborative efforts of the readers of *El beso de la mujer araña,* he ultimately "retrieves and refashions works made for indoctrination and manipulation" (181). Moix's autobiography thereby offers insight into the interconnectedness of popular culture and gay self-representation, positing gay sexuality not as an essence but as a gaze through which the seemingly natural constructions of modern heterosexual ideology are denaturalized and queered.

Moix, who undertook his autobiographical project in the wake of the liberationist years of the 1980s, manipulates the Peter Pan narrative to affirm male homoeroticism and his own identity as a gay man, even if the childhood fantasy of Peter as ideal lover eventually eludes him in adulthood. In the texts of the preeminent Catalan feminist writers, Esther Tusquets and Montserrat Roig, produced during the period of transition from fascist dictatorship to democracy in the late 1970s, lesbian desire is more ephemeral. As Emilie L. Bergmann explains in "Lesbianism, Female Homosociality, and the Maternal Imaginary in Montserrat Roig's *L'hora violeta*" (The violet hour), Tusquets associates lesbian fantasy with the myth of Peter Pan, but in *El mismo mar de todos los veranos* (The same sea of every summer) lesbian desire is limited to childhood, and when her "'Wendy' grows up, she leaves homosexuality behind." In *L'hora violeta* lesbianism is a marginal discourse, despite the effort of the narrator to recover the voice of her lost mother and define her relationship with another woman. Lesbian desire is inscribed through a dream, only to be disrupted by the intrusion of the archetypal figure of Spanish heterosexual patriarchy, Francisco Franco. But the dream of *L'hora violeta* is a potent one, disturbing the official history of life under Francoism and obfuscating the conventional taxonomies of fictional and historical discourses.

The protagonist of *L'hora violeta* aspires to reconfigure the pieces of the past through the imaginary and to effect "the revenge of literature against History," even if she ultimately realizes that this might be accomplished only through practical struggle. In the age of AIDS, literature itself becomes an instrument of survival. Indeed, gay-male autobiographers of the 1980s and 1990s are less concerned with speculations regarding the rhetorical death of the author than with their own imminent demise from disease. As I have elsewhere observed (*The Hispanic Homograph*), many gay-male life-writers have shifted their emphasis from the inscription of the *autos* to that of the *bios,* and in so doing have transformed autobiography from a vehicle for identity formation into an affirmation of life. In "Arenas's *Antes que anochezca:* Autobiography of a Gay Cuban Dissident," Emilio Bejel reads the autobiography of Arenas as an assertion of the self in the face of both AIDS and what Arenas experiences as an equally life-threatening, heterosexist political regime. Bejel marshals the deconstructionist theory of Paul de Man to argue that autobiography, as prosopopoeia, seeks to give "life to the dead" by endowing the voiceless with a voice and the faceless with a face (in the context of Arenas, the political dissident, the homosexual, and the person with AIDS), but that autobiography concomitantly "de-faces" the living by rendering them other through writing.

As Irwin has demonstrated through his reading of Villaurrutia, the inscription of homosexuality is a contradictory enterprise, and in the case of Arenas, the bios is incessantly "described" as the Thanatos. Bejel deconstructs the various binaries informing the Arenas text, chief of which is the desire/power opposition. Arenas implicitly rejects both the Freudian and Foucauldian paradigms that posit power as an external, but nevertheless requisite, condition of desire and its expression. Instead, he disengages the two, conceiving of desire as a presocial force capable of resisting and even undoing power. As Bejel's reading makes clear, however, Arenas's desire, like his idealized natural world with its polymorphous sexuality, is already mediated by power, and his first homoerotic encounter in a "natural" setting is fraught with the socially constructed guilt of the homosexual within a heterosexist society. Bejel finds the *raison d'être* of the Arenas autobiography in a crisis of authority resulting from the absence of the father figure. As autobiographer, Arenas responds to this crisis by constituting Virgilio Piñera as the "law," in the Lacanian sense. But Piñera, according to Bejel, is the dissident gay writer par excellence, and by inscribing him as the bearer of the Cuban literary tradition, Arenas's writing approaches what for Bejel is the very limit of modernity. Through dissidence, Arenas aims to recover and reaffirm the self and its history and, as Thomas Yingling indicates with regard to AIDS writers, to effect a "repair of broken subjectivity" and construct a "meaningful death" (306). Yet Arenas's modernist project in effect undoes itself through constant hyperbole in the narration of his dramatic escapes from power and his numerous sexual adventures. By pressing modernism to the edge of night, as it were, Arenas in fact begins to discern the place of the queer as an in-between zone, as Bejel puts it, that is perhaps a more viable "biosphere," or *ambiente,* for the gay male with AIDS than is the utopian realm of Arenas's nostalgic longing, which is itself shot through with the oppression and violence that he so desperately struggles to escape.

Reading and Writing the Ambiente closes on the topic of AIDS because, despite the recent development of life-prolonging therapies, AIDS still ravages Latino communities in the United States and throughout the world to a degree often exceeding that of other social and racial groups.

AIDS, moreover, has been and remains an overdetermining condition of women and gay men. As a matter of fact, it has led to a reexamination of identities based solely on sexual orientation, gender, and race, and to the formation of new coalitions. Yet AIDS continues to be posited, at least in the Western imagination, as a gay-male disease rather than as a Latino or woman's disease. Indeed, it is typically construed as the ultimate meaning of homosexuality as defined in heterosexist discourse, that is, as a moral, psychological, organic, and ontological deficiency. From this perspective the gay/AIDS *ambiente* is not an *ambiente* at all but a nonspace tantamount to death. As Juan Goytisolo writes in his AIDS fable, *Las virtudes del pájaro solitario:* "Vivíamos en un vacío de campana neumática" (20) ["We lived amid the vacuum of a bell jar" (published in English as *The Virtues of the Solitary Bird* 21)]. It is precisely to infuse this space with the conditions necessary for life, that is, to "ambientize" it, that Latino and Hispanic AIDS writers choose to write. Similarly, by engaging and joining in their vital project, readers begin to approximate the "moral position of a true reader" imagined by Severo Sarduy (206). It is the hope of the authors of this volume that their work will in some way help to delineate this position.

Note

1. Significant in this regard are the pioneering studies of Foster, *Gay and Lesbian Themes in Latin American Writing;* and Smith, *Laws of Desire.* Foster compiled the first sourcebook, *Latin American Writers on Gay and Lesbian Themes;* and Smith, along with Bergmann, edited the first collection of essays, ¿Entiendes? *Queer Readings, Hispanic Writings.* More recent collections include Foster and Reis, *Bodies and Biases;* Balderston and Guy, *Sex and Sexuality in Latin America;* and Molloy and Irwin, *Hispanisms and Homosexualities.*

Works Cited

Arenas, Reinaldo. *Arturo, la estrella más brillante.* Barcelona: Montesinos, 1984.

Arenas, Reinaldo. *The Brightest Star.* Trans. Andrew Hurley *Old Rosa: A Novel in Two Stories.* New York: Grove P, 1989. 45–104.

Balderston, Daniel, and Donna J. Guy, eds. *Sex and Sexuality in Latin America.* New York: New York UP, 1997.

Bergmann, Emilie L., and Paul Julian Smith, eds. ¿Entiendes? *Queer Readings, Hispanic Writings.* Durham: Duke UP, 1995.

Berlant, Lauren, and Michael Warner. "What Does Queer Theory Teach Us about *X?*" *PMLA* 110.3 (1995): 343–49.

Bredbeck, Gregory W. "The New Queer Narrative: Intervention and Critique." *Textual Practice* 9.3 (1995): 477–502.

Caminha, Adolfo. *Bom-crioulo: Texto integral.* São Paulo: Atica, 1983.

Carrasco, Rafael. *Inquisición y represión sexual en Valencia: Historia de los sodomitas (1565–1735).* Barcelona: Laertes, 1985.

Copi. *Plays.* Trans. Anni Lee Taylor. London: John Calder, 1976.

de Man, Paul. "Autobiography as De-Facement." *Modern Language Notes* 94 (1979): 919–30.

Denning, Michael. "The End of Mass Culture." *Modernity and Mass Culture.* Ed. James Naremore and Patrick Brantlinger. Bloomington: Indiana UP, 1991. 253–68.

Edelman, Lee. *Homographesis: Essays in Gay Literary and Cultural Theory.* New York: Routledge, 1994.

Ellis, Robert Richmond. *The Hispanic Homograph: Gay Self-Representation in Contemporary Spanish Autobiography.* Champaign-Urbana: U of Illinois P, 1997.

Foster, David William. *Gay and Lesbian Themes in Latin American Writing.* Austin: U of Texas P, 1991.

Foster, David William. *Latin American Writers on Gay and Lesbian Themes: A Biocritical Sourcebook.* Westport, Conn.: Greenwood, 1994.

Foster, David William, and Roberto Reis, eds. *Bodies and Biases: Sexualities in Hispanic Cultures and Literature.* Minneapolis: U of Minnesota P, 1996.

García-Moreno, Laura. "Situating Knowledges: Latin American Readings of Postmodernism." *Diacritics* 25.1 (1995): 63–80.

Genette, Gerard. *Narrative Discourse.* Ithaca: Cornell UP, 1980.

Goytisolo, Juan. *Las virtudes del pájaro solitario.* Barcelona: Seix Barral, 1988.

Goytisolo, Juan. *The Virtues of the Solitary Bird.* Trans. Helen Lane. London: Serpent's Tail, 1991.

Moix, Terenci. *El beso de Peter Pan.* Vol. 2 of *El Peso de la Paja: Memorias.* Barcelona: Plaza y Janés, 1993.

Molloy, Sylvia. "Too Wilde for Comfort: Desire and Ideology in *Fin-de-siècle* Latin America." *Negotiating Lesbian and Gay Subjects.* Ed. Monica Dorenkamp and Richard Henke. New York: Routledge, 1995. 35–52.

Molloy, Sylvia, and Robert Irwin, eds. *Hispanisms and Homosexualities.* Durham: Duke UP, 1998.

Piedra, José. "Nationalizing Sissies." *¿Entiendes? Queer Readings, Hispanic Writings.* Ed. Emilie L. Bergmann and Paul Julian Smith. Durham: Duke UP, 1995. 370–409.

Puig, Manuel. *El beso de la mujer araña.* Barcelona: Seix Barral, 1976.

Puig, Manuel *Kiss of the Spider Woman.* Trans. Thomas Colchie. New York: Vintage, 1980.

Richard, Nelly. "The Latin American Problematic of Theoretical-Cultural Transference: Postmodern Appropriations and Counter-appropriations." *South Atlantic Quarterly* 92.3 (1993): 453–59.

Sarduy, Severo. "The Explosion of Emptiness." Trans. Suzanne Jill Levine. *Life Sentences: Writers, Artists, and AIDS.* Ed. Thomas Avena. San Francisco: Mercury House, 1994. 197–207.

Sartre, Jean-Paul. *Critique of Dialectical Reason, Theory of Practical Ensembles.* Trans. Alan Sheridan-Smith. Ed. Jonathan Rée. London: Verso/NLB, 1982.

Sebreli, Juan José. *Eva Perón: ¿Adventurera o militante?* 4th ed., ampl. Buenos Aires: Editorial La Pleyade, 1971.

Sedgwick, Eve Kosofsky. *Epistemology of the Closet.* Berkeley: U of California P, 1990.

Smith, Paul Julian. *Laws of Desire: Questions of Homosexuality in Spanish Writing and Film 1960–1990.* Oxford: Clarendon, 1992.

Tusquets, Esther. *El mismo mar de todos los veranos.* Barcelona: Editorial Lumen, 1978.

Wittig, Monique. "One Is Not Born a Woman." *The Lesbian and Gay Studies Reader.* Ed. Henry Abelove, Michèle Aina Barale, and David M. Halperin. New York: Routledge, 1993. 103–9.

Wyers (Weber), Frances. "Manuel Puig at the Movies." *Hispanic Review* 49.2 (1981): 163–81.

Yingling, Thomas. "AIDS in America: Postmodern Governance, Identity, and Experience." *Inside/Out: Lesbian Theories, Gay Theories.* Ed. Diana Fuss. New York: Routledge, 1991. 291–310.

Part 1

Reading Slant: Daring to Name

1

María de Zayas and Lesbian Desire in Early Modern Spain

Sherry M. Velasco

Seldom contested in Zayas criticism is the textual preference for the exclu-
sionary community of women in the climactic finale of the *Desengaños
amorosos* (1647) (published in English as *The Disenchantments of Love*),
which articulates the protagonist's decision to reject marriage as a separatist utopian space for women only. However, because this homosocial resolution, with its emphatic challenge to all women to eliminate men and
heterosexual relations from their lives, does not specify how desire functions in this nonheteronormative system, the reader is allowed to consider
multiple options, depending on his or her own tastes and experiences. By
contextualizing María de Zayas's work in terms of a queer(ed) position,
which invites a reading of the text from perspectives that disrupt heterobiased discourses, this study questions the author's portrayal of same-sex
desire in comparison to other early modern depictions of female homoeroticism and then shows how these representations function in her two
best-selling collections of framed novellas, the *Novelas amorosas y ejemplares* (1637) (published in English as *The Enchantments of Love: Amourous
and Exemplary Novels*) and the *Desengaños amorosos*.[1] In two of Zayas's
novellas, *Amar sólo por vencer* (Love for the sake of conquest) and *La burlada Aminta y venganza del honor* (Aminta deceived and honor's revenge),
the author engages various arguments that defend desire among women.[2]
At the same time, however, despite the consistent defense of same-sex love

between women, these plots may also be read as normative within dominant discourses, since they, initially at least, appear to be based on patriarchal constructions of female homoeroticism rather than on transgressive expressions of lesbian subjectivity. Nonetheless, within the possibilities of orthodox representations of lesbian behavior in early modern Spain, an analysis of how Zayas's text portrays female homoeroticism compared with its depiction of male homosexuality leads the reader to reconsider the "normative" function of same-sex desire in the text.

Desire between Women during the Early Modern Period

Most critics maintain that there was a more general awareness of male than of female homosexuality in early modern Spain. The existence of fewer documented cases during this period that involve woman-to-woman genital contact than those involving male sodomy seems to confirm this belief. Despite the tendency to minimize lesbian relations, nonetheless, philosophers, lawmakers, and theologians had discussed the possibility of their occurrence for centuries.[3] As Louis Crompton points out, the "Spanish seem to have been preeminent in Renaissance Europe as specialists on the subject of lesbianism and the law" (18). Crompton notes the importance of Gregorio López's 1556 revision of *Las siete partidas,* which argued that the medieval Spanish law on sodomy applied to women as well as to men.

In the late sixteenth century Pierre Brantôme (1540–1614) referred to lesbian women as "two ladies that be in love one with the other, . . . sleeping together in one bed" (128–29). He also points out the increasing popularity of sexual encounters between women, especially in Spain, Italy, Turkey, and France.[4] Describing what were also called *donna con donna,* tribades, and fricatrices, Brantôme concluded that lesbian relations may be less sinful than heterosexual affairs outside the confines of matrimony:

Still excuse may be made for maids and widows for loving these frivolous and empty pleasures, preferring to devote themselves to these than to go with men and come to dishonour, . . . they do not so much offend God, and are not such great harlots, as if they had to do with the men, maintaining there is a great difference betwixt throwing water in a vessel and merely watering about it and round the rim. . . . this alone will make no man cuckold. (133–34)

This apparent tolerance of desire between women is presumably based on a male-centered view of female sexuality that assumes that sexually transgressive acts must involve penetration by the phallus or its imitation. As a result, sexual relations between women have been silenced or minimized in many early modern as well as contemporary commentaries. In the sixteenth century, Gregorio López called female sodomy the "silent sin" (*peccatum mutum*) or "the sin which cannot be named" (qtd. in Brown, "Lesbian" 75). Judith Brown argues that even though lesbian sexuality was considered a sin and a crime in early modern Europe, it did not receive the attention given to male homosexuality during the same period, since the European view of human sexuality was phallocentric; it was difficult to believe that women could be more attracted to other women than to men (*Immodest* 6). The notion that lesbian desire was not taken seriously or was not threatening is also supported by Rudolf M. Dekker and Lotte C. van de Pol in their study of female transvestism in early modern Europe: "In spite of the prescribed death penalty for tribady, amorous relationships between women, even when these were coupled with physical caresses, were rarely viewed as serious throughout Europe" (57). Other critics, nonetheless, question the assumption that passion between women was widely tolerated. Emma Donoghue argues that "seventeenth- and eighteenth-century words do not seem to refer only to isolated sexual acts, as is often claimed, but to the emotions, desires, styles, tastes and behavioral tendencies that can make up an identity" (3).

Cultural documents from the early modern period indicate that there are, in fact, numerous examples of female homoeroticism in literature, theater, legal proceedings, medical treatises, pornographic pictures, songs, and anecdotes.[5] Fictional scenes of same-sex attraction between women, even though they most often end with a heterobiased resolution, can be found in works such as Montemayor's *La Diana*, Rojas's *La Celestina*, Ariosto's *Orlando furioso*, Villalón's *El Crótalon de Cristóforo Gnofoso*, Cubillo de Aragón's play *Añasco el de Talavera*, Pérez de Montalbán's play *La monja alférez*, the poetry of Sor Violante del Cielo,[6] and so forth. Whether or not these images of passion between women were intended as mere titillation for male readers/spectators, the effect of such images put forth the idea of women as the objects of desire for other women.[7] Referring to sex between women in early modern Europe, Ian McCormick concludes that "we should not rule out the possibility that female readers experimented themselves in the light of such episodes, or that they found a measure of legitimation in these textual/sexual encounters" (176–78).

Historical episodes, on the other hand, do not always mirror the traditional patriarchal plots that are so frequent in fictional works. Cases such as that of Elena de Céspedes (Eleno/Elena) and Catalina de Erauso (La Monja Alférez) provide valuable clues to the popular, legal, and religious attitudes toward early modern transgenderism in Spain.[8] While Céspedes was punished for having married another woman while living as a man,

Erauso was rewarded for her transgenderism by the king of Spain and by the pope, because it was proved that she was a virgin, despite stories of romantic relationships with other women. Interestingly, it seems probable that in *El juez de su causa* (Judge thyself), Zayas used Erauso (more commonly known as La Monja Alférez) as her inspiration for Estela, who, like the historical "Lieutenant Nun," dons male garb, enlists as a soldier, and is ultimately more successful as a heroic warrior than many men are. Considering that most seventeenth-century versions of the "Monja Alférez" story (in news pamphlets, letters, Pérez de Montalbán's play *La monja alférez,* Castillo Solórzano's picaresque novel *Aventuras del Bachiller Trapaza,* and so forth) include references to Erauso's presumed lesbian identity, it could be argued that, despite the heterosexual plot in *El juez,* the early modern reader would have provided a simultaneous queer reading of Zayas's narrative, given that many of the details of Estela's story conjure images of the transgender Erauso.[9] According to Alicia Yllera, seventeenth-century readers would have made the connection between Estela and Erauso, which also would have made Zayas's story more believable in their minds (Zayas, *Desengaños* 41).

Amar sólo por vencer

Perhaps the most extensive explicit discussion of lesbian desire in Zayas's work is found in *Amar sólo por vencer.* In this novella, Esteban, disguising himself as a woman, transforms himself into "Estefanía" in order to gain access to his love interest, Laurela. Despite the heterosexual motivation behind the disguise, some critics such as Inés Dolz-Blackburn see Estefanía as a spokesperson for Zayas: "Estefanía seems to transmit the opinion of the author, given the continual defense of love between women" (77). Salvador Montesa Peydro also concludes that Zayas is using Estefanía (or Esteban) to express her support for same-sex love: "The author defends love between women as less selfish and more pure than that between men and women. . . . doña María speaks with complete freedom because her ideas come from the mouth of a gentleman, and therefore free of suspicion, she can express her ideology regarding homosexual love" (208–9).

Clearly in *Amar sólo por vencer* female homoeroticism is more acceptable than heterosexuality outside the confines of marriage. Only as Estefanía is Esteban free to display his passion for Laurela openly. Moreover, other women in this story join Estefanía in discussing the spiritual advantages of love between women. This Neoplatonic expression of same-sex desire attempts to define romantic relationships between women as chaste and therefore morally superior to the physically based heterosexual love:

El alma es toda una en varón y en la hembra, no se me da más ser hombre que mujer; que las almas no son hombres ni mujeres, y el verdadero amor en el alma está, que no en el cuerpo; y el que amare el cuerpo con el cuerpo, no puede decir que es amor, sino apetito, y de esto nace arrepentirse en poseyendo; porque como no estaba el amor en el alma, el cuerpo, como mortal, se cansa siempre de un manjar, y el alma, como espíritu, no se puede enfastiar de nada.

—Sí; mas es *amor sin provecho amar una mujer a otra* —dijo una de las criadas.

—Ese —dijo Estefanía— *es el verdadero amor, pues amar sin premio es mayor fineza.*

—Pues ¿cómo los hombres —dijo una de las hermanas de Laurela— a cuatro días que aman le piden, y si no se le dan, no perseveran?

—Porque no aman —respondió Estefanía—; que si amaran, aunque no los premiaran, no olvidaran. Que amor verdadero es el carácter del alma, y mientras el alma no muriere, no morirá el amor. . . .

—Pues según eso —dijo otra doncella—, los hombres de ahora todos deben de amar sólo con el cuerpo, y no con el alma. (*Desengaños* 317; emphasis mine)[10]

["Since the soul is the same in male and female, it matters not whether I'm a man or a woman. Souls aren't male or female and true love dwells in the soul, not in the body. One who loves the body only with the body cannot truly say that that is love; it's lust, which brings only repentance after physical satisfaction because that love wasn't in the soul. The body, being mortal, tires of its food, while the soul, being spirit, never tires of its nourishment."

"All right, but for one woman to love another woman is a fruitless love," one of the maids commented.

"No," said Estefanía, "it's true love, for loving without reward is the purest kind."

"Well how come men," asked one of Laurela's sisters, "ask for their reward after they've loved for only four short days and if they don't get it, they give up?"

"Because they don't really love," Estefanía responded; "if they did love, even unrewarded, they'd never give up. True love is the very substance of the soul and so long as the soul doesn't die, love won't die. Since the soul is immortal, so love will be also. But in loving only with the body, if they don't enjoy the body, they'll soon desist and forget and go seek satisfaction elsewhere. If they do attain their ends, surfeited, they move on to seek more of the same elsewhere."

"Well, if that's the way it is," said another maid, "then nowadays men must all love just with the body and not with the soul."] (*Disenchantments* 224)[11]

The Neoplatonic defense of love between women, then, attempts to distance female homoeroticism from corporeal lust. The assumption is that lesbian attraction is "amor sin provecho" [fruitless love] and "amar sin premio" [love without reward]. Consequently, true (same-sex) love between women does not yield the *provecho* and *premio* associated with phallic-based carnal lust. Regardless of intention, Estefanía's arguments protect lesbian desire from attack, since this seemingly "nonphysical" love is exempt from scrutiny on the basis of honor and chastity.

Despite its insistence on the spiritual nature of same-sex love between women, the text emphasizes Estefanía's physical attraction for Laurela: "Estefanía con su señora, asistiéndola hasta que se puso en la cama, gozando sus ojos, . . . juzgando a Laurela aún más linda desnuda que vestida" (*Desengaños* 309). ["Estefanía went with her mistress to attend her until she was tucked in. By virtue of the deception, her eyes enjoyed sights they could never have seen had it not been for her false disguise. Finding Laurela far more beautiful undressed than dressed . . ." (*Disenchantments* 217).] Although only the reader knows that Estefanía is actually Esteban, the other household members are well aware of the nature of Estefanía's passion for Laurela, without the privileged knowledge of the cross-dresser's true identity.

Ultimately, the reaction of others provides an important indication of the attitude toward female homoeroticism in Zayas's text. When those close to Laurela believe that Estefanía is a woman passionately in love with her, their reaction is jovial, for they find amusement at the idea of lesbian desire:

El poder de amor también se extiende de mujer a mujer, como de galán a dama. Dioles a *todas gran risa* oír a Estefanía decir esto. . . . Volviéronse a *reír todas,* confirmando el pensamiento que tenían de que Estefanía estaba enamorada de Laurela. . . . Empezaron *todas a reírse,* . . . con esto y otras *burlas* . . . *en todas ocasiones le daba a entender su amor, ella y todas* lo juzgaban a locura, antes les servía de *entretenimiento y motivo de risa,* siempre que la veían hacer extremos y finezas de amante, llorar celos y sentir desdenes, admirando que una mujer estuviese enamorada de otra, sin llegar a su imaginación que pudiese ser lo contrario. . . . empezóse a *reír.* . . . *reían todas.* (*Desengaños* 306–11; emphasis mine)

[For the power of love can also include a woman's love for another woman just as it does a suitor's love for his lady. . . . Estefanía's words followed by a deep sigh, made them all laugh at the notion that she had fallen in love with Laurela. . . . Again they all laughed, further convinced that Estefanía had fallen in love with Laurela. . . . They all burst out laughing . . . this kind of joking. . . . In spite of the fact that Estefanía was always telling her of her love, she and everyone else thought it was simply folly. It amused them and made them laugh whenever they saw her play the exaggerated and courtly role of lover, lamenting Laurela's disdain and weeping from jealousy. They were surprised that a woman could be so much in love with another woman, but it never crossed their minds that things might be other than they seemed. . . . She burst out laughing and her sisters and the other maids joined in.] (*Disenchantments* 214–25)

Apparently the idea of passionate love between women was a source of humor and entertainment for the women close to Laurela. Not surprisingly, female homoerotic passion in Álvaro Cubillo de Aragón's play *Añasco el de Talavera* elicits a similar response in Dionisa's family when they discover her love for Leonor. They "are not scandalized; they just refuse to take Dionisa seriously, and one wonders whether contemporary audiences did not react in the same way" (McKendrick 315).

The idea of lesbian desire as nonthreatening entertainment is supported by the comic element present in many female homoerotic images. The humor and erotic tension created by lesbian scenes in paintings, literature, and theater are described by many critics as a popular device used to titillate male viewers.[12] However, according to Brantôme, same-sex desire portrayed in paintings could also arouse sexual feelings in heterosexual women:

They beheld a very beautiful picture, wherein were pourtrayed a number of fair ladies naked and at the bath, which did touch, and feel, and handle, and stroke, one the other, and intertwine and fondle with each other, and so enticingly and prettily and featly did show all their hidden beauties that the coldest recluse or hermit had been warmed and stirred thereat. Wherefore did a certain great lady, as I have heard it told, and indeed I do know her well, losing all restraint of herself before the picture, say to her lover, turning toward him maddened as it were at the madness of love she beheld painted; "Too long have we tarried here. Let us now straightway take coach and so to my lodging; for that no more can I hold in the ardour that is in me. Needs must away and quench it; too sore do I burn." And so she did haste away to enjoy her faithful lover. (33)

Patricia Simons likewise demonstrates how early modern depictions of the goddess Diana bathing with her nymphs could also have an erotic effect on female viewers as well as on male spectators: "Any woman daring enough to recognize her own sexual orientation outside the norm might also have surreptitiously enjoyed some images of sensual women produced for heterosexual men, 'cross-viewing' as it were" (83). Similarly, in Zayas's text both men and women are amused by lesbian passion; the women are frequently entertained by the idea ("reían todas"), as the patriarch of the family is. Laurela's father entrusts the most intimate aspect of his daughter's care (dressing, undressing, and so forth) to a woman who has openly declared her physical attraction and love for Laurela. Despite this knowledge, Laurela's father finds the situation amusing and is clearly not worried about the family's honor: "—Bien me parece —respondió don Bernardo—, pues de tan castos amores bien podemos esperar hermosos nietos" (*Desengaños* 308) ["'That's splendid,' don Bernardo responded, 'and we can expect lovely grandchildren from such a chaste love'" (*Disenchantments* 216)]. One could assume from the father's joke here that honor, chastity, and the control of female sexuality are solely related to issues of reproduction and paternity.[13]

After returning to male garb, Esteban's comments reveal an equally phallocentric view of female sexuality. While trying to convince Laurela that he is really a man, Esteban exposes his skepticism regarding the possibility of erotic feeling between women:

—¿Es posible que has estado tan ciega que en mi amor, en mis celos, en mis suspiros y lágrimas, en los sentimientos de mis versos y canciones no has conocido que soy lo que digo y no lo que parezco? Porque, ¿quién ha visto que una dama se enamore de otra? (*Desengaños* 320; emphasis mine)

["Is it possible that you've been so blind that you haven't seen in my love in my jealousy, in my sighs and tears, in the feelings expressed in my songs and poems, that I really am what I say and not what I seem? Who's ever seen a woman fall in love with another woman?"] (*Disenchantments* 227)

Esteban is not the only character who openly questions the benefits of lesbian passion. One of the young women of the household also wonders what Estefanía plans to gain by loving another woman:

—Qué piensa sacar Estefanía de amar a mi señora Laurela, que muchas veces, a no ver su hermosura, y haberla visto algunas veces desnuda, me da una vuelta el corazón pensando que es hombre. (*Desengaños* 318)

["Of course, but what I'd like to know," the other maid commented, "is what Estefanía thinks she'll get out of loving my mistress Laurela. If I hadn't beheld her beauty and seen her a few times undressed, my heart has often leapt at the thought that she might be a man."] (*Disenchantments* 225)

One might question whether the young woman is referring to the phallocentric *provecho* or *premio* when she asks what might be gained from female homoerotic desire. The speaker implies that this passion would make sense if Estefanía were a man. However, given Estefanía's beauty, this possibility is doubtful, and, perhaps more important, the idea that Estefanía could be a man is scandalous considering that she has seen Laurela naked on numerous occasions.

Laura J. Gorfkle has examined how Esteban's cross-dressing "highlights the ambiguity and indeterminacy of gender identity and desire (sexuality) in the text of his/her body and discourse" (77).[14] This ambiguous and arbitrary nature of gender identity and desire is perhaps best enacted in Esteban/Estefanía's promise to Laurela that her identity is a choice and not a fixed entity: ". . . que Estefanía sería mientras ella gustase que no fuese don Esteban" (*Desengaños* 321) [". . . she'd be Estefanía so long as Laurela didn't want her to be don Esteban" (*Disenchantments* 228)].[15] Gorfkle concludes that Zayas's text is subversive precisely because it seeks to deprive "hegemonic culture of the claim to naturalized or essentialist (gender) identities" (86).

Nonetheless, there is no liberation for Laurela at the end of *Amar sólo por vencer*. After Laurela submits to a heterosexual affair with Esteban, her father orchestrates a violent retaliation to punish his daughter's transgression. While the patriarch of the family may have been pleasantly amused by Estefanía's passion for Laurela, he later ensures the death of his daughter to punish her for a heterosexual relationship with the same person in the form of Esteban. Likewise, when Laurela ponders such a scandalous situation ("caso tan escandaloso" [*Desengaños* 321]), she is not referring to Estefanía's lesbian desire for her but rather to a heterosexual male who is disguised as a woman in order to disrupt the private sphere of a protected virgin. The message remains clear: desire between women does not pose a threat to the patriarchal order as heterosexual love outside the legal confines of marriage does.

After engaging in physical relations with Laurela, Esteban's attitude is drastically different in comparison to Estefanía's previous declarations of love:

—Las cosas, hermosa Laurela, que se hacen sin más acuerdo que por cumplir con la sensualidad del apetito no pueden durar, y más cuando hay tanto riesgo como el que a mí me corre, sujeto al rigor de tu padre. (*Desengaños* 325)

["Beautiful Laurela, the things one does simply to satisfy one's physical appetite cannot last, particularly when they involve as much danger as I now face. I am prey to harsh revenge from your father."] (*Disenchantments* 231)

Like the Dorothy/Michael character from the popular film *Tootsie,* who declared, "I was a better man with you as a woman than I ever was with a woman as a man," Estefanía was more capable of true love than was Esteban, who knew only sexual appetite.[16] Not only does Esteban change his tune with the change of dress, but also the general tone of the story shifts from the jovial and pleasant discussion of lesbian desire to the ominous and sinister chain of events involved in heterosexual passion that results in a violent homicide. Similar to Brantôme's assessment of lesbianism compared with heterosexuality outside the confines of marriage, Zayas's story graphically demonstrates how homoerotic desire between women is preferable to the real transgressive sexual relations, which are performed with men.

La burlada Aminta y venganza del honor

As *Amar sólo por vencer* discusses attraction for partners of the same sex in chaste entertainment, so does *La burlada Aminta y venganza del honor* present homoerotic desire in these terms. Flora's declaration, "—Ya sabes que tengo el gusto y deseos más de galán que de dama, y donde las veo y más tan bellas, como esta hermosa señora, se me van los ojos tras ellas, y se me enternece el corazón" (*Novelas amorosas* 94)[17] ["'You know my tastes are more those of a gallant than of a lady, and wherever I see a lady, particularly one as beautiful as this lady, I can't take my eyes from her beauty and my heart grows tender'" (*Enchantments* 55)],[18] has typically led critics to describe her as the only woman in Zayas's work who explicitly expresses her own lesbian desire. Although I agree with this assessment, I would propose that homoerotic passion here functions in a manner quite different from what might initially be expected. If we consider Flora's comments in their context, we find that they are used by the speaker to manipulate another listener: Aminta. Again, the reaction of the listener may tell more about the role of lesbian passion than simply the potential intention of the expression of same-sex desire. First of all, although Flora is talking directly to Jacinto, her statements are clearly articulated for the benefit of the nearby Aminta. Flora audibly expresses her physical attraction to Aminta as a way of endearing herself to the latter. Aminta's reaction to Flora's declaration of lesbian desire indicates that Flora's strategy worked:

—Donde haya tanta hermosura, que es cierto que más puede dar envidia que tenerla, no sé para qué buscáis otra, pues tomando un espejo en las manos, y mirándoos en él, satisfaréis vuestros deseos, porque más os merecéis que os enamoren, que no que enamoréis. Mas por lo menos me pienso estimar desde hoy en adelante en más que hasta aquí, y enriquecerme con la merced que me hacéis, *pues de amores tan castos,* no podrá dexar de sacarse el mismo fruto; y así, os suplico me digáis qué es lo que de mí más os agrada y enamora, para que yo lo tenga en más, y me precie dello. (*Novelas amorosas* 94; emphasis mine)

["With your great beauty, which certainly should cause envy rather than suffer it, I don't know why you seek any other. If you take a mirror in your hands and look at yourself, you will satisfy all your desire. Your beauty deserves more to be loved than to love. But I shall now have higher regard for myself; I'm flattered by the favor you've shown me because pure love gives pure fruit. I beg you, please tell me what it is in me that most pleases and delights you so that I may esteem it more and prize it in myself."] (*Enchantments* 56)

Far from being scandalized or even surprised, Aminta is clearly flattered by Flora's attraction to her. Reminiscent of the comments expressed by Laurela's father in *Amar sólo para vencer,* Aminta assumes that this same-sex passion is chaste and does not pose a threat to her honor "because pure love gives pure fruit." Despite Aminta's belief that Flora prefers women, comments made by the narrator lead the reader to another conclusion. We soon learn that Flora's flattering statements about Aminta were designed to trick her: "Diestramente iba la cauta Flora poniendo lazos a la inocente Aminta para traela a suma perdición. . . . Disimuló

Flora su mentira con tantas muestras de verdad, que no fué mucho que Aminta la creyese" (*Novelas amorosas* 95). ["With great skill, the crafty Flora gradually placed bonds on the innocent Aminta to bring about her total downfall. . . . Flora disguised her lies with such color of truth that it was no wonder Aminta believed every word" (*Enchantments* 56).] Given that Flora is described as having lied to manipulate Aminta, it would be hard to accept her prior statements as a sincere expression of lesbian desire. Moreover, Flora's sexual behavior elsewhere in the story seems to be decidedly heterosexual: she orchestrates the cruel deception in order to assure herself of ultimately maintaining her affair with Jacinto: "Aguardando por premio destos engaños, quedarse con su amante, dexando a Aminta con su deshonor y desventura" (*Novelas amorosas* 99) ["As a reward for her resourcefulness, she expected to end up with her lover, abandoning Aminta to her misfortune and dishonor" (*Enchantments* 60)]. In fact, the narrator condemns Flora, not because she is attracted to women, but because she manipulates and deceives them: "— . . . en siendo una mujer mala, lleva ventaja a todos los hombres. A don Jacinto disculpa amor, a la triste Aminta el engaño, mas para Flora no hay disculpa" (*Novelas amorosas* 98). ["' . . . as a woman who's evil, you have the advantage over men. Love excuses don Jacinto, deception excuses the unfortunate Aminta, but for Flora there is no excuse'" (*Enchantments* 59).] Although the text plays with the idea of physical attraction between Flora and Aminta—"Recibiéronse con los brazos Aminta y Flora, dando a don Jacinto justa envidia" (*Novelas amorosas* 97) ["Flora and Aminta greeted each other with an embrace, causing proper envy in don Jacinto" (*Enchantments* 58)]—these comments seem to function more in accord with the intricate "engaño" plotted by Flora and Jacinto against Aminta.

Neither Estefanía (Esteban) in *Amar sólo por vencer* nor Flora in *La burlada Aminta* are reliable characters who express sincere feelings of female homoeroticism. However, through their comments and the more telling reactions of those around them, we can approach a possible view of same-sex love between women in Zayas's text. In both cases, this passion is received with a positive attitude and without threat, whereas heterosexual love (as well as male homosexual love in *Mal presagio casarse lejos*) proves to be destructive for women.

Mal presagio casarse lejos

Considering the absence of scandal surrounding female homoeroticism in Zayas's text, it is significant to note that male homosexuality is treated in a very different way. In fact, a comparison is difficult to avoid given the structure of the text. When Margaret R. Greer notes the lesbian attraction between Laurela and Estefanía in *Amar sólo por vencer,* she connects the possible importance of this theme to the novella that immediately follows, *Mal presagio casarse lejos* (Marriage abroad: portent of doom) (Greer 114). Given that Zayas's text seems to silence any specific details of physical relations among women, we might question why she allows the reader to witness a physically explicit homosexual episode involving two men in *Mal presagio casarse lejos.* Compared with the jovial and positive depiction and reception of female homoeroticism in *Amar* and *Burlada,* the explanation of how doña Blanca's husband preferred his handsome young male servant to his wife is presented with implied reprobation by the narrator doña Luisa:

Tenía el príncipe un paje, mozo, galán, y que los años no pasaban de diez y seis, tan querido suyo, que trocara su esposa el agasajo suyo por el del paje, y él tan soberbio con la privanza, que más parecía señor que criado. El tenía cuanto el príncipe estimaba, con él comunicaba sus más íntimos secretos, por él se gobernaba todo, y él tan desabrido con todos, que más trataban de agradarle que al príncipe. Pues, como doña Blanca muchas veces que preguntaba qué hacía su esposo, y le respondían que estaba con Arnesto (que éste era su nombre), y algunas que, o por burlas o veras, le decía que más quería a su paje que no a ella. (*Desengaños* 350–51)

[The prince had a page who wasn't over sixteen, young and handsome. The prince loved him so dearly that he would have exchanged his wife's favor for the page's, and the page was so proud in his privilege that he seemed more the lord than the servant. He ruled over everything and acted so ill-tempered that people tried harder to please him than the prince. The prince confided his most intimate secrets in this page and valued him above everything. Whenever doña Blanca would ask what her husband was doing, she'd be told he was with Arnesto (which was the page's name). Sometimes, half in jest, half in earnest, people would tell her that the prince loved his page more than her.] (*Disenchantments* 255–56)

When doña Blanca eventually finds the two men together in bed, the narrator and the protagonist are equally repulsed by what is characterized as a hideous and sinister display of male homosexuality:

Quisiera, hermosas damas y discretos caballeros, ser tan entendida que, sin darme a entender, me entendiérades, por ser cosa tan *enorme* y *fea* lo que halló. Vio acostados en la cama a su esposo y a Arnesto, en deleites tan *torpes* y *abominables,* que es *bajeza,* no sólo decirlo, mas pensarlo. Que doña Blanca, a la vista de tan *horrendo* y *sucio* espectáculo, más difunta que cuando vio el cadáver de la señora Marieta, mas con más valor, pues apenas lo vio, cuando más apriesa que había ido, se volvió a salir, quedando ellos, no vergonzosos ni pesarosos de que los hubiese visto, sino más descompuestos de alegría, pues con gran risa dijeron:— Mosca lleva la española. (*Desengaños* 360; emphasis mine)

[Beautiful ladies and discreet gentlemen, I wish I could be so subtle that you would understand what she found without my having to say point-blank because of its *hideousness* and *enormity*. In the bed she saw her husband and Arnesto engaged in such *gross* and *abominable* pleasures that it's *obscene* to think it, let alone say it. At the sight of such a *horrendous* and *dirty* spectacle, doña Blanca was more stunned than when she had beheld Lady Marieta's corpse, but she was braver. The moment she set eyes upon them, she left more quickly than she had come. They weren't ashamed or embarrassed by her having seen them, instead they were amused and roared with laughter. One of them said: "That sure spooked the Spanish woman!"] (*Disenchantments* 264–65; emphasis mine)

Since Zayas's text clearly criminalizes this sexual relationship between men, we might assume that if genital relations between women were likewise presented they would also be subjected to criticism, especially given the legal and religious response to sexual activity among women.[19] According to early modern legal records, the apparent tolerance of lesbian relations discussed earlier seems to be contigent upon the absence of any instrument, which would indicate penetration or masturbation as well as a replacement of the phallus.[20] Antonio Gómez wrote of two nuns who were accused and eventually burned at the stake for sexual relations using a prosthetic phallus, but if lesbian relations did not include an instrument, a more lenient punishment would be considered (Crompton 19).[21] As Jacqueline Murray concludes: "In the absence of either a penis or a substitute, male writers minimized the seriousness of the sin" (199).

The interpretation of the lesbian sexual activity of the seventeenth-century abbess Benedetta Carlini, as well as the punishment of life in prison, clearly demonstrates the lack of tolerance for genital contact between women in the convent: "For two continuous years, . . . after disrobing and going to bed waiting for her companion . . . to disrobe also, she would force her into the bed and kissing her as if she were a man she would stir on top of her so much that both of them corrupted themselves" (qtd. in Brown, *Immodest* 162–63).

Scenes of sexual contact between women in the convent are also present in fictional works. Jean Barrin's *Venus dans la cloitre* (1683) (published in English as *Venus in the Cloister; or, The Nun in Her Smock*) recounts the sexual pleasures between an older and a younger nun: "Angel: '. . . Let me embrace thee, that our hearts may talk to each other in the tumult of our kisses.' Agnes: 'Ah Lud! how you squeeze me in your arms: don't you see I am naked to my smock? Ah! you have set me all on fire'" (qtd. in McCormick 189).

It would seem, however, that physical contact between nuns was not the only concern of theologians and legislators.[22] Verbal displays of affection among the nuns were also admonished by Santa Teresa in chapter 7 of her *Camino de perfección* (published in English as *The Way of Perfection*):

—Mejor amistad será esta que todas las ternuras que se pueden decir, que estas no se usan ni han de usar en esta casa, tal como «mi vida», «mi alma», «mi bien», y otras cosas semejantes, que a las unas llaman uno y a las otras otro. Estas palabras regaladas déjenlas para su Esposo. (Teresa de Jesús 308)

["This will be a much truer kind of friendship than one which uses every possible loving expression (such as are not used, and must not be used in this house): 'My life!' 'My love!' 'My darling!' and suchlike things, one or another of which people are always saying. Let such endearing words be kept for your Spouse."] (Teresa of Ávila 78–79)

Similarly, according to Fray Félix de Jesús María's biography of María de Jesús, the nun was horrified by the "amor particular" that some of the sisters had for one another (Lavrin 48).[23] Even Brantôme in the late sixteenth century suggests that seclusion or women-only communities (convents, prisons, and so forth) foster same-sex passion: "And wherever the women are kept secluded, and have not their entire liberty, this practice doth greatly prevail" (130).

Perhaps the concern for female homoeroticism within convent walls is significant in light of the ambiguous convent resolution in the denouement of the *Desengaños*.[24] Lisis's final decision to break her engagement to Diego and live instead among women disrupts the heterosexual plot resolution that traditionally has been believed to neutralize the temporary yet potentially transgressive same-sex flirtation scenes involving the *mujer vestida de hombre* (cross-dressed woman) motif that was so popular, especially on the early modern stage.[25] At the end of Zayas's novella the protagonist does not die, marry, or become the bride of Christ: "Doña Isabel tomó el hábito y Lisis se quedó seglar" (*Desengaños* 510) ["Doña Isabel took the habit but Lysis remained secular" (*Disenchantments* 404)]. Lisis's decision to reject marriage is motivated more by a desire for freedom from the suffering in heterosexuality than by a calling to become a nun: "—Me voy a salvar de los engaños de los hombres" (*Desengaños* 509) ["'I'm going to save myself from the deceptions of men'" (*Disenchantments* 403)]. Through Lisis's declaration, the text offers a glimpse of a separatist utopian vision, for the text clarifies that Lisis's actions show the best possible option for women:

. . . la hermosa Lisis queda en clausura, temerosa de que algún engaño la desengañe, no escarmentada de desdichas propias. *No es trágico fin, sino el más felice que se pudo dar, pues codiciosa y deseada de muchos, no se sujetó a ninguno.* (*Desengaños* 510–11; emphasis mine)

[. . . the beautiful Lysis lives in the cloister, still fearful that some deception might disenchant her because she did not learn directly from her own misfortune. This end is not tragic but rather the happiest one you can imagine for, although courted and desired by many, she did not subject herself to anyone.] (*Disenchantments* 405)

Perhaps this "Amazonian call to forget about men and be true to the collectivity of women" (Ordóñez 9) marks the completion of Lisis's earlier promise to show "que no sea el mundo el que siempre ha sido" (*Desengaños* 469) ["the world to be different from the way it's always been" (*Disenchantments* 367)]. By presenting the renunciation of heterosexuality as the ideal arrangement for women, the text proposes separatism as a "final solution to the problems of women's oppression in male-dominated society" (Andermahr 134).[26]

Many critics have argued that Zayas's ending reflects a preference for female bonding that may or may not lead to a "utopian model of sexuality" (Gorfkle 86). Margaret Greer defines the female bonding in Zayas as a process in which the woman proceeds from the "mother through men back to women" (107) and "not as sexual objects but as the ideal family" (114). Although homoerotic issues in Zayas's fiction have been acknowledged by many scholars, these "female-only" relationships have been described as nonsexual. Marcia Welles interprets Zayas's version of the love between two women to be spiritual as opposed to physical: "The rejection of corporeality and adherence to spirituality can be interpreted as a form of protest, . . . only as a 'disembodied' asexual being can she attain independence" (308). When Ruth El Saffar describes Zayas's text as a "female utopia outside the bounds of male-female intercourse" (211), she argues that the textual separation of the sexes shows a favoring of "celibacy and female bonding" (205). Similarly, Amy Kaminsky believes that Lisis does not take vows upon entering the convent because she "merely wishes to remain celibate and live her life among her women friends and relatives. For that, holy vows are unnecessary" (391).[27]

I would argue that Zayas rejects the traditional patriarchal models for a cathartic resolution and instead creates an ambiguous utopia that does not limit the options for female sexuality within the prescribed separatist community. While the portrayal of female homoeroticism in *Amar sólo por vencer* and in *La burlada Aminta* seems to follow other early modern models of tolerance for nonpenetrative same-sex desire (as long as these depictions are designed for the male spectator's pleasure and the final resolution is heteronormative), Zayas's ending creates tension by not adhering to expected patriarchal plots. The author anticipates this reader discomfort when she justifies her conclusion: "Ya, ilustrísimo Fabio, por cumplir lo que pedistes de que no diese trágico fin a esta historia, la hermosa Lisis queda en clausura. . . . No es trágico fin, sino el más felice que se pudo dar . . ." (*Desengaños* 510). ["Now, illustrious Fabio, to comply with your request that I not give a tragic end to this story, the beautiful Lisis lives in the cloister. . . . This end is not tragic but rather the happiest one you can imagine . . ." (*Disenchantments* 405).] Like the silencing of specific sexual details in the representation of desire between women, the transgression of Zayas's separatist resolution proves that what is *not* included is just as telling as what *is* included; if not more so.

Notes

A preliminary version of this essay was first presented on October 15, 1993 at the Mid-America Conference on Hispanic Literatures at Washington University in St. Louis ("Felices en el convento: Lesbianism or Asexuality in the Utopian Vision of Maria de Zayas").

1. See Goldman; and Beemyn and Eliason.
2. See Gossy for discussion of lesbianism in Zayas. Unfortunately I was unable to incorporate Gossy's argument here since my chapter was already completed and this volume in press.
3. See Boswell; Bradbury; McCormick; and Sanfeliú.
4. Other concepts suggesting possible female homoerotic themes, such as hermaphrodite, romantic friend, particular friend, Sapphist, and so forth, were used throughout the early modern period in Europe. See Brown *Immodest;* Donoghue; Dekker and van de Pol; Crawford and Mendelson; Lavrin; and Traub.
5. See Donoghue; Dekker and van de Pol; Simons; Murray; Vicinus; Crompton; Sanfeliú; and Yarbro-Bejarano 111–13.
6. See Olivares and Boyce for Sor Violante de Cielo's poetry.
7. Donoghue 87; and Simons.
8. For discussion of Céspedes, see Bullough and Bullough; Burshatin; and Barbazza. For Erauso see Vallbona; Merrim; and Velasco 2000.
9. Jiménez also notes that "Zayas seems to recreate the most exaggerated qualities and virtues of the lieutenant nun in Estela, a perfect example of the manly woman" (120).

Interestingly, just as Erauso's masculine appearance is well-documented both in portraits and in written comments such as "parece más capón, que muger" (qtd. in Vallbona 128) [she seems more like a eunuch than a woman], Zayas was also described in terms of the *mujer varonil* (manly woman) in the satirical work of Francesc Fontanella:

> Doña María de Sayas
> viu ab cara varonil,
> que a bé que «sayas» tenia,
> bigotes filava altuis.
> Semblava a algun cavaller,
> mes jas' vindrà a descubrir
> que una espasa mal se amaga
> baix las «sayas» femenils.
>
> (qtd. in K. Brown 231)

[Doña María de Sayas
with her manly face,
although she wore a skirt,
she played with her moustache proudly.
She looked like a gentleman,
but it will soon be discovered
that a sword is not easily hidden
under feminine "skirts."]

See also Welles and Gossy 508. Also, except where otherwise noted, all translations from the Spanish original are my own.

10. All quotations from the text in Spanish are from Alicia Yllera's edition of Zayas, *Desengaños amorosos.*

11. All quotations from the text in English are from H. Patsy Boyer's translation of Zayas, *The Disenchantments of Love.*

12. See Donoghue; Inamoto; Smith; Luna; McKendrick; Maroto Camino; Bradbury; and Yarbro-Bejarano. Interestingly, the reaction of early modern female audiences to lesbian scenes has been little studied. According to Donoghue, erotic incidents portraying female transvestites courting other women were not only popular among women spectators during the early modern period, but more important, these plots undermine marital loyalty while showing a different way of imagining female sexuality (89, 91).

13. According to Valerie Traub, women's desire for other women on the early modern stage, and only when the women were not performing acts that could be construed as phallically imitative, was implausible precisely because it was "nonreproductive" (163).

14. See also Garber.

15. See Gorfkle 84.

16. Marjorie Garber argues that the ultimate message in *Tootsie* and other Hollywood movies (such as *Mrs. Doubtfire*) is conservative, since men dressed as women not only are better men but also are better than women (6).

17. All quotations from the text in Spanish are from Amezúa's edition of Zayas, *Novelas amorosas y ejemplares.*

18. The passages in English are from H. Patsy Boyer's translation of Zayas, *The Enchantments of Love.*

19. Accordingly, Melveena McKendrick explains that Cubillo de Aragón most likely omitted a physical component from Dionisa's love for Leonor in his lesbian play *Añasco el de Talavera* "to avoid the inevitable censure of the authorities and obtain his *licencia*" (314).

20. Cristóbal de Chaves claimed that some female prisoners in Seville "made themselves into roosters" by tying an artificial phallus to themselves (J. Brown, *Immodest* 166; Perry 125).

21. Gómez describes a specific case in Granada in which the women "were whipped and sent to the galleys" (qtd. in Crompton 19).

22. St. Augustine's warning to his sister against similar practices before she took holy vows also confirms an awareness of the possibility of same-sex desire between women: "The love which you bear one another ought not to be carnal, but spiritual: for those things which are practiced by immodest women, even with other

females, in shameful jesting and playing, ought not to be done" (qtd. in Boswell 158). In a less serious vein, Erasmus likewise hints at lesbianism in the convent in his colloquy entitled "The Girl with No Interest in Marriage": "Not everything is virginal among these virgins. . . . Because there are more who copy Sappho's behavior than share her talent . . ." (qtd. in Raymond 95).

23. See also Ibsen.

24. See Velasco 1994–95.

25. See Ashcom; Bergmann; Bradbury; Bravo-Villasante; Cotarelo y Mori; Inamoto; Luna; Matulka; McKendrick; Romera Navarro; and Yarbro-Bejarano.

26. According to Kristine Anderson, the feminist separatist utopia is usually categorized under lesbian utopia. Anderson notes that "not all utopias 'for women only' are explicitly lesbian, however, although it is difficult to see how they could be otherwise in the absence of men" (85).

27. Female-only relations are also treated in Zayas's play *La traición en la amistad*. In act 1 Laura expresses her attraction for Marcia:

> Marcia hermosa, perdonadme,
> que es vuestro talle extremado;
> me ha turbado, y casi estoy
> muerta de amores en veros;
> no hay más bien que conoceros
> dichosa en miraros soy.
> (qtd. in Serrano y Sanz 599)

> [Beautiful Marcia, forgive me,
> for your figure is so exquisite;
> it has troubled me, and I am almost
> dying of love upon seeing you;
> there is nothing finer than knowing you
> so I can have the good fortune of seeing you.]

Although Montesa Peydro notes the sexual attraction between Laura and Marcia in Zayas's play (210), Matthew Stroud insists that these relationships are based on a platonic female friendship that, in the end, proves to be more valuable than marriage (545).

Works Cited

Andermahr, Sonya. "The Politics of Separatism and Lesbian Utopian Fiction." *New Lesbian Criticism.* Ed. Sally Munt. New York: Columbia UP, 1992. 133–52.

Anderson, Kristine J. "The Great Divorce: Fictions of Feminist Desire." *Feminism, Utopia, and Narrative.* Ed. Libby Falk Jones and Sarah Webster Goodwin. Knoxville: U of Tennessee P, 1990. 85–99.

Ariosto, Lodovico. *Orlando furioso.* Ed. Guido Waldman. New York: Oxford UP, 1983.

Ashcom, B. B. "Concerning 'La mujer en hábito de hombre' in the *comedia.*" *Hispanic Review* 28 (1960): 43–62.

Barbazza, Marie-Catherine. "Un caso de subversión social: El proceso de Elena de Céspedes (1587–1589)." *Criticón* 26 (1984): 17–40.

Barrin, Jean. *Venus in the Cloister; or, The Nun in Her Smock.* Trans. Robert Samber. 2d ed., 1725. Rpt. in Ian McCormick, *Secret Sexualities: A Sourcebook of 17th and 18th Century Writing.* London: Routledge, 1997. 187–97.

Beemyn, Brett, and Mickey Eliason, eds. *Queer Studies: A Lesbian, Gay, Bisexual, and Transgender Anthology.* New York: New York UP, 1996.

Bergmann, Emilie L. "(Re)writing History in Lope: Cross-Dressing and Feminism in *La vengadora de las mujeres.*" *Indiana Journal of Hispanic Literatures* 2.1 (1993): 29–48.

Boswell, John. *Christianity, Social Tolerance, and Homosexuality.* Chicago: U of Chicago P, 1980.

Bradbury, Gail. "Irregular Sexuality in the Spanish 'Comedia.'" *Modern Language Review* 76.3 (1981): 566–80.

Brantôme, Pierre. *Lives of Fair and Gallant Ladies.* Trans. A. R. Allinson. New York: Liveright, 1933.

Bravo-Villasante, Carmen. *La mujer vestida de hombre en el teatro español.* Madrid: Temas, 1976.

Brown, Judith C. *Immodest Acts: The Life of a Lesbian Nun in Renaissance Italy.* New York: Oxford UP, 1986.

Brown, Judith C. "Lesbian Sexuality in Medieval and Early Modern Europe." *Hidden from History: Reclaiming the Gay and Lesbian Past.* Ed. Martin Duberman, Martha Vicinus, and George Chauncey, Jr. New York: Penguin, 1989. 67–75.

Brown, Kenneth. "Context i text del *Vexamen* d'academia de Francesc Fontanella." *Llengua i Literatura* 2 (1987): 173–252.

Bullough, Vern L. *Sexual Variance in Society and History.* New York: John Wiley and Sons, 1976.

Bullough, Vern L., and Bonnie Bullough. *Cross Dressing, Sex, and Gender.* Philadelphia: U of Pennsylvania P, 1993.

Burshatin, Israel. "Elena Alias Eleno: Genders, Sexualities, and 'Race' in the Mirror of Natural History in Sixteenth-Century Spain." *Gender Reversals and Gender Cultures: Anthropological and Historical Perspectives.* Ed. Sabrina Petra Ramet. London and New York: Routledge, 1996. 105–22.

Castillo Solórzano, Alonso de. *Aventuras del Bachiller Trapaza.* Ed. Jacques Joset Madrid: Cátedra, 1986.

Charnon-Deutsch, Lou. "The Sexual Economy in the Narratives of María de Zayas." *María de Zayas: The Dynamics of Discourse.* Ed. Amy R. Williamsen and Judith A. Whitenack. Madison, N.J.: Fairleigh Dickinson UP, 1995. 117–32.

Cotarelo y Mori, Emilio. *Bibliografía de las controversias sobre la licitud del teatro en España.* Madrid: Real Academia Española, 1904.

Crawford, Patricia, and Sara Mendelson. "Sexual Identities in Early Modern England: The Marriage of Two Women in 1680." *Gender & History* 7.3 (1995): 362–77.

Crompton, Louis. "The Myth of Lesbian Impunity Capital Laws from 1270 to 1791." *Journal of Homosexuality* 6. 1–2 (1980–81): 11–25.

Cubillo de Aragón, Álvaro. "Añasco el de Talavera." Ms. University of Minnesota Rare Book Collection, n.d.

Dekker, Rudolf M., and Lotte C. van de Pol. *The Tradition of Female Transvestism in Early Modern Europe.* New York: St. Martin's, 1989.

Dolz-Blackburn, Inés. "María de Zayas y Sotomayor y sus *Novelas ejemplares y amorosas.*" *Explicación de Textos Literarios* 14.2 (1985–86): 73–82.

Donoghue, Emma. *Passions between Women: British Lesbian Culture 1668–1801.* London: Scarlet, 1993.

El Saffar, Ruth. "Ana/Lysis and Zayas: Reflections on Courtship and Literary Women in the *Novelas amorosas y ejemplares.*" *María de Zayas: The Dynamics of Discourse.* Ed. Amy R. Williamsen and Judith A. Whitenack. Madison, N.J.: Fairleigh Dickinson UP, 1995. 192–216.

Erauso, Catalina de. *Lieutenant Nun: Memoir of a Basque Transvestite in the New World.* Trans. Michele Stepto and Gabriel Stepto. Boston: Beacon, 1996.

Garber, Marjorie. *Vested Interests: Cross-Dressing and Cultural Anxiety.* New York: HarperPerennial, 1993.

Goldman, Ruth. "Who Is That *Queer* Queer? Exploring Norms around Sexuality, Race, and Class in Queer Theory." *Queer Studies: A Lesbian, Gay, Bisexual, and Transgender Anthology.* Ed. Brett Beemyn and Mickey Eliason. New York: New York UP, 1996. 169–82.

Gorfkle, Laura. "Re-constituting the Feminine: Travesty and Masquerade in María de Zayas's 'Amar sólo por vencer.'" *María de Zayas: The Dynamics of Discourse.* Ed. Amy R. Williamsen and Judith A. Whitenack. Madison, N.J.: Fairleigh Dickinson UP, 1995. 75–89.

Gossy, Mary S. "Skirting the Question: Lesbians and María de Zayas." *Hispanisms and Homosexualities.* Ed. Sylvia Molloy and Robert McKee Irwin. Durham: Duke UP, 1998.

Greer, Margaret R. "The M(Other) Plot: Psychoanalytic Theory and Narrative Structure in María de Zayas." *María de Zayas: The Dynamics of Discourse.* Ed. Amy R. Williamsen and Judith A. Whitenack. Madison, N.J.: Fairleigh Dickinson UP, 1995. 90–116.

Ibsen, Kristine L. *Women's Spiritual Autobiography in Colonial Spanish America.* Gainesville: U of Florida P, 1999.

Inamoto, Kenji. "La mujer vestida de hombre en el teatro de Cervantes." *Cervantes* 12.2 (1992): 137–43.

Jiménez, Lourdes Noemi. "La novela corta española en el siglo XVII: María de Zayas y Sotomayor y Mariana de Caravajal y Saavedra." Diss. University of Massachusetts, 1990.

Kaminsky, Amy Katz. "Dress and Redress: Clothing in the *Desengaños amorosos* of María de Zayas y Sotomayor." *Romanic Review* 79.2 (1988): 377–91.

Lavrin, Asunción. "La vida femenina como experiencia religiosa: Biografía y hagiografía en Hispanoamérica colonial." *Colonial Latin American Review* 2.1–2 (1993): 27–51.

Luna, Lola, ed. *Valor, agravio y mujer.* Madrid: Castalia, 1993.

Maroto Camino, Mercedes. "*Spindles for Swords:* The Re/Dis-covery of María de Zayas' Presence." *Hispanic Review* 62 (1994): 519–36.

Matulka, Barbara. "The Feminist Theme in the Drama of the Siglo de Oro." *Romanic Review* 26 (1935): 191–231.

McCormick, Ian. *Secret Sexualities: A Sourcebook of 17th and 18th Century Writing.* London and New York: Routledge, 1997.

McKendrick, Melveena. *Woman and Society in the Spanish Drama of the Golden Age: A Study of the* Mujer Varonil. London: Cambridge UP, 1974.

Merrim, Stephanie. "Catalina de Erauso: From Anomaly to Icon." *Coded Encounters: Writing, Gender, and Ethnicity in Colonial Latin America.* Ed. Francisco Javier Cevallos-Candau et al. Amherst: U of Massachusetts P, 1994. 177–205.

Montemayor, Jorge de. *Los siete libros de La Diana.* London: Tamesis, 1996.

Montesa Peydro, Salvador. *Texto y contexto en la narrativa de María de Zayas.* Madrid: Gráf. Maravillas, 1981.

Murray, Jacqueline. "Twice Marginal and Twice Invisible: Lesbians in the Middle Ages." *Handbook of Medieval Sexuality.* Ed. Vern L. Bullough and James A. Bundage. New York: Garland, 1996. 191–222.

Olivares, Julián, and Elizabeth S. Boyce. *Tras el espejo la musa escribe: Lírica femenina de los Siglos de Oro.* Madrid: Siglo Veintiuno, 1993.

Ordóñez, Elizabeth J. "Woman and Her Text in the Works of María de Zayas and Ana Caro." *Revista de Estudios Hispánicos* 19.1 (1985): 3–15.

Pérez de Montalbán, Juan. "La Monja Alférez: Comedia famosa." *Spanish Drama of the Golden Age: The Comedia Collection.* Microfilmed from *Comedias varias de diferentes autores de España.* 17—? New Haven, Conn.: Research Publications, 1972.

Perry, Mary Elizabeth. *Gender and Disorder in Early Modern Seville.* Princeton: Princeton UP, 1990.

Raymond, Janice G. *A Passion for Friends: Toward a Philosophy of Female Affection.* Boston: Beacon, 1986.

Rojas, Fernando de. *La Celestina.* Ed. Bruno Mario Damiani. Madrid: Cátedra, 1982.

Romera Navarro, M. "Las disfrazadas de varón en la comedia." *Hispanic Review* 2 (1934): 269–86.

Sanfeliú, Luz. *Juego de damas: Aproximación histórica al homoerotismo femenino.* Málaga: Atenea, 1996.

Serrano y Sanz, Manuel. "Doña María de Zayas y Sotomayor." *Apuntes para una biblioteca de escritoras españolas desde el año 1401 al 1833,* vol. 2. Madrid: Tipografía de la Revista de Archivos, Bibliotecas y Museos, 1905. 582–621.

Simons, Patricia. "Lesbian (In)visibility in Italian Renaissance Culture: Diana and Other Cases of *donna con donna.*" *Journal of Homosexuality* 27.1–2 (1994): 81–122.

Smith, Paul Julian. *The Body Hispanic: Gender and Sexuality in Spanish and Spanish American Literature.* Oxford: Clarendon, 1989.

Stroud, Matthew D. "Love, Friendship, and Deceit in *La traición en la amistad,* by María de Zayas." *Neophilologus* 69.4 (1985): 539–47.

Teresa de Jesús. *Camino de perfección. Obras completas.* Madrid: Aguilar, 1988.

Teresa of Ávila. *The Way of Perfection.* Trans. E. Allison Peers. New York: Doubleday, 1964.

Traub, Valerie. "The (In)significance of 'Lesbian' Desire in Early Modern England." *Erotic Politics: Desire on the Renaissance Stage.* Ed. Susan Zimmerman. New York and London: Routledge, 1992. 150–69.

Vallbona, Rima de, ed. *Vida i sucesos de la monja alférez: Autobiografía atribuida a doña Catalina de Erauso.* Tempe: Arizona State U, 1992.

Vega Carpio, Lope de. *Arte nuevo de hacer comedias.* Ed. J. M. Rozas. Madrid: SGEL, 1976.

Velasco, Sherry M. "Contradiction, Control and Utopia in María de Zayas." *Journal of Hispanic Philology* 19.1–3 (1994–95): 201–12.

Velasco, Sherry M. *The Lieutenant Nun: Transgenderism, Lesbian Desire, and Catalina de Erauso.* Austin: U of Texas P, 2000.

Vicinus, Martha. "'They Wonder to Which Sex I Belong': The Historical Roots of the Modern Lesbian Identity." *Feminist Studies* 18 (1992): 467–97.

Villalón, Cristóbal de. *El Crótalon de Cristóforo Gnofoso.* Ed. Asunción Rallo Gruss. Madrid: Cátedra, 1982.

Welles, Marcia L. "María de Zayas y Sotomayor and Her *Novela cortesana:* A Re-evaluation." *Bulletin of Hispanic Studies* 54–55 (1977–78): 301–10.

Welles, Marcia L., and Mary S. Gossy. "María de Zayas y Sotomayor (1590?–1661?/1669)." *Spanish Women Writers: A Bio-Bibliographical Source Book.* Ed. Linda Gould Levine, Ellen Engelson Marson, and Gloria Feiman Waldman. Westport, Conn.: Greenwood P, 1993.

Yarbro-Bejarano, Yvonne. *Feminism and the Honor Plays of Lope de Vega.* West Lafayette: Purdue UP, 1994.

Zayas y Sotomayor, María de. *Desengaños amorosos.* Ed. Alicia Yllera. Madrid: Cátedra, 1983.

Zayas y Sotomayor, María de. *The Disenchantments of Love.* Trans. H. Patsy Boyer. Albany: State U of New York P, 1997.

Zayas y Sotomayor, María de. *The Enchantments of Love: Amorous and Exemplary Novels.* Trans. and intro. H. Patsy Boyer. Berkeley: U of California P, 1990.

Zayas y Sotomayor, María de. *Novelas amorosas y ejemplares.* Ed. Agustín G. de Amezúa. Madrid: Real Academica Española, 1948.

2

Concealing Pleasures
Cross-dressers, Tribades, and Sodomites in Lope de Vega's *El rufián Castrucho*

Harry Vélez Quiñones

> Que sea Escobar, puede ser,
> ¡mas, vive Dios que es mejor!
> —Lope de Vega, *El rufián Castrucho*

It is easy to read *El rufián Castrucho* (Castrucho the pimp [ca. 1598]) as one of the many *comedias* written by Lope de Vega that in some fashion or other remind us of Fernando de Rojas's *La Celestina* (1499). Indeed, Teodora, an old hag and Fortuna's *madre* (madam) in the business of prostitution, is described as a veritable double of the "tercera de Calisto" (Calisto's go-between), the troubled *galán* (male lead) of *La Celestina*.[1] For his part, Castrucho is related to the lineage of *valentones* (braggarts) or *rufianes cobardes* (cowardly pimps) that begins with Rojas's Centurio and the Galterio of the anonymous *Comedia Thebaida* (1521) and continues with the likes of Pandulfo, Bravonel, Barrada, and so on, in other imitations of *La Celestina*. Similarly, Fortuna is closely linked to *mochachas* (girls) of the sort of Elicia, Parmenia, Ancora, and Libertina.

Differences abound, nonetheless. The celestinesque story tells of the amorous struggle of a young nobleman in hot pursuit of a virtuous maiden. A cunning and duplicitous *alcahueta,* or go-between, who ultimately is able to change the lady's righteous ways, aids him in this difficult enterprise. The final failure or success of such a love is also mediated to a lesser degree by the young couple's servants, the *alcahueta*'s *mochachas*—semiprofessional prostitutes—and one or more braggarts at the service of either household. Castrucho's story, however, centers around the lusts of Spanish soldiers in Italy and the travails of pimping and prostitution.

43

Teodora does not act as a go-between but more as Fortuna's madam, and Fortuna, a professional and itinerant harlot, has but the appearance of virtue and the promise of pleasure to offer to her paying clients. Yet, this is also a world of masks and deception, a realm of countless uniformed men, scheming scoundrels, and wandering trollops. The most interesting type of craftiness in this milieu, though, may not be as blatantly manifest for some readers despite its high degree of visibility. What Marjorie Garber calls "transvestite effects," however, prevails in the military order of desire depicted in *El rufián* (17). It is only through cross-dressing that both male and female characters satisfy their sexual appetites and achieve their goals in this *comedia*.

More important, transvestite effects dramatize the characters' struggle for sexual and affective fulfillment. Sex and gender in their social and physical practice are in effect being "queered" in this multilayered display of garments, identities, and performances. In this fashion, *El rufián* helps us understand the extent to which the presentation and circulation of alternative modalities of desire point toward an emergent queer identity in early modern Spain.

The plot of *El rufián* is fairly simple. In an unspecified Spanish military encampment in Italy, three comrades in arms, Sergeant Álvaro, Ensign Jorge, and Captain Héctor, meet and succumb to the charms of a beautiful prostitute, Fortuna. First to fall is Álvaro, who appears in the first scene of the play recounting to his superior, Jorge, the many graces of the lovely Fortuna. Soon enough, Jorge and Héctor get a chance to meet the ravishing *mochacha,* and a contest of wits and deceptions ensues between the three smitten friends. Two additional characters come into play from the outset: Teodora and Castrucho. A celestinesque *puta vieja* (old bawd) if there ever was one, Teodora is a comic avatar of the figure as it had appeared in works such as Gáspar Gómez de Toledo's *Tercera parte de la tragicomedia de Celestina* (Third part of the tragicomedy of Celestina [1539]), Sancho de Muñón's *Tragicomedia de Lisandro y Roselia* (Tragicomedy of Lisandro and Roselia [1542]), Sebastián Fernández's *Tragedia Policiana* (The tragedy of Policiana [1547]), and others.[2] Her relation to Fortuna can best be described as a composite of teacher, manager, and guardian in the business of whoredom. Early on in the play we learn that this living and commercial arrangement has been imperiled since some time ago as a result of the advent of Castrucho, an amalgam of pimp, braggart, gambler, and swindler. After meeting Teodora and Fortuna in their native Seville, Castrucho becomes the prostitute's lover and exploiter all in one. He has taken both women with him to Italy to sell the charms of the younger one, live off their wealth, gamble away their meager savings, and slap them both at the smallest sign of rebellion, much to the financial and physical ruin of Fortuna and Teodora.[3]

At this juncture we must turn our attention to a couple of highly instru-
mental characters in this *comedia de enredo* (play of high intrigue): a pair
of servant boys called Escobarillo and Beltranico. As in so many other
comedias, under the names, garments, and discourse of a young and handsome page one will in time uncover the likeness of a woman. In *El rufián*
we eventually come across Brisena and Lucrecia, young women from Valladolid and Milan, respectively. They have made their way to the military
encampment in search of their *burladores* (deceivers), Álvaro and Jorge,
former lovers who had promised to marry them but fled rather than live
up to their words. The other characters only discover their so-called true
identities as females at the very end of act 3, just before a semblance of
order finally emerges amidst this rather twisted community of dramatis
personae. At that time, Fortuna's last client, the general of the Spanish
army, intervenes, sorts out the *enredo,* and marries off everybody to his or
her corresponding mate. However, questions arise as to whether these
three heterosexual couples—Brisena and Álvaro, Lucrecia and Jorge, and
Fortuna and Castrucho—are as well matched as it might seem. Further,
even if one accepts the restoring effect of their marital unions, one still is
forced to contend with the disturbing and ultimately fascinating effects of
cross-dressing and transvestism in the presentation and development of
these characters, especially in the context of sex, gender, and desire.

The opening scenes in *El rufián* strongly suggest that we may well read
the events represented therein under the sign of the cross-dresser. Ardently
enamored of Fortuna, Álvaro, however, lacks anything of value with which
to satisfy the whims and needs of a professional of her sort. Fortuna, it
turns out, has rather peculiar and expensive sartorial tastes. Thus, at the
beginning of act 1, Álvaro visits his superior, Ensign Jorge, with a view to
borrowing from him a luxurious military suit that, in turn, he has promised to lend to his darling:

ÁLVARO: Aquel vestido con que el otro día
    de nuestro emperador en la presencia
    metistes vuestra guarda y compañía
    la llevaré, como me deis licencia;
    que me ha pedido alguna gala mía
    para cierto disfraz o impertinencia.
                (30, vv. 105–10)

[The suit that days ago,
in our emperor's presence,
you dressed your guard and company
I will present her, if you so allow it,
for she has requested one of my uniforms
for some masquerade or cheeky deed.][4]

Although Ensign Jorge quickly lends Sergeant Álvaro the uniform and has his page deliver it at once, never do we come to know what need Fortuna had of such a costume or what sort of impudent diversion she was contemplating. Certainly, given the particular demands of her profession, Fortuna in military garb would have been considered an erotically stimulating sight. As the cross-dressed Teodora/Lelio in Lope's *Los bandos de Sena* (The leagues of Sena [1597–1603]) remarks of her own self-made self:

TEODORA: Esto de ser desbarbado
  es apetecible cosa,
  el pie firme
  y pierna airosa,
  y esto de pluma y soldado,
  no sé qué tiene atractivo.
(Vega, Los bandos 551a)

[This beardless condition
is a luscious thing;
a firm stance
and handsome legs,
and these feathers and soldierly attire
have a certain attractive something.]

Clearly, the figure cut by these female transvestites in military attire is sufficiently beguiling to incite not only the lascivious soldiers in the encampment but other subjects as well.[5] No doubt, the price fetched by Fortuna's transvestite *no sé qué* in the market of desire in this military setting is quite high. It is by coming across as a charming and beardless young recruit or, more precisely, by acting out such a role—by *passing*—that Fortuna can stand out professionally. This is evidently so, since the practice appears to have the approval of her *madre,* Teodora, without whose erotic shrewdness Fortuna is incapable of undertaking any professional transaction.[6] Yet, the fact that Fortuna's impertinent need to cross-dress is never again brought up in the play is in and of itself revealing. Although we may never see her/him in drag, her penchant for transvestism is one of her initially salient characteristics, one that we should keep in mind.

In their study on female transvestism in early modern Europe, Rudolf M. Dekker and Lotte C. van de Pol affirm that "in periods of war we usually find peaks in the numbers of women dressed as men" (30). They go on to quote the case of a woman soldier, Margarita, who in the early years of the the Dutch revolt against Spain (1568–1648) became a heroine to the Flemish and even wrote rousing patriotic poetry aimed at inspiring young women to follow her example (30). In Spain the often-quoted case of the prodigious Catalina de Erauso—nun, soldier, murderer, and hero—

was widely known. Through her autobiography, *Historia de la monja alférez doña Catalina de Erauso escrita por ella misma* (History of the nun ensign donna Catalina de Erauso, written by herself [1625]), and a play attributed to Juan Pérez de Montalbán, *La monja alférez* (The nun ensign [ca. 1626]) the impact of her story reached sensational proportions in the first half of the seventeenth century.[7] As a creature of fiction, Fortuna's case cannot be measured with the same tools as those of the case of Margarita, Catalina, and her sisters, yet it is curious that both of them are either prey or part of the same army. Dekker and van de Pol assure us that Margarita can be counted as not only among the lucky few who managed to get away with cross-dressing and joining the army but also as someone who won the admiration of many and secured for herself a solid economic future as a shopkeeper (83). Catalina's fortune was no worse. Having won papal dispensation to wear men's clothing, she eventually returned to the New World, where, when she was last seen, she had set up shop transporting merchandise from incoming ships in Mexico (Perry, *Gender* 130–31). In all respects Fortuna's luck pales in comparison with theirs and poses many interesting questions. Subjugated by Castrucho's wretched control, Teodora's exploitative ways, and the erotic needs of multiple select customers, she emerges as a prisoner of the wills and desires of others. It is precisely because her situation as a desiring subject is so dire that her subsequent appearance as an ardently passionate woman is so full of potential meanings, as we will see.

As a "lost woman" Fortuna occupies a precarious position in the social order explored here.[8] Her services are immensely sought after, yet she is also reviled as a *dueña* (duenna) and constantly abused by her clients or lovers, especially Castrucho. She is loved, yet bought, esteemed, yet discarded and despised. Her borderline location acquires further importance because of the apparent confusion that surrounds her origins. Entranced by Álvaro's glowing description of the young prostitute, Jorge affirms:

En efecto, la dama es forastera,
¿qué digo forastera?, es castellana,
que aquí en el campo nuestro y dondequiera
se lleva, como Venus, la manzana.
(28, vv. 33–36)

[Indeed, the lady is a foreigner,
foreigner? what am I saying? she is a Castilian,
who, here in our encampment or elsewhere,
like Venus, wins the apple.]

Jorge's slip of the tongue underscores the ambivalence that informs the attitudes surrounding this coveted public woman. Can she be *castellana*

and a common whore? If this were so it would constitute an affront to the
honor of all Castilian women. Then again, can such a uniquely disquieting
and beautiful harlot be anything but *castellana?* That is, can any other
women aspire to the charm of Castilian ladies? Later we learn that she is
indeed *castellana* but that she hails not from the pure and *castizo* towns
of Valladolid, Burgos, or Toledo but from Seville, "la Gran Babilonia de
España" (the Great Babylon of Spain [Perry, *Crime* 1, n. 1]).[9] The liminality of individuals such as she, as Dekker and van de Pol remind us,
engenders not only positive reactions but also, and even more often, negative reactions because they do not conform to normal social categories,
they are threatening. They disturb the natural order of things and cause
disorderliness, chaos, and filth (41). Indeed, Fortuna's uncertain origins,
profession, and fondness of cross-dressing point toward further destabilizing traits.

The first one of such characteristics to stand out has to do with Fortuna's dubious health. Pondering his decision to lend Álvaro the military
outfit, Jorge speculates:

> Será, si viene a mano, esta señora
> alguna ninfa de color quebrado
> que me deje en el término de un hora
> de humor el vestidillo inficionado;
> ¡Oh cuerpo de la pobre pecadora,
> que el alma de don Álvaro has robado
> trátame bien, si pueden oraciones,
> las inocentes calzas que te pones!
>   (32, vv. 147–54)

> [I bet that, if at all, this lady
> is but some sallow slut
> that in the course of an hour
> will infect with her excretions my poor suit;
> O, body of this wretched sinner,
> you that have stolen don Álvaro's soul,
> treat kindly, if you heed any prayers,
> my innocent and spotless stockings!]

Jorge's description of Fortuna as a pallid ill trollop who contaminates the
clothes that she wears with her sickly secretions is revealing. Written thirty
years after the first syphilis epidemic in Seville, although set in an earlier
historical period, the dread of venereal afflictions is quite apparent in *El
rufián.*[10] Jorge's concerns show a keen anxiety about "secondhand clothing
and bedding, both of which carried disease in this period" (Perry, *Crime*
238). In this context, Fortuna's inclusion in the realm of the plague

stricken conjures images of hideous disfiguration, pustules, pain, and death. This stresses her contradictory nature—she is both Venus and the source of the *contagio de San Gil* (San Gil's disease).[11]

Much later, in the second half of act 2, the reader again becomes aware of Fortuna's conflicting psyche. The suspicions raised by her "cierto disfraz o impertinencia" at the outset now gather strength. Introduced to the pageboy Beltranico, Lucrecia in drag, we see Fortuna as she falls head over heels in love for the first and only time "Tan pagada estoy del paje, / que no me ha hecho otro gusto / tu amo que a éste aventaje" (83, vv. 651–53) [I am so charmed by the page, / never has your master pleased me / in a way that this one surpasses]. When this experienced sexual worker uses the word "gusto,"[12] which we must understand as "deléite ù deséo de alguna cosa . . . vicios" (delight, desire, voluptuousness, and vices), to describe the pleasure derived from consorting with someone, the reader ought to take notice. It is extremely intriguing that such a veteran in the art of love, as well as an occasional cross-dresser, does not exhibit any misgivings about Beltranico's self-made persona. Gifted with as keen an eye as Fortuna, Castrucho had concluded after inquiring about his hometown, his lineage, and his name that the little page was not a boy, but a girl or, at the very least, a catamite, an ingle, or a hermaphrodite.[13] "Eres mujer" (72, vv. 327) [You are a woman], says he, much to the surprise of Beltranico, who mounts a desperate defense of his cross-dressed self "No juzguéis por la corteza, / que tengo el alma de roble" (72 vv. 333–34) [Judge not by the facade; / my soul is as hard as an oak]. Clearly, to this sagacious pimp this boy looks like someone who either for pleasure or profit, by nature or by perversion, belongs in bed with men rather than women. Why then, the reader should wonder, is Fortuna so silent about the highly ambiguous sex appeal of he who "en talle y compostura / parece tan caballero / cuanto hembra en la hermosura" (73, vv. 353–55) [in figure and composure / seems as much a gentlemen / as a woman in her beauty]?

Fortuna and Beltranico's brief liaison is the only source of steamy scenes in *El rufián*. While the three soldiers and Castrucho go about the business of tricking and deceiving each other, attempting to lay their hands on the voluptuous dame, we hear from Beltranico how Fortuna fools her suitors in order to spend time with him/her. Next we also learn about other more saucy goings-on behind the scenes:

LUCRECIA: Al fin le dio cantonada
　　y a una casa me llevó,
　　donde a los dos recibió
　　una buena vieja honrada.
　　Luego los brazos traviesos,
　　llamándome un ángel bello,

me echó mil veces al cuello,
y pensó comerme a besos.

                    (99, vv. 53–60)

[Finally, she lost him in the street
and she took to me a house
where an honest and good duenna
welcomed the two of us.
Then, calling me a beautiful angel,
her mischievous arms
she threw around me a thousand times,
wanting to devour me with her kisses.]

Although Beltranico escapes Fortuna before being "devoured" by her, his/ her effect on Fortuna is indelible. No wonder, much later when Fortuna is getting ready to visit the Spanish general's bed, we see the young prostitute lamenting the absence of her self-made boyfriend and crying for "aquel pobre pajecillo, / que era para estas cosas un tesoro" (103, vv. 185–86) [that poor little page, / who was a darling in these matters].

Fortuna's attachment to Beltranico is indeed troublesome and calls for further thought. In a study of female theatrical cross-dressing in eighteenth-century London, Kristina Straub posits the existence of "safe" limits of the cross-dressed actress role in performances, affirming that the gender and sexual confusion associated with the actress could be a source of pleasure as long as it did not contaminate or compromise dominant narratives of heterosexual desire (145). In my view, *El rufián* comes perilously close to endangering heterosexual male dominance symbolically, and in effect, by awarding Beltranico and Fortuna's ephemeral flirtations center stage in this parade of lustful appetites, it opens the door to alternative configurations of desire. The tribade, a homoerotically disposed woman, appears visibly in the staging of Beltranico's transvestite effect on Fortuna. Fortuna's crush on Beltranico constitutes more than merely one more comic interlude. The release of pent-up desires that her aggressive performance of sex and gender, as directed toward the ambiguously clad "boy," puts in circulation is telling and points to an awareness of different conceptions of *gusto*.

At the end of act 3, pressed by the rigorous demands of the three angry and lecherous soldiers, Castrucho conceives a plan, a "graciosa niñería" (119, vv. 643) [an amusing prank], to defraud his customers:

CASTRUCHO: Dos mozos tengo, que son
    Escobarillo y Beltrán,
    en el talle y además
    de mujeril condición.

A estos dos vestiré
como mujeres, y luego
a uno y otro amante ciego
la palabra cumpliré.
                    (113, vv. 452–59)

[Two lads I have,
Escobarillo and Beltrán,
who in their figure and demeanor
are of a womanish sort.
These then I will dress
like women, and thus
to both blind lovers
I shall keep my word.]

When Castrucho decides to cross-dress the boys so as to pass them as Fortuna, he exhibits more than mere resourcefulness, he reveals a heretofore hidden aspect of his métier as pimp and exploiter of the flesh. By providing young boys to the soldiers, Castrucho promotes a trade that, according to historical sources, involved close to 30 percent of those processed by the Spanish Inquisition on charges of sodomy (Carrasco 222).[14] In addition, Castrucho's action further complicates our reception of Fortuna's role in Teodora's *casa de placer* (house of pleasure). Obviously, "everything goes" in the liminal setting of the military encampment: all desires are admitted, and there are providers for each desire.

Dressed as a woman, Fortuna's self-made boy, Beltranico, and his partner in cross-dressing, Escobarillo, spend the night with Ensign Jorge and Sergeant Álvaro. The magnitude of this deception is truly formidable. What Castrucho is peddling to these ardent males is not Fortuna herself, not even a woman, but boys who are in fact not truly so but rather female cross-dressers remade once more as females in order to impersonate simultaneously the same prostitute, Fortuna. Two respectable if dishonored ladies from Valladolid and Milan, proficient cross-dressers, are *also* Beltranico and Escobarillo, a couple of salacious and sexually ambiguous lads, who both impersonate for a night the same lower-class prostitute and apparent tribade. Out of this perversely twisted layering of garments, personal identities, class, gender, and sex eventually emerge Brisena and Lucrecia, but this is hardly a natural, obvious, or logical result. Quite to the contrary, Castrucho appears at this juncture as a producer of monsters or prodigies in an open economy of desire.

As the *comedia* comes to a close, the general of the Spanish forces summons all the principal male characters and compels them to account for their actions. As that moment gets closer, Castrucho feels quite confident

that he has been dealt a winning hand. If he opens his mouth, Jorge and
Álvaro might very well end up in a bonfire:

CASTRUCHO: Paso, nadie me haga mal,
  que descubriré la fiesta.
ÁLVARO: ¿Qué fiesta?
CASTRUCHO: Fiesta de fuego;
  denme campo franco luego
  o cantaré lo que resta.
ÁLVARO: ¿Qué has de cantar, sentenciado?
CASTRUCHO: ¿Luego Escobar y Beltrán
  no son las damas que han
  el uno y otro gozado?

                        (126, vv. 822–31)

[CASTRUCHO: Hold it, no one dare harm me
  else I uncover your game.
ÁLVARO: What game?
CASTRUCHO: A game of fire;
  quickly grant me safe passage
  or I will divulge the rest.
ÁLVARO: What are you going to disclose, you felon?
CASTRUCHO: Well then, are not Escobar and Beltrán
  the ladies with whom
  the two of you have made love?]

Of course, the public and the reader may reasonably assume that no instances of *pecado nefando* (nefarious sin) or *crimen inter christianos non
nominandum* (a crime not to be named among Christians) have actually
taken place. However, whether such a presumption is warranted must remain an open question, given the wicked confusion of garments, personal
identities, class, gender, and sex that surrounds the soldiers' sexual partners. If one reads Escobarillo and Beltranico exclusively as *mujeres vesti-
das de hombres* (women in men's clothing), the question is much simpler.
However, at this time in the play, only the two transvestites know that
Beltranico and Escobarillo are the cross-dressed self-made identities of
Lucrecia and Brisena. Castrucho and the smitten Fortuna are completely
unaware that this is so, and thus the former is convinced that the soldiers
are sodomites. Jorge and Álvaro are equally ignorant of the fact, and,
surprisingly, they appear to have serious doubts as to whether their bed-
mates were male or female, Fortuna or someone else:

ÁLVARO: ¿Yo a Escobar?
JORGE: ¿Yo a Betranico?

ÁLVARO: Que sea Escobar, puede ser;
   ¡mas, vive Dios que es mejor! . . .
JORGE: Yo a Beltranico no creo
   que pueda ser. . . .
   Digo que es, sin falta alguna,
   mujer, y que sea Fortuna
   yo no lo afirmo.
(126, vv. 832–43)

[ÁLVARO: Me, Escobar?
JORGE: Me, Beltranico?
ÁLVARO: That it be Escobar, is possible;
   but, by God he is better! . . .
JORGE: That I had Beltranico, I do not think
   that can be. . . .
   I tell you that she/he is, a perfect
   woman, but that she/he is Fortuna
   I do not confirm.]

Álvaro's remarks are positively astonishing. Not only does he reveal his innocence in regard to his sexual partner's identity and sex, but also he is open to the possibility that the person with whom he has just had sex might have been Escobarillo, after all. Moreover, he swears to God that if that has been the case, sleeping with him was a magnificent experience. Jorge's simplicity regarding his bedfellow's identity is also startling, as is his use of the term "mujer" in proclaiming that person's sex. Earlier, Castrucho had employed this same ambiguous term to question Beltranico's self-definition as a boy. Further, since in Spanish it is common to omit the personal pronoun before the verb, the sex of the subject of the sentence "Digo que es, sin falta alguna, mujer" is impossible to determine, and thus it is difficult to ascertain exactly what Jorge is saying. If in effect he were using "*ella*" (she) in reference to whomever it was that he slept with, it would be clear that by "*mujer*" he would mean what is generally understood as "woman," that is, a female of the human species. However, if he were using the masculine pronoun "*él*" (he) in reference to Beltranico, Jorge would be concurring with Castrucho's earlier assessment that the lad is as much a *mujer* "sin falta alguna" [a perfect woman] as the prettiest of catamites, ingles, or hermaphrodites. Moreover, given Jorge's willingness to admit that it probably was not Fortuna, the person with whom he spent the night can also be read as ambiguous. In the first instance his words would seem to indicate that the subject in question is a woman "sin falta alguna," as Fortuna presumably is. On the other hand, his assertion may be casting doubt on the stability of Fortuna's own biological sex and gender performance. After all, we must not forget that Fortuna is as much

a cross-dresser as Lucrecia and Brisena are and, further, that the configuration of her sexual desire had already been exposed as atypical.[15]

At this point, the last scene of the *comedia,* the general finally confronts
all the characters. His intervention forcefully displaces all these troubling
uncertainties, temporarily at least. Castrucho states his side of the story
and, upon removing the shawls covering the upper body of the subjects in
question, the field marshall, don Rodrigo, establishes the facts as he sees
them "Estas mujeres son" (128, v. 879) [These are women]. At this juncture
the restoration of order, or better yet the containment of ambivalence, is
deployed. In a predictable display of virtuosity, the general acknowledges
Lucrecia's and Brisena's claims to marriage with their respective *burladores,* weds Fortuna, now also manifestly *burlada,* to her pimp, and confers
upon Castrucho the rank of infantry captain.

Castrucho, the intriguing hero of this work and the architect of this
labyrinth of errors, emerges triumphant at the conclusion of the *comedia*
after having stood at the center of all the dramatic hubbub. This puzzling
figure deserves closer scrutiny. If, as Garber has asserted, "*all* of the figures
on stage are impersonators" (40), no one is more so than this astute *rufián
cobarde.* That he is an impersonator by virtue of being who he is comes
across quite clearly in the following exchange between Héctor's servants,
Belardo and Pradelo:

BELARDO: ¿No es gracioso el fanfarrón?
PRADELO: ¿Cuándo has visto tú rufián
  que no parezca Roldán
  y sea después lebrón?

                    (65–66, vv. 138–41)

[BELARDO: Isn't the braggart funny?
PRADELO: When have you seen a pimp
  who does not look like Roland
  but isn't later a coward?]

Castrucho is a persistent dramatic contradiction; dressed with the garb
and verb of a bully, he is treated as such by most characters, though they
simultaneously regard him as a pantywaist, as it were. Indeed, it is because
he brings together opposite extremes of being that he is an effective figure.
As a truly bold scoundrel or, alternatively, as a declared wimp, Castrucho
would lose interest and power as a dramatic persona. My reading of Castrucho as the quintessential cross-dresser gains legitimacy by his classi-
fication as such toward the end of act 2. It is while trading insults with
Teodora that she labels him "Hombre con faldas, / bellaco, medio mujer" (94, vv. 980–81) [Skirt-wearing man, scoundrel, hermaphrodite]. The
reader must reconcile the image of this skirt-wearing womanish scoundrel

with his own claim of being an "hombre de vida airada" (96, v. 1037) [angry young man] and his earlier description as an "espadachín / destos que viven, en fin, / sin otra renta y caudal" (49, vv. 678–80) [swordsman / of the sort that live, well, / of no other income or riches].[16] Ironically, when the general raises Castrucho above the rest to the rank of captain, saying, "porque de un hombre tan astuto espero / que se han de ver grandezas en un día" (129, vv. 922–23) [because from such an astute man I hope / that some day we will see great wonders], he is recognizing the merits of an outstanding cross-dresser and impersonator.

Then again, the sort of "grandeza" that informs Castrucho's greatest achievements has already been witnessed by the public viewing the *comedia*. His prodigious intervention with his staff of cross-dressed boys manages to set "straight" a sorely unbalanced heterosexual community. He achieves that through repeatedly dressing both himself and others as what they are not. His magic is that of producing myriad "transvestite effects."

At this point we must entertain a few more questions. Must we think of Beltranico and Escobarillo as women dressed as men or as something else entirely? Most Hispanists who have addressed the *mujer vestida de hombre* from Romera Navarro and Bravo-Villasante on have been timorous in confronting the implications of this phenomenon. On the other hand, as Gail Bradbury, Lorraine Daston and Katharine Park, Ursula K. Heise, Mary Beth Rose, and others remind us, the relation of the female cross-dresser to the realm of irregular sexuality is undeniable.[17] What then are we to conclude about the lovely Beltranico, whose conflictive liminality is highlighted from the moment he appears on stage and becomes the only attractive object of desire in Fortuna's eyes? It is difficult to discount the young page's quite active role in promoting this sadly fatal attraction. To borrow Jane E. Howard's words concerning Viola and Olivia in Shakespeare's *Twelfth Night* (ca. 1600): "It is Viola who provokes the love of Olivia, the same-sex love between women thus functioning as the marker of the 'unnatural' in the play and a chief focus of its comedy" (432). Like Viola, Beltranico's actions render visible the suggestion of Fortuna's tribadic preferences, which, in turn, indicate the eventual sterility of the ardorous attempts of her many suitors at having her. In point of fact, at the end of *El rufián* not even the general of the Spanish forces, Fortuna's wealthiest and most powerful client, is able to enjoy her immensely desired services. In addition, when both Beltranico and Escobarillo are cross-dressed as women and sold for the night to eager soldiers, the trace of the "unnatural" is displaced from the field of female homoeroticism, tribadism, to that of male homoeroticism, sodomy. This *comedia*'s reiteration of the motif of acts *contra natura,* whether in the guise of tribadic flirtations or masculine prostitution, supports Bradbury's thesis that "for some

Spaniards, certain aspects of abnormal sexuality were a source of delight and intrigue, rather than of horror and repulsion" (569).

The repeated instances of cross-dressing in *El rufián* bring to the fore these suggestions of homoerotic desire. This process speaks to the device's potential to reveal unsettled and unsettling cultural tensions. "The transvestite in this scenario," states Marjorie Garber, "is both terrifying and seductive precisely because s/he incarnates and emblematizes the disruptive element that intervenes, signaling not just another category crisis, but—much more disquietingly—a crisis of 'category' itself" (32). It is this crisis that *El rufián* advertises and *attempts* to resolve. I emphasize "attempts" because the identity of those who, with so little trouble, speak under the names of "Lucrecia que era Beltrán, Escobar que es Brisena" (127) [Lucrecia who was Beltrán, Escobar who is Brisena] at the end of act 3 is to me quite a problem to determine. Under each of these alarmingly charming counterfeit Fortunas there hides a cross-dressed pageboy, Beltranico or Escobarillo, under which we are to believe one might find two outrageous female cross-dressers, Lucrecia and Brisena, respectively. When, at the close of the play, Brisena affirms having secured for a second time a marriage promise from Álvaro, this time "con el vestido propio" (128, vv. 890) [wearing the proper clothing], one cannot be but puzzled. Is the *vestido propio* to be understood as "the proper garment" or "my own attire," and, if the latter, well, what does it consist of exactly? What is, indeed, the proper garment of human bodies on or off stage? As a *curioso lector* (curious reader) of *El rufián* I am left wondering what gender construction informs the body that the said *vestido propio* covers? Moreover, I continue asking myself, what does that body look like and, further, how does it perform its gender practice? These are questions that matter some whether we concern ourselves with the study of literary characters in seventeenth-century Spanish texts, or the exploration of artists and writers of the late nineteenth and twentieth centuries, or, closer to home, our relations with students, colleagues, and friends as we are fast approaching a *fin de siglo* that promises change in all categories of human interaction.

By focusing on the especially poignant suggestions that cross-dressing helps bring about in *El rufián*, I have aimed to show how that, no matter what the degree to which this conceit constitutes an "incipient threat to heterosexual male dominance" (Straub 146), it arises, in all its pleasurable ambiguity, as the only way in which this heterosexual order of desire can contain its own underlying instability and mend itself. This operation's questioning of the established paradigms of sex and gender and their social and physical performances as officially promoted both in early modern Spain and in our times is an additional consequence, the relevance of which is perhaps better to discuss extensively elsewhere. If nothing else, the outrageous suggestions of gender and sexual turmoil that this *comedia* shamelessly parades on stage under the garb of entertainment constitute one more indication that the "natural" order of things is always much less so than it is generally regarded to be. However, like the bodies of this cross-dressed corps, ultimate identities, final definitions, and absolute truths are, mercifully, rather impossible to lay bare.

Notes

1. Lope de Vega Carpio, *El galán Castrucho,* 30, v. 92. Subsequent citations to this source occur in the text as only page and verse numbers. Although originally titled *El rufián Castrucho,* the word *rufián* (pimp) in the title turned into *galán* (gallant) by the time the *comedia* was first published. Such an euphemistic move is not followed in these pages.

2. The seven principal members of the *celestinesca* family are: Anonymous, *Comedia Thebaida* (1521); Feliciano de Silva, *Segunda comedia de Celestina* (1534); Gáspar Gómez de Toledo, *Tercera parte de la tragicomedia de Celestina* (1539); Sancho de Muñón, *Tragicomedia de Lisandro y Roselia* (1542); Sebastián Fernández, *Tragedia Policiana* (1547); Juan Rodríguez Florián, *Comedia llamada Florinea* (1554); and Alonso Villegas Selvago, *Comedia llamada Selvagia* (1554). The *Comedia Eufrosina* (1555), written by the Portuguese Jorge Ferreira de Vasconcellos, does not fit exactly within the parameters of the genre. Much like Lope de Vega's *La Dorotea,* the *Comedia Eufrosina* lacks a true avatar of Celestina and her fellow characters. This means not that both works are not celestinesque, but that their structural differences separate them from their generic precursors. See Heugas.

3. Fortuna and Castrucho's situation is rather unliterary. It recalls the condition of many young women in early modern Seville. Writing at the end of the sixteenth century, the lawyer Cristóbal de Chaves reports the case of a certain Ana and her lover-pimp Juan de Molina. After seducing her, "he gave her lessons every day in how to be a successful prostitute, and he placed her in a brothel on the Calle del Agua. On the days that she did not take in much money, he beat her, for he wanted the money for gambling. He taught her how to call out and get clients, and he showed her many tricks for getting money from them" (Perry, *Crime* 218).

4. All translations from the original Spanish sources are my own.

5. The erotic attraction of cross-dressed women was significant. Among others, Rudolf Wittkower and Margot Wittkower report that in late fifteenth-century Italy. ". . .Venetian prostitutes found it more profitable to don mannish clothes in order to attract customers . . ." (170).

6. Much later Fortuna spells out for Ensign Jorge the rules of her game.

Mi madre gobierna en mí;
ésta quita, veda y pone,
y pues ella no está aquí,
que es la que de mí dispone,
podéis perdonarme a mí.
(86–87, vv. 748–52)

[My *madre* rules over me,
she discharges, proscribes, and confirms,
and since she is presently not here,
the one who manages me,
you will do well in excusing.]

7. See Perry, *Gender* 127–35, and McKendrick 213–17. *The Nun Ensign* is J. Fitzmaurice-Kelly's translation of Erauso's autobiography.

8. The term "lost woman" is revealing. "The euphemism that city fathers used suggests that the women were outcasts who had completely lost their way in the dominant culture of the city, but historical evidence shows that 'lost women' were an integral part of their community, just as prostitutes are in present-day society" (Perry, *Crime* 212).

9. A Sevillian citizen would write the following about his city in the early seventeenth century. "For six years I have not seen a thief hung in Seville, nor will such a thing be seen, since there are swarms of them like bees. . . . the majority in Seville are bullies, pimps, false beggars, ruffians, assassins, money lenders, hucksters, vagabonds that scrape a living from Mohammed and from those that play and rob in gambling houses and at gaming tables, for we pass from 300 gambling houses to 3000 brothels" (qtd. in Perry, *Crime* 66).

10. The first appearance of this terrifying new plague in Seville took place in 1568. See Perry, *Crime* 227–30.

11. "The 1568 syphillis epidemic in the city was called *el contagio de San Gil* because it first broke out in San Gil, another parish bordering the city's walls" (Perry, *Crime* 227). The expression of Fortuna's paradoxical self can be seen as well in one of the first glimpses of her that Álvaro remembers:

El día que yo ví, volviendo al cuento,
esta dama gentil, esta hermosura,
ví detrás della un negro paramento
y una fantasma de la noche oscura:
una vieja, señor, bebiendo el viento,
que, cual suele la sombra en la pintura,
parecía detrás del ángel bello,
junto al realce y luces del cabello.
                                    (29, vv. 57–64)

[The day in which I first saw, returning to the story,
this gentle lady, this lovely creature,
I saw behind her a black apparition
and a ghost from darkest night:
an old hag, sir, scouting for profit,
who, like the shadows in a portrait,
stood behind the beautiful angel,
next to the luster and shine of her mane.]

As in a painting, Fortuna's very shadow, and thus a part of her symbolic self, is composed of no other than Teodora. The *dama gentil* is also a potential *puta vieja*.

12. *Diccionario de autoridades* (1984), s.v. "gusto."

13. Castrucho uses the term "mujer" as an adjective (womanly) rather than as a noun (female). It is not that he reads Beltranico as a biological woman but rather as a womanlike boy, that is, as a boy who may be "used" as a female. Later, in act 3, he describes Escobarillo and Beltranico as such, using the adjective "mujeril" (womanish):

CASTRUCHO: Dos mozos tengo, que son
  Escobarillo y Beltrán,
  en el talle y ademán
  de mujeril condición.

(113, vv. 452–55)

[Two lads I have,
Escobarillo and Beltrán,
who in their figure and demeanor
are of a womanish sort.]

As Gregory Bredbeck points out, a catamite is defined as "a boy hired to be abused contrary to nature," whereas an ingle is "a boy kept for Sodomy" (17).

14. Addressing the issue of male prostitution, Carrasco underlines the sociological conditions that made possible "una infancia marginada y excluida, desposeída e ignorada como tal, donde la aventura homosexual no representa sino una imposición más del mundo de los adultos" (225) [a marginated and excluded childhood, dispossessed and ignored as such, in which the homosexual escapade represents but one more imposition of the adult world].

15. Daston and Park mention the case of a young chambermaid named Marguerite Malaure, whom Dr. Veay of Toulouse presented to the Royal Society of London. Marguerite was diagnosed by him "as a male-dominant hermaphrodite, despite the fact that she was in every other way a well-made girl and indeed 'bien jolie.'" After such a diagnosis Marguerite became Arnaud. As the authors point out, although personality traits (boldness versus timidity, for instance) and secondary external traits (such as the presence of breasts or facial hair) were used in sexing hermaphrodites, the absence or, more important, "the presence of functional male genitals was conclusive" in most cases to pronounce the subject a man. See Daston and Park 4.

16. In some aspects Castrucho's lifestyle recalls that of a certain Martín de Castro, who was burned at the stake in Madrid in 1574. Besides having one or more prostitutes working for him in the streets, Castro made a handsome living as a hustler for very rich and noble men such as the count of Ribagorza and the master of the Military Order of Montesa, don Garcerán de Borja. As he himself put it in his deposition before the inquisitors "Él no se echaba ni cabalgaba a hombres pobres sino a señores que le daban muchos dineros" [he did not sleep with nor sodomize poor men, but gentlemen that gave him lots of money]. A braggart and a pimp, Castro despised the nobles for whom he "worked" as much as he looked down to the inquisitors who prosecuted him. Secure in the economic and legal protection that he could extort from his male clients, he spent his time with his female prostitute-lovers and at his monies in brothels and gambling houses. At

least once, he sent to his "whore's house" for money, adding "mi puta es el Maestre de Montesa" (my whore is the master of Montesa). See Carrasco 204.

17. Gail Bradbury posits that the representation of irregular sexuality in the *comedia* had a place in the prevailing economies of desire. Ursula K. Heise finds similarities in the cultural anxieties surrounding masculine and feminine cross-dressing in Spain and England. Jane E. Howard examines the subversive potential of cross-dressing in early modern England. Ann Rosalind Jones and Peter Stally-brass look at the instability of gender in Renaissance Europe betrayed by the notion of hermaphroditism. And Mary Beth Rose explores the moral ambiguity and sexual challenges posed by the practice of cross-dressing on and off stage in early modern England. Dan Heiple's recent study, "Lope de Vega Explores Homoerotic Desire," has appeared in *Selected Proceedings. Louisiana Conference on Hispanic Languages and Literatures,* ed. Joseph V. Ricapito, 121–31 (np, nd). In LA CHISPA '95, Eugenia Ramos read a highly provocative paper entitled "La subversividad sexual de la comedia barroca española" (unpublished), which further addressed some of the issues raised by the above scholars. My paper entitled "Monstrous Friendship. The Dynamics of Homosocial Desire in Lope de Vega's *El amigo hasta la muerte*" was also discussed in this congress and can now be found in the *Journal of Interdisciplinary Literary Studies.*

Works Cited

Bradbury, Gail. "Irregular Sexuality in the Spanish *Comedia.*" *Modern Language Review* 76.3 (1981): 566–80.

Bredbeck, Gregory W. *Sodomy and Interpretation.* Ithaca: Cornell UP, 1991.

Carrasco, Rafael. *Inquisición y represión sexual en Valencia.* Barcelona: Laertes, 1985.

La comedia Thebaida. Ed. G. D. Trotter and Keith Whinnom. London. Támesis, 1968.

Criado de Val, Manuel, et al., eds. *Las Celestinas.* Barcelona: Planeta, 1976.

Daston, Lorraine, and Katharine Park. "Hermaphrodites in Renaissance France." *Critical Matrix* 1.5 (1985): 1–19.

Dekker, Rodolf M., and Lotte C. van de Pol. *The Tradition of Female Transvestism in Early Modern Europe.* New York: St. Martin's, 1989.

Erauso, Catalina de. *The Nun Ensign.* Trans. J. Fitzmaurice-Kelly. London, 1908.

Ferreira de Vasconcellos, Jorge. *Comedia Eurfrosina.* Ed. Eugenio Asensio. Madrid: C.S.I.C., 1951.

Garber, Marjorie. *Vested Interests: Cross-Dressing and Cultural Anxiety.* New York: Routledge, 1992.

Gómez, de Toledo, Gaspar. *Tercera parte de la tragicomedia de Celestina.* In *Las Celestinas.* Ed. Manuel Criado de Val et al. Barcelona: Planeta, 1976. 609–943.

Heiple, Dan. "Lope de Vega Explores Homoerotic Desire." *Selected Proceedings: Louisiana Conference on Hispanic Languages and Literatures.* Ed. Joseph V. Ricapito. N.p., n.d. 121–31.

Heise, Ursula K. "Transvestism and the Stage Controversy in Spain and England, 1580–1680." *Theatre Journal* 44 (1992): 357–74.

Heugas, Pierre. *La Célestine et sa descendance directe.* Bordeaux: Bordeaux UP, 1973.

Howard, Jane E. "Crossdressing, the Theatre, and Gender Struggle in Early Modern England." *Shakespeare Quarterly* 39.4 (1988): 418–40.

Jones, Ann Rosalind, and Peter Stallybrass. "Fetishizing Gender: Constructing the Hermaphrodite in Renaissance Europe." *Body Guards: The Cultural Politics of Gender Ambiguity.* Ed. Julia Epstein and Kristina Straub. New York: Routledge, 1991. 80–111.

McKendrick, Melveena. *Woman and Society in the Spanish Drama of the Golden Age: A Study of the* Mujer Varonil. London: Cambridge UP, 1974.

Muñón, Sancho de. *Tragicomedia de Lisandro y Roselia llamada Elicia y por otro nombre quarta obra y tercera Celestina.* In *Las Celestinas.* Ed. Manuel Criado de Val et al. Barcelona: Planeta, 1976. 947–1144.

Perry, Mary Elizabeth. *Crime and Society in Early Modern Seville.* Hanover, N.H. UP of New England, 1980.

Perry, Mary Elizabeth. *Gender and Disorder in Early Modern Seville.* Princeton: Princeton UP, 1990.

Rodríguez Florián, Juan. *Comedia llamada Florinea.* In *Orígenes de la novela.* Vol. 3. By Marcelino Menéndez Pelayo. 3 vols. Madrid: Bailly Bailliére, 1910. 157–311.

Rojas, Fernando de. *La Celestina.* Madrid: Alianza, 1979.

Rose, Mary Beth. "Women in Men's Clothing: Apparel and Social Stability in *The Roaring Girl.*" *English Literary Renaissance* 14 (1984): 367–91.

Silva, Feliciano de. *Segunda comedia de Celestina.* In *Las Celestinas.* Ed. Manuel Criado de Val et al. Barcelona: Planeta, 1976. 262–605.

Straub, Kristina. "The Guilty Pleasures of Female Theatrical Cross-Dressing and the Autobiography of Charlotte Charke." *Body Guards: The Cultural Politics of Gender Ambiguity.* Ed. Julia Epstein and Kristina Straub. New York: Routledge, 1991. 142–66.

Vega Carpio, Lope Félix de. *Los bandos de Sena: Obras de Lope de Vega publicadas por la Real Academia.* New ed., vol. 3. Ed. Emilio Cotarelo y Mori. Madrid: Tipografía de la Revista de Archivos, Bibliotecas y Museos, 1916.

Vega Carpio, Lope Félix de. *La Dorotea.* Ed. Edwin S. Morby. Berkeley: U of California P, 1958.

Vega Carpio, Lope Félix de. *El galán Castrucho.* Valencia: Albatros Hispanófila, 1983.

Vélez Quiñones, Harry. "Monstrous Friendship: The Dynamics of Homosexual Desire in Lope de Vega's *El amigo hasta la muerte.*" *Journal of Interdisciplinary Literary Studies* 7.1 (1995): 45–56.

Villegas Selvago, Alonso de. *Comedia llamada Selvagia.* Madrid: n.p., 1873.

Wittkower, Rudolf, and Margot Wittkower. *Born under Saturn.* New York: Norton, 1969.

3

Queer Reader/Queer Muse
Romantic Friendships, Sexual Identity, and Sapphic Representations in Gómez de Avellaneda's Poetry

Librada Hernández

With the recent academic impulse to focus on the issue of sexuality, it has become clear that during the nineteenth century modern conceptions of sexual identity were formed. As Eve Kosofsky Sedgwick has established in *Epistemology of the Closet,* the nineteenth century was the historical moment in which the political and cultural parameters of modern gay and lesbian identity were firmly established (67–90). Sedgwick, together with Foucault, among others, points out that the term "homosexual" was constructed around the year 1870, following the development of legal, medical, and pedagogical discourses of sexuality.[1] These discourses did not appear overnight, and in fact we may safely assume that a gestating period occurred with their founding. For this reason, it is crucial that we rethink the writings of both canonical and noncanonical figures of the time who deal with issues of gender.

It was during this period of gestation that the Cuban-born Gertrudis Gómez de Avellaneda's writings began exploring sexual identity. In the limited world of sexuality that the mid-nineteenth century afforded Spanish women writers, she understood that gender roles are socially imposed and are a reflection of patriarchal society. From the outset of her literary career, and especially in the theater, she exposed artificially created gender roles and challenged their imposition by making her dramatic characters rebel against them (Hernández, "El *no*" 28). Through this questioning and rebellion and through an actual inversion of gender, she indirectly reveals erotic desire. In fact, many of her characters escape the confines of gender by concealing sexual and erotic experience. As Teresa de Lauretis has affirmed, "A way of escaping gender is to so disguise erotic and sexual experience as to suppress any representation of its specificity" (145). In the novel *Dos mujeres,* a woman learns to control erotic desire in solidarity with her female counterpart (Picón Garfield 137); in the play *Tres amores,* a woman resolves to give up sexual desire for a more asexual relationship (Hernández, "On the Double" 46). The suppression of the representation of sexual desire by female writers manifests itself in different forms according to contemporary critics of sexuality. Scholars such as Lillian Faderman, Bonnie Zimmerman, Martha Vicinus, and Adrienne Rich, when trying to chart a lesbian identity, claim that women's writing needs to be explored for its buried desires. Faderman proposes that passionate love between women was not labeled abnormal or undesirable in the past because women were considered to be asexual (18). Vicinus asserts that when we discuss women's sexuality we are venturing onto "covered" ground, since historically women were not associated with sexuality (434).

Avellaneda's sexuality was an issue of much controversy during her life, if not on account of identity, then certainly for its perceived deviancy. Witness the constant comments regarding her assertive feminism, her various failed love affairs, her passionate soul, her admiration of women writers of the avant-garde, such as Georges Sand and Madame de Staël. The poet herself gives us an account of how she was perceived:

> No hay dia en el que no me oiga llamar escéntrica, y a veces por personas para las que dicha voz es sinónima de *estrafalaria,* y le aseguro á V. que jamas se me ha ocurrido el reputarlo agravio. (*Cartas inéditas* 15)[2]

> [There is no day that I don't hear my name associated with the word eccentric, and by persons who believe that such a word is synonymous with *bizarre,* and I assure you that it has never occurred to me to find it an insult.][3]

She confesses to her lover that she is aware of having broken sexual taboos and confirms that she has done so consciously:

> Mi posicion es indudablemete la mas libre y desembarazada que puede tener un individuo de mi sexo en nuestra actual sociedad. Viuda, poeta, independiente por caracter, sin necesitar de nadie, ni nadie de mi, con hábitos varoniles en muchas cosas, y con edad bastante para que no pueda pensar el mundo que me hacen falta tutores, es evidente qe estoy en la posicion mas propia para hacer cuanto me dé la gana, sin mas responsabilidad qe la de dar cuenta a Dios y á mi conciencia. (*Cartas inéditas* 31)

[Undoubtedly my position is the freest and most unencumbered that an individual of my sex can have in our present society. Widowed, poet, of independent character, without need of anyone, nor anyone of me, with masculine habits in many things, and old enough so that the world may not deem that I am in need of tutors, it's evident that I am in the most suitable position to do whatever I please, with the only responsibility to account to God and my conscience.]

Her literary persona and her characters present an uneasiness with heterosexuality and an impulse to sublimate erotic love. In her letters to her lover Antonio Romero Ortiz, she appears to want to interpret their love as a mystical experience:

Es cosa horrible que el alma esté asociada à este cuerpo miserable. Que para espresar las mas altas aspiraciones de aquella, tengamos que valernos del lenguaje de los hombres mas comunes: que no alcance el amor mas puro y mas espiritual, otras satisfacciones qe. aquellas qe estan à la disposicion del mas rudo patan. (*Cartas inéditas* 29)

[It is a horrible thing that the soul is associated with this miserable body. That in order to express the highest aspirations of the former, we have to use the language of the most common of men: that the purest and most spiritual of loves cannot reach other satisfactions than those that are available to the crudest of workers.]

And she makes a further request of her lover:

Hazte ángel, amigo mío, hazte ángel, aun cuando me quieras menos. Ten un idealismo superior á mi propio idealismo. . . . Sé muy espiritual, amigo mio, te lo pido à nombre de nuestra felicidad futura. (*Cartas inéditas* 29)

[Become an angel, my love; become an angel, even if you were to love me less. Have a superior idealism to my own idealism. . . . Be very spiritual, my love, I beg of you in the name of our future happiness.]

This avoidance of physical love appears frequently in Avellaneda's woman-centered texts. Picón Garfield has already alluded to the subversive intent encountered in Avellaneda's dealing with sexuality in some novels:

Desde la posición de una doble alteridad, Gómez de Avellaneda forja su propia identidad estética. Por un lado, se distancia del centro en un desafío a la hegemonía del poder político, y por otro impone la autoridad de su propio contradiscurso engendrado mediante la inversión y la subversión del discurso hegemónico social de la sexualidad. (10)

[From the position of a double alterity, Gómez de Avellaneda forges her own aesthetic identity. On the one hand, she distances from the center in a contestation to the hegemony of political power, and on the other, she imposes the authority of her own counterdiscourse engendered through the inversion and subversion of the hegemonic social discourse of sexuality.]

But not only did Avellaneda challenge and subvert social sexual discourse, her own life revolved around physical transgression. Consider Hugh Harter's portrait in his biography of a flirtatious young woman who rejoiced in tempting her male colleagues: "Her dark beauty as a young woman, and later on as a stately matron, is still striking to us today as we see her in portraits and engravings. It is not surprising that when the lovely Tula first appeared in the literary circles of Madrid in 1840, twenty-five years old . . . she dazzled the most distinguished writers of the capital. She also soon caused malicious tongues to wag, and not wholly without reason" (17).

Male critics, while exhibiting an uncomfortable attitude toward her ("malicious tongues" wagging?), exalted her poetry for its "versificación robusta" [robust versification], which made her more "un escritor y no, . . . una del sexo bello" [a (male) writer and not one of the fair sex] (Cotarelo 257). This frequent association of masculinity with her verse, coupled with her perceived lack of femininity, makes Avellaneda what some historians of sexuality might call a butch/femme. Yet, as a matter of fact, her femininity was seen as inadequate, and she was placed outside the binary masculine/feminine.

The consciousness of sexual orientation is not very applicable to any of the Spanish women writers of the nineteenth century. The idea was too new, and women writers were in fact struggling to authenticate themselves as women and writers without losing their femininity. However, the Romantic ethos that advocated confronting society at all levels manifested itself in the group of women writers that marched forward to claim a space in the literary world. In their writing, these women expanded the domain of domesticity to include female friendships. The important part is that in their writings these women focused on women and on women's emotional lives with one another, and above all many of the relationships described directed erotic feelings toward female friends. By doing this, in some instances, they turned the domestic sphere into a queer site for women, beyond male social and sexual identity formation. Avellaneda's personal experience in sexual relationships is not in question here, I am interested in her imaginative projection of an alternative kind of same-sex relationship that was unidentified at the time and that is charged with sexual tension that I read as queer. This relationship has not escaped the scrutiny of current scholars, and it has been brought forth by the leading feminists in Hispanic studies. But until the present this has been done on the assumption that both the reader and writer are heterosexuals, through a normalizing matrix of presumptive heterosexuality. By queering Avellaneda's attempt to speak to other women, I will try to elucidate her attitude toward sexual identity at the historical moment when such an identity is being constructed. While literary characters in her novels and plays themselves queer gender roles and sexuality, I will focus on certain poems dedicated to women in which the relationship of the poetic "I" to the object "friend" is one where there seems to be an erotic love playing a central role.

Avellaneda and the Sapphic Tradition

Joan DeJean has noted that many literary women assume authorial power by means of their identification with Sappho. Women writers actually come of age when Sappho is recovered for modern literature. Sometimes, to overcome the supposedly literary deviant role of the woman writer, they propose Sapphic fictions alternative to the plots used by their male contemporaries; at other times, they are complicit with the myths created by their male colleagues and propagate an erroneous Sapphic figure (DeJean 15). In Spain, although male writers and critics ridiculed the figure of Sappho, she served as a mentor for many of the women writers that form part of Spanish Romanticism. Amy Kaminsky, in her study of Carolina Coronado's article on Sappho and Santa Teresa, confirms that authorial identity was forged by developing a history of women's writings all the way back to Sappho. Many writers such as Coronado, although aware that they had received a twisted version of Sappho through history, nevertheless used her to validate their writing as women. Thus confronted with a tradition of writings where women are excluded, and in possession of a Sappho misread by males, these women opt for misreading her poetry (Kaminsky, "Construction" 7). In fact, they were projecting their experiences on Sappho rather than identifying with her feelings for women sex partners. However, as Kaminsky advocates, there is a need to examine "repressed sexual desires" that might better come through the language used by these women (Kaminsky, "Lesbian Cartographies" 223). Writers of the stature of Avellaneda and Coronado used Sappho as an inspiration in their works, that they identified her as the woman of genius who elevated the woman poet does not mean that they were totally ignorant of the other cultural value of the "Sapphic" figure—the love for other women—since this Sappho was part of the literary air of the time as well. DeJean reminds us that it was precisely during this century that Sappho's sexual identity becomes a central issue. "In the course of the 19th century, Sappho leaves behind the often modest and always timid heterosexuality in which she had been disguised for nearly a century to reemerge as a figure of highly charged sexuality, first a courtesan, later a (sometimes depraved, sometimes oversexed) lesbian" (13). Yet the poet of Lesbos was important in European literature in formulating an environment where women communicated the love of learning and friendship among themselves. As we know today, there was an obsessive drive to contain female excess when it came to passion, as evidenced, according to DeJean, in the drive to desexualize Sappho. The leap of Sappho, though viewed by many men as a madness, allowed these women a free expression of the feeling of love and passion. They saw the poet of Lesbos leaping from the rock at Leucades, not as an act of madness, but as an act of passion. Since Romanticism was historically a masculine phenomenon in which the male-female relationship predicated by society and nature was one of complementarity, women were seen as deviant if they confronted and usurped the male subject's attributes. Thus the connection with Sappho was seen as one of madness: women who abdicated their feminine roles were mad, as Sappho was mad. However, there was one side of Sappho that was skirted in the Spanish mythifying of this figure, the side of desire for a female object. Kirkpatrick affirms that "erotic desire and gratification meant the death of a female social identity defined by the absence of sexual pleasure; this ideological imperative is evident in the writing of all Spanish women of the time" (*Las Románticas* 119). Therefore, it should not come as a surprise that the other side of Sappho's love is never articulated and that it appears only obliquely in women's poetry. Even in such works as Foucault's *History of Sexuality,* Sappho's challenge to what sometimes has been seen as monolithic phallic economy is omitted, as Dubois concludes in her study (Dubois 145). To be sure, by the end of the nineteenth century, Sapphism was beginning to be defined as an aberration, and women who had erotic feelings for other women became freaks. The idea that women were outside the realm of the erotic and passion led to the conclusion that women could express sexuality only through their masculinity. Thus, the mannish woman becomes a monster, an invert, and a femme fatale by the end of the century (Vicinus 439).

The relationships that these women formed came under scrutiny as well. The increased visibility of women's friendships, as well as the growing number of women writers, was seen as a challenge to patriarchy. Both were the result of women's greater economic freedom. This was the age of Georges Sand, Madame de Staël, and many other women who usurped male space through their lives or literature. Women had not been punished in previous centuries for advocating and maintaining same-sex relationships, only for breaking the patriarchal code of femininity. Only when a woman seemed to break masculine priorities and privileges was she punished. During the eighteenth century such relationships had been marginalized by men under the psychological rubrics of "hermaphrodism" or "tribadism." However, when these friendships interfered with male space, women were identified as flaunters of a dangerous and monstrous sexuality (Vicinus 439).

In the world of Avellaneda, the separation of the genders encouraged women to form close affectional bonds with each other. Despite the relative inferiority of the domestic sphere, they could develop friendships that affirmed their female power, bonded and solidified their love. It is within this separate domestic space of womanhood and affection that Avellaneda develops her interpretation of Sappho, focusing on the love of women writers for each other, a marginal love, a sort of new relationship beyond the structures of love, respect, and friendships of the time. Lillian Faderman defines the nineteenth century as the heyday of romantic friendships; it is at this time that women could love each other without fear of social stigma (17–18). However, this was true only as long as love was not associated with sexuality. The options of the Spanish writers were limited, either they assumed the position of passive "normal" femininity, or they were perceived as reversing that position and appropriating masculine subjectivity and desires, in which case they could express sexuality but only by becoming masculinized. But it is the love of learning that for Faderman corresponds with same-sex desire. Passionate love between women had not been labeled either abnormal or undesirable—probably because women were perceived to be asexual—until the sexologists led by Krafft-Ebing and Havelock Ellis "morbidified" female friendship at the end of the century (Faderman 18).

The suspicion of sexual ambiguity is always part of the reaction of male critics who see women as crossing the literary boundary reserved for male intellectual superiority "Siempre por detrás de las críticas aparece esta sospecha de que la mujer literata es sexualmente ambigua, es hombruna y tiende a lo masculino ya que ha usurpado intelectualmente ese espacio" (Picón Garfield 15) [There is always behind the criticism the suspicion that the woman writer is sexually ambiguous, is mannish, and leans toward the masculine precisely because she has intellectually usurped that male space]. Thus in the world of love in the nineteenth century, women who took control of their own sexuality violated an unwritten rule that made men the sole arbiters of sexual behavior. By imitating Sappho, the Spanish poets were expressing an ease with romantic friendships and making visible the space to which women's eroticism had been relegated. The presence of Sappho in their writing was not enough to cast doubt on sexuality, since women like Coronado were considered feminine even when they admired Sappho. But even in the case of Coronado, the use of Sappho was a delicate one, her "Odas a Safo" were not included in her works and have been revived only recently by Susan Kirkpatrick (*Las Románticas*). In the case of Avellaneda, it was her active invasion of a male space that cast her as a mannish woman. This association came about because of her dealing openly with the erotic world of passion, a territory that was reserved for men. She herself recognized and often welcomed this reference to her masculinity, as we have seen previously. Nonetheless, her obsession with passion was seen as a result of unrequited love:

. . . un profundo denominador llenó casi toda su juventud, de amor por un hombre frío, . . . que miraba con temor y a veces con reconcentrada desconfianza de sí mismo la superioridad inmensa de la mujer que amaba. (*Obras de . . . Avellaneda* 173)

[. . . a profound denominator filled almost all of her youth, of love for a cold man, . . . one that was afraid and at times suspicious and insecure of the immense superiority of the woman he loved.]

Kirkpatrick points out that Avellaneda appropriates romantic tropes of masculinity to reconfigure the romantic subject (*Las Románticas*). This incursion into male subjectivity was often ridiculed, since Avellaneda did not conform to the concept of femininity validated by the discourse of her time. Her letters to her lovers reveal a so-called sexually troubled woman.[4] However, Avellaneda's interest in Sappho is not an issue with contemporary critics. Although she imitates Sappho's sensual poetic voice where women's friendships are centered within erotic love, her critics insist that Avellaneda interprets Sappho as a woman of genius and as a poet oppressed by jealous male writers. This is no doubt true, for in some poems she makes reference to Sappho's mad passion for Faon. But in other poems, the interest in Sappho is paired with a tension in sexual desire. This deviant sexual discourse is one of the reasons behind the "slanderous gossip" that Harter finds, as well as the name "doña Safo" (Ms. Sappho), used for Avellaneda when she applied to the Real Academia (Royal Academy) (Harter 159). And the name resounds as well in the often-quoted reaction to her daring request to enter the Academia: "Es mucho hombre esta mujer" [This woman is too much of a man]. It is the privileging of sexuality and women that leads Marcelino Menéndez Pelayo to try to salvage Avellaneda's femininity by affirming that she is a feminine writer despite her "masculine" temperament:

La expresión robusta, grandilocuente, magnífica, prueba que era artista y espíritu muy literario quien acertó a encontrarla, pero no espíritu que hubiese cambiado de sexo ni renegado en la envoltura en que Dios quiso encerrarle. (Menéndez Pelayo 265–66; also qtd. in *Obras de . . . Avellaneda* 171)

[The robust expression, grandiose and magnificent, proves that it was an artist and a literary spirit who was able to find it, but not a spirit that would have changed sex or negated the wrapping in which God tried to enclose it.]

Menéndez Pelayo wants us to disregard the possibility of a transsexual poetics as well as the monster phenomenon that the lesbian was becoming in the medical literature of Europe at the time he was writing. Picón Garfield talks about a "discurso masculinizante" [masculinizing discourse] and relates it to a subtext of subversiveness rather than to sexual identity (127). Kirkpatrick comments on the "uneasy awareness of gender as an issue of poetic voice in Avellaneda's translation of male poets" (*Las Románticas* 180).

In her poetry, Avellaneda's relationship with other women is interesting in that it often departs from the romantic friendships of her contemporaries by feminizing both subject and object. What is more, some of her poems even associate sexuality and femininity. In them, as in most of her poetry, the exotic and exuding tropical nature becomes eroticized and feminized. Female desire is expressed though rhythmic palm trees, myriad flowers and butterflies, and undulating rivers. In many of her translations and imitations, the poetic voice is "transvoiced" from a male "I" to sing of erotic love for a woman and from a Sapphic "I" to speak of erotic love as a woman. Although the inclusion of the erotic female body and the usurpation of the male and female voice in women's poetry are no evidence of same-sex experience, even when it is directed to a female object, in Avellaneda's poems these images are charged with a sexual tension which made contemporary readers uneasy.

Marina Mayoral has studied the romantic friendships of a group of minor poets that wrote around the middle of the century, the "hermandad lírica," and suggests a sort of veiling that implies same-sex relations through the use of heterosexual erotic images as a "confusión de formas y de sentimientos" [confusion of forms and feelings] but that is related to their identity as women writers ("Las amistades" 70).[5] Mayoral contends that this confusion is not in any way related to a same-sex desire but is the result of a lack of models for expressing an asexual love between women; the poetry sounds lesbian because the only models available were those of heterosexual love poetry:

Hay un cariño en estas relaciones [entre mujeres] hay dolor, quizá el inevitable dolor de toda relación humana y hay un sentimiento que no veo otra manera de nombrar sino con la palabra que ellas mismas utilizan amor, un amor espiritual, que nace de identidad de sentimientos y aspiraciones, de una hermandad del alma que ellas se esfuerzan por dejar de manifiesto. La impresión equívoca que producen hoy muchos de estos poemas procede en gran parte del uso de un lenguaje y unas fórmulas expresivas tomadas de la poesía a erótica masculina. ("Las amistades" 44)

[There is a love in these relationships [between women], there is pain, maybe the inevitable pain of every human relationship, and a feeling that I can't see any other way of identifying than with the word that they themselves used, love, a spiritual love born of the same feelings and aspirations, of a sisterhood of the soul that they try to inscribe in their text. The ambiguous impression that today produces many of these poems is due to the use of a language and expressive forms taken from the male erotic poetry.]

Today's readers must not, according to Mayoral, apply a different meaning to this poetry because there is no other interpretation than a straight one. Their love is different because it occurs only between women, a feeling that is parallel to heterosexual erotic love but that surpasses it as well:

Las mujeres escritoras parecen encontrar en el trato con otras mujeres una complacencia y una afinidad espiritual que no se da en su relación con los hombres y que provoca en ocasiones un entusiasmo sentimental que si no es enamoramiento lo parece. ("Las amistades" 44)

[Women writers find in their relationships with other women a satisfaction and spiritual affinity that is not found in their relationship with men and that at times provokes a sentimental enthusiasm that if it is not an erotic attraction, it is something very similar.]

Whether these writers speak of a dangerous friendship, or of a special feeling that we may call lesbian, following Faderman's designation, or simply of "a special kind of friendship," the fact remains that erotic love is being expressed between two women. Are they timid ladies writing erotic love to their women friends because they don't have a tradition of writing erotically to men? That was indeed the explanation given for Sappho's erotic poetry to young women: they were learning how to love a man by practicing with their lady teacher (Stigers 45)!

In the case of Avellaneda, whom Mayoral does not include in her studies (she is not considered a minor figure), we find that she also partakes of this friendship formation; however, Avellaneda does not eroticize her language in the way the other poets do. She directs her poems to them as heterosexual friends. While we cannot clearly elucidate a "romantic friendship" in Avellaneda's poetry, we do detect an erotic impulse from a female subject to a female object. Avellaneda then partakes of this veiling of form and feelings that shape the minor writers' poetic friendships in a more original way, and she goes beyond using masculine erotic language to privilege the images Sappho used to talk to women about love. The fact that in Avellaneda's poems some female friendships are not eroticized while others are makes me as a queer reader suspect that, in those poems to women in which she introduces an erotic tension framed by Sapphic subjectivity, the author is intentionally expressing a different kind of love. What Avellaneda discovers in Sappho is women's subjectivity in erotic feelings. Interestingly, she also discovers this when she appropriates the male persona to talk to women about love, in which case she uses the heterosexual erotic model to describe her relationships with her women friends.

Whether Avellaneda's discovery is obfuscated by her projection of a heterosexual desire or is in fact a hidden lesbian desire need not disturb us.
But it did disturb the male writers of the time, who tended to see her
incursion into the world of passion as an intent to usurp their place. Even
when the academicians protested that if women were allowed into the Real
Academia the spirit of intellectuality would suffer because males would
be distracted by the disturbing presence of a female, it was actually the
ability of women to take away male spaces (*escaños*) that bothered them.
And they reacted with a vengeance, as this poem published at the time
shows:

> Yo, doña Safo segunda,
> entre avellaneda y fresca;
> musa que soplo a las nueve
> y hago viento a los poetas.
> (qtd. in Cotarelo 254)

> [I am Ms. Sappho the Second,
> a bit hazelnut[6] and a bit fresh;
> I am a muse that sings to the other nine,
> and blows away (male) poets.]

With this poem, titled "Protesta de una 'individua' que solicitó serlo de
la Academia Española y fué desairada" (Protest of a "female individual"
that solicited to become a member of the Royal Academy and was rejected), written at the time of Avellaneda's attempt to enter the all-male
Real Academia, the author voices the wrath of writers who feared Avellaneda's usurpation of an entirely male space. The poem aims to degrade
her poetry by making reference to her sexual persona. The attack exposes
masculinist fears that she is writing outside the parameters of femininity,
and it focuses on the invasion of the masculine world of letters by appropriating the muses. Indeed, the poem presents her as a destroyer of male
writers "hago viento a los poetas." At the same time, Avellaneda's literary
career is ridiculed by associating it with Sappho. This reference to a
woman that incompetently sings ("soplo" [blow]) to the muses, that from
them receives the inspiration to do away with male poets, is a recognition
that women writers pose a threat to the male institution of literature. It is,
nonetheless, an oblique recognition that if women writers don't have
power, they do have influence; it is also an admission that this influence is
pernicious to the male writer. Indeed, the poem was written by don Luis
Fernández Guerra to criticize Gómez de Avellaneda's standing in the way
of the Conde de San Luis entering the Academia (Cotarelo 255). The use
of Sappho ("Safo segunda") follows a tradition of ridiculing women writ-

ers who turned the world upside down by dedicating themselves to letters (Kirkpatrick, *Las Románticas* 87). The poem reflects as well the rumors of her sexual promiscuousness with the adjective "fresca." This sort of defeminization of the woman writer was common in nineteenth-century Spain, as Susan Kirkpatrick, Evelyn Picón Garfield, Amy Kaminsky, and Noel Valis, among others, have pointed out in their studies. Women writers represented a threat, yet male writers recognized that women's influence was there to stay. To avoid having such influence become too powerful, the literary critics associated any expression of passion with masculinity and power, and thus feminine passion in writing became an issue. Even though Avellaneda enjoyed the support of prominent men of letters of the time, what becomes distinctive about her behavior is her sexual transgression as evinced by the poem quoted above.

Throughout Europe during the course of the nineteenth century, masculinist images of women were frequently assigned to women writers who dared invade a male space. Much of the criticism focuses on the identity of the woman writer as a feminine writer. Thus a writer was good if she was feminine, if she dealt with tender feelings but not with passions. If she delved into history, passion, philosophy, this was seen as masculine because the intensity of study was believed to atrophy her sexual body. In other words, in the male mind, women were born tied to their biology, and they were identified as such.[7] At the same time, the change in the conception of sexuality as part of identity makes the pretense of a woman being a man a disturbing one, since it threatens to replace the male as subject.

Not only does Avellaneda disturb the boundaries of gender, but also, as Kirkpatrick concludes, the duplicitous character of the lyrical self in her poetry leads to a disintegration and annihilation of the feminine (*Las Románticas* 179). Avellaneda's textual self-representation and affirmation are therefore achieved through a sort of transvestism in which she rehabilitates her feminine self by writing in a masculine voice. The "extrañas cosas" [peculiar things] that resound in Cotarelo's response to Avellaneda's discussion of transvestism in nineteenth-century women writers in her article "La mujer . . ." (Woman) (1860) is an example of a masculine reaction to women delving into passion, sexuality, and writing (Cotarelo 255). In this article, Avellaneda confronts the insistence of male writers that women write within their biology. She makes it clear that women's sexuality has nothing to do with their writing, but she also notes that women could overcome their biological sexuality and assume the personality of a male writer by masking their sex. Avellaneda is lauding those women who were perceived as sexual troublemakers, women who somehow disturbed and tipped the scales and who at times were forced to atrophy their sexual identity to be able to write. In opposition to the received wisdom of the time, Avellaneda views these women not as inverts or nymphomaniacs but as individuals of superior intelligence:

> Pero ¡admirad la audacia y la astucia del *sexo débil*! Hay *ellas* que no sé cómo se alzaron súbitamente con borlas de doctores. Otras que cubriendo con sus lampiñas caras con máscara varonil, se entraron sin más ni más, tan adentro del templo de la fama que cuando vino a conocerse que *carecían de barbas* y no podían, por consiguiente, ser admitidas entre las capacidades académicas, ya no había medio hábil de negarles que poseían justos títulos para figurar eternamente entre las capacidades europeas. . . . Nos contentaremos con citar a Jorge Sand, jefe de todas esas *lampiñas disfrazadas*. El nombre varonil que supo ilustrar con sus escritos, figuraría indudablemente entre los más notables de la Academia francesa, pero ¡oh dolor! se supo demasiado pronto que eran postizas las *barbas* de aquel gran talento verdadero. . . . ("La mujer" 303; emphasis in original)

> [But behold the brazen and astute *weaker sex!* There are *shes* that have surprisingly raised themselves to the level of doctors. Others covering their hairless faces with a masculine mask penetrated without qualms so far into the temple of fame that when it was known that they *lacked beards* and could not, for that reason, be admitted among the academic talents, there was no clever way to deny that they possessed the right titles to figure eternally among the European talents. . . . We are glad to cite only Georges Sand, chief among all of those *masked beardless.* The masculine name that she was able to illustrate with her writings would figure undoubtedly among the most notables of the French Academy, but what a painful surprise it was. It was found out too soon that the *beard* of that true talent was false. . . .]

Sexuality is separate from writing; the *mujer de genio* (woman of genius) demonstrated, when she disguised her sexuality, that she was as intelligent as men. Dressing up as or identifying with a male subject is a transvestite or "transvoicite" means to write outside socially assigned gender roles.

From the Pen of a Woman to the Lips of Sappho

The community of women writers that Mayoral studies claimed Sappho as their older sister or a great-grandmother to validate their sex as writers. In the process of affirming a community of writers, they circumvented Sappho's sexuality or at times turned it into a heterosexual transgression of passion (Kaminsky, "Construction" 4). The image of the Greek poet brought together acknowledged poetic genius and emotional qualities desirable and acceptable in the feminine world (Kirkpatrick, *Las Románticas* 79). For the Romantic women poets, Sappho represented the quintessential form of female poetic creativity. But the image of Sappho that was propagated in nineteenth-century Spain had to do with a woman of unbridled passion who was mad and who killed herself for her lover Faon. In this sense, Sappho was not seen as a muse by the male writers. She was deemed a perverse figure. Therefore, the parodic literature that evolved around the figure of women writers associates the figure of Sappho with the usurpation of masculinity.

In the case of Avellaneda, the association with Sappho was used to deride her achievement in her literary career. While the poet subscribed to the general interpretation of Sappho as the woman who had been scorned by her lover and who died of passion, she also incorporated the other Sappho, the Sappho in whose poetry reverberates an impulse to reconfigure the feminine subject in light of desires within a feminine world. In "Despedida a la señora Da D G C de V." (1843) (in *Obras de . . . Avellaneda*), dedicated to her friend Lola, the Sapphic trope of the loss of the beloved through parting is used to cast the feminine poetic voice as the lover who is left in solitude after departure. As Sappho does in her poetry in general, and in poem 14[8] in particular, Avellaneda focuses on the moment of departing as a means of expressing the love for the other. In her poem 14, Sappho re-creates a scene of departure in which feelings of loneliness and happiness affirm the intimacy of love. Sappho's reminder of the beautiful experience shared with the lover assigns value to their sexual closeness (Rayor 13). Avellaneda takes the point of view of the departing lover who feels the solitude, but she is able to incorporate the intimacy as well. The poem starts with sadness and reproach in which the poetic voice joins with a community to lament the departure:

> ¿Y nos dejas, cruel? ¿Y nada alcanza
> El tierno llanto, el suplicar ferviente?
> ¿Senda hallarás de fácil bienandanza
> Dejando atrás a la amistad doliente?
> ("Despedida" 277–78)[9]

> [Can you be so cruel as to leave us? Can't the tender weeping, the impassioned supplication stop you? Will you find a better road by leaving behind our wounded friendship?]

The poetic voice then turns into a solitary feminine "I" that assumes the role of a lover and, on probing her friend's motives for departure, reproaches the friend for deceitfulness. She then introduces the only physical caress in the poem, a kiss of departure. In the coming together of the lips, the erotic stimulus is not in the kiss itself, but in the words not pronounced. Thus the erotic agent is to be found in the impulse to articulate a language of silence:

¿Qué engañosa esperanza,
Presto tal vez deshecha,
Hoy seduce tu pecho, que resiste
A la voz del amor, y el adios triste
Dicta a tu labio, que mi labio estrecha?

("Despedida" 278)

[What illusory hope, soon to be undone, today seduces your
bosom that resists the voice of love and dictates a sorrowful
farewell to your lip, as my lip embraces it?]

She goes on to tempt Lola with the "gloria" that staying would allow
her while sharing with her the lyre of Sappho:

¡Si! ¡Tente! ¡Mira! ¡Toma! ¡Que en tu mano
Torne a vibrar la lira
De la de Lesbos malograda musa!

("Despedida" 278)

[Yes! Stop! Look! Take it! Let your hands vibrate once again
the lyre of the wasted muse of Lesbos!]

On the one hand, this sharing/transferring of Sappho's lyre and voice
through the kiss and the gesture of extending the hand begs the friend to
continue the tradition of women communicating their love and their learning to one another, on the other hand, the kiss stops words from being
said and implies that what the poet transfers to her friend can be said only
through the caress itself. The tension in the poem mounts when the name
of Sappho is transmitted by the kissing lips. This mere Sapphic reference
causes a paralyzing fear that is recorded by the lyrical subject:

Mas, ¿qué pavor insano
Este recuerdo súbito me inspira,
Que el conturbado corazón rehusa
La voz a mi garganta? . . . ¿Por qué cunde
Por mis venas un hielo, que sofoca
El entusiasmo que en el pecho infunde
La augusta sombra que mi labio evoca!
¡Oh, Safo! ¡Oh, Safo! . . .

("Despedida" 278)

[But, why does this sudden memory inspire in me an insane
fear that my disturbed heart rejects and that stops words from
coming to my throat? Why this ice that runs through my veins,
that suffocates the enthusiasm that is in my heart when my lip
evokes the majestic shadow? Oh, Sappho! Oh, Sappho! . . .]

Is this eloquent statement of speechlessness a fear of the solitary life of the woman of genius? Or is this "pavor insano" one that is produced by the feelings provoked by identifying with the voice of Sappho? The descriptions of feelings and experience are directly borrowed from Sappho's poem 8, a poem which Avellaneda would imitate seven years later and in which the Greek poet describes her feelings upon thinking of her lover with another:

> I say nothing, my tongue broken,
> a delicate fire runs under my skin,
> my eyes see nothing, my ears roar,
> cold sweat rushes down me,
> trembling seizes me . . .
>
> (qtd. in Rayor 57)

In Avellaneda's poem the physical reaction occurs not upon remembering her friend once she is gone but upon pronouncing the words of Sappho as she kisses her friend. This "Sapphic feeling" that causes fear and pain is what Lola must seek to escape. In the poem Avellaneda goes on to urge Lola away from the "amistad doliente." Thus, "tente" [stop], in the name of Sappho, turns into a warning against her inarticulate desire:

> Huye, triste mujer! Mi ruego loco
> Desestima prudente:
> Yo lo condeno ya, yo lo revoco.
>
> ("Despedida" 279)

> [Run away, sad woman! Be prudent before my insane plea,
> for I myself already have revoked it and condemned it.]

And the kiss that brought the lips together is now given to the forehead:

> Vete! . . . Tu noble frente,
> Do por última vez mi labio imprimo,
> Jamás, jamás, ostente
> La corona fatal.
>
> ("Despedida" 279)

> [Leave me! . . . Your noble forehead, where for the last time
> my lip shall rest, never, never should wear the fatal crown.]

She presses her friend to search for love away from the dangerous world that her mouthful of Sappho implies. Her "ruego loco" to remain and enjoy a sort of literary bliss that would lead them down the path of Sappho presents a sort of temptation that the poet acknowledges to be imprudent. Whereas Sappho is left in a state of satisfaction, telling her lover, "go happily / and remember me" (qtd. in Rayor 60), Avellaneda is left in turmoil while she urges her friend to cling to her domestic happiness "cual ama el náufrago la tabla" ("Despedida" 279) [as the shipwrecked loves the plank]. At this point, the salvation of the other is seen within a domestic sphere. It is precisely here that the poem becomes truncated as Avellaneda questions Sappho's destiny to die for love:

> ¿No fue de rosas para ti el camino
> Cuando pasaste abrillantando el suelo?
> ¿Pudiste hallar abrojos en la vida?
> ¿Pudo vil cieno salpicar tus galas,
> Y el tirano dolor causarte herida,
> Cuando la gloria te prestaba asilo
> Y te dio el genio sus brillantes alas? . . .
> ¡Ay! ¡No respondas tú! . . . Leucades, dilo!
> . . . .
> . . . . [*sic*]
> ("Despedida" 278)

[Was the road not paved in roses when you passed enlightening the soil? Is it possible that you found thorns in life? Is it possible that your regalia was muddied, and could pain have hurt you when glory was yours and genius gave you brilliant wings? . . . Ah! Don't respond! . . . Let Leucades speak!]

I think these two blank lines following the evocation of Sappho's suicide at Leucades represent for Avellaneda the silence and emptiness that is the answer to Sappho's life. Interestingly, at this point, she does not refer to the assumption that Sappho killed herself out of desperation for a male lover. So it seems that even with her genius and glory she was consumed by an unhappy experience in love. After this coda of silence, Avellaneda goes on to desex the experience of death as a result of painful existence by comparing Sappho's suffering with that of other male poets (Ovid, Camoens, Cervantes, Tasso). In this sense her poetic "I" is tainted or equated to that male subjectivity that was annihilated by suffering.

The warning to her friend to avoid the painful existence of geniuses who have endured the hard life of the artist is followed by a different revelation which introduces one more Sapphic trope, that of the separate feminine space. As Sappho does in her odes, Avellaneda evokes a space which serves as a metaphor for emotional openness in a bucolic setting apart from the "normal": separate from marriage, home, society, from everything experienced by ordinary women in the course of domestic life. In her poetry, Sappho uses the bucolic setting in a sensual manner. Jack Winkler confirms that the physical landscape in Sappho is a metaphor for the female sexual body ("Double" 591). In the same manner, Lola's departure allows Avellaneda to transmute the sensuous nature of her "patria" [motherland] to her present loss with images that are eroticized in a feminine Sapphic mood:

> ¡Nunca igual dicha gozaré! Los montes
> Que se encumbran al sol; los silenciosos
> Bosques espesos, do jamás penetra;
> Las sabanas de inmensos horizontes,
> No existen para mí. No más mi diestra,
> Ligera, armada de cincel agudo,
> —Cual en un tiempo de memoria eterna—
>
>   . . .
>
> Irá ufana grabando,
> Del verde mango en la corteza tierna,
>   Dulces versos de amores,
> Encubiertos después con gayas flores.
>
>   ("Despedida" 279)

> [Never such joy shall I have! The mountains that rise toward the sun, the silent and thick forests where the sun never penetrates, the savannas of ample horizons do not exist for me any longer. . . . No more my hand, agile, and armed with a sharp easel—as ingrained in an eternal remembrance—shall happily engrave the tender skin of the unripe mango with sweet songs of love concealed afterwards with bright flowers.]

Nature becomes an extended and multiperspectived metaphor for women's sexuality: the "montes," "bosques espesos," "sabanas," "corteza tierna," "verde mango," and "gayas flores" render an erotic landscape that suggests the experience of female sexuality. The hand that holds the "cincel" [easel] to the juicy mango leaves a sensation of a diffuse lovemaking, so that the lost paradise of her native island turns into a way of expressing female desire. In Sappho's poem 8, a mutual understanding and desire are expressed to recall in an affirmative and orgasmic manner the experience of love. In the poem there is confirmation of intimacy between two women and an attempt to continue it (Winkler, "Garden" 77). In Avellaneda's poem, the erotic impulse is diffused within a literary friendship; and the desire that engages the narrator, although placed within the Sapphic bucolic setting, culminates in the solitude of the poet. Instead of an attempt to continue the intimacy, there is an impulse to break it, and the poet ends alone. Kirkpatrick interprets this solitude and the painful existence to which it leads as the result of being a woman writer in a hostile male world. Thus in her reading, the solitude of the subject becomes an annihilation of the self (*Las Románticas* 79–80). This reading centers on a subjective heterosexual discourse where women suffered for stepping into the male literary world, but if we locate this solitude within the Sapphic reading that Avellaneda adds, we can discern a reconfiguration of the subject–object relation as articulated by Simone de Beauvoir. "Between women love is contemplative; caresses are intended less to gain possession of the other than gradually to re-create the self through her, separateness is abolished, there is no struggle, no victory, no defeat, in exact reciprocity each is at once subject and object, sovereign and slave, duality becomes mutuality" (Beauvoir 465).

While duality does not become completely mutual in the relationship described in "Despedida," the solitary caress equates Sappho's suffering with that of Avellaneda for Lola. In the natural landscape, moreover, Avellaneda speaks of a love that erases the distinction between self and other, so that the poet incorporates suffering for her Sapphic love as part of her fulfillment. At the end there is an acceptance of a different kind of love, one that can live only in the memory of the poet:

> Para gemir tu ausencia
> Me quedan los insomnios devorantes
> De una soledad larga existencia
> ¡Sé dichosa sin mí!
>
>   ("Despedida" 279)

[To cry for your absence I am left with devouring sleepless nights of a lonely and long existence. Be happy without me!]

Unlike Sappho's "go happily / and remember me," Avellaneda's focus is on her own state of sadness as she says farewell to her friend: "¡Sé dichosa *sin mí!*"

As revealed in "Despedida," Avellaneda appropriates the voice of other poets to talk of passion and in doing so becomes a sort of transvestite, or transvoicite, expressing the love between women. Further examples of this strategy include two poems invoking Sappho, "El último acento de mi arpa" and "Soneto imitando una oda de Safo," and one imitating Byron, "Conserva tu risa." In 1851 Avellaneda wrote a poem in which Sappho becomes central in speaking to women. "El último acento de mi arpa: A mi querida amiga doña Leocadia de Zamora" (The last note of my harp: To my dear friend Ms. Leocadia de Zamora). Picón Garfield mentions this poem as an example in which the poet imitates Sappho by singing to women as a means of making them famous through their association with her (37). This is true, for the poet makes it clear that she, like Sappho, is glorifying this woman. "¡Yo quiero mostrarte mi afecto / ¡Yo quiero en mis versos tu gloria fijar!" ("El último acento" 320) [I want to show you my affection, and in my verses I want to affix your glory.]

But Avellaneda does not limit herself to consecrating the friend's name to posterity, she uses male erotic language to speak of women's love and to express their beauty. As writers have done through the ages, she compares Leocadia's body with Venus's. The poetic voice assumes the role of an older woman singing to a younger one who inspires her with a "canto" [song] as a "tributo de amor" [tribute of love] ("El último acento" 320):

> ¡Del Tínima esbelta ondina!
> ¡Rosa del trópico ardiente!
> ¡Pura estrella de Occidente!
> ¡Sirena hermosa del mar!
> ("El último acento" 320)

> [You are a water nymph from the Tínima![10] You are a rose from the ardent tropic! You are a pure Western star, and a beautiful siren from the sea!]

At the same time as she includes love and glory for her friend, she focuses on sensual parts of the body that have been the staple of erotic male poetry through the ages, such as *ojos* (eyes), *labios* (lips), and *profusa melena* (abundant long hair). Since the poem contrasts an older woman with a younger one, one wonders if Avellaneda is not lamenting the loss of her own sensual body. The poetic voice contrasts as well "el genio" [genius] with physical beauty and concludes that both, beauty and intelligence, are what make her friend attractive:

> El genio anima tu mente
> La virtud rige tu alma;
> Por eso pasión y calma
> Unidas sueles mostrar.
> ("El último acento" 321)

> [Genius animates your mind and virtue reigns in your soul; hence passion and serenity you usually reveal in unison.]

This beauty is so stunning that it turns the poet into a silent lover of a goddess:

> ¡Quisiera tu voz divina
> Para poderte alcanzar;
> Pues siento la mía turbada y mezquina,
> Y sólo en silencio te debo admirar!
> ("El último acento" 321)

> [I wish for your divine voice so that I could reach you, for I feel mine disturbed and wretched, and only in silence can I admire you.]

In "Soneto imitando una oda de Safo" (1850), written seven years after "Despedida," Avellaneda again speaks of female desire, but this time she clarifies for her readers her unison with the voice of Sappho:

> Ante mis ojos desaparece el mundo,
> Y por mis venas circular ligero
> El fuego siento del amor profundo.
> ("Soneto" 257)

> [Before my eyes the world disappears, and through my veins I feel
> the light fire of profound love.]

The literary friendship implied in "El último acento de mi arpa" turns into a lyric expression of passion for a desexualized love object with the very sexually charged words of Sappho. The poet here turns again to the same passage of Sappho in poem 8, but now she has framed that passage in a love poem rather than in a poem to a friend. By imitating Sappho, she clearly implies that this is a love poem, not a poem of friendship. Avellaneda inscribes Sappho and her erotic language, assuming and validating the experience of Sappho as subject in open desire for her love object. The fear of speaking with the voice of Sappho implicit in "Despedida" acquires a female orgasmic ecstasy as the poem re-creates an erotic surrender to passion uncharacteristic in the poetry written by women at this time. Mutuality is confirmed through the act of passion and through the metaphor of total fusion with the other:

> Trémula, en vano resistirte quiero . . .
> De ardiente llanto mi mejilla inundo
> Deliro, gozo, te bendigo y muero!
> ("Soneto" 258)

> [Tremulous, in vain, I want to resist you . . .
> And I cover with hot tears my chin.
> I am delirious yet joyous as I bless you and die!]

While there is no doubt that the subject is feminine, the sexual identity of the object is not identified as male or female. Is it male? This is how it was understood at the time. And it is this reading that one critic points out:

La señora de Avellaneda ha querido, por ultimo, pintarnos el paso más doloroso y temible de la pasión de amor, y nos le ha pintado superándose a sí misma y dejandonos entrever, . . . la tempestad que agitaría el pecho de la desdeñada de Faón. . . . [sic]

(Juan Valera, qtd. in *Obras de . . . Avellaneda* 167)

[Mrs. Avellaneda wants to draw for us the most painful and fearful step of passionate love, and she has done so, outdoing herself and letting us see the tempest that agitated the heart of the scorned of Faeon. . . .]

Valera here chooses the word "desdeñada" to identify Avellaneda's interpretation of Sappho as a "scorned" woman, and thus the possible lesbian erotic meaning of the poem is completely erased. But could the object have been female, as it was in Sappho's poem? This is a possibility, since Avellaneda is imitating a poem in which the object is clearly a woman. Avellaneda is joining Sappho to talk about the voice of the lover as the catalyst for ecstasy. So in this later poem, as in the earlier poem to Lola, words are the erotic agent that connect the subject and object of desire. The veiling of sexuality here is a sort of transvoicing through which the author talks of sexual passion by appropriating a lesbian desire.

While in these poems Avellaneda transvoices a female poetic voice, in other poems the process of transvoicing becomes more complex. On occasion she borrows a male voice to speak of love, but again the sexual identity remains fluid. In "Conserva tu risa: Imitación de las estrofas a Inés, del Child Harold, de Byron" (Save your smile: Imitation of Byron's Child Harold verses to Ines), the poet adopts the voice of Byron to sing to her female friend. The poet starts by focusing on the "labios bellos" [beautiful lips] that render her speechless with a sensuous smile: ". . . mis labios mustios, / Que agito con esfuerzo" [my wilted lips, which I agitate with compulsion]. Transgression here is analogous to the love and fear expressed in "Despedida." However, in this poem there is a silent impulse that struggles to articulate an unnamed feeling. This silence is caused by the object of her love; the poem is dedicated to an unidentified woman. "Dedicada a mi amiga C***" ("Conserva" 298) [Dedicated to my friend C—]. The male voice is taken over by a feminine subject to talk to a friend of her unspoken feelings captured at the moment of the smile. The poem is subtitled "Malestar inmenso" (Immense malady), which alludes to the romantic ethos of a philosophical angst and responds to the masculine anxiety of the *mal du siècle*. The poem is, after all, an imitation of Lord Byron's. In the original Byronic poem, the authorial voice is masculine and the object is feminine. By changing the sex of the subject but not that of the object, Avellaneda transvoices the poem and speaks as if she were a man, but with the gender mark that corresponds to the feminine. "Huir de mí misma necesito . . ." ("Conserva" 298) [I need to flee away from myself . . .]. The feminine figure becomes a parody of the masculine romantic figure, for it is philosophically trapped in a painful world:

> Mi mal estriba en esto . . .
> ¡Me ensangrienta el azote de la vida!
> ¡Me agobia el pensamiento!
> ("Conserva" 298)

> [My malady consists in the following . . . I am bloodied by life's blast, I am oppressed/overwhelmed by thought!]

This would be a mere usurpation of masculine erotic poetry were it not for the erotic beginning, in which the lips, as in "Despedida," become the focal point at which the eyes are directed and which desire mutuality:

> En vano la sonrisa alagadora
> Vaga en tus labios bellos,
> Y otra demanda de mis labios mustios,
> Que agito con esfuerzo.
>
> ("Conserva" 298)

[In vain your praising smile wanders in your beautiful lips and demands another from my wilted lips, which I agitate with compulsion.]

Thus the poetic persona, after receiving a sort of erotic gaze from her young friend, warns her about her feelings while tentatively asking the friend to look at her again:

> ¡Ah, no puedo reir! Mira esta frente,
> Que marca infausto sello. . . .
> Mas no la mires, no; guarda tu risa
> Y hágala eterna el cielo!
>
> ("Conserva" 299)

[Ah!, I can't return your smile! Look at this forehead marked with an ill-fated seal. . . . But alas, don't dare return my gaze, save your smile and let the heavens make it eternal!]

And at the end of the poem the poetic voice returns to the gaze:

> Al cielo mira y a la luz sonríe
> Yo en verte me recreo. . . .
> Mas nunca intentes penetrar en mi alma,
> Que en ella está el infierno!
>
> ("Conserva" 299)

[Toward the heavenly light, direct your look and your smile, and I will rejoice in watching you. . . . But never try to penetrate in my soul for in it evil reigns!]

In these verses there is a tension between the friends that goes beyond the erotic love veiled in the romantic friendships. This poem, however, is different from the Sapphic poems, since the poet now appropriates and feminizes the male voice to speak to a woman, whereas in the previous two poems she speaks as a woman with the voice of a woman. As if Avellaneda wants us to make sure that we understand the poem as a love poem to a woman, she writes another poem to explain her meaning in this one. In "Versos que acompañaron a los anteriores cuando fueron enviados a la persona a quien están dedicados" (Verses accompanying the previous ones when they were sent to the person to whom they are dedicated), the poet explains how she came to speak with the voice of Byron. It was after seeing her friend's happiness turn to sorrow in an attempt to understand her suffering that she thought of Lord Byron's verses:

> Mas, ¡ay!, cuando miraba
> Tu alegre y lindo rostro,
> Pensaba que en un tiempo
> (¡Cercano, no remoto!)
> Un bardo—que fue gloria
> Del Támesis brumoso,—
> Mirando igual cariño
> En otros bellos ojos,
> Mirando igual sonrisa
> En otro labio hermoso . . .
>
>   ("Versos" 299)

> [But when I was looking at your happy and beautiful face, I thought of that Thames's bard, who once—not long ago—finding a similar love in other beautiful eyes, looking at a similar smile in another beautiful lip . . .]

This explanation of her transvoicing that follows the Sapphic poems is a queer explanation indeed. Avellaneda has affirmed herself as a lover, able to express passion. But she has also realized that passion is problematic because, in her relationship with her young woman friend, she understood Child Harold's passion for Ines. Is this a lesbian love? Yes. Is it evidence of a consummated sexual relationship between women? Probably not. But Avellaneda's exploration seems to me to express a side of passion that had not been dealt with by those male writers who wrote of erotic love. She has discovered and understood passion for women. To be sure, this is not the only poem in which Avellaneda transvoiced the female subject; there are others in which she talks with the voice of male poets. But it is a clear example of the "uneasiness" that many literary critics have found in the lyrical subject and object of Gertrudis Gómez de Avellaneda.

In contrast with Coronado, who aimed to normalize and sanitize the figure of Sappho, and with other women poets who veiled their erotic friendships with women, Avellaneda presents a more complex relationship with her women friends. She does not defend Sappho from the accusations of impropriety, but she ignores the readings that present Sappho as a woman of unbridled passion. On the one hand, Gómez de Avellaneda has much in common with Sappho, for through the ages, and especially in the nineteenth century, the Lesbian poet was criticized for and interpreted on the basis of her sexual transgression and her exorbitant passion. Avellaneda was aware that she was an object of sexual desire, but she also knew that she had stepped beyond the boundaries of contemporary sexuality, and she was judged for this. At the time, Sappho is very much in the air. There are French and Spanish translations of her poetry as well as the interpretations that Madame de Staël and Georges Sand included in their works.

Thus, the tenuous introduction of Sappho in Avellaneda's poetry focuses on the feminine as special and renders the sexual poetic subject as problematic in many of her poems. Silence seems to be her response when she is in need of expressing her affection to her women friends. Unlike the group of writers that wrote love poetry to other women, Avellaneda's poems to her women friends present a more complex relationship, one that can in fact be deemed queer. A critic of her time confirms this when he comments that Avellaneda's "inconcreto y vago" [inconcrete and vague] love seems never to have found an adequate love object "no descubre objeto adecuado y digno de adorar y querer" (Juan Valera, qtd. in *Obras de . . . Avellaneda* 166) [does not discover an adequate object to adore and love]. Through recourse to Sappho, Avellaneda participates with other women who sought to establish a community that would validate their writings, but at the same time, her poems were charged by the sexuality that Sappho brought to nineteenth-century Europe. By transvoicing Sappho she comes to perform a female sexuality that disrupts dominant gender binaries. In her poetry we learn how she spoke of passion as a woman, and in these poems we are able to elucidate how that passion will open a queer space where passion for women begins to be articulated.

Notes

1. For a detailed history of the appearance and coinage of the word "homosexual," see the introduction to Fuss; and Jagose 10–21.

2. In quoting from Avellaneda's *Cartas inéditas,* I have been careful to transcribe her wording exactly as it was published, preserving misspellings and so on. Throughout the chapter, in citing works of Gómez de Avellaneda, I have omitted the author's name and included only the title of the source.

3. Unless otherwise noted, all translations in this chapter are my own.

4. See *Cartas inéditas;* as well as Hernández, "On the Double."

5. Susan Kirkpatrick refers to the group of women writers that evolved around the middle of the century as the "Románticas" in her book, *Las Románticas.* Kirkpatrick focuses on Carolina Coronado, Gómez de Avellaneda, and Cecilia Bohl as the key figures of this group. In her study "La 'hermandad lírica' en la década de 1840," she cites the periodical literature of the time that coined the phrase "hermandad lírica" (lyrical sisterhood) for the group of writers who were active around the middle of the nineteenth century and who developed a loving, supportive, and noncompetitive relationship with each other (30). Marina Mayoral includes in her study minor figures of this group who wrote about that friendship that flourished

between the women writers ("Las amistades"). Among the writers that she studies are: Vicenta García Miranda, Victoria Merida y Piret, Amalia Fellonosa, Manuela Cambronero, Robustiana Armiño, and María Teresa Verdejo y Durán.

6. The poet-satirist is demeaning the author by making fun of her name, Avellaneda, by using its literal meaning. An *avellana* is a hazelnut, and the adjective form, "*avellaneda*," refers to the nut's color, which suggests something hazy and unclear.

7. The arguments about women's biology and their incapacity to write has been treated by many contemporary feminists that have delved into nineteenth-century women writings. Gilbert and Gubar in their chapter "Infection in the Sentence" discuss the issue of patriarchal society's attributing writing to certain maladies and its attempt to prove that writing in fact atrophies the female body (298). Elaine Showalter (280–81) and Wendy Martin have also focused on this issue.

8. I am using Diane Rayor's translation of Sappho, and the numbers refer to her designation of Sappho's poems.

9. Avellaneda's poems cited in this section are from Gómez de Avellaneda, *Obras de doña Gertrudis Gómez de Avellaneda*. All citations of these poems will be identified by a short title form followed by the page numbers in which they appear in *Obras de . . . Avellaneda*. I will summarize the poems in English rather than give a direct translation from the Spanish. No attempt at versification will be made, but I will try to be specific in terms of the meaning.

10. The Tínima is a river from Avellaneda and Leocadia's native city, Camagüey, Cuba.

Works Cited

Beauvoir, Simone de. *The Second Sex*. Trans. H. M. Parshley. New York: Vintage Books, 1974; first published 1952.

Cotarelo y Mori, Emilio. *La Avellaneda y sus obras: Ensayo biográfico y crítico*. Madrid: Tipografía de Archivos, 1930.

DeJean, Joan. *Fictions of Sappho: 1546–1937*. Chicago: U of Chicago P, 1989.

Dubois, Page. *Sappho Is Burning*. Chicago: U of Chicago P, 1995.

Faderman, Lillian. *Surpassing the Love of Men: Romantic Friendship and Love between Women from the Renaissance to the Present*. New York: Morrow, 1981.

Foley, Helene P., ed. *Reflections of Women in Antiquity*. New York: Gordon and Breach, 1981.

Foucault, Michel. *The History of Sexuality*. Trans. Robert Hurley. New York: Pantheon, 1978.

Fuss, Diane, ed. *Inside/Out: Lesbian Theories, Gay Theories*. New York: Routledge, 1991.

Gilbert, Sandra M., and Susan Gubar. "Infection in the Sentence: The Woman Writer and the Anxiety of Authorship." *Feminisms: An Anthology of Literary Theory and Criticism*. Ed. Robyn R. Warhol and Diane Price Herndl. New Brunswick: Rutgers UP, 1991. 289–300. Originally published in *The Madwoman in the Attic*, by S. M. Gilbert and S. Gubar (1979).

Gómez de Avellaneda, Gertrudis. *Cartas inéditas existentes en el Museo del Ejército*.

Ed. José Priego Fernández del Campo. Madrid: Fundación Universitaria Española, 1975.

Gómez de Avellaneda, Gertrudis. *Dos mujeres.* Vol. 4 of *Obras literarias de la Sra. Gertrudis Gómez de Avellaneda.* 5 vols. Madrid: Rivadeneyra, 1869.

Gómez de Avellaneda, Gertrudis. "La mujer considerada particularmente en su capacidad científica, artística y literaria" (in the section "La mujer"). Vol. 5 of *Obras literarias de la Sra. Gertrudis Gómez de Avellaneda.* 5 vols. Madrid Rivadeneyra, 1869. 302–6.

Gómez de Avellaneda, Gertrudis. *Obras de doña Gertrudis Gómez de Avellaneda.* Ed. José María Castro y Calvo. 1st vol. of 5: 272, 273, 278, 279, 288. Biblioteca de Autores Españoles. Madrid: Atlas, 1974.

Gómez de Avellaneda, Gertrudis. *Tres amores* (Comedia en prosa y en tres actos, precedidos de un prólogo). Vol. 2 of *Obras dramáticas de la Sra. Gertrudis Gómez de Avellaneda.* 2 vols. Madrid. Rivadeneyra, 1877.

Grahn, Judy. *The Highest Apple: Sappho and the Lesbian Poetic Tradition.* San Francisco: Spinsters, Ink, 1985.

Harter, Hugh A. *Gertrudis Gómez de Avellaneda.* Boston: Twayne Publishers, 1981.

Hernández, Librada. "El *no* de las niñas: Subversive Female Roles in Three of La Avellaneda's *Comedias.*" *Hispanic Journal* 12.1 (1991): 27–45.

Hernández, Librada. "On the Double: *Tres amores* and the Postponement of Love in La Avellaneda's Theater." *Letras Femeninas* 20 (Número Extraordinario Conmemorativo: 1974–94): 39–49.

Jagose, Annemarie. *Queer Theory: An Introduction.* New York: New York UP, 1997.

Kaminsky, Amy. "The Construction of Immortality: Sappho, Saint Theresa and Carolina Coronado." *Letras Femeninas* 19.1–2: 1–14.

Kaminsky, Amy. "Lesbian Cartographies: Body, Text, and Geography." *Cultural and Historical Grounding for Hispanic and Luso-Brazilian Feminist Literary Criticism.* Ed. Vidal Hernán. Minneapolis: Institute for the Study of Ideologies and Literature, 1989. 223–56.

Kirkpatrick, Susan. "The Female Tradition in Nineteenth-Century Spanish Literature." *Cultural and Historical Grounding for Hispanic and Luso-Brazilian Feminist Literary Criticism.* Ed. Vidal Hernán. Minneapolis: Institute for the Study of Ideologies and Literature, 1989. 343–70.

Kirkpatrick, Susan. "La 'hermandad lírica' de la década de 1840." *Escritoras románticas españolas.* Ed. Marina Mayoral. Madrid: Fundación Banco Exterior, 1990. 25–41.

Kirkpatrick, Susan. *Las Románticas: Women Writers and Subjectivity in Spain, 1835–1850.* Berkeley: U of California P, 1989.

Lauretis, Teresa de. "Sexual Indifference and Lesbian Representation." *The Lesbian and Gay Studies Reader.* Ed. Henry Abelove, Michèle Aina Barale, and David M. Halperin. New York: Routledge, 1993. 141–58.

Martin, Wendy. *The American Sisterhood: Writings of the Feminist Movement from Colonial Times to the Present.* New York: Harper and Row, 1972.

Mayoral, Marina. "Las amistades románticas: Confusión de formulas y sentimientos." *Escritoras románticas españolas.* Ed. Marina Mayoral. Madrid: Fundación Banco Exterior, 1990. 43–72.

Mayoral, Marina, ed. *Escritoras románticas españolas.* Madrid: Fundación Banco Exterior, 1990.

Menéndez Pelayo, M. *Historia de la poesía hispano-americana.* Vol. 1. Madrid: n.p., 1911.

Picón Garfield, Evelyn. *Poder y sexualidad: El discurso de Gertrudis Gómez de Avellaneda.* Amsterdam and Atlanta: Rodopi, 1993.

Rayor, Diane. *Sappho's Lyre: Archaic Lyric and Women Poets of Ancient Greece.* Berkeley: U of California P, 1991.

Rich, Adrienne. *On Lies, Secrets, and Silence: Selected Prose, 1966–1978.* New York: Norton, 1979.

Sedgwick, Eve Kosofsky. *Epistemology of the Closet.* Berkeley: U of California P, 1990.

Showalter, Elaine. "The Female Tradition." *Feminisms: An Anthology of Literary Theory and Criticism.* Ed. Robyn R. Warhol and Diane Price Herndl. New Brunswick: Rutgers UP, 1991. 269–88. Originally published in *A Literature of Their Own,* by E. Showalter (1977).

Stigers, Eva Stehle. "Sappho's Private World." *Reflections of Women in Antiquity.* Ed. Helene P. Foley. New York: Gordon and Breach, 1991. 45–61.

Snyder, Jane McIntosh. *Lesbian Desire in the Lyrics of Sappho.* New York: Columbia UP, 1997.

Valera, Juan. *Disertaciones y juicios literarios.* Madrid: Biblioteca Perojo, n.d.

Valis, Noel. *In the Feminine Mode: Essays on Hispanic Women Writers.* Lewisburg, Pa.: Bucknell UP, 1990.

Vicinus, Martha. "They Wonder to Which Sex I Belong: The Historical Roots of the Modern Lesbian Identity." *The Lesbian and Gay Studies Reader.* Ed. Henry Abelove, Michèle Aina Barale, and David M. Halperin. New York: Routledge, 1993. 432—52.

Winkler, Jack. "Double Consciousness in Sappho's Lyrics." *The Lesbian and Gay Studies Reader.* Ed. Henry Abelove, Michèle Aina Barale, and David M. Halperin. New York: Routledge, 1993. 577–94.

Winkler, Jack. "Gardens of Nymphs: Public and Private in Sappho's Lyric." *Reflections of Women in Antiquity.* Ed. Helene P. Foley. New York: Gordon and Breach, 1991. 63–87.

Wittig, Monique. "One Is Not Born a Woman." *The Lesbian and Gay Studies Reader.* Ed. Henry Abelove, Michèle Aina Barale, and David M. Halperin. New York: Routledge, 1993. 103–9.

Zimmerman, Bonnie. *The Safe Sea of Women: Lesbian Fiction, 1969–1989.* Boston: Beacon, 1990.

Part 2

Si(gh)ting the *Armario:* Restoring Visibility

4

"Para objetos solamente"
The Silencing of a Voice

Carmen Tisnado

As I was reading Mario Benedetti's first novel, *Quién de nosotros*,[1] I was captivated by the overriding power of the "unsaid" as that which creates and shapes the story. The more I read Benedetti the more I regarded silence, in its many forms, as a recurrent motif in his narrative, especially in his short stories.

In his first collection of stories (*Montevideanos*, 1959), in which the focus is on individuals and their personal circumstances, silence permeates the relations among characters, primarily couples and people who work together. It is in his second book of short stories (*La muerte y otras sorpresas*, 1968) where silence, for the first time, reflects the effects of political repression, abuse, and torture. This volume of stories marks a definite transition in Benedetti's narrative from mainly existential themes to themes that deal with strictly political issues, in which torture is one of the inevitable topics when referring to the situation in Uruguay in the late 1960s and early 1970s. In *La muerte y otras sorpresas* there are stories which include, among other topics, the apathy of office workers ("Musak"), the sexual exploitation of women ("Miss Amnesia"), the experience of political activists and their consequent arrest and torture ("El cambiazo").

In this collection Benedetti portrays what it is like to be neglected, ignored, silenced, with the same clarity as he portrays what it is like to be on the side of the powerful, perpetrating the abuse and silencing those who are on the margin. Although I do not intend to attribute intentionality to the author, it seems as if he assumed the silenced voice of the oppressed and delivered it as such to his readers.

The stories in *La muerte y otras sorpresas* were written during a period of unrest, when Uruguay was going through its worst economic crisis, and socially there was uncertainty and fear. As it is explained in the introduction of *Uruguay nunca más:*

All that [Uruguayan stability] changed with astounding rapidity during the decade and a half after 1960. The roots of that transformation are complex. . . . In essence, the economic model that undergirded the prosperity that in turn sustained Uruguay's generous system of public entitlements began to falter seriously during the 1950s, and the country's political classes seemed utterly incapable of confronting the developing crisis; in fact, corruption and complacency were rampant. Some kind of calamitous outcome was perhaps inevitable, but it was doubtlessly hastened along by the increasingly disruptive provocations of a new generation of political radicals, the almost legendary Tupamaros, whose initially uproarious high jinks progressively degenerated into more and more violent confrontations. The political and financial establishment increasingly began relying on its security apparatus to enforce public order. The police and armed forces in turn grew both larger and more independent of their civilian overlords; they also underwent a marked ideological transformation, their worldview becoming more and more aligned with that of their neighboring security elites. (Servicio Paz y Justicia, Uruguay xviii–xix)

The stories in *La muerte y otras sorpresas,* then, were written when the police had started a repression that was directed not only at terrorists but also at whomever was suspected of disapproving of the government. Although in this collection of stories Benedetti portrays victims—and victimizers—of oppression of different kinds, "Para objetos solamente" (1966) (For objects only)[2] is the only story in which the author deals, even if obliquely, with the theme of homosexuality. This story is not "political": it does not deal with the crisis itself, the protests it provoked, or the repression that ensued. Yet a queer reading would describe "Para objetos solamente" as a deeply political short story. As Paul Burston and Colin Richardson state,

Queer Theory is both "political" and "cultural": political because it seeks to expose and problematise the means by which "sexuality" is reduced to the definitions of gender; cultural, because just about everything we might call Queer Theory concerns itself with the ways in which cultural texts . . . condition understandings of sexuality. (1)

Benedetti's text seems to have assimilated the "understandings of sexuality" at the time it was written. The author depicts gays (and, indirectly, lesbians) as any other oppressed group: as objects of social prejudice, of lack of acknowledgment, of neglect, of negation. He shows that homosexuals are victims of oppression and abuse just by systematically being denied and consequently deprived of their identity. At the time the story was written, discussion of (homo)sexuality was socially proscribed, and gay men and lesbians were suppressed to the point of being tacitly regarded as nonexistent. Apart from showing this suppression in the story itself, Benedetti exhibits it in his narrative technique by only alluding to the topic. In its explicit form, homosexuality—or rather sexuality—is thematically and narratively silenced, and this silence represents the taboo that for such a long time made sexuality belong to the realm of the unsayable.[3] In his text, Benedetti mirrors the social oppression of homosexuals by silencing Fernando, the gay character: Fernando has no voice at all. This silencing has an inevitable double-edged effect. On the one hand, it could be understood as a complicit, even if unconscious, alliance of Benedetti with the oppressors. On the other hand, the author does manage to show what this oppression consists of, and by showing it, he makes the reader witness it and thus become more aware of it.

However, whether Benedetti is basically complicit with the oppressors or whether he denounces this oppression by showing it in his text is not a dilemma that would be easily resolved as if it were an "either-or" option. If we place "Para objetos" within the context of Benedetti's writings, we cannot but assume that he sides with the marginalized, whether they are the political prisoner, the raped woman, the exploited worker, or the gay character. Yet by presenting homosexuality in an oblique way, Benedetti indirectly renders obedience to the oppressors. The author internalizes— or rather has internalized—the "rules of society," and even when he exposes their harms, he abides by them.

One of the main features of Benedetti's narrative technique in "Para objetos" is the very limited presence of a narrator: the story mainly consists of the meticulous enumeration of objects in an apartment. In the beginning, a barely noticeable narrative voice gives the context and proposes a hypothesis to the reader: that she or he imagine that somebody enters a room in the apartment where, we discover later, Fernando's dead body is lying. The voice invites the reader to go over the inventory of the objects in the room:

Por el momento nadie entra en la habitación, pero si alguien entrara, o mejor aún, si sólo penetrara una mirada, sin tacto, sin gusto, sin olfato, sin oído, sólo una mirada, y decidiera fríamente hacer un ordenado inventario visual de sus objetos, comenzando digamos, por la derecha, lo primero que habría de encontrar sería . . . (90)

[For the moment no one enters the room, but, if anyone would enter, or, better yet, if only a stare would pierce through the door, a stare with no sense of touch, or taste, or smell, or hearing, just a stare intent upon making a cold and well-ordered visual inventory of the room's objects, beginning, let's say, on the right, the first thing it should meet would be . . .]

As soon as the inventory of objects begins, the narrative voice assumes mainly the role of "focalizor"[4] and refers only to what is statically there, without alluding to any action. It is when the gaze stops at a dead male body that we realize there must be a story which is never "told." The inventory—*inventario visual*—of objects "shown" leads the reader to reconstruct the events that constitute the story underneath.[5]

What kind of gaze, then, is given at the apartment? Who gives it? Although the narrative voice seems neutralized, mainly because it does not "tell" a story, the assumption that most readers would make is that it is a male voice: detectives or police officers are the ones responsible for making an inventory of the objects at the scene of a homicide or suicide. In South America, especially at the time "Para objetos" was written, the vast majority of the police force was male. What is not necessarily expected is the inventory to be done exclusively as an enumeration of things, without any comment or speculation that might guide a discovery or a further inquiry. Yet there is not a single word leading to any interpretation of the events that have occurred. If there were any attempt for an interpretation, the narrative voice would inevitably have to refer to Fernando's sexuality. However, Fernando's body is just looked at and listed as another object in the room. Not only is the gaze male, then, but also voyeuristic and homophobic. By making the gay character's body and his apartment be simply looked at, the text, out of its own homophobia, is imprisoning the character in his gay closet.

Although in this short story there is no direct speech from a character, the text of "Para objetos" constitutes discourse. As Caroline Evans and Lorraine Gannan say, "Context is important, but the text also is a structuring discourse. Cultural meanings are actively generated through representation . . ." (45). In this sense, "Para objetos" not only generates homophobia but also stimulates the "différance"[6] of gay characters in that they deserve an inspecting gaze, which adds otherness and strangeness to them.

Furthermore, another aspect of the narrative technique in "Para objetos" is that there is no action performed, nor is there a character to perform an action. Only by treating the objects in the list as pieces in a puzzle and by interpreting them as signs and symbols can we go beneath the surface of the objects and enter the sphere of the action. Only then can the reader obtain an approximate understanding of the characters' "mind and heart."[7] The idea is that there are characters behind these objects, yet as long as the objects are not touched by human presence they lack meaning. It is human action upon the objects that makes them acquire meaning in a specific situation.

Gerard Genette indicates that "the very idea of showing, like that of imitation or narrative representation (and even more so, because of its naively visual character), is completely illusory: in contrast to dramatic representation, no narrative can 'show' or 'imitate' the story it tells" (163–64). However, in "Para objetos," it is the telling which is illusory. This story exemplifies what "showing" is through a cameralike technique. There is a narrative silence throughout the whole text, so that in essence the reader becomes the teller of the story when she or he is finally able to put the pieces together. Without this "telling," the story does not exist. What actually shapes the story is the reader's interpretation of signs and reconstruction of the action, which makes the reading of the text somewhat ambiguous. As Evans and Gannan remark,

While there might be consensus on the denoted meaning, there is always ambiguity in the realm of connotation. For example, in texts with a homosexual subtext D. A. Miller has argued that the love that dares not speak its name, except ambiguously, is relegated by virtue of its very ambiguity to a system of connotation. . . . Miller goes on to say that connotation is the very signifying process of homophobia, denying homosexuality even as it reiterates it. (45)

Evans and Gannan refer to D. A. Miller's reading of Alfred Hitchcock's *Rope,* where, Miller states, the homosexuality of the protagonists "has been consigned to connotation" (123). Connotation, according to Miller, imposes silence but at the same time seeks confirmation. The result is then a sort of urgency to prove what is otherwise unspoken. Therefore, in *Rope,* connotation "has the advantage of constructing an essentially insubstantial homosexuality, [but] it has the corresponding inconvenience of tending to raise this ghost all over the place" (Miller 125). Accordingly, in "Para objetos," homosexuality has been consigned to connotation, quoting Miller. Both the structure of the narrative and the gaze that dominates the text from within deny homosexuality by making it invisible and unspoken. The gaze, needless to say, cannot "look at" what is not visible, but it does stare at Fernando's body as an object, and this objectification is what makes Fernando completely invisible as a character.

King-kok Cheung, when analyzing Hisaye Yamamoto's texts, which have different kinds of silences, notes that "because the relationship between life and art is here as elsewhere indirect, these texts demand and deserve meticulous close reading. Only by anchoring them culturally and historically, however, can we fully disclose the author's formally complex design and the layers of emotion embedded in her ellipsis" (73). Given the history of homosexuality, it is to be assumed that "by anchoring culturally and historically" Benedetti's text, we can understand that the narrative silence in "Para objetos" mirrors (and also happens because of) the silence inflicted upon homosexuals for a long time, especially in Latin America: homosexuality was hardly mentioned, and therefore gays and lesbians were rendered invisible and thus were unable to voice their identity in any way. As Susan Friedman notes, "Textual repression can reflect cultural and political oppression" (qtd. in Cheung 29).

A very significant quality of "Para objetos" is its absence of characters on a first level of fictionalization. On a second level—in the story that is reconstructed by the readers—there are three characters: Fernando, Manuel, and Beatriz. They are only alluded to, however, and not directly presented in the text. They emerge only through certain objects. In this sense, they are objectified. Manuel appears first as the initial "M." written on a calendar and later as the name "Manuel." Beatriz also appears as the name "Beatriz" on a signed photograph Fernando has in his apartment. The pieces of a letter Beatriz writes to Fernando are also shown in the text. Finally, even Fernando's body becomes another object in the room.

The dead body suggests that there must be a story, but in order to discover it, the reader is invited to engage in detective strategies. Just as a detective takes an inventory of the objects at the scene of a crime, retrieving as many clues as possible, so too readers must start associating and interpreting signs in order to discover the story which is not told.

The presence of Fernando's dead body brings about many questions to ponder. How does he die? Why does he feel he has to die? Within the context of a detective "inventory," is he responsible for a crime? Or is he a victim of one? And so on. Whatever the answers, Fernando is present in the text as a would-be character, since we encounter only his body. Moreover, we learn later that this male body we first come upon belongs to a gay man. Hence, "Para objetos" includes the inscription of "the gay body." Lee Edelman suggests that "the . . . tropology of the inscribed gay body indicates, by its defensive assertion of a visible marker of sexual otherness, a fear that the categorical institutionalization of 'homosexual différance' might challenge the integrity and reliability of anatomical sameness as the guarantor of sexual identity" (12).

Fernando's body is inscribed as a gay body, and its inclusion as yet another object in the room accentuates a certain otherness. In other words, it is hard for any reader to identify with a dead body at all, yet within this otherness is included a "sexual otherness," which would ensure that the straight-identified male reader will not identify with the gay male character.

The language in the text also invites the reader to keep a distance. The words used in "Para objetos" are devoid of any emotion or judgment. There is an objective description of what can be seen in a room without any mention of an inner state. It is as if the author were "writing at a zero degree." Roland Barthes indicates that writing at a zero degree is

basically in the indicative mood, or if you like, amodal; it would be accurate to say that it is a journalist's writing, if it were not precisely the case that journalism develops in general, optative or imperative (that is, emotive) forms. The new neutral writing takes its place in the midst of all those ejaculations and judgments, without becoming involved in any of them; it consists precisely in their absence. But this absence is complete, it implies no refuge, no secret; one cannot therefore say that it is an impassive mode of writing; rather, that it is innocent. (76–77)

"Para objetos" has no voice which takes a side. In this sense, it conforms to the Barthean idea of an "innocent" text. Benedetti, employing the same blinding devices that the repressive society uses, shows how innocence could be confused with support of oppression just by omission. He portrays the dangerous and harmful angles the so-called innocence could take. By the same token, when analyzing torture in repressive societies, Kate Millett emphasizes that "the silence must end, must be broken, the victim's voice must be restored, since otherwise the torturers are never negated or defeated or even counterbalanced, they are merely in and out of power. . . . And how easy it is to become complicit" (301–2).

Following this idea, we see that not saying anything about repression to gays contributes as much to their isolation and loneliness as repression does directly. The text itself is the example: the word "homosexuality" is not mentioned, and it is the lack of acknowledgment and recognition which ends up, to an extent, making "Para objetos" a heterosexist text. As Judith Butler affirms,

Oppression only works through the production of a domain of unthinkability and unnameability. Lesbianism is not explicitly prohibited in part because it has not even made its way into the thinkable, the imaginable, that grid of cultural intelligibility that regulates the real and the nameable. How, then, to "be" a lesbian in a political context in which the lesbian does not exist? That is, in a political discourse that wages its violence against lesbianism in part by excluding lesbianism from discourse itself? To be prohibited explicitly is to occupy a discursive site from which something like a reverse-discourse can be articulated; to be implicitly proscribed is not even to qualify as an object of prohibition. (312)

Although Butler refers to lesbianism, the concepts are undoubtedly applicable to the oppression of gay men as well. "Para objetos" represents an analogy of how silence can be heard as consent of oppression, that is, as homophobia by omission.

In the text of "Para objetos" there is an initial fluctuation between the conditional and the indicative, which gives the reader a very succinct description. Regardless of the mood, we can say that "Para objetos" has a structure of absence in its writing. There is absence of emotion or any other personal involvement in the description. Any feelings are shown only through written words in some of the described objects. It is only because of those words that we are able to reconstruct the story. If only the objects as such were considered, we would have bits and pieces with hardly any connection. If only objects were mentioned, some of them would be:

a sofa
a heap of newspapers and magazines
a book with a paper cutter between the first pages
a calendar
a theater program
an ashtray full of cigarette butts, all of them bent in the same way
a single bed
a torn piece of a letter
a pad of paper with a written message
an oak wardrobe
men's clothes
an inscribed photograph of a young woman
a small gas stove with two burners, one on and one off
the dead body of a young man with blue shorts and a red scarf on
a second torn piece of a letter

Trying to attribute significance to each object would be a useless activity. It is only when we see objects in relation to each other that we can gather meaningful information. With this list, very few things can be inferred: a young man commits suicide by leaving the gas on in his apartment. He is involved with a woman in some way. He smokes a lot before his final action.

Only when we read what is written on some of the objects mentioned can we start establishing connections. This implies a second level of writing as well as a second level of reading. The first level refers to the "visual inventory" of what is seen in the room. The meaning of the objects is strictly limited to the objects themselves, since no context is given. For example, an ashtray is no more than an object used to collect butts of cigarettes; a picture frame is nothing but a frame in which one can place photographs. On the second level of description, the objects are given significance through written messages or words contained in them. It is inscribed language that brings meaning to the objects. The written messages presented on this second level of description are:

> *Claudia,* the title of the magazine at the top of the heap of magazines
> names, initials, and events written down on the calendar: "Beatriz,"
>   "M." and "ensayo general" [general rehearsal]
> the content of the first piece of the torn letter
> the word "Chau" (the Spanish version of "*ciao*") written on the first
>   page of the pad
> an inscription on the photograph of the young woman: "A Fernando,
>   con fe y esperanza pero sin caridad. Beatriz" [To Fernando, with faith
>   and hope but without charity. Beatriz].
> names of actors in the play whose program is on the floor; among others: Fernando Montes and Manuel Solano
> the content of the second piece of the torn letter

It is actually the content of the letter which clarifies the story. The letter is first presented as another object in the room. Its content is described from a graphic point of view: the reader is presented with a reproduction of its handwritten form. In this sense, it is the reader herself or himself who reads the letter. No one else does, not even the narrator-focalizor, who can see only the handwriting and describe the style but who does not read or interpret the message. Both pieces of paper are described with nearly the same words. When the focalizor—or the imaginary eye—pauses on the first piece of paper, it is described as

un papel irregularmente rasgado, algo así como la mitad de una hoja de carta, color crema, que alguien hubiera partido en dos. Está escrito con una letra menuda y muy pareja, de curvas suaves, con los puntos de las jotas y las íes muy por encima de su ubicación clásica. Si la mirada quisiera detenerse a leer, podría comprobar que las palabras, y trozos de palabras, que contiene el papel, son los siguientes: . . . (91)

[a piece of paper unevenly torn, something like half of a piece of cream-colored letter paper, as if someone had cut it in two. The handwriting on it is rather small and very even, with delicate curves and the dots on the *j*'s and the *i*'s far above their usual place. If the stare should want to stop and read, it could verify that the words and fragments of words on the piece of paper are as follows: . . .]

The focalization continues, following the order of the objects as they appear in the room. A few other things are described before the second piece of paper is met by the imaginary eye. The description of this second piece is almost identical to that of the first one, except for a few changes at the beginning:

un trozo de papel crema, algo así como la mitad de una hoja de carta que alguien hubiera partido en dos, escrito con una letra muy menuda y muy pareja. . . . (94)

[a piece of cream-colored paper, something like a half of a piece of paper, as if someone had cut it in two. The handwriting on it is rather small and very even. . . .]

The rest of the words are the same as those used to describe the first piece. Although it is not stated that there is one letter torn vertically into two pieces, the reader, seeking to find out the story behind it, has to piece the two fragments together. Only the letter, that is, the object containing the most words, can resolve the enigma of the story. Until this moment the reader has knowledge of a suicide but does not know the motives that might have led to it. The letter, pieced together, is as follows:

masiado para mí. Bien	sabés cómo aprecio
tu inteligencia y tu sen	sibilidad, bien sabés
la imprudente esperan	za que puse en vos,
en tu *capacidad de*	*recuperación,* en tus
esfuerzos por *volve*	*r a la normalidad* como
única y comprensible	exigencia que te impongo
para compensar mi a	mor de tantos años, de
tantos desencantos, de	tantas hermosas y falsas
pistas. Creo que en	el fondo estarás de
acuerdo conmigo: es i	nútil insistir. Estoy
segura de que me q	uerés y que querés
mi modesta felicidad	tal como yo quiero
la tuya, pero, buen	as o malas, hay en ti
y en mí, zonas inco	mpatibles; la de *tu*
inevitable y morbos	*a inclinación por Manuel,*
y la de mi incurab	le resistencia (llamale
prejuicios, anacronis	mo, lo que quieras) a
insistir en quererte	, consciente como soy de que
no podés ni podr	ás nunca entenderte con un
cuerpo de mujer, as	sí sea tan corriente como el
mío. Te juro que	miro mi propia e irrevocable
decisión con extr	aña melancolía. Acaso se deba
a que nunca h	asta ahora había querido resig
narme a enfren	tar la realidad, que en mi caso
es sencillamente	TU realidad. Mira si seré in-
corregible que a	quí te dejo aquel pañuelo
rojo que María	Elena me trajo de Italia y
(92; emphasis mine)	(95; emphasis mine)

[much for me. You know very well how much I value your intelligence and sensibility, you know very well how unwisely I believed in you, in *your ability to recover,* in your efforts to *return to normality* as my only and understandable demand in compensation for so many years of love, for so many disappointments, for so many beautiful and false clues. I believe that, at heart, you will agree with me: it's of no use to insist. I am sure that you care for me and for my modest share of happiness as I care for yours, but, be they good or bad, there are, in you and in me, some incompatible regions: that of *your morbid and irresistible attraction to Manuel,* that of my incurable resistance (call it prejudice, anachronism, whatever you want) to insist on loving you, aware, as I am, that you are not and never will be able to know how to deal with a woman's body, even one as ordinary as mine. I swear that I look at my own and irrevocable decision with a strange nostalgia. Perhaps it is that I had never until now resigned myself to face reality, which in my case is simply YOUR reality. Look how incorrigible I am that I am leaving for you here that red scarf María Elena brought me from Italy and][8]

Only when putting those pieces of paper together can we understand the action: Fernando is a young actor who has had a close, platonic relationship with a woman (Beatriz) for a number of years. Beatriz wants a romantic relationship with him. Fernando feels an attraction to Manuel, who is also an actor in the company in which he performs. It is never clear whether he and Manuel are romantically and/or sexually involved or not. Beatriz knows about Fernando's attraction, and for some time she hopes he will forget what she calls that "morbosa inclinación" [morbid attraction]. In the end she realizes this will not happen and leaves Fernando behind. She writes a letter to him explaining what she feels and leaves him a scarf. Fernando reads the letter, tears it into pieces, and throws the pieces on the floor. He turns on the gas, possibly takes his clothes off, leaving the blue shorts on, writes the word "Chau" on a pad, and puts on the red scarf. He dies.

If we take into account that the scarf is a present given to Beatriz by a friend, who is also female, it could be assumed that it is a female piece of clothing. Although her reasons for leaving it to him are not explicit, Fernando chooses the scarf, along with the shorts, as the pieces of clothing to wear for his suicide. It is to be inferred that in the apartment there are no other female clothes. Quite the contrary, the visual inventory includes only men's clothes—"ropa de hombre" (91)—in the wardrobe. Why, then, does Fernando choose to have the red scarf on? Is his choice acknowledging his gayness and therefore stating his belief in the stereotyped binary opposition homosexual/masculine?

I would like to leave these questions aside for a while because, in order to attempt any answers, there may be a need to pose other questions before: Do the shorts have a function? What do they suggest, especially if contrasted with the scarf? If Fernando were alive, his having shorts on would not be a matter of any discussion. In his society, as in ours, men and women are expected to cover their genitals. Yet it is precisely the possession of a penis, or the lack of one, that has falsely determined gender over the years. There is the assumption, Butler indicates, "that gender is the rightful property of sex, that 'masculine' belongs to 'male' and 'feminine' belongs to 'female'" (312). But, as Butler herself points out, "there is no 'proper' gender, a gender proper to one sex rather than another, which is in some sense that sex's cultural property. Where that notion of the 'proper' operates, it is always and only *improperly* installed as the effect of a compulsory system" (312–13).

Fernando, immersed in the "compulsory system" of heterosexual dominance, feels compelled to act according to what society expects of him as male. In other words, he has always, in a literal and a metaphoric sense, worn *ropa de hombre.* Not only does Fernando dress as a man, but he also brings into a public sphere a supposedly manly behavior, namely, a heterosexual behavior. He is acting out gender or what he believes to be expected of his gender. It would seem, then, that Fernando is unable to confront the rules of society when alive, but by committing suicide, by leaving the pieces of Beatriz's letter on the floor, and by exposing most of his body, he is figuratively disclosing his sexuality. Yet he is actually covering his penis. Why is he? Does he still want to act according to the rules of society? Does he need to, especially when, after his death, he will not have to face any reaction against him? Furthermore, his mere act of suicide is already an affront to these rules. Why, then, does he choose to wear the shorts and cover his penis? These questions take me back to the one I previously left pending.

Why does Fernando choose to have the scarf on, then? And, again, why does he have the shorts on? He may well be claiming his femininity by wearing the scarf, but his wearing the shorts seems more ambiguous. It is a fact that shorts are worn by both men and women. Since there is no specification, it is to be assumed that Fernando's shorts are men's. If we stress this, we could see his wearing the shorts as a claim of masculinity. Yet, if we emphasize the fact that his genitals are covered, especially since most of his body is not, we could interpret his wearing the shorts as a disclaimer of masculinity.

The latter interpretation, combined with the idea of his claiming femininity by wearing the scarf, may lead us to think that Fernando, only after his death, is disclosing his feminine or even effeminate side, as popular culture insists on depicting gays. In this regard, the scarf is the item that shows Fernando's appropriation of the feminine. This appropriation of gender suggests the idea of drag, which, according to Butler, "constitutes the mundane way in which genders are appropriated, theatricalized, worn and done; it implies that all gendering is a kind of impersonation and approximation" (313). We may agree, then, that Fernando is appropriating the feminine, but, what else is he doing through this action? It appears that he is finally reclaiming his sexuality. Yet he does this by accepting the opposition gay/masculine, which is proven not to be true. We have to conclude that, in several ways, Fernando agrees with Beatriz in that he is not "normal": he is gay, so he is not masculine; or, he is a man, *but* he is gay.

To some extent the text of "Para objetos" also represents a latent agreement with the opposition gay/masculine. In this story we find conventional (heterosexist) representations of gender and sexuality, which Butler proves wrong when she declares that if the idea that all gendering is a kind of impersonation and approximation is true, "it seems, there is no original or primary gender that drag imitates, but *gender is a kind of imitation for which there is no original*" (313). This concept takes away any grounds for a "pure heterosexual identity." As Butler points out, "Compulsory heterosexual identities, those ontologically consolidated phantasms of 'man' and 'woman,' are theatrically produced effects that posture as grounds, origins, the normative measure of the real" (313).

Benedetti, seemingly unintentionally and unconsciously, abides by the heterosexist rules of society. Ideology is inscribed in the discourse of "Para objetos." As Catherine Belsey explains:

A *discourse* is a domain of language-use, a particular way of talking (and writing and thinking). A discourse involves certain shared assumptions which appear in the formulations that characterise it. This discourse of common sense is quite distinct. . . . Ideology is *inscribed in* discourse in the sense that it is literally written or spoken *in it;* it is not a separate element which exists independently in some free-floating realm of "ideas" and is subsequently embodied in words, but a way of thinking, speaking, experiencing. (qtd. in Evans and Gannan 19)

"Para objetos," merely because it is shaped as a list of objects, may give the impression that it is not ideological or political. Yet a queer reading will show that it is a text charged with ideology. Beatriz's letter, for instance, is structured by a system of oppositions that suggest a homophobic and heterosexist point of view. The pairings found include: value/disapproval; recovery/worsening; normality/abnormality; morbidity/health; "reality"/Fernando's reality. These oppositions lie under the reading of the whole text.

Beatriz insists that Fernando should be aware of how much she values his intelligence and sensibility. Yet this value seems to be swept away by her disapproval of his attraction to Manuel. Although both her value and disapproval are focused on specific objects, the latter overpowers the former, and, in the end, Beatriz appears not only to disapprove of Fernando but also to reject him as a person.

She regrets having hoped for Fernando's recovery as if he had an illness or a certain syndrome which prevented him from being heterosexual. Since Beatriz sees her hopes shattered, her understanding is that Fernando has worsened, or reached a chronic state of either morbidity or abnormality, or both. Beatriz confuses Fernando's gay identity with a condition that could change as if it were mainly circumstantial.

Beatriz's expectations for Fernando to "return to normality" are also broken. Beatriz assumes heterosexuality as the norm and understands homosexuality as a transgression. Her attitude reflects a somewhat stereotypic viewpoint toward gays and lesbians. Furthermore, the opposition morbidity/health, which she implicitly suggests, follows the ideas proposed by the pairing abnormality/normality. There is an implied analogy among homosexuality, morbidity, and abnormality. Not being homosexual is assumed as being heterosexual, and this is rendered as "the healthy normality."

Finally, Beatriz's letter also implies a clash of realities. She talks about resigning herself to accept "reality," but she adds that the reality that influences her life is Fernando's reality. She does not show respect for Fernando, since she dismisses his being gay as a reality but categorizes it as only a perspective Fernando is temporarily giving to his life. The possessive *tu* when she says "TU realidad" [your reality] suggests a transitory state, a phase. Since points of view or perspectives which constitute "our" reality in the here and now may vary according to circumstances, Beatriz renders homosexuality as a stage but heterosexuality as an identity, thus attributing qualities of essentiality to it.

Lee Edelman, talking about *The Picture of Dorian Grey,* says that Dorian becomes aware of his identity when he hears Lord Henry speak. Edelman declares that "this moment of recognition retroactively produces the various 'meanings' that it appears, instead, to reveal" (19). Just as Dorian's is, Fernando's perception of himself is influenced by somebody else's speech. Beatriz's words reveal to Fernando her view of his identity. It seems that when he reads the letter he assumes and internalizes as his the "abnormality" and "morbidity" associated with his situation.

Fernando leaves no written message but the word "Chau." His voice is nullified. He is under the yoke of the silence imposed on him. Silence has been externally imposed on him in so many different ways that Fernando has internalized it as an integral part of himself. Evans and Gannan point out that the Foucaldian model of the "panopticon"—"the perfect prison, where the controlling gaze is used at all times as surveillance" (15)—is also applied to the female experience of being looked at by the male. They quote Sandra Lee Bartky, who concludes that "a panoptical male connoisseur resides within the consciousness of most women" (20). Applying the same model, we can argue that a panoptical homophobic connoisseur resides within the consciousness of some gays and lesbians, who exercise the surveillance against themselves. In "Para objetos" it is Beatriz who, within the story, portrays the homophobic surveillance and who makes Fernando exercise this surveillance against himself.

In the inscription she writes on the photograph, Beatriz says that she has "fe" [faith] and "esperanza" [hope]. Although the object of her faith and hope is not conveyed, we can understand that she hopes that Fernando will be able to love her as a woman. She will have no "caridad" [charity] for him if he assumes his gay identity. Beatriz is honest when expressing her feelings to Fernando, but she is inflicting pain on him nonetheless. Her words have a punitive effect on Fernando, even if she does not wish this. Although this punishment is figurative, Fernando takes a final step that permanently silences his voice: he commits suicide. Beatriz discards him in a figurative way, and he kills himself literally. Fernando is so unable to accept the social pressure—the inspecting gaze—on his sexuality that he ends up unable to accept his gayness himself. His death reveals that he actually cannot live as a gay man.

In an interesting twist, we can assume that in her own heterosexual world Beatriz, because she is female, is the object of a male gaze. Why, then, if she is being oppressed herself, does she act as an agent of oppression? However, her oppressive act is disguised by her portraying herself as a victim of Fernando's gayness. Beatriz presents herself as the suffering female, partly deceived by the gay male. Fernando's rejection of a female romantic partner accentuates his identity and, especially in the context of the 1960s in South America, serves as an accusation against him: not only are gay men "morbid" and "abnormal," but they also victimize women by making them feel inadequate and unloved. Beatriz, although also oppressed in a patriarchal society, assumes the heterosexist oppression that the patriarchal society invokes.

Fernando's self-imposed silence prevents him from explaining an act as meaningful and irreversible as suicide. As Cheung points out, "Because there are different degrees of access, different ways of (and barriers to) communication, not all those on the margins will speak. Before they can be heard in a 'democracy,' someone will have to learn their discourse of silence and make it audible" (172). Who makes Fernando's silence audible? I would say it is not the narrative voice, since Fernando is present only as a dead body. He is narratively silent, in a literal and a metaphoric way. It is not even Benedetti, who adopts this silence in his choice of nar-

rative technique and strategies. Is Fernando's silence made audible in the
text at all, then? In my opinion it is only the reader who can potentially
turn this silence into something else. Of course, Benedetti *is* the author of
the short story, so the structure he creates for the text allows, even if indirectly, this possibility of reading—of reaching a certain level of connotation. However, it also allows some ambiguity. We have, on the one hand,
Fernando's silence functioning as a statement to show, and therefore denounce, the oppression of gays in the same way as "Para objetos" may
denounce it. On the other hand, both Fernando and the structure of "Para
objetos" surrender to the regulations of the oppressive and homophobic
society they emerge from and act according to those regulations. This duality should remind us of the degree to which ideology is imposed on our
minds, and even if we consciously denounce abuse and oppression, we
may unconsciously act as agents of the same abuse and oppression we
denounce.

It is only when we are able to transcend the limits of the first level of
fictionalization in the text that we understand what happens in the story
and why. What is the component that gives meaning to the second level of
fictionalization? Language is what first comes to my mind. The written
elements make it possible to understand "Para objetos." Only when reading what Beatriz has written on two occasions (the message on the framed
photograph, and her letter torn into pieces) can we perceive her ambivalence toward Fernando: in the same text she expresses her care for him as
well as her apprehension due to his homosexuality.

"Para objetos," thematically and structurally, describes the silence of
social taboos and, specifically, the silence of homosexuality. Homosexuality is the unsayable. Benedetti's story has the structure of a puzzle that the
reader must solve. The reader sees with the help of the focalizor, but only
the reader can reach an understanding, since she or he is able to hypothesize and draw conclusions. In other words, only the reader can interpret
the signs that the focalizor sees but cannot interpret. While reading the
story, the reader creates suspense, since each object mentioned and described becomes a clue to a hypothesis that is ultimately supported by the
combination of clues. Suspense increases throughout the story. Mieke Bal
states that

suspense can be generated by the announcement of something that will occur later,
or by temporary silence concerning information which is needed. In both cases,
the image which is presented to the reader is manipulated. The image is given
by the focalizor. In principle, it coincides with the image that the focalizor has
himself. (114)

Sexuality is announced—rather, hinted—in the structure of suspense
created in the text. The first name we are able to see is Beatriz's, written

on a calendar. It is to be assumed that somebody has made an appointment with her or has to establish contact with her on a certain date. On the same calendar, marked at a different date, we see the initial "M." and this is when suspense starts. Why do we have Beatriz's name written in full but only an initial in the other case? To add mystery to this suspense, we can see what is written next to the initial: "M. ¿O.K.? OK" (90). Whatever is at stake has been cleared (it is "OK"), but the inscription of the doubt involved contributes to create a hidden agenda, a subtlety. Later, there are two objects that make us realize that the "stare" is focusing on a man's apartment: the cigarette butts without lipstick marks and men's clothes in the wardrobe. When both elements are linked, issues of sexuality begin to take shape. There are no indications about the sexual orientation of the man who lives in the apartment, but, in a society which preserves a heterosexual hegemony, it is easy to assume the character's heterosexuality. The name "Beatriz" reinforces this idea. Even the letter M could be taken as the initial of a secret woman, "the other woman." There are further objects that help readers maintain this first hypothesis: the male character keeps a framed photograph of Beatriz in his apartment. She, therefore, fits the role of the "official" partner, contrasted with the "unofficiality" suggested by simply "M." Besides, the written inscription on the photograph implies that there is an untold story. Beatriz has faith and hope but not charity. If we give a heterosexual reading to this message, the attribution of sex to the initial "M." might be more than viable: Fernando has a mistress, but Beatriz hopes that he will come back to her. However, the inscription on the theater program breaks all assumptions: "Manuel" (Solano) is the only first name in the program with the initial "M." Some readers might reach this conclusion more quickly than others, but whatever suspicion may arise is confirmed by Beatriz's letter, when she refers to Fernando's morbid attraction to Manuel. Even then, we cannot read this directly. The letter, as presented, breaks the reading of the story, and it is impossible to understand its meaning until we piece together the two fragments and see them as a whole. The suspense created is finally clarified, but the clarity arrives as an explosion, breaking assumptions and earlier interpretations.

In "Para objetos," silence is a permanent element found throughout the text. The silences are initiated by an impartial enumeration of objects, without any presence or even indication of emotions that may surround the hinted actions that the hinted characters may have performed. These silences are filled in by the reader's interpretation, which is shaped by clues and covert allusions.

The suspense is manipulated by the author. It is just this manipulation which leads the reader to hypothesize. In effect, the reader is encouraged to attribute sense to things that seem senseless; this constitutes a method of acquiring knowledge. Likewise, "Para objetos" is also a story about the adventure of making sense. It is a story that proves that "las cosas tienen un ser vital"[9] [things have a life all their own] whenever there is human presence behind them. And human presence is primarily expressed through language. Only the words written on pieces of paper or on photographs provide us with the elements for a global comprehension of the story. The pieces of the puzzle would be isolated without the words which link them cohesively and coherently, and the objects listed would not make much sense without those words.

"Para objetos" expresses the adventure of making sense through reading notes and messages within the level of the story and also through reading the title and the epigraph within the level of the narrative. The title, by suggesting that the "imaginary stare" will focus only on objects, reinforces the repression shown in the story: nothing will be seen but objects; what is not an object will be suppressed. Just after reading the title, though, the reader finds the epigraph, "Las cosas tienen un ser vital," which enables her or him to observe that, despite having to narrow the vision to objects, there will always be a story to be told and that the narrowing could merely signify the necessity of adapting to the repressive rules in order to function. "Para objetos" can be understood as an allegory of reading. Reading is an adventure in which readers hypothesize, associate events, and draw conclusions.

Thematically, this story also refers to the expression—or rather, the nonexpression—of identity. Fernando, in order to express one aspect of his identity, would have to assume and accept his homosexuality, what is now known as "coming out." The term "coming out," as Rebecca Mark reminds us,

has many performative meanings. It is simultaneously the statement of a moment, and a continuous process. Because of the charged political nature of homosexuality, coming out is never simply personal disclosure, but instead a willingness to align oneself with a certain set of assumptions, stereotypes, inconsistencies, incoherences, irrationalities, and projections. Because of this bewildering confusion and profusion of meanings, beyond the statement "I am" is a lifetime of creating understanding of what "I am" means. (245–46)

Fernando does not have a chance to express who he *is*. On the one hand, he is textually dead; on the other, the lack of understanding and the complaints from the outside, represented by Beatriz, are mainly connected to what Fernando *is not*. The basis for Fernando's identity is that he is not heterosexual rather than that he is homosexual. Fernando does not see a way out and opts for the maximum expression of "not being," that is, death.

The reading of "Para objetos" confirms that, as Eve Kosofsky Sedgwick states, "the closet is the defining structure of gay oppression in [the twenti-eth] century" (71). The listing of the objects in Fernando's apartment func-tions as an outing, and his apartment symbolizes the gay closet. The imag-inary stare, through its gaze, then, violates the privacy of Fernando's closetedness. Moreover, the inventory brings this privacy into a public realm. Fernando is outed, but he is put into another closet, and in the end, even in his silence and his death, he is surveilled by a homophobic gaze.

In its manifest form, "Para objetos solamente" is a story about the op-pression of gays, but in its latent form it is much more than that. It is also an allegory of all kinds of repression and of how objects of this repres-sion are nullified, annihilated. The story suggests that governments or "regimes" in power are not necessarily the only agents of oppression and repression. Society in general can be as repressive, even without weapons. Repression from society is harder to identify and, therefore, harder to admit, probably because it does not belong to anything "official" and its methods are not specific, and because it is repression by omission instead of repression by commission. It is as spiteful and harmful, however, as any armed repression. Its weapons are so disguised that they are incorporated as part of "the people." So long as societies base their beliefs on the grounds of oppositions—black/white; Christian/Jew; professional/blue-collar worker; straight/gay, to name a few—the weapons will be "the oth-ers" themselves. Because of their conviction, sometimes groundless or blind, they may hurt and wound to the point of causing death, even if figurative.

"Para objetos solamente" illustrates the forceful invasion of ideology. When reading Benedetti's fictional as well as nonfictional works, we can-not but conclude that he is a committed, progressive author who de-nounces numerous types of abuse and oppression. Yet when denouncing oppression toward gays, his text, even if in indirect ways, still follows the rules and uses the tools that belong to the oppressive system. In Bene-detti's texts, oppression is articulated in terms of political positions. The polarization Left/Right, at the time, invaded all aspects of life. Even the leftists, who denounced abuse and sided with those who were oppressed, were somewhat oblivious of marginal groups other than the workers and intellectuals. It does not come as a surprise, then, that the gay topic has no specific space in Benedetti's literature.

However, "Para objetos solamente" still presents the idea that oppres-sion is generalized. Social oppression of a specific group—in this precise case, gays—causes loss of individual identities and, consequently, collec-tive identities, preventing people from gathering as a community. On the same line, political repression also takes away the identity of individuals. It gives license to, even encourages, social repression. In both ways, either through political or through social repression, the effect is the same: the silencing of a voice, either individual or collective, or both. Society becomes the daily panopticon to any marginalized individual and group. And the most painful and harmful result of it is the self-surveillance, which could lead to self-alienation and self-destruction.

Notes

1. *Quién de nosotros* tells the story of three characters (two male and one female) involved in a triangle. All actions are based on assumptions about what the others do not say. At the end the three characters feel at a loss. The misunderstandings are clarified, but it is too late for them to reorganize their lives.

2. All English translations from the Spanish are done by Inés Azar.

3. I am using the distinction Patricia Ondek Laurence makes among "the unsaid" (something one might feel but does not say), "the unspoken" (something not yet formulated or expressed in voiced words), and "the unsayable" (something not sayable because of social taboos) (20).

4. Mieke Bal defines "focalization" as "the relationship between the 'vision,' the agent that sees, and that which is seen. The subject of focalization, the *focalizor*, is the point from which the elements are viewed" (104).

5. I am referring to the concepts of showing and telling as discussed by Genette in *Narrative Discourse*, 163–66. "Showing" suggests a minimal presence of the narrator. "Telling" implies saying something *about* something. As Genette says, "'Showing' can be *a way of telling*, and this way consists of both *saying about it* as much as one can, and *saying this 'much'* as little as possible." In other words, "pretending to be silent" (166).

6. See Derrida.

7. Wayne Booth points out that "one of the most obviously artificial devices of the storyteller is the trick of going beneath the surface of the action to obtain a reliable view of a character's mind and heart" (3).

8. In its translation the letter is presented as a unit, without the tear.

9. I am using the epigraph at the beginning of the story, a quotation from Rubén Darío.

Works Cited

Bal, Mieke. *Narratology*. Toronto: U of Toronto P, 1985.

Barthes, Roland. *Writing Degree Zero*. New York: Hill and Wang, 1967.

Benedetti, Mario. *Montevideanos*. 1959. Mexico City: Nueva Imagen, 1978.

Benedetti, Mario. "Para objetos solamente." 1968. *La muerte y otras sorpresas*. 20th ed. Mexico City: Siglo XXI, 1986. 90–95.

Benedetti, Mario. *Quién de nosotros*. 1st ed. Mexico City: Nueva Imagen, 1977.

Booth, Wayne. *The Rhetoric of Fiction*. 2d ed. Chicago: U of Chicago P, 1983.

Burston, Paul, and Colin Richardson, eds. *A Queer Romance: Lesbians, Gay Men and Popular Culture*. London: Routledge, 1995.

Butler, Judith. "Imitation and Gender Insubordination." *The Lesbian and Gay*

Studies Reader. Ed. Henry Abelove, Michèle Aina Barale, and David M. Halperin. New York: Routledge, 1993. 307–20.

Cheung, King-kok. *Articulate Silences*. Ithaca: Cornell UP, 1993.

Derrida, Jacques. "Différance." *Margins of Philosophy*. Chicago: U of Chicago P, 1982. 1–27.

Edelman, Lee. *Homographesis: Essays in Gay Literary and Cultural Theory*. New York: Routledge, 1994.

Evans, Caroline, and Lorraine Gannan. "The Gaze Revisited, or Reviewing Queer Viewing." *A Queer Romance: Lesbians, Gay Men and Popular Culture*. Ed. Paul Burston and Colin Richardson. London: Routledge, 1995. 13–56.

Genette, Gerard. *Narrative Discourse*. Ithaca: Cornell UP, 1980.

Laurence, Patricia Ondek. *The Reading of Silence*. Palo Alto: Stanford UP, 1991.

Mark, Rebecca. "Teaching from the Open Closet." *Listening to Silences*. Ed. Elaine Hodges and Shelley Fisher Fishkin. New York: Oxford UP, 1994. 245–59.

Miller, D. A. "Anal Rope." *Inside/Out: Lesbian Theories, Gay Theories*. Ed. Diana Fuss. New York: Routledge, 1991. 119–41.

Millett, Kate. *The Politics of Cruelty*. New York: Norton, 1994.

Sedgwick, Eve Kosofsky. *Epistemology of the Closet*. Berkeley: U of California P, 1990.

Servicio Paz y Justicia, Uruguay. *Uruguay nunca más: Human Rights Violations, 1972–1985*. Trans. Elizabeth Hampsten. Philadelphia: Temple UP, 1989.

5

As Invisible as He Is
The Queer Enigma of Xavier Villaurrutia

Robert McKee Irwin

> . . . Mi oreja sigue su rumor secreto,
> oigo crecer sus rocas y sus plantas
> que alargan más y más sus labios dedos.
> Lo llevo en mí como un remordimiento,
> pecado ajeno y sueño misterioso
> y lo arrullo y lo duermo
> y lo escondo y lo cuido y le guardo el secreto.
>
> [. . . My ear follows its secret rumors,
> I hear its rocks and plants growing
> lengthening further and further its fingers and lips.
> I carry it in me like a regret,
> someone else's sin, a mysterious dream
> and I lull it and put it to sleep
> and I hide it and care for it and for it I keep the secret.]
>
> —Xavier Villaurrutia,
> "Nocturno mar"
> (Nocturnal sea, 1937)

The enigma of Xavier Villaurrutia has been a kind of romantic attraction for literary critics. Frank Dauster, writing in the early 1970s, is intrigued by the "pervasive mystery" surrounding Villaurrutia, spanning his whole life, from birth to death (17). Merlin Forster adds to the eerie atmosphere of mystery by juxtaposing Villaurrutia's private life, "a region of shadows," with a description of the poet as "notably superstitious and obsessed by fears" such as that of being buried alive (12). Octavio Paz merely writes of his "reserve" and complains about never having been invited to his apartment (*Xavier* 19). Even as recently as 1994, scholars were still looking to "decipher a secret" in the poetry of Villaurrutia (Kirkpatrick 92). José Joaquín Blanco, on the other hand, calls Villaurrutia his personal "high point" because to him there is no mystery surrounding the poet, his work

114

is "closely linked to a definite person, with a precise temperament, with an intimate history, such that even his thinnest abstractions are as intimate and habitable as a confidence" (*Crónica* 172–73).

How is it that Blanco has solved the riddle so perfectly, pulled the mystery out of Forster's gruesome burial pit, and outsmarted all the other critics? Fabienne Bradu (writing in *Vuelta* and praising her editor-in-chief Paz's reading of Villaurrutia to the hilt) recognizes that "young" critics like Blanco may have overcome the "spell of the personage" Villaurrutia, but calls him "victim of the emotion which the work evokes" as if naïve Blanco (a youthful 37 at the time, but a prominent literary critic in Mexico for over a decade) needs to mature a bit and become more impartial (56). Although Bradu has gotten further than some critics in penetrating what seems to be the primary enigma of Villaurrutia, his sexuality, she can do no more with it than cite a sordid anecdote, related in Luis Cardoza y Aragón's memoirs, about Villaurrutia's being caught dancing with a "driver" in an "atmosphere thick with smoke, reeking of underarm odor and tequila" (58). I contend that Blanco's lack of fear and disapproval regarding Villaurrutia's sexuality grants his examination of the poet's work a greater profundity than any of the sources cited above. And the even franker and more extensive treatment of Villaurrutia, the man, in Guillermo Sheridan's *Los Contemporáneos ayer* is, thus, even more significant (although the latter covers only the early part of his career, prior to the publication of Villaurrutia's most well-known work, *Nostalgia de la muerte* [published in English as *Nostalgia for Death*]).[1]

It has been said that some writers write "under the influence of sexuality" (Lucey 4). André Gide, an early inspiration of Villaurrutia, saw writing, particularly writing about sexuality and sexual desire, as an exploration of and challenge to boundaries of self (Lucey 3–8). To imagine that Villaurrutia—who, if not "openly gay" in the sense of current-day identity politics as some would have it,[2] never went out of his way to hide or deny his homosexuality—wrote erotic poems of desire that have nothing to do with homosexual desire is absurd. While it would be equally absurd to imagine that there is some sort of "homosexual essence" to his writing, the fact that most critics, even in recent years, have skirted the topic of Villaurrutia's homosexuality when discussing even his most homoerotic work has denied Villaurrutia's work the importance it deserves not just nationally but internationally. How many early twentieth-century writers were dealing with homosexual themes? Or more important, why don't we know about anyone besides Whitman, Wilde, Gide, and Proust?

This critical blind spot relates to Sylvia Molloy's observation that homosexual panic has been the cause of "a near total suppression of the male body from Latin American literature" of the twentieth century. She goes on to say that "as the body is hidden, so have all sexual and erotic manifestations deviating from 'healthy,' patriarchal heterosexual norms successfully remained in the closet of literary representation and, especially, in the closet of literary criticism" ("Too Wilde" 49). I would argue that in many cases (including that of Villaurrutia, whose poetry is characterized, as I will show, by the erotic representation of implicitly male body parts and male homosexual desire) this homosexual panic has been less an affliction of Latin American literature than of Latin American literary criticism.

Thus, perhaps it took an "out" homosexual such as Blanco to break through the big enigma, prying Villaurrutia's work out of its critical "closet." Blanco is open to a range of possibilities of theme and content in Villaurrutia's work, a range of representations of masculinities and sexualities, and not just versions that are uncontroversial enough for narrow-minded or paranoid critics. As Sedgwick has noted, "the closet" has been a "shaping presence" in gay people's lives through this century (*Epistemology* 68),[3] and its inevitable presence is, I think, both an obstruction and a clue toward understanding Villaurrutia's work. For Villaurrutia, the closet was both a repressive force, which Pozo Pietrasanta has referred to (with some exaggeration, I think) as "castrating" to him, and a creative one, which, to a large degree, shaped his career as a poet.

Before discussing the particular case of Villaurrutia's homosexuality, the word itself warrants a brief digression. "Homosexuality," it has been shown, has meant different things in different places and at different times. In the case of Mexico, there is often said to be more concern with homosexual acts and roles than with homosexual identities. And while I believe this case is often overstated,[4] the use of words such as "*maricón*" (big Mary) and "*loca*" (crazy woman) to refer to homosexuals indicates a tendency to blur male effeminacy into homosexuality in popular discourse. I will assume, then, that the homophobic critics of Villaurrutia equated effeminacy and (homo)sexual "passivity" (in the Freudian sense); however, there is no reason to suspect that such tropes could define Villaurrutia's sexuality (nor is it worthwhile or even feasible to attempt such a definition).

Homosexuality (in whatever form) has hardly been an absent theme in Mexican literature, appearing in a central role in dozens of novels in recent decades. A handful of review essays have broached the topic, yet even the most popular of the Mexican novels with clearly homosexual themes (written by openly homosexual authors) remain largely unexamined by literary critics. And those critics who have been brave enough to confront the topic have committed historical errors inevitable in addressing works up to three decades old which have been actively ignored by academia.

Furthermore, it would be difficult to defend an origin point (usually cited as 1964) for Mexican queer literature.[5] What about "masculine" novels such as *Los de abajo* (The underdogs)? Or why not the foundational *El periquillo sarniento* (The itching parrot)? Or what about the earliest written works in Mexico (i.e., New Spain) such as the *Códice Chimalpopoca* or the *Florentine Codex*?[6]

Despite this critical silence, and even though Villaurrutia himself has never been cited as having come out and said "I am homosexual," his public personage was always suspicious, and he was often the object of homophobic attack in his lifetime. The early years of Villaurrutia's development as a poet were, in fact, fraught with controversy. Mexico, in the space of a few decades, was moving from a literary environment in which decorum prevented the discussion of homosexuality to one in which the presence of homosexuals within it could no longer be ignored.[7]

A certain literary homophobia became apparent during the great virility debates of the 1920s. With precursors in the shrill propaganda of the Estridentistas (who in a manifesto of 1923 proclaimed: "To be an Estridentista is to be a man. Only eunuchs will not be with us." [quoted in Schwartz 171]), a number of prominent journalists became engaged in a debate about the "feminization" of Mexican letters. In late 1924, Julio Jiménez Rueda raised the issue, slipping freely into his discourse from literature to *literatti,* by claiming that "today . . . even the type of man who thinks has degenerated. We are no longer valiant, lofty, rough, . . . we are now used to finding success, not so much at penpoint as in the complicated arts of the dressing table."[8] He was mainly concerned with what he saw as a need to establish a literature of the Mexican revolution which would somehow rival that inspired by the Russian revolution: "The 'revolutionary' proposal finds its paradigm in Soviet literature. These works . . . 'reflect' a nation 'shaken, in disarray, in full creative madness, in constant action [, of a] people of clear profiles, a people colored, brilliant and tragic.' . . . those works contain a feeling which is 'masculine in every acceptation of the word'" (qtd. in Díaz Arciniega 55). The political element of the debate is clear, and eventually a tendency developed "to associate 'virile literature' with the idea of 'social literature'" (Sheridan, *Los Contemporáneos* 258)—social in the sense of "socialist." Yet this is not all that is going on.

Jorge Ruffinelli points to "the sexism and machismo . . . increased by the violence of the revolution" (187), which came across in this debate, while other critics would prefer to ignore its more controversial elements by portraying it as a debate about Mexico's needing a "vital" (in place of "virile") literature (Leal 30). However, recent critics have begun to take into account the homophobic element of the debate, attributing it to a certain "anti-homosexual paranoia," in the Hocquenghemian sense (Hoc-quenghem 55–72),[9] directed toward a group of up-and-coming young writ-ers, among them Xavier Villaurrutia, who would later become known as the Contemporáneos. Víctor Díaz Arciniega, furthermore, goes on to find in these attacks traces of jealousy inspired by the fact that certain mem-bers of the cenacle (which Villaurrutia famously referred to as a "group without a group"), most notably Jaime Torres Bodet, held positions of relative importance on the staff of José Vasconcelos, the flamboyant minis-ter of public education.[10] His education ministry was nicknamed "the little chamber [*camarilla*] of shorties" by Pedro Henríquez Ureña, who char-acterized Vasconcelos's young followers as "effeminate and wretched."[11] Sheridan paraphrases Paz as once having said, "It's incredible the number of writers who have raised their prestige by denouncing homosexuals . . . as criminals" (*Los Contemporáneos* 259). Over the next 15 years, such veiled attacks would become more and more openly homophobic and per-sonally directed, creating an increasingly menacing atmosphere, especially for the group's two most openly homosexual members, Salvador Novo and Xavier Villaurrutia.

Painters (among them Rivera, Orozco, Ruiz el Corzo) ridiculed Villau-rrutia and Salvador Novo in paintings with titles such as "the anal ones"; the "30–30" group of realist painters demanded the resignation from gov-ernment posts of those exhibiting "homosexualism" and those in "doubt-ful psychological condition"; a group of prominent intellectuals in 1934 repeated the gesture, demanding the ouster of "hermaphrodites" from the federal government; Villaurrutia and several colleagues were forced to re-sign their government posts in 1932 after obscenity charges were filed against fellow Contemporáneo Jorge Cuesta's magazine, *Examen.* Diffi-culties with the government continued throughout the populist/nationalist presidential regimes of the 1930s and 1940s, practically right up to Villau-rrutia's suicide in 1950.[12]

The feelings between the nationalists and Villaurrutia were so un-friendly that, according to a legend, Villaurrutia repeatedly snubbed invi-tations by Lázaro Cárdenas to visit him "to exchange ideas." When con-fronted directly by the president at a public gathering, Villaurrutia's reply was biting: "Well, . . . you said that you wanted to exchange ideas, and frankly, Mr. President, that didn't strike me as a fair trade."[13]

Personal attacks masquerading as literary criticism also abounded dur-ing the period. For example, one contemporary critic referred specifically to Novo and Villaurrutia as part of a "queer" (*jotista*) literary group. In 1940, Manuel Maples Arce of Estridentismo fame, in his anthology of modern Mexican poetry, pointed to Villaurrutia's use of "inversion as a poetic method" (366). Maples Arce was also the one who, as a congressman in the 1930s, tried to reinstate severe nineteenth-century laws against homosexual acts (see Monsiváis 274; Sheridan, *Los Contemporáneos* 133, 391).

Despite the hostile atmosphere, Villaurrutia did not find himself without safe haven during many years in government jobs under the protection of sympathetic cabinet ministers such as Vasconcelos, Bernardo Gastélum, and Genaro Estrada. Similarly, literary criticism's silence on the subject of Villaurrutia's homosexuality is not just a result of the critics' own fear of seeming to know too much or appearing to be too interested (which Sylvia Molloy sees as yielding "readings that . . . 'dare not speak their name' for fear of contamination" ["Speaking/Reading" 20]), but also perhaps at times due to a sympathetic desire to protect Villaurrutia's public image. Forster tells us discreetly that Villaurrutia "never married, but lived with his mother," though "he kept a study-apartment in the downtown area and there often received friends and visitors" (12). Eugene Moretta goes beyond discretion into the realm of invention, referring repeatedly to female lovers in Villaurrutia's works and life (e.g., he alludes to "a passionate love affair between the poet and his mistress" [ch. 7: 18–19]).[14] But, in some ways, sympathetic blindness confounds more than the smear campaigns, and both tactics are clearly marred by homophobia.

Some might object that Villaurrutia was not really in the closet; Paz points out that Villaurrutia "did not hide himself and was capable of facing public condemnation," but he also underlines that, unlike his friend Novo, "Xavier defended his private life. . . . He was discreet" (*Xavier* 19). Villaurrutia indeed defended certain aspects of his private life, at times with a vengeance. Novo relates how Villaurrutia once broke into a locker and stole some of Novo's autobiographical writings because they explicitly named him, associating him with certain "crudeness" ("Memoir" 37). Years later, Sheridan describes an argument between Villaurrutia and Gilberto Owen over Xavier's translation of Gide's *La retour de l'enfant prodigue* (published in Spanish as *El regreso del hijo pródigo*) (The return of the prodigal son). Gide's concept of a "voyage toward oneself," in which "one runs the risk of finding oneself," was a key one for Villaurrutia and at times a euphemism for "coming out." Is Villaurrutia's "discretion" the reason, to Owen's annoyance, that Villaurrutia timidly translated "*embrasser*" as "*abrazar*" (hug)—as opposed to "*besar*" (kiss)—in a scene in which two young men express their mutual affection (Sheridan, *Los Contemporáneos* 222, 77)? Is this also why, in his novella *Dama de corazones* (Dame of hearts), he introduces the character Xavier Villaurrutia, "as invisible as he is[,] . . . inclined more and more every day to disappear," to fade into the crowd (*Obras* 582)? If Villaurrutia was afraid to be "out," it was not because of an irrational and homophobic "homosexual panic," but because of the experience of years of attacks launched at a figure just far enough out of the closet to make an easy target.

Gide was often a key symbolic figure in the attacks on Villaurrutia and his cohorts. Although perhaps few had read *Corydon,* Gide, along with Wilde, Proust, and Whitman and even Langston Hughes, was often employed to evoke homosexuality, both by homophobic critics and by Villaurrutia himself.[15] Ironically, Villaurrutia enjoyed not flaunting his sexuality but subtly hinting at it by frequently mentioning these "tainted" writers and attaching his name to theirs. For example, in "Debate en torno de Walt Whitman," Villaurrutia alludes to Gide's criticism (in *Corydon,* as anyone in the know will recall immediately) of Bazalgette's translations of Whitman for being too timid and even touches on Whitman's reputed homosexuality. Villaurrutia's name, in fact, is often associated with that of Gide, whether for his translations of Gide's works, the abundant mentions of Gide in his critical writing, his designation of some of Gide's most controversial (i.e., sexually explicit) works as his "favorites," or his references to Gide in his own book titles.[16] In fact, Villaurrutia saw his own name so entangled with that of Gide that in an interview, when asked in a general way about "influences," he assumed that the question referred to André Gide. He admitted to being influenced by Gide; however, he called this influence "not aesthetic" but "moral" (Ortega 25).

These deliberate links of his own person to such scandalous figures as Gide reflect a rather daring game of self-outing in which Villaurrutia liked to engage. He revealed his point of view (and his homosexuality) in another interview in 1930. When accused, in jest, of being an egoist, he responded: "Egoist? Perhaps, but in the manner of the hero of an English novel at whose name I blush to mention. A disinterested egoist, I occupy myself with others for the pleasure of surprising them one day, suddenly, with a gesture, with a word, with a moral reaction, something that I consciously let slip" (qtd. in Rojas 278).

Villaurrutia's friend and contemporary Salvador Novo was perhaps more flamboyant (recently described in a Mexican queer journal, with obvious irony, as "the most macho of the queer poets") and as a result was the most attacked of the generation (his enemies gave him such nicknames as "Nalgador Sobo," which might be roughly translated as "Pawing Assman"). He had to devise his own public personage, that of a nasty epigrammatist who defended himself ably with cutting wit.[17] But, are we to label Novo "out" and Villaurrutia "in," as Octavio Paz seems to want to do?

Paz writes, "Novo made a spectacle of his sexual inclinations," but criticizes Villaurrutia for not being enough of a gay rights activist: "We do not find in his writings the moral independence and intellectual coherence of a Gide or the rebelliousness of a Cernuda" (*Xavier* 19, 29). However, Villaurrutia's mere playful excursions "out of the closet" can be taken as valuable (and risky) political acts in themselves. As Paz would have it, every homosexual would have to write his or her own treatise on sexual morality. Imagine if all the well-known homosexual figures of the early twentieth century had written awkward, ill-prepared dissertations like *Corydon*. Apparently, for Paz, it is fine to be homosexual, as long as you act in a certain way (i.e., as a rebel, not a sissy). We also ought to consider the financial security which was involved in such rebellious acts, acts which posed less risk to Gide or Novo than to Villaurrutia. Novo clarifies his financial position with relation to his buddy: "My economic practicality had distanced us without distancing us. I got money, and he preferred satisfaction. The result was that I have aged, and he has not" (*La vida en México . . . M. Ávila Camacho* 57).

José Luis Martínez, a few years ago, recalled Villaurrutia as follows: "I esteemed him for that capacity he had to keep his distance. He had a wild private life . . . but he kept his different lives perfectly separate, his literary friendships and his personal nocturnal world" (qtd. in Otero, Martínez, and Solana 276). José Gorostiza, in a letter to his younger brother, Celestino, makes a somewhat similar bifurcation. "In the case of Xavier and his friends, before anything I distinguish between their intelligence and their conduct" (qtd. in Gorostiza et al. 10 [letter dated Feb. 7, 1928]). Fabienne Bradu, too, insists on separating the private person from the public personage, this time coinciding with Blanco, who stresses in his study of Villaurrutia the need to "enter into the secret."[18] Villaurrutia, as well, would agree; in a letter, again to Celestino Gorostiza, he writes, "I only live a life which is not made to my scale, a life which, more than living it, obliges me . . . to see myself living from the outside, as if I were a stranger, an imposter, a fantasm of little flesh and blood" (*Cartas* 37–38 [letter dated Jan. 1936]). The public poet is not the same person as the private homosexual man (with the former being the easier to grasp and control).

Leaving aside Villaurrutia himself, another question comes to mind: How do we fit his poetry into this scheme? Blanco calls his poetry "intimate" (*Crónica* 174). Yet, is there any basis by which we might read his poetry as "homosexual" or "queer" just because we know he was? Does it make any sense to do as past literary critics have done and read his poetry as "straight," even knowing that he was not?

I would suspect that Villaurrutia would be uncomfortable with either choice, since both appear to be constricting labels. Villaurrutia, it must be remembered, was something of a Gidean but also a Heideggerian.[19] His eternal quest for self-discovery (Gide) would be inevitably incomplete (Heidegger) because the self which he sought was anything but fixed, reachable, or knowable. Gide has been accused of being an "essentialist," which would by association taint Villaurrutia from a poststructuralist point of view, but I would argue that while Gide may have written about a human "essence," he never believed it to be something attainable, stable, understandable (or even really essential).[20]

In Villaurrutia's case, the only times he attempted explicit self-portraits (drawings), they were invariably of fragmentary body parts or, in his novella *Dama de corazones,* of a figure who appeared as nearly invisible.[21] The same is true in his poetry. There are never "people" present in them, only lips, fingers, shoulders, thighs, never clearly defined human figures, only supernatural phantasms such as angels. For Villaurrutia, fixed or definite subjectivity was not possible, whether in terms of sexual identity or anything else. In this way, it makes sense to discuss homosexual elements of Villaurrutia's poetry openly but without assuming these elements to have a defining or essential role.

Some critics make the jump from author to work without hesitation. In the case of Villaurrutia's drawings, Luis Mario Schneider, discussing Villaurrutia's painting, writes: "To retain the fleeting presence of anonymous loves he utilized the portrait. . . . Thus Villaurrutia poetizes his autobiography in his painting, . . . another means of making transparent the secret, for those who know how to read enigmas" (see Villaurrutia, *Xavier Villaurrutia entre líneas* 22–23). Despite his essentialist assumptions, Schneider's romantic vision may not be far from Villaurrutia's own in some ways; an early poem, "Poesía" (Poetry, 1926), concludes as follows:

> . . . el menor ruido te ahuyenta
> y te veo salir
> por la puerta del libro
> o por el atlas del techo,
> por el tablero del piso,
> o la página del espejo,
> y me dejas
> sin más pulso ni voz y sin más cara,
> sin máscara como un hombre desnudo
> en medio de una calle de miradas.
>
>   (*Obras* 26)

> [. . . the least noise scares you off
> and I see you leave
> by the door of the book
> or by the atlas of the ceiling,
> by the floorboards,
> or the page of the mirror,
> and you leave me

with no more pulse or voice and without any more face,
without a mask like a naked man
in the middle of a street of gazes.]

The poet is stripped naked by the words that flee his soul through his pen (although there is nothing to indicate that the poet can be fully seen or known through his poetry). In the same poem Villaurrutia describes poetry's "voice" as "echo," its "skin" as "mirror." His critics accept a link between poet and poetry at this moment without question; Villaurrutia couldn't be more literal here. And yet when his poems become erotic, masculine spaces, this link is forgotten in a manifestation of what can be seen only as homosexual panic. The prime example of such homophobia appears in the criticism of what Villaurrutia calls his "poem with a 'subject' [*asunto*],"[22] "Nocturno de los ángeles" (Nocturn of angels or Nocturn of Los Angeles, 1936).

On a trip to California in the summer of 1936, he finds Los Angeles "marvelous at night. Not even in New York do desire and its satisfaction flow as they do here." Of course, New York, a city which "is populated by angels," is where he confesses to taking advantage of opportunities for "always discreet . . . nocturnal escapes." In San Francisco, he writes, "All the last few days I have lived times of extraordinary passion. It scares me sometimes, but, how to resist a temptation without making it stronger? I prefer to fall into it" (Villaurrutia, *Cartas* 75–78).[23] This desire and passion seem to relate directly to the homosexual desire and passion in this poem, which is made even more explicit by the illustrations that appeared in its manuscript, discovered a few years ago among Carlos Pellicer's papers. It includes faces of blond sailors melding into the words, some in each other's arms, others kissing, reminiscent of Jean Cocteau's drawings in *Le livre blanc* (published in English as *The White Book*).[24] Thus, discreet Merlin Forster is forced to admit the homoerotic content of the poem, although he homophobically refuses to accept that the angels of the poem could be sailors (126); presumably sailors do not fit into his stereotyped conceptions of homosexuality. Villaurrutia's drawings tell us otherwise; nor is "Nocturno de los ángeles" itself at all opaque in this regard:

> Se diría que las calles fluyen dulcemente en la noche.
> Las luces no son tan vivas que logren desvelar el secreto,
> el secreto que los hombres que van y vienen conocen,
> porque todos están en el secreto
> y nada se ganaría con partirlo en mil pedazos
> si, por el contrario, es tan dulce guardarlo
> y compartirlo sólo con la persona elegida.
>
> (*Obras* 55)

[It might be said that the streets flow sweetly in the night.
The lights are not bright enough to unveil the secret,
the secret known by the men who come and go,
because they are all in on the secret
and nothing would be gained by smashing it up into a thousand pieces
if, on the contrary, it is so sweet to keep it
and share it only with the chosen person.]

If "the secret" is not made clear enough in the first stanza, the theme of clandestine homosexual desire and its satisfaction leap out soon after:

Si cada uno dijera en un momento dado
en sólo una palabra, lo que piensa,
las cinco letras del DESEO formarían una enorme cicatriz luminosa,
una constelación más antigua, más viva aún que las otras.
Y esa constelación sería como un ardiente sexo
en el profundo cuerpo de la noche,
o, mejor, como los Gemelos que por vez primera en la vida
se miraran de frente, a los ojos, y se abrazan ya para siempre.
De pronto el río de la calle se puebla de sedientos seres.
Caminan, se detienen, prosiguen.
Cambian miradas, atreven sonrisas.
Forman imprevistas parejas.

                                                                    (*Obras* 55)

[If each one were to say at a given moment
in a single word, what he is thinking,
the six letters of DESIRE would form a huge luminous scar,
a constellation more ancient, more alive than any other.
And that constellation would be like an ardent sex
in the profound body of the night,
or, better yet, like the Twins who for the first time in life
look at each other face to face, eye to eye, and embrace forever.
Suddenly the river of the street is populated with thirsty beings.
They walk, they pause, they proceed.
They exchange glances, they venture smiles.
They form haphazard couples.]

Villaurrutia confides to Novo in April 1936 that these have been months of revelation that changed his outlook profoundly (*Cartas* 79). Perhaps this is why this poem seems so uninhibited, unlike many of his other poems. What could these "thirsty beings," analogous to the embracing twins, be if not men in pursuit of their mirror image in other men? The sailor allusion—and it is not surprising that there were homosexual or, in this case, bisexual sailors cruising around California ports in the 1930s[25]—appears a bit later:

Son los Ángeles.
Han bajado a la tierra
por invisibles escalas.
Vienen del mar, que es el espejo del cielo,
en barcos de humo y sombra,
a fundirse y confundirse con los mortales,
a rendir sus frentes en los muslos de las mujeres,
a dejar que otras manos palpen sus cuerpos febrilmente,
y que otros cuerpos busquen los suyos hasta encontrarlos
como se encuentran al cerrarse los labios de una misma boca . . .

(*Obras* 56)

[They are the Angels.
They have dropped down to earth
on invisible ladders.
They come from the sea, which is the mirror of the heavens,
on ships of smoke and shadow,
to fuse and confuse themselves with the mortals,
to surrender their foreheads in the thighs of women,
to allow other hands to grope their bodies feverishly,
and other bodies to search for theirs until they find them
like the lips of a single mouth find themselves upon closing . . .]

These angels of the sea, it seems, whether sailors or not, seem to fit the U.S. archetype of "trade" or heterosexual-identifying men who participate in sexual acts with women and men but who treat homosexual men differently from women, actively giving oral sex to women but letting themselves be touched only by men, in order (in both cases) to prove their "manhood."

Ironically, homophobic Forster is actually the bold one here, having admitted a possible homoeroticism. Dauster, Paz, and even Blanco avoid examining this blatantly homoerotic poem. Kenneth Massey identifies this poem as one of a few that constitute "the best of his poetic creation," then never mentions it again (17). Manuel Martín-Rodríguez uses it to sum up a series of arguments on Villaurrutia's poetry but treats it as "humoristic," not erotic (1126–27)—in contrast with Paz, whose unique and very brief mention of the poem identifies it only as "one of Villaurrutia's few erotic poems" (*Xavier* 64)—and links it to "the trauma of birth" and "the relation with the mother," never mentioning (despite references to Villaurrutia's revealing letters to Novo from California) the word "homosexual." Daniel Balderston, then, is the first, to my knowledge, to state the obvious, comparing Villaurrutia's angels to the hustlers of John Rechy's *City of Night* (Balderston 13–15).

Yet as Balderston notes, Villaurrutia's poems are not usually so frank, or "obvious." More often, his poems depict shadowy, surreal spaces inhabited by equally shadowy, surreal figures (65–66). However, his poems are not so opaque that some critics might not occasionally draw conclusions such as those of Enrique Franco Calvo: "His poetry on not a few occasions declares an impassioned homosexual love for another man" (132). Certainly some of his poems are dedicated to known homosexuals ("Nocturno amor" to Manuel Rodríguez Lozano, "Nocturno de los ángeles" to Agustín Fink, "Nocturno de la estatua" to longtime companion Agustín Lazo, "Nocturno mar" to Novo), although there is nothing in them to indicate that these men were his lovers.[26] And if all the poems are not as explicit as this one, I would still contend that the *oeuvre* as a whole is characterized by an eroticism that can only be read as homosexual. As in the case of his contemporary Gabriela Mistral, his sexuality is "at once hidden and obvious" (Fiol-Matta 227), which is not to say that he suffered from homosexual panic; on the contrary, he played with language, denuding himself and his sexual desire repeatedly in his poems, but at the same time protecting himself from his ever-vigilant homophobic enemies.[27]

Thus, while few of Villaurrutia's poems could be described as blatantly homoerotic, it is a mistake to read them simply as if they were not at all queer.[28] For example, Forster's analysis of the early "El viaje sin retorno" (The voyage without return, 1926) points to an almost mathematical formula ("*sinalefa* linkings," "hendecasyllabic quatrains," "breath groups controlled by successive *enjambement*") but does not note the voyage theme's link to coming out, which we have seen mentioned by Sheridan (see Forster 110; Sheridan, *Los Contemporáneos* 222). This voyage out "without return" seems to indicate a definitive coming out experience, or an ultimate release of oneself into uninhibited sensuality. The poem begins:

> Contigo está mi sangre, silenciosa;
> mi sangre, ayer fervor, torrente ayer,
> sobre tus brazos leales se rebosa
> —¡qué asombro el que en los ojos se me posa!—.
> A un nuevo ritmo debe obedecer.
>
> Yo iba a ti en mi clamor, alucinante
> y alucinado, como en un irreal
> Mediterráneo, Ulises delirante.
> ¡Qué gritos en aquella soledad!
>
> (*Obras* 22–23)

> [With you is my blood, silent;
> my blood, yesterday fervor, torrent yesterday,
> over your loyal arms it overflows

—your eyes present me with such astonishment!—.
A new rhythm it must obey.

I went to you in my clamor, hallucinating
and hallucinated, as in an unreal
Mediterranean, delirious Ulysses.
What cries in that solitude!]

"Delirious Ulysses," the bold voyage out from his solitude into the world
of self-discovery leads the narrator into someone's arms, where he finds a
new corporeal rhythm to obey. The narrator is driven by a "thirst," which
is quenched in a certain delight and tenderness that allows the poem to
conclude with a new certitude for the narrator, a self-assurance as the
result of a new sensual self-knowledge:

Por esa sed que al corazón abría
ávido con mis labios y mis brazos,
y por la llaga que en mi carne hundía
la angustia de las uñas, llegué un día:
certidumbre entre todos los acasos.

Mas contigo mi sed halló frescura
y en tu blando mirar halló deleite;
y sin que fluya un ansia prematura
siento cómo me invade la ternura
con que unges a mi llaga con tu aceite.

(*Obras* 23)

[For this thirst which opened my heart
avid with my lips and my arms,
and for the wound which in my flesh submerged
the anguish of my fingernails, I arrived one day:
certitude among all the maybes.

But with you my thirst found freshness
and in your soft look it found pleasure;
and without a premature anxiety pouring forth
I feel how your tenderness invades me,
the tenderness with which you anoint my wound with your oil.]

It is extremely difficult to read the nocturnal world of desire, vice, fear,
secrets, and furtive contact as something other than a thinly veiled symbolic of a homosexual underworld. The absence of people and the men
who would have to be there to prove that the male narrator is desiring,
pursuing, and making erotic homosexual contact with tangible beings, and
not just dream figures, shadowy fantasies, or even women (as some would
have it), form a paradox only if one ignores what people might logically

be doing in the erotic and romantic poems of Villaurrutia if they were present there. Could the clandestine nocturnal life, the shadowy sexual encounters of homosexuals such as Villaurrutia in Mexico City in the 1920s and 1930s be the "enigma" hidden in his poetry? Or, better: What else could it be?

The epigram which starts off the "Nocturns" section of his *Nostalgia de la muerte* collection, "Burned in a sea of ice, and drowned amidst a fire" (*Obras* 44),[29] points immediately to a paradox, an impossibility which recalls the impossibility of writing unequivocally homoerotic poetry, the paradox of writing a love poem to a man who can*not* be the object of desire. The first poem, "Nocturno" (Nocturn, 1938), is the perfect introduction to this subterranean, nocturnal world of forbidden homosexual pleasure, empty of humans except for shadowy, elusive figures, because of the danger of the surrounding homophobic world.

Todo lo que la noche
dibuja con su mano
de sombra;
el placer que revela,
el vicio que desnuda.

Todo lo que la sombra
hace oír con el duro
golpe de su silencio:
las voces imprevistas
que a intervalos enciende,
el grito de la sangre,
el rumor de unos pasos
perdidos.

Todo lo que el silencio
hace huir de las cosas:
el vaho del deseo,
el sudor de la tierra,
la fragancia sin nombre
de la piel.

Todo lo que el deseo
unta en mis labios:
la dulzura soñada
de un contacto,
el sabido sabor
de la saliva.

Y todo lo que el sueño
hace palpable:

la boca de una herida,
la forma de una entraña,
la fiebre de una mano
que se atreve.

¡Todo!
circula en cada rama
del árbol de mis venas,
acaricia mis muslos,
inunda mis oídos,
vive en mis ojos muertos,
muere en mis labios duros.

(*Obras* 44–45)

[All that the night
sketches with its hand
of shadow;
the pleasure it reveals,
the vice it denudes.

All that the shadow
makes heard with the hard
blow of its silence:
the unexpected voices
which at intervals it ignites,
the cry of the blood,
the rumor of some footfalls
lost.

All that the silence
makes flee from things:
the vapor of desire,
the sweat of earth,
the nameless fragrance
of skin.

All that desire
smears over my lips:
the dreamed sweetness
of a contact,
the known taste
of saliva.

And all that the sleep
makes palpable:
the mouth of a wound,
the form of an entrail,

the fever of a hand
that dares.

All!
circulate in each branch
of the tree of my veins,
caress my thighs,
flood my ears,
live in my dead eyes,
die in my hard lips.]

The images here are of the nocturnal world where pleasure and vice are sought so furtively, where "contact" is dreamed of, where a hand feverishly "dares" to touch, recall, although romanticized in quite a different way, a homosexual underworld of the repressed, but active, Mexico City precisely like the one described by Novo; a world of furtive contacts, of secret desires, of daring nocturnal adventures. As usual, the poem is enigmatic because "people" never appear, only voices, footfalls. The pleasure and vice alluded to at the beginning of the poem are never illustrated; instead there are only fragmentary sensual encounters: the scent of skin, the taste of saliva, the feverish heat of a hand. What would the vice be if it were only his veins caressing his thighs; what pleasure is revealed if "the vapor of desire" is only "the sweat of the earth" and not "the fragrance" of *someone's* skin?

Dauster is in agreement that Villaurrutia is attempting here to "express the inexpressible" (43); however, for him the poem reflects an existential search for a mysterious, unknown self. Of course, Villaurrutia did see himself as engaging in a Gidean voyage toward himself, an ever-evolving self; but to say simply that Villaurrutia was a follower of Gide and Heidegger is insufficient. What of the poet's own erotic and romantic life, his own secret, shadowy life, life toward death, death approached through the endless, somnambulistic, nocturnal contacts? It would be a mistake to ignore the context in which this work was produced, not just because we would thus lose valuable insight into how it was "intended," but also because we would otherwise be unable to imagine how it might have been read by Villaurrutia's readers *and,* in particular, by homosexuals of the time who may have been in on "the secret." As Michael Lucey has argued with respect to André Gide, I would agree that particularly in terms of sexual expression, Villaurrutia might easily have gone beyond his conscious intention (4).[30] A few critics (Dauster, Moretta, Massey) are at a great disadvantage because they apparently do not suspect (or at least refuse to recognize the possibility) that Villaurrutia was a homosexual and thus was not writing from the same subject position as many of his heterosexual contemporaries.

Paz, who acknowledged Villaurrutia's homosexuality and whose literary biography, in fact, outed him to many, was more on the right track with his interpretation of the famous "enigma" as not just a self-searching but also a controlled and deliberate contradiction that was "existential and verbal, vital and rhetorical" and that set up what he called a "poetic drama" (*Xavier* 59). Certainly an important part of this drama was an exploration of what the poems might have hinted at that could not be said, a probing of sorts, to be carried out by the curious reader, into "the enigma." While it would be going too far to say simply that *Nostalgia de la muerte*'s surrealistic atmosphere was *only* masking unspeakable homosexuality, it would be irresponsible to relate his work to dreams as, for example, Forster does—and with good reason, since Villaurrutia himself wrote "the theme of the poet is the dream"[31]—without recognizing the full range of desires which might appear in dreams. Villaurrutia, at the very least, had read Freud.

Blanco, without saying the *h* word, analyzes this poem more rigorously, not playing down the eroticism, but instead tracing the path of desire. Blanco's progressive summary of the atmosphere, only part of his analysis, will give a good idea of his approach. His summary proceeds stanza by stanza: "clandestineness/pleasure = vice/night = truth; espionage/desire = lurking; persecution/silence = scenting out; encounter/dream = contact; recognition/acquaintance = touch; circular totality (a spiral which drops while narrowing itself with its sensorial organs until it coagulates in the mouth)/death = poem" (*Crónica* 178–79). To Blanco the poem is about a quest for a criminal pleasure in which contact is essential and in which death is only symbolic. In fact, Sheridan concurs that in Villaurrutia's nocturns, the author "associates . . . sexual experience with death, death with dreams, dreams with sex," a point which Paz had offered up years before.[32]

Villaurrutia might have been describing in "Nocturno" *any* desire that is repressed or considered sinful. But the critic who does the "universal" reading without considering the particular case of the homosexual author ignores the male homosexual subject's reality in the 1930s in Mexico: *all* desire he might have felt for a man was forbidden and vicious. Villaurrutia did not choose to confine his sexual images to the atmosphere of dreams, darkness, and death because it was picturesque and because surrealism was in vogue; he was forced to locate desire and eroticism there because that is where it lurked in his own life.

One of the most frequently studied among the *Nostalgia de la muerte* poems is "Nocturno de la estatua" (Nocturn of the statue, 1938).

> Soñar, soñar la noche, la calle, la escalera
> y el grito de la estatua desdoblando la esquina.

Correr hacia la estatua y encontrar sólo el grito,
querer tocar el grito y sólo hallar el eco,
querer asir el eco y encontrar sólo el muro
y correr hacia el muro y tocar un espejo.
Hallar en el espejo la estatua asesinada,
sacarla de la sangre de su sombra,
vestirla en un cerrar de ojos,
acariciarla como a una hermana imprevista
y jugar con las fichas de sus dedos
y contar a su oreja cien veces cien cien veces
hasta oírla decir: "estoy muerta de sueño."

(*Obras* 46–47)

[To dream, to dream the night, the street, the staircase
and the cry of the statue unfolds the corner.

To run toward the statue and find only the cry,
to long to touch the cry and find only the echo,
to long to seize the echo and find only the wall
and to run toward the wall and touch a mirror.
To find in the mirror the assassinated statue,
to pull it out of the blood of its shadow,
to dress it in a closing of eyes,
to caress it like an unexpected sister
and to play with the chips of its fingers
and to whisper in its ear a hundred times a hundred hundred times
until hearing it say: "I am dead of dreaming."][33]

What is the statue? And why is it so elusive? And how is it that it at last turns up in a mirror, dead, feminized? Certainly that is the oddest part; the statue is presumably male, especially since it appears initially as a mirror image, yet Villaurrutia's statue becomes like a sister. In this way, not only is the object of desire (the statue) feminine, but so too is the desiring subject. The statue is not made a "sister" to make the caress seem an expression of heterosexual desire; on the contrary, the mirror reveals a narcissistic, homosexual desire which is subverted further by the effemination of the presumed male subject (and object). Again, the elusive eroticism is clearly homosexual, even "queer," in its subversion not just of heterosexuality but also of gender. Even if the sexuality of the author were not taken into account, it would be difficult to read this play of gender roles differently. But what have the critics said?

Dauster seems to have caught on when he begins by noting how Villaurrutia's passion "blurs the distinction between modes of existence." Unfortunately, his modes of existence turn out to be "real life" and dreams, and he later demonstrates that he does not see any blurring of identity, especially in terms of gender and sexuality. For Dauster, the subject (which he assumes to be Villaurrutia himself) remains male, and the statue, female. He chooses to ignore the narcissism implied by the metaphors of mirror and echo. His subject suffers a "hell" of "solitude" and "failure," not because he is a sexual outcast but because of his obsession with death (Dauster 48).

Forster's analysis of the poem is more detailed. He provides an analysis of the use of the infinitive verb form to emphasize the lack of person and time through much of the poem. This is an important point overlooked by Dauster: there is, in fact, no subject, no first-person narrator, let alone the presence of the author in the poem. However, there is an implied subject. Someone pursues the statue, and someone finds it as his (or her) reflection in a mirror. It is interesting to note that in this poem with its strong homosexual overtones, in fact, no person appears—only a statue and the implication of a human subject who is attracted to it. Even when there is homosexual desire, no one is there, except for the statue, which is both "dead" and the product of dreaming. The infinitive form, however, not only conceals subjectivity but also embodies desire. Desire (to dream, to run, to touch, to seize) itself is the grammatical subject (technically speaking, it is the verb, not the subject, that is missing); the human subject who ought to be present is overwhelmed and made invisible by this desire. Ironically, despite his grammatical insight, Forster himself assumes a male subject who "comes face to face with himself" (30, 86–87).

Again, Forster posits the poem as a self-searching exercise, ignoring the possibility that it may have been about a self-discovery which occurs through a Freudian "narcissistic homosexuality."[34] For Villaurrutia, the narcissistic mirror is related to self-portraiture, but not of the body. For him, narcissism is something more transcendental ("outside of time"), more along the lines of Gide's vision of narcissism as a sublime timelessness that comes about in poetic creation.[35] Moreover, in Villaurrutia's poems, narcissistic self-discovery so often occurs through the faces of passing strangers in the streets or through a consuming desire that unites two lovers. Recall the twins of "Nocturno de los ángeles" or the "mirrors" encountered in the early poem "Calles" (Streets, 1926) and later in "Nocturno en que nada se oye" (Nocturn in which nothing is heard, 1938) ("a silence deserted like the street before a crime . . . the anxious game of one mirror in front of another" [*Obras* 47]) or lovers who seem to meld into one being in "Nocturno de la alcoba" (Nocturn of the bedroom, 1938). Narcissism is embodied through both poetic creation and sexual desire, a theme with which critics such as Forster would prefer not to deal, especially if that sexual desire might be homosexual.

Blanco's interpretation is more similar to mine: he sees in the poem a

process of identification of "the ego with the other" (*Crónica* 183). It is not
an internal self-searching so much as a Lacanian process of recognition
which takes place from outside in. And while it is true that the statue might
just be a "poetic ego," as Martín-Rodríguez suggests (1123), the night
street setting combined with the obsessive physical desire (desire to touch,
to seize, to caress) suggests more strongly a narcissistic self-exploration that
happens through the pursuit of an "other," an other of the same gender(s)
as the narrator, of a gender which is not fixed, which seems to be feminine
when at the same time it *must* be masculine. We now see emerging in
Villaurrutia's work, despite the absence of "men," a masculinity, a peculiar
(queer) masculinity which is not easily defined or contained.

Again in "Nocturno eterno" (Eternal nocturn, 1938), it is difficult to
ignore the homosexual atmosphere:

> Cuando los hombres alzan los hombros y pasan
> o cuando dejan caer sus nombres
> hasta que la sombra se asombra . . .
>
> (*Obras* 51)

> [When men shrug their shoulders and pass by
> or when they drop their names
> until even the shadows are startled . . .]

Who are the men who pass, some indifferently, others stopping, saying
their names, shockingly? Why shockingly, unless these are forbidden (homosexual?) encounters? And why is it that life itself in this context is nameless (or would it be better to say that it dare not speak its name)?

> cuando la vida o lo que así llamamos inutilmente
> y que no llega sino con un nombre innombrable
> se desnuda para saltar al lecho
> y ahogarse en el alcohol o quemarse en la nieve
>
> (*Obras* 51)

> [when life or what we uselessly call life
> which does not arrive but with an unnameable name
> undresses in order to jump into bed
> and drowns itself in alcohol or burns itself in snow]

More questions: Why is this life linked so closely with the bed? Why is it
undressed only in bed? Could it be not just a dream life but also a sexual
life? And why the alcohol or drugs?[36] Might they signal not just an escape
into a dream world but also a breaking down of inhibitions to commit
certain forbidden sexual acts? In the context of other poems such as those
mentioned above, it would seem naïve to ignore the erotic elements of the

poem. And again, we can link the erotic to the hidden; again, the metaphor of the closet is apparent.

The narrator is not sure that he exists, and he concludes that all these
things are no more than "shadows of words":

> . . . vida silencio piel y boca
> y soledad recuerdo cielo y humo
> nada son sino sombras de palabras
> que nos salen al paso de la noche.
> (*Obras* 52)

> [. . . life silence skin and mouth
> and solitude memory sky and smoke
> none are anything but shadows of words
> that come forth from us in the passing of the night.]

This almost Saussurian ending might imply that the unnameability or un-
speakability of this life requires a sort of shadow-symbolic which reflects
not so much the inadequacy or instability of signifiers to express specific
signified concepts, as the need for a camouflaged symbolic of double enten-
dres, which we see in Villaurrutia's poetry, where instead of "male body"
it is necessary to say merely "mouth" or "skin" and where "death" refers
to love or sex (see Sheridan, *Los Contemporáneos* 236).

Again Dauster situates this poem within Villaurrutia's endless existential search for meaning in life (and death). He focuses on the atmosphere
of confusion, concentrating on the men who shrug their shoulders and
ignoring the others who give their names; interpreting "drown oneself in
alcohol" not as getting drunk but as killing oneself and ignoring the fact
that life, which Dauster has described as "the utter desolation of life without life," is revealing itself at the moment of jumping into bed (44). Does
he think that *life* is jumping into bed? Why not those men who were telling
us their names earlier? When Villaurrutia writes, "I no longer exist," is he
in existential crisis or is the narrator, drunk, in bed with a strange man,
realizing a complication which causes him to doubt his identity and perhaps be drawn toward a different identity, one which is either ill-defined
or simply impossible for him to have?

Forster's reading also refers to existential confusion and a general questioning of "existence and meaning." Again, I would not disagree with this
reading but would add the possibility that the questioning of existence is
the questioning of the place of the homosexual man in a world which
does not permit his existence, and that the questioning of meaning is the
questioning of the use of signifiers developed in a heteronormative (and
moreover homophobic) society to describe elements of a homosexual life-

style, which it does not recognize to exist except as a crime, sin, aberration, and/or illness.

I might go on with examples of how for Villaurrutia the association of death, darkness, night, silence, shadows, smoke, dreams, emptiness, and a lack of bodies with love, lust, touch, and desire indicates his inability to write frankly about homosexuality. I might find more examples of his consciousness of the inability of language to be used to express this homosexuality (or even gender) forthrightly and the need for subterfuge in an alternate symbolic. I might also go on to show Villaurrutia's poems' questioning of life as it is normally (or normatively) represented in his world and how these works shed light on sexual difference, on the power exerted over male sexuality in society, and on the subversiveness of simple acts of expression among those of outlaw sexualities. Villaurrutia's silence, the words he has left unsaid, and his personal symbology, his alternative symbolic which *must* subvert hegemonic language because of who he is and how he desires, etch meanings upon his poems which ought not to be ignored.

Thus, the enigma of Villaurrutia seems less a mystery than one might imagine reading most recent criticism of his work. It is more an enigma emerging out of certain critics' homosexual panic. And while Villaurrutia does avoid presenting an overt eroticized male body in his work, in accordance with Molloy's aforementioned observation on twentieth-century Latin American literature, it is more his critics who have kept Villaurrutia's homoeroticism hidden by failing to follow up on the many clues he left, by ignoring what they would rather not deal with, the unmistakable "homographesis" (see Edelman) in Villaurrutia's work.

Villaurrutia's later poems are more raw and less stylized than his more famous poems collected in the classic *Nostalgia de la muerte* (1938). The playful eroticism is replaced by a greater emotiveness; the furtive glances are displaced by confessions of unrequited love and heartache. These poems are more often directed *to* someone, although gender is never revealed, and whole bodies never appear (only fragments, as before). Yet, they are no less revealing than his earlier works. In "Décimas de nuestro amor" (*Décimas* [ten-line stanzas] of our love, 1948), the "secret" is now only too transparent:

> A mí mismo me prohibo
> revelar nuestro secreto,
> decir tu nombre completo
> o escribirlo cuando escribo.
> Prisionero de ti, vivo
> buscándote en la sombría
> caverna de mi agonía.

Y cuando a solas te invoco,
en la oscura piedra toco
tu impasible compañía.

(*Obras* 79)

[I prohibit myself
from revealing our secret,
from saying your full name
or from writing it when I write.
Your prisoner, I live
searching for you in the shadowy
cavern of my agony.
And when alone I invoke you,
in the dark stone I touch
your impassive company.]

Thus, despite attempts by critics to fix Villaurrutia "in" the closet through their performative silence on the subject of his sexuality, a close reading of his poems (along with his critical works and interviews mentioned earlier, and even his plays)[37] reveals less an impenetrable secret than the expression of secrecy. Villaurrutia may prohibit himself from revealing his secret, as he writes above, but he does not make it impossible for the secret to be glimpsed. Perhaps if he had never written a word, we would not have suspected anything, but his *writing* silence is what most reveals the closet door which we might otherwise not have suspected to exist. Thus, Villaurrutia's writing reveals the closet to be, as Sedgwick suggests, not an absolute structure which divides into in and out, but a structure which exists between, which includes both in and out, but which permits neither as an absolute. Villaurrutia's secret is known and yet it is not: his enigma is both murky and transparent.

Oddly, it was Octavio Paz who first noted this rather poststructuralist aspect of Villaurrutia's poetry, which he referred to precisely as "between," a form which assumes a "question which has no answer" (*Xavier* 83–85). Perhaps this is why so many critics see an enigma, a secret, or a mystery in Villaurrutia's work. Perhaps if H-O-M-O-S-E-X-U-A-L-I-T-Y is not spelled out in every word of his writing, it will never be detected by some. It might seem counterproductive to have given so much space here to apparently homophobic critics, but given that this is pretty much the extent of criticism of Villaurrutia's poetry since 1970, I felt it necessary to present it in order to contest it. The homoerotic desire of Villaurrutia's poetry remains an enigma for those who do not dare to see, a secret for those who refuse to notice, yet it is there, and undeniably so, accessible to anyone who wants it, available for anyone who needs it, knowable for anyone in the know. Given that desire is a key thematic component of his poetry, it is nothing less than cowardly for critics to ignore the homosexual traces within his work. In fact, extensively, throughout Villaurrutia's poetic work, homosexual desire and homoeroticism are inscribed, though they may be "as invisible as he is."

Notes

All translations from Spanish-language sources, except those noted, are my own; however, it should be noted that I am greatly indebted to Eliot Weinberger for his recent translation of *Nostalgia for Death*. I chose to use my own translations because, while his often skillfully capture the romantic mood of vacuity, desire, somnambulance, and anguish of Villaurrutia's poems, my own argument often requires a more literal translation. Villaurrutia's poetry has been quoted with the permission of el Fondo de Cultura Económica.

1. Sheridan's interesting work of literary history and criticism traces the development of the Contemporáneos from 1917, when Villaurrutia was just a high school student, to 1928, with some further analysis up to about 1932. Villaurrutia's *Nostalgia de la muerte* was first published in 1938. The poems in Spanish can be found both in Villaurrutia's *Obras* and in the recent bilingual edition published as *Nostalgia for Death*. Page references of poems cited herein pertain to *Obras*.

2. See "Editor's Note" by Eliot Weinberger in Villaurrutia, *Nostalgia for Death* 1.

3. Note that while Sedgwick's work focuses on the literature and culture of the United States and western Europe, the closet metaphor is equally fitting for Mexico, as evidenced by the adoption of the English word into Mexican slang.

4. For example, Almaguer 255–73; and Carrier 103–24. The often-argued case that Mexican men are stigmatized as homosexual only when they are known to play a passive sexual role or to appear effeminate is true to an extent, but it is far from absolute; it is unlikely that a "straight" man would be willing to have an openly public relationship with a homosexual in most Mexican communities. See, for example, the novel *En jirones* by Luis Zapata. Additionally, José Piedra (370–409) argues interestingly that this active/passive sodomy-based view of homosexuality is a remnant of a European colonizing discourse (and is by no means universal in the hybrid culture of places like Mexico). For additional discussion of Mexican views on male homosexuality, see Paz, *El laberinto* 33, 74; also Lumsden.

5. See the following review essays: Schneider, "El tema homosexual"; Foster; and Muñoz. These essays are valuable sources, although none is complete. For example, all three make the mistake of naming Miguel Barbachano Ponce's *El diario de José Toledo,* originally published in 1964, as the "first" Mexican novel with a central homosexual theme, when in fact Paolo Po's forgotten *41, o un muchacho que soñaba en fantasmas* predated it by several months. In the mainstream of Mexican literary criticism, however, despite the international renown of such novels as Luis Zapata's *El vampiro de la colonia Roma,* which has been translated into English and French and is now in its tenth edition in Mexico, and despite the

quantity (several dozen) of such novels published in Mexico in the last thirty-odd years, the "genre" has been largely ignored. For example, in Aralia López González's review essay "Quebrantos, búsquedas y azares de una pasión nacional," the various novels mentioned in the essays of Schneider, Foster, and Muñoz are given less than a paragraph's space under the subheading "marginality." Zapata's *Vampiro* is ignored completely, although López does briefly note that Zapata's novels generally remind her of those of Manuel Puig. (What is the point of this comparison? Are we to conclude that novels with homosexual themes are inherently similar? If you've read one, you've read them all?) Also, most noteworthy is the recent work of literary criticism by Claudia Schaefer, *Danger Zones.*

6. See, for example, my "*Los de abajo* y los debates sobre la identidad masculina nacional." Regarding José Joaquín Fernández de Lizardi's *El periquillo sarniento,* see my "El Periquillo Sarniento y sus cuates." With regard to the early colonial period, see my "Tezcatlipoca, Nefarious Sodomite."

7. There may or may not have been "homosexual" writers prior to the 1920s; certainly the case of Sor Juana Inés de la Cruz is still debated today. Nonetheless, prior to the twentieth century, there were rarely even veiled allusions to such topics in literary discourse. Villaurrutia and a few of his friends had the honor of being the first major Mexican literary figures vociferously attacked by name for being (perceived as) homosexuals.

8. Quoted in Díaz Arciniega 57. This text contains a detailed discussion of this debate and also includes an index of journal articles. Daniel Balderston's "Poetry, Revolution, Homophobia: Polemics from the Mexican Revolution" discusses both the homophobia of these debates and that of the Estridentistas' discourse. See also Sheridan, *Los Contemporáneos;* Monsiváis; and Schneider, *El estridentismo.*

9. Hocquenghem refers to a common social phenomenon in which, put simply, a fear of one's own latent homosexuality leads one to persecute others perceived as homosexual.

10. While Vasconcelos maintained close friendships with certain homosexual writers, most notably Carlos Pellicer, his own homophobia would become apparent a decade or so later with the publication of his memoirs. See *Memorias,* 2 vols, originally published in the late 1930s and, for his most rabid homophobia, the companion fifth volume, *La flama,* published several decades later.

11. Henríquez Ureña did not actually engage in the public debate; this quotation is taken from a letter, quoted in Díaz Arciniega (68). However, these homophobic comments represented quite clearly the feelings of some with regard to Vasconcelos's staff. Ironically, they seem to have been inspired less from professional jealousy (after all, Henríquez Ureña was considered one of the masters of the day in Mexico) than from the Dominican's ambiguous relationship with Villaurrutia's close friend and fellow Contemporáneo, Salvador Novo, a relationship tinged by contradictory rumors of homophobic violence and homosexual desire. See Novo, "Memoir" 41, for an account of his mentor's angry and ridiculing dismissal of Novo; see also Alderson in his introduction to Novo's *The War of the Fatties and Other Stories from Aztec History;* Alderson mentions rumors of an amorous relationship between the two men (xx).

12. See Monsiváis 273–77; Paz, *Xavier* 24; Alderson xxvi. Villaurrutia's suicide itself has contributed to his enigma. Hushed up for decades (Dauster thought he had died of a heart attack), it has only recently been mentioned at all by critics. The only source of any details is "fictional"; see Pedro Ángel Palou's "biographical novel," *En la alcoba de un mundo.*

13. Quoted in Forster 13. Such directly antagonistic remarks hardly seem characteristic of Villaurrutia; however, there is little doubt that this quip would have accurately expressed his sentiments at the time.

14. See also Moretta, ch. 2: 8, ch. 3: 10 and 17, ch. 4: 29–38.

15. On *Corydon,* see Novo, *La vida en México . . . M. Alemán* 470 (originally published in *Hoy,* 10 Mar. 1951); see also, for example, pp. 121–23 of *La flama,* the late "autobiographical novel" of José Vasconcelos, who mentioned Gide in an attempt to blame the suicide of his lover Antonieta Rivas Mercado on her close association with Villaurrutia and other homosexuals involved in the theater group Ulises. See also Capistrán 11–44; in yet another public debate, this time in the journal *El Nacional* in 1932 (7 May), Héctor Pérez Martínez complains to Alfonso Reyes (referring to Villaurrutia and his cohorts) about "what is . . . appalling in this new mistaken generation, wise in the tricks of unanimity and outstanding in its promulgation of the even more mistaken morals of André Gide. Mexican literature is lacking a lesson of virility in the most complete human sense . . ." (qtd. in Capistrán 29). Regarding Langston Hughes's visits to Mexico (and his publication in the journal *Contemporáneos*), see Rampersad. Villaurrutia dedicated the erotic poem "North Carolina Blues" to Langston Hughes.

16. See Villaurrutia's "Debate en torno de Walt Whitman" (*Obras* 948; originally published in *Cima* 5 [Feb. 1942]); also, *Obras* 605, 610, 948 for some examples of Villaurrutia's references to Gide; also "Un juego literario: La isla desierta" (*Obras* 952; originally published in *Imagen* 2 [30 June 1933]), in which Villaurrutia lists *Les faux monnayeurs* and *Si le grain ne meurt* among the books he wouldn't want to do without if stranded on a desert isle. Gide is mentioned in Villaurrutia's "Carta a un jóven," published in Capistrán 78–82. Also see Villaurrutia's translations of Gide, *El regreso del hijo pródigo* and *La escuela de las mujeres,* the latter a collaborative translation with Antonieta Rivas Mercado. Finally note that Villaurrutia's first volume of collected essays was titled *Textos y pretextos* after Gide's *Prétextes* (*Obras* 639–763).

17. For more on Novo, see Barrera López's article; also Monsiváis's *Amor perdido* contains a chapter listed under the heading "Que sí esto es escandaloso" (Now *this* is scandalous), 265–96; also see Blanco, *Crónica* 168–69.

18. See Bradu 55; Blanco, *La paja* 89; and also Blanco, *Crónica* 174.

19. As Villaurrutia himself said, "Every poet discovers his philosopher and I have found mine in Heidegger." This is taken from an interview with José Luis Martínez, "Con Villaurrutia" 78; however, note that Paz believes that "Villaurrutia came to Heidegger very late, when most of the poems of *Nostalgia for Death* had already been written. He himself made it clear that his encounter with Heidegger was more a confirmation than a revelation." See Paz, *Xavier* 66.

20. See Dollimore 3–21, 335–44. I argue that Dollimore oversimplifies Gide in order to set up a rather forced binary opposition to Oscar Wilde. Michael Lucey's

recent study, which concerns itself more with literary analysis than political theorizing, more accurately captures Gide. "Sexual experience, Gide claims, is more
than just physical pleasure. As an experience, it challenges the boundaries of the
self; it furthers an understanding of how those boundaries are drawn and re-
drawn. . . . Gide's writings on sexuality and sexual experience investigate sexuality's challenges to the boundaries of a self . . ." (7).

21. See Villaurrutia's *Xavier Villaurrutia entre líneas* for a review of his many
self-portraits on canvas; also see the description of the character Xavier Villaurrutia in *Dama de corazones* (*Obras* 582).

22. Quoted in Sheridan, "Villaurrutia" 59.

23. N.B. According to Blanco, these letters were published censored (see *Crónica* 184). They had previously been published in Novo's newspaper column and
are collected in Novo, *La vida en México . . . M. Alemán* 444–46.

24. While Cocteau's drawings are clearly more overtly erotic than Villaurrutia's,
the resemblance not just in style but also in content (handsome blond men) is clear.
Villaurrutia's drawings are reproduced in his *Xavier Villaurrutia entre líneas* 60–63.

25. See Chauncey 76–90; see also Rifkin.

26. We do know that Lazo and Villaurrutia were lifelong friends, that they were
lovers at least for a time in the 1920s, and that they lived together. See Novo,
"Memoirs" 46. In fact, they were so close that upon Villaurrutia's death, Lazo
gave up his career as a painter, forever. See Sheridan, *Los Contemporáneos* 208.
For a semifictionalized account of their relationship, see Palou's novel.

27. Mistral's case was a bit different; according to Fiol-Matta, she was able to
get away with certain indiscretions while remaining protected by her public persona; Villaurrutia's public persona was always as controversial as his work, and
yet, he played with veiling and unveiling, getting away, like Mistral, with whatever
he thought safely viable.

28. I use this term, a term not translatable to Spanish, not to define Villaurrutia's homosexuality but to emphasize its lack of specificity, its indeterminate nature.

29. The quotation, attributed to Michael Drayton, appears in English.

30. In the case of Villaurrutia, who never wrote about his "intentions," we can
only guess at them. Even more than in the case of Gide, it becomes relevant to
focus not on what Villaurrutia intended to write but on what he did write under
the influence of sexuality.

31. Quoted in Paz, *Xavier* 59. Freud's linking of dreams to wish fulfillment and
sexual repression was hardly radical stuff in the 1970s. Yet Forster's analysis of
"Sleeping and Dreaming" does not touch on erotics and concludes blandly, "The
nocturnal street, along with the figure of personified night, functions as an important motif in the representation of the dream state of Villaurrutia's poems, and is
the most important concrete representation of this subterranean dream world"
(84–87).

32. Paz, *Xavier* 78–79; Sheridan, *Los Contemporáneos* 236. Sheridan sees this
as an influence of Cocteau and cites *Plain-chant* and *Orphée*.

33. This final clause would normally be translated as "I am dead tired," but
given that Villaurrutia never writes of fatigue, though frequently deals with dream
motifs, I believe the more unusual translation of "dreaming" for "*sueño*" makes

more sense. (N.B. Weinberger also rejected the more literal translation in favor of "I'm dying of sleep." See Villaurrutia, *Nostalgia for Death* 13.)

34. See Silverman 367–73 for a discussion of what she calls Freud's "Leonardo Model" of narcissistic male homosexuality.

35. See "Meditación ante el retrato" (*Obras* 1072–77, esp. 1073–74; originally published in *Vida* 15 [7 Oct. 1947]). Villaurrutia had most assuredly read Gide's "Narcissus: A Treatise on the Theory of Symbolism."

36. See Sheridan, *Los Contemporáneos* 225; "la nieve" probably refers to cocaine. See also Novo, "Memoirs" 27–28 on his and Villaurrutia's experiments with drugs.

37. For example, in Héctor Martínez Tamez's recent adaptation of *Invitación a la muerte* (Invitation to death), the play is outed; Martínez and director Gonzalo Valdés Medillín present the version that, according to the liner notes of Gonzalo Pozo Pietrasanta, Villaurrutia would have written in a less homophobic epoch. This revised version ends with a kiss between the two male protagonists who then go off to bed together.

Works Cited

Alderson, Michael. Introduction. *War of the Fatties and Other Stories from Aztec History.* By Salvador Novo. Trans. Michael Alderson. Austin: U of Texas P, 1994.

Almaguer, Tomás. "Chicano Men: A Cartography of Homosexual Identity and Behavior." *The Lesbian and Gay Studies Reader.* Ed. Henry Abelove, Michèle Aina Barale, and David M. Halperin. New York: Routledge, 1993. 255–73.

Azuela, Mariano. *Los de abajo.* 1915. Edición crítica. Coord. Jorge Ruffinelli. Buenos Aires: Colección Archivos/UNESCO, 1988.

Balderston, Daniel. "Poetry, Revolution, Homophobia: Polemics from the Mexican Revolution." *Hispanisms and Homosexualities.* Ed. Sylvia Molloy and Robert Irwin. Durham: Duke UP, 1998. 57–75.

Barbachano Ponce, Miguel. *El diario de José Toledo.* 1964. Mexico City: Prémia, 1988.

Barrera López, Reyna. "Novo en la memoria." *Del Otro Lado* 13 (spring 1994): 40–41.

Blanco, José Joaquín. *Crónica de la poesía mexicana.* 4th ed. Mexico City: Katún, 1983.

Blanco, José Joaquín. *La paja en el ojo.* Puebla: ICUAP, 1980.

Bradu, Fabienne. "Presencia y figura de Xavier Villaurrutia en la crítica mexicana." *Vuelta* 137 (Apr. 1988): 55–58.

Capistrán, Miguel, ed. *Los Contemporáneos por sí mismos.* Mexico City: Consejo Nacional para la Cultura y las Artes, 1994.

Carrier, Joseph. "Cultural Factors Affecting Urban Mexican Male Homosexual Behavior." *Archives of Sexual Behavior* 5.2 (1976): 103–24.

Chauncey, George. *Gay New York.* New York: Basic Books, 1994.

Cocteau, Jean. *Orphée.* Paris: Stuck, 1927.

Cocteau, Jean. *Plain-chant.* Paris: Stuck, 1922.

Cocteau, Jean. *The White Book.* Trans. P. Owen. San Francisco, City Lights Books, 1989.

Códice Chimalpopoca. Trans. Primo Feliciano Velázquez. Mexico City: Universidad Nacional Autónoma de México, 1992.

Dauster, Frank. *Xavier Villaurrutia.* New York: Twayne, 1971.

Díaz Arciniega, Víctor. *Querella por la cultura "revolucionaria" (1925).* Mexico City: Fondo de Cultura Económica, 1989.

Dollimore, John. *Sexual Dissidence.* Oxford: Oxford UP, 1993.

Edelman, Lee. *Homographesis.* New York: Routledge, 1994.

Fernández de Lizardi, José Joaquín. *El periquillo sarniento.* 1816. Mexico City: Proxema, 1979.

Fiol-Matta, Licia. "The 'Schoolteacher of America': Gender, Sexuality, and Nation in Gabriela Mistral." *¿Entiendes? Queer Readings, Hispanic Writings.* Ed. Emilie L. Bergmann and Paul Julian Smith. Durham: Duke UP, 1995. 201–29.

Forster, Merlin. *Fire and Ice: The Poetry of Xavier Villaurrutia.* Chapel Hill: University of North Carolina, Department of Romance Languages, 1976.

Foster, David William. *Gay and Lesbian Themes in Latin American Writing.* Austin: U of Texas P, 1991.

Franco Calvo, Enrique. "Notas sobre Xavier Villaurrutia y la crítica de arte." *Los Contemporáneos en el laberinto de la crítica.* Ed. R. Olea Franco and A. Stanton. Mexico City: El Colegio de México, 1994. 119–35.

Gide, André. *Corydon.* Paris: Gallimard, 1924.

Gide, André. *La escuela de las mujeres.* Trans. Xavier Villaurrutia and Antonieta Rivas Mercado. Mexico City: La Razón, 1931.

Gide, André. "Narcissus. A Treatise on the Theory of Symbolism." *The Return of the Prodigal, Preceded by Five Other Treatises with Saul: A Drama in Five Acts.* Trans. D. Bussy. London: Secker and Warburg, 1953. 1–15.

Gide, André. *El regreso del hijo pródigo.* Trans. Xavier Villaurrutia. Mexico City: Séneca, 1942.

Gorostiza, J., J. Cuesta, A. Reyes, X. Villaurrutia, J. Torres Bodet, and G. Owen. *Cartas a Celestino Gorostiza.* Mexico City: Equilibrista, 1988.

Hocquenghem, Guy. *Homosexual Desire.* Trans. D. Dangoor. Durham: Duke UP, 1993.

Irwin, Robert. "*Los de abajo* y los debates sobre la identidad masculina nacional." *La otredad: Los discursos de la cultura hoy: 1995.* Coord. Silvia Elguea Véjar. Mexico City: UAM-Azcapotzalco/Centro de Cultura Casa Lamm/Universidad de Louisville, Ky., 1997. 71–82.

Irwin, Robert. "El Periquillo Sarniento y sus cuates: El 'éxstasis misterioso' del ambiente homosocial en el siglo diecinueve." *Literatura Mexicana* 9.1 (1998): 23–44.

Irwin, Robert. "Tezcatlipoca, Nefarious Sodomite. *Codex Chimalpopoca* and 16th-Century Discourse on Homosexuality in Mexico." Paper, University of Iowa, 6th North American Lesbian, Gay and Bisexual Studies Conference, Nov. 1994.

Kirkpatrick, Gwen. Review of *Nostalgia for Death and Hieroglyphs of Desire,* by

Xavier Villaurrutia and Octavio Paz. *Latin American Literary Review* 12.44 (July–Dec. 1994): 90–92.

Leal, Luis. *Mariano Azuela.* New York: Twayne, 1971.

López González, Aralia. "Quebrantos, búsquedas y azares de una pasión nacional (dos décadas de narrativa mexicana 1970–1980)." *Revista Iberoamericana* 164–65 (July–Dec. 1993): 660–85.

Lucey, Michael. *Gide's Bent.* Oxford: Oxford UP, 1995.

Lumsden, Ian. *Homosexualidad: Sociedad y estado en México.* Trans. Luis Zapata. Mexico City: Solediciones, 1991.

Maples Arce, Manuel. *Antología de la poesía moderna.* Rome: Poligráfica Tiberina, 1939.

Martínez, José Luis. "Con Villaurrutia." *Tierra Nueva* 1.2 (Mar.–Apr. 1940): 74–81.

Martínez Tamez, Héctor. Adaptation of *Invitación de la muerte,* by Xavier Villaurrutia. Mexico City: Universidad Nacional Autónoma de México/Teatro Rosario Castellanos de la Casa del Lago, 1995.

Martín-Rodríguez, Manuel. "El fondo angustiado de los 'Nocturnos' de Xavier Villaurrutia." *Revista Iberoamericana* 148–49 (July–Dec. 1989): 1119–28.

Massey, Kenneth W. "La poesía de Xavier Villaurrutia." *Chasqui* 1.2 (Mar.–Apr. 1972): 6–19.

Molloy, Sylvia. "Speaking/Reading Silence: Queer Traces in Latin American Writing." Keynote address, Twentieth-Century Spanish and Spanish-American Literatures International Symposium, University of Colorado, Boulder, Nov. 1993.

Molloy, Sylvia. "Too Wilde for Comfort: Desire and Ideology in *Fin-de-siècle* Latin America." *Negotiating Lesbian and Gay Subjects.* Ed. Monica Dorenkamp and Richard Henke. New York: Routledge, 1995. 35–52.

Monsiváis, Carlos. *Amor perdido.* Mexico City: Era, 1990.

Moretta, Eugene L. *The Poetic Achievement of Xavier Villaurrutia.* Cuernavaca: Cidoc Cuaderno, 1971.

Muñoz, Mario. "En torno a la narrativa mexicana de tema homosexual." *La Palabra y el Hombre* 84 (Oct.–Dec. 1992): 21–37.

Novo, Salvador. "Memoir." *Now the Volcano: An Anthology of Latin American Gay Literature.* Ed. W. Leyland. San Francisco: Gay Sunshine, 1979. 11–47.

Novo, Salvador. *La vida en México en el periodo presidencial de Manuel Ávila Camacho.* Mexico City: Consejo Nacional para la Cultura y las Artes/Instituto Nacional de Antropología e Historia, 1994. Originally in *Hoy* (3 Dec. 1943).

Novo, Salvador. *La vida en México en el periodo presidencial de Miguel Alemán.* Mexico City: Consejo Nacional para la Cultura y las Artes/Instituto Nacional de Antropología e Historia, 1994.

Ortega, [Gregorio]. "Conversación en un escritorio con Xavier Villaurrutia." *Revista de Revistas* 1143 (10 Apr. 1932): 25–26.

Otero, C., J. L. Martínez, and R. Solana. "Los Contemporáneos en familia." *Los Contemporáneos en el laberinto de la crítica.* Ed. R. Olea Franco and A. Stanton. Mexico City: El Colegio de México, 1994. 269–88.

Palou, Pedro Ángel. *En la alcoba de un mundo.* Mexico City: Fondo de Cultura Económica, 1992.

Paz, Octavio. *El laberinto de la soledad.* 18th ed. Mexico City: Fondo de Cultura Económica, 1989.

Paz, Octavio. *Xavier Villaurrutia en persona y en obra.* Mexico City: Fondo de Cultura Económica, 1978.

Piedra, José. "Nationalizing Sissies." ¿Entiendes? *Queer Readings, Hispanic Writings.* Ed. Emilie L. Bergmann and Paul Julian Smith. Durham: Duke UP, 1995. 370–409.

Po, Paolo. *41, o un muchacho que soñaba en fantasmas.* Mexico City: B. Costa-Amic, 1963.

Pozo Pietrasanta, Gonzalo. Playbill notes to *Invitación a la muerte,* by Xavier Villaurrutia. Mexico City: Universidad Nacional Autónoma de México/Teatro Rosario Castellanos de la Casa del Lago, 1995.

Rampersad, Arnold. *The Life of Langston Hughes.* Vol. 1: *1902–1941: I, Too, Sing America.* New York: Oxford University Press, 1986.

Rechy, John. *City of Night.* 1963. New York. Grove Weidenfeld, 1988.

Rifkin, Adrian. *Street Noises: Parisian Pleasure, 1900–1940.* Manchester: Manchester UP, 1993.

Rojas, Marcial. "Xavier Villaurrutia, entrevisto." *Revistas literarias mexicanas modernas: Ulises (1927–1928).* Mexico City: Fondo de Cultura Económica, 1980. Originally published in *Escala* 1.1 (Oct. 1930).

Ruffinelli, Jorge. "La recepción crítica de *Los de abajo.*" *Los de abajo.* By Mariano Azuela. Edición crítica. Coord. Jorge Ruffinelli. Buenos Aires: Archivos, 1988. 185–213.

Sahagún, Fray Bernadino de. *Florentine Codex.* Trans. Charles E. Dibble, Arthur J. D. Anderson. Santa Fe: School of American Research/University of Utah, 1961.

Schaefer, Claudia. *Danger Zones: Homosexuality, National Identity, and Mexican Culture.* Tucson: U of Arizona P, 1996.

Schneider, Luis Mario. *El estridentismo o una literatura de la estrategia.* Mexico City: Instituto Nacional de las Bellas Artes, 1970.

Schneider, Luis Mario. "El tema homosexual en la nueva narrativa mexicana." *Casa de Tiempo* 5.49–50. (Feb.–Mar. 1985): 82–86.

Schwartz, Jorge. *Las vanguardias latinoamericanas: Textos programáticos y críticos.* Madrid: Cátedra, 1991.

Sedgwick, Eve Kosofsky. *Between Men.* New York: Columbia UP, 1985.

Sedgwick, Eve Kosofsky. *Epistemology of the Closet.* Berkeley: U of California P, 1990.

Sheridan, Guillermo. *Los Contemporáneos ayer.* Mexico City: Fondo de Cultura Económica, 1993.

Sheridan, Guillermo. "Villaurrutia habla dos veces." *Vuelta* 222 (May 1995): 58–59.

Silverman, Kaja. *Male Subjectivity at the Margins.* New York: Routledge, 1992.

Vasconcelos, José. *La flama.* Mexico City: Continental, 1959.

Vasconcelos, José. *Memorias.* Vol. 1: *Ulises criollo, La tormenta.* Mexico City: Fondo de Cultura Económica, 1983.

Vasconcelos, José. *Memorias.* Vol. 2: *El desastre, El proconsulado.* Mexico City: Fondo de Cultura Económica, 1984.

Villaurrutia, Xavier. *Cartas de Villaurrutia a Novo 1935–1936.* Mexico City: Instituto Nacional de las Bellas Artes, 1966.

Villaurrutia, Xavier. *Obras.* 2d Ed. Mexico City: Fondo de Cultura Económica, 1966.

Villaurrutia, Xavier. *Xavier Villaurrutia entre líneas: Dibujo y pintura.* Ed. Luis Mario Schneider. México: Trabuco y Clavel, 1991.

Villaurrutia, Xavier, and Octavio Paz. *Nostalgia for Death/Hieroglyphs of Desire.* Trans. Eliot Weinberger and Esther Allen. Port Townsend, Wash.: Copper Canyon Press, 1993.

Zapata, Luis. *En jirones.* Mexico City: Consejo Nacional para la Cultura y las Artes, 1994.

Zapata, Luis. *El vampiro de la colonia Roma.* Mexico City: Grijalbo, 1979.

6

Alternative Identities of Gabriel(a) Mistral 1906–1920

Elizabeth Rosa Horan

This chapter registers expressions of sexual dissidence in the earlier life and work of Chilean poet Gabriela Mistral (born Lucila Godoy Alcayaga, 1889–1957; winner of the Nobel Prize for literature, 1945). Such a survey is necessary to counter, explain, and move past the reactionary appropriation of Gabriela Mistral as "la Divina Gabriela," "Santa Mistral," "*la maestra*," and ultimately "Madre de América."[1] Although the writer's status as the continent's first Nobel laureate has led to her singular and solitary acceptance into a literary elite otherwise loathe to acknowledge women writers, a feminist approach is necessary, both to sort out the ways that her canonization is profoundly enmeshed in clichés of femininity and to examine how she almost certainly deployed such clichés to her own use. In probing the work that Gabriela Mistral produced in the years prior to her fame, my intent is to reveal the wide range of potentially queer identifications that she and others explored and invoked in early twentieth-century Chile. I am not looking to pigeonhole "Gabriela Mistral" into the category of lesbian, a category which print discourse, in her youth, did not acknowledge. Rather, I find that her early writings reveal a profoundly ambiguous figure, utterly unrecognizable and alien to the frozen image of the Nobel queen, a plaster saint enthroned just to the right of the Mother.

For Gabriela Mistral (as for others involved in the bohemian worlds of poetry and theosophy) queerness is constituted (subversively) by the ten-

sion between historical context and her writing. The evidence of that subversion appears in her early, explicit, reiterated rejection of heterosexuality
and in her multiple efforts to express an erotic subjectivity beyond the
simplistic male/female binary. Rejecting the bounds of decorum that re-
stricted women's emergence into the public sphere, challenging heterosexual hegemony, she uses mixed genre forms and personal letters to imagine
a wide range of alternatives to the bovarism of the era, which postulates
women solely in terms of heterosexual desire.

Like other writers of the era, Gabriela Mistral draws from theosophy
and from modernism to construct alternative sexualities and express a
bohemian, international sensibility. The former, an alternative spiritual
movement, and the latter, Latin America's highly successful heir to and
variant on symbolism, simultaneously helped and hindered Gabriela Mistral, as well as other independently minded writers and intellectuals. Theosophy allowed women to speak, but not as sexual beings. Modernism
championed the language of sensuality while offering scant room for elab-
orating an explicitly female subjectivity. When from 1911 onward Gabriela
Mistral wrote for the all-female worlds of the time, such as the *liceos de
las niñas* (girls' public high schools), and when in 1914 her work came to
the attention of Santiago's literary elite, she drew from theosophy and
modernism to develop a highly codified language of desire. As Martínez
has suggested, that language is lesbian in that it constantly and consistently evades specifying the gender of subject or object. As Franco, Pizarro, and others point out, her language is curiously antimodern, looking
backward in its self-conscious archaism and concentration on infancy. In
the affective centrality that her poetry and prose-poetry accord to the female body, however, Gabriela Mistral shows how same-sex desire might be
inscribed even within the highly constrained set of conditions and options
available to women writers in early twentieth-century Latin America.

Early Ventures in Identity Formation: Publications of 1905–8

Gabriela Mistral's dissent from normative sex roles begins as early as 1906,
when she criticizes marriage as hypocrisy and low-pay prostitution. Her
publications that do so are consistent with the editorial policy of the two
provincial newspapers that printed her work, poetry and prose, from 1905
onward, in the rural province of Coquimbo, four hundred kilometers to
the north of Santiago. These publications appear in a context of support
for the radical, that is, secularizing, politics of *La Voz de Elqui* and *El
Coquimbo: Diario Radical,* which criticized landowners and local poli-
ticians who protected church interests. In the tradition of nineteenth-
century radicalism and internationalist discourse, they stress lay public

education and advocate science and progress (see Góngora; Santa Cruz et al.). The investment of "radicals" in such provincial newspapers was crucial in developing a modern sensibility among the nascent middle class in early twentieth-century Latin America. In the context of selling papers, educating the public, and promoting the Radical Party agenda, there were furious debates over questions of decorum, taste, and propriety, debates to which the young writer contributed in the pieces she wrote for the literary sections of *La Voz de Elqui, El Coquimbo, El Mercurio de Antofagasta,* and elsewhere. Such literary sections were typically quite extensive, amounting to several pages of poetry and sketches by local authors, as well as synopses of books originally published abroad.

In essays that mix poetry and prose, local with global concerns, and that set the exploration of subjective aesthetic sketches in the context of calls for social change, Lucila Godoy's work (she sometimes wrote under her original name until 1908, when she was nineteen) was particularly marked by the writer's self-presentation as an artist for whom emotion is thematically and affectively central. Her first published pieces, melancholy texts such as "Ecos" and "Amor imposible," are prose essays written in the first person, employing hyperbole and metaphor to assert the supremacy of inspiration descending in the form of (imagined?) "nights . . . tears . . . caresses . . . black-clad phantoms . . . sorrows" ("Ecos," 21 Mar. 1905; qtd. in *Gabriela Mistral en La Voz de Elqui* 11–12; hereafter cited as *Voz*).[2]

The poet's stated aim of expression is not to be understood but to find relief in the hope that similar souls might share in her complicated sorrows:

No reclamo para estas incoherencias del delirio de mi alma, nada sino una lágrima de tus ojos: la mirada ajena que se pose en estos fragmentos no encontrará sino oscuridades de misterios i de enigmas en ellos. . . . canto para arrancarme un jiron de sombra, para ensanchar el pecho i dejar el vacio que reclama la gota de hiel que rueda eternamente en los flancos heridos del corazón. ("Carta íntima," 30 Nov. 1905, *Voz* 32)

[For these incoherencies from the delirium of my soul I ask nothing, nothing save a tear from your eyes: the alien glance that would settle on these fragments will find nothing but the darkness of mystery and enigma in them. . . . I sing to pull myself out of darkness, to swell my breast and leave the emptiness that reclaims the drop of gall that eternally turns in the heart's wounded chambers.]

The writer's express pessimism, here and elsewhere articulated as disappointment with her surroundings, provoked controversy among the newspapers' readers. The tone of the initial responses could be categorized as polite incomprehension, as in a sonnet dedicated to Lucila Godoy, signed "Bohemio," that asks:

Ave errátil que cantas i que lloras
Al compas dulce de inspiradas notas
¿Si eres hermosa i buena, por qué imploras?
¿Por qué de tu suerte ignota?
¿Por qué de tu alma el sentimento brota
I evocas al dolor horas tras horas?

(7 July 1905, *Voz* 15)

[Wandering bird who sings and weeps
to the sweet compass of inspired chords,
If you are beautiful and good, why do you implore?
Why lament your hard luck?
Why does feeling sprout from your soul,
why evoke pain, hour after hour?]

The poet's reply, printed in the following month as a poem entitled "Flores negras," begins: "Yo no puedo cantar porque no brota / El verso ya de mi alma entristecida" (10 Aug. 1905, *Voz* 18) [I cannot sing because verses do not sprout from my saddened soul]. Another reader responded with a poem, "'Flores blancas,' dedicada a la inspirada autora de 'Flores negras,' respetuosamente." Signed "Goliat Petit," this writer suggests that the poet disdain both love and excessive sadness (13 Aug. 1905, *Voz* 22).

In contrast with such typically respectful responses, a letter to the editor, signed with the cryptic pseudonym "Abel Madac," responds to Lucila Godoy's next publication, entitled "Voces," by attacking her work and underlying sensibility, calling her mental competence into question. Abel Madac describes himself as an enthusiastic and experienced admirer of literature and poetry who has but recently moved to the area, "donde florecen con igual prodigalidad las flores i las mujeres hermosas" [where the flowers and the women blossom with equal beauty]. Questioning Lucila Godoy's right to the sentiment articulated in "Voces," he asks, rhetorically, "¿Cuál es el orígen de ese amargo pesimismo, ese lúgubre acento. . . ?" [What is the origin of this bitter pessimism, this gloomy accent. . . ?]. He condemns her work as "frases huecas; espresiones antisonantes, llenas de enfasis, que no dicen nada a la mente, i mucho ménos al corazon" [empty sentences, harsh-sounding and emphatic expressions, that say nothing to the mind and even less to the heart]. He concludes that the writer may be mentally unbalanced and intellectually overextended. "Ella me da solo la idea de un cerebro desequilibrado, talvez . . . por el exceso de pensar" ("Crítica y réplica literaria," 26 Nov. 1905, *Voz* 26; ellipsis in the original) [She gives me only the idea of a brain unbalanced, perhaps . . . by thinking too much].

Printed alongside this attack, which argues that women's value is primarily a decorative one, is Lucila Godoy's reply, which defends her work from an intellectual and aesthetic perspective:

No hago en él el relieve absoluto de mi vida, hago una imitación de la vida de todos los infortunados, por lo cual empiezo: Habla el alma infortunada, ¿O es que me equivoco i escribo: Habla mi alma infortunada? (*Voz* 27)

[I did not try in my article "Voices" to put my life in absolute form, but to make an imitation of the life of all unfortunates; therefore I begin "the unfortunate soul speaks," or am I mistaken, and I write, "my unfortunate soul speaks"?]

She points to his male chauvinism, commenting,

¡Qué poca penetración de hombre pensador tiene al creer que todas las mujeres sueñan con idilios i viven de aquellas esperanzas! (*Voz* 28)

[How shallow in his thinking the man who thinks that all women dream of idylls and live from those hopes!]

She underscores the error in this line of thought when she indicates that

hai almas que, saliendo de la mediocridad, no esperan ver iluminarse aquel con los fulgores de dos ojos apasionados, sino con la luz única que existe sobre la Tierra, la luz intelectual, la luz de la gloria. (*Voz* 28)

[there are souls who, coming out of mediocrity, seek enlightment not through a pair of flashing, impassioned eyes, but through that only light that exists on the Earth, the intellectual light, the light of glory.]

The controversy raged on, with neither the side of "Abel Madac" (who continued to hide behind his pseudonym) nor that of Lucila Godoy and her defenders conceding any ground. Madac insisted that the writer lacked "educación," a code word for taste and good manners, while she maintained that she was being unfairly attacked.

Such critical responses to the young writer's expressions of sadness and alienation are among the earliest indications of a pattern recurring over the poet's life. Accused of excessive emotion, disorder, bitterness, and pride, she defends herself by maintaining that her expression is an abstract plea on behalf of hypothetical others who might share such feelings of alienation. Challenged to justify a poetics of emotional extremity and verbal excess, she presents art as a way out, not just for individuals, but for a society mired in mediocrity and cowardice. Fundamental to her expression is an atmosphere of intense yet disembodied emotion, which, she argues, speaks to "those in the know."

The episode with "Abel Madac" seems to have spurred the writer to reconfigure her public identity, formulating an aesthetics of speaking on

behalf of others and setting her work in the larger context of calls for
social change. The combination counters Abel Madac and others who felt
that girls' primary value was decorative rather than intellectual. In "La
instrucción de la mujer" (The education of woman), the young writer
takes the then-controversial stance of supporting women's education.[3] Her
line of argument attacks as hypocrisy the premise that women should be
kept ignorant in order to protect their honor:

Es preciso que la mujer deje de ser la mendiga de protección y pueda vivir sin que
tenga que sacrificar su felicidad con uno de los repugnantes matrimonios mo-
dernos, o su virtud con la venta indigna de su honra. (8 Mar. 1906, *Voz* 44)

[It's necessary that woman stop being a beggar needing protection and be able to
live without having to sacrifice her happiness in the repugnant modern marriages,
or her virtue with the undignified sale of her honor.]

She follows this social commentary with a poem, "El final de la vida,"
which describes the sad and lonely final days of "a heart" devoted to faith
and blind adoration (*Voz* 47).

The attacks on and defense of women writers expose a fundamental
problem confronting provincial girls such as Lucila Godoy, as well as urban girls and women in Santiago: the notion of *pudor* held that decency
forbade women's entry into the public sphere in anything but a silent,
decorative capacity. Subscribing to this notion of decency were the few
exclusively upper-class women regularly publishing their writing prior to
1920 in Chile. Their manifestly allegorical pen names fooled no one and
were not intended to. Rather, they did lip service to the idea that these
women needed to protect their decency (that is, their family's decency
or husband's honor, all amounting to the same thing). Inés Echeverría
de Larraín wrote as "Iris" (messenger of the gods), while Mariana Cox
Stueven wrote as "Shade." With surnames that already linked them to the
nation's oligarchy, Iris and Shade each sought refuge, not in alternate civil
identities (hardly needed!), but in the abstract realms of feeling and the
spirit. In the same generation as Lucilla Godoy/Gabriela Mistral, the
writer later known as Winnet de Rokha, after her more famous husband,
began her literary career as "Sor Juana" (see Nómez).

The young, unknown writer Lucila Godoy Alcayaga initially looked to
older writers' example as she cast about for ways to hide or create a new
identity. She wrote as "Alma" (Soul), "Alguién" (Somebody), and "Soledad" (Solitude), abstract pen names that compose an alternate identity in
personal and spiritual rather than in sociohistorical terms. With her 1908
invention of the pseudonym "Gabriela Mistral," the young writer addressed head on the distinction of class that separated her from her aristo-

cratic predecessors. It solved the problem of the unfamiliarity of her civil surnames, Godoy Alcayaga (which merely associate her with Basque colonizers, and not property or prestige). "Gabriela Mistral" could plausibly serve as a civil name (the given name of an angel, the surname of the mistral wind crossing Provence). The letter *a* tacked onto the "given" name "Gabriel," God's messenger angel, minimally meets the requirements for a feminine identity, yet the overall weight of the pseudonym's associations, for those literarily in the know, is with two renowned European male writers, Italian writer Gabriele D'Annunzio and Provençal poet Frederic Mistral (the former, a nationalist patriot; the latter, a writer articulating an alternative, premodern identity for southern rural France). The newly invented identity is superficially but not profoundly female, sounding very spiritual and close to the natural world, even as the weight of its authority appeals to and claims association with a heftily European, male literary heritage.

Interlude: Caveats of the Smoking Vibrator and the Soap Opera

To understand how the writer who became famous as Gabriela Mistral would stand in relation to an as-yet-unwritten history of sexual sensibility in Latin America requires confronting the reception of her work as an example of how women's writings are regularly co-opted, enlisted to support projects for repressive versions of femininity. Mistral's later work exists in a problematic relation to the state, which limits the recognition of women as speaking, historical subjects, casting the female into the mono-dimensional role of republican mother (see Pratt; Fiol-Matta). A pseudo-Marianic projection of symbolic motherhood onto Gabriela Mistral's work and life unites her as a woman with the patria (see Horan, "Santa Maestra muerta"). Her expressions of desire and longing have been shoehorned into a formula of suffering and transcendence through devotion to the nation's future citizens (i.e., children).

In distinction to the symbolic or allegorical inscription of Gabriela Mistral as a figure for national or universal devotion, the real-life Gabriela Mistral presents a figure that flatly contradicts a national mythology of "*la chilena*" as petite, fashion-conscious, coquettish, home-loving, devoted to family (see Horan, "Gabriela Mistral"). Precious little space, here, for Gabriela Mistral, whom her friend from these years, sculptor Laura Rodig, later described as a "cariátide en movimiento" (285) [caryatid in motion], that is, a priestess of Artemis serving as an architectural support. In her size forty shoes, standing 1.8 meters tall, usually hatless and wearing the same clothes for months on end, the *paticaliente* (lit., "hot-footed," or restless) and work-driven Gabriela Mistral, never married, chain smoking, exceeds the category of the exception that proves the rule. As Bianchi points out, this real-life figure proves the impossibility of the categories: "Por sus largas vestimentas, su cabello corto y escasos afeites, se espía casi como sinónimo de ambigüedad sexual" (11) [With her long robes, cropped hair and seldom shaving, she is almost a synonym for sexual ambiguity].

On the one hand, the construction of a saintly vita flattens, narrows, and shrinks this large, uncontainable figure, so that she may enter Chilean and Latin American literary canons without disrupting them too much. Suppressing the eroticism in her work does not, on the other hand, erase what brought her to attention in the first place: the perverse and violent and ambiguously directed emotion that haunts her verse. By redirecting attention to the conditions making possible as well as hindering the emergence of "Gabriela Mistral" (superbly represented in Patricia Rubio's comprehensive bibliography), the palimpsest of identity shows through: the experimentation of youth, the erased alternatives, the faded yet rescued earlier drafts, all reveal the multiplicity of possible identifications within a historical "*ambiente*" of *fin-de-siècle* queerness.

The problem with the figure of "la Divina Gabriela" is not just the way that the subject's personal eccentricity is suppressed but also that reinforcing a rigid division of gender depends on pushing aside the sexually dissident *ambiente* from which Gabriela Mistral emerged. Failure to acknowledge her engagement with the legendary bohemianism, internationalism, and avant-garde experimentation of early twentieth-century Chile belongs to the larger, ongoing, willed amnesia of the postdictatorship, post–cold war as the triumph of market-based neoliberalism.

Too great a stress on historicist specificity perhaps runs the risk of deteriorating into what I call the hunt for the smoking vibrator, that is, the phallocentric attempt to locate some hard-and-fast proof that la Divina Gabriela was really "la Divina lesbiana." The hunt for the smoking vibrator, analogous to the idea of a smoking gun that would identify the perpetrator of a crime, conjures up the archivist's search for "was-she-or-wasn't-she" evidence. Such an approach is misguided: we need not "prove" lesbianism any more than we need "prove" heterosexuality. Discovering the repression of sexuality in Gabriela Mistral is useful for comprehending the real and potential multiplicity of women's sexual identities and desires. Such comprehension requires returning to the very items and qualities that made her raw, embarrassing, almost inarticulate expressions of longing so sensational in the first place.

Gabriela Mistral's inclusion in the canon begins with construing her as a figure of self-abnegating devotion to a male child-lover. This is especially evident in the fascination of critics with a handful of so-called love poems, written early in her career, appearing in *Desolación* (1922).[4] Drawing from the group of poems subtitled "Dolor," which are dedicated "a su sombra," critics from Figueroa onward have cast the poet as an innocent country girl betrayed by a young man after he degrades their chaste love, first by engaging in a consensual physical relationship with another woman, and subsequently when he kills himself in despair over what he has become. Palma Guillén points to the motivations of this interpretation:

Los comentadores (no sé cuántos libros y artículos se han escrito sobre G. M. machacando sobre esta imagen que tan satisface el orgullo varonil) nos imponen la silueta simplificada de una mujer haciéndose pedazos al borde de un sepulcro en un amor único y terrible. Seguramente esos comentadores han soñado con un amor así para ellos mismos y han querido una mujer así—parecida a una fuerza de la Naturaleza—que se destroza en un nudo fatal de amor y muerte del que ellos mismos son motivo y objeto. (x)

[The commentators (I don't know how many books and articles have been written about G. M. chewing over this image that so satisfies manly pride) impose on us the simplified sillouhette of a woman going to pieces alongside a tomb in a single, terrible love. Surely these commentators have dreamed of such a love for themselves and have wanted such a woman—resembling a force of Nature—who is destroyed in a fatal knot of love and death in which they themselves are origin and object.]

   Guillén's analysis suggests that it is impossible to underestimate the impact, extension, and durability of this *historieta,* or soap-operatic narrative, in which male vanity readily, eagerly projects itself. It creates a hierarchy in which the love-elegy as *plegaria* (prayer) in behalf of the beloved (e.g., "El ruego," which Gabriela Mistral later repudiated) reigns supreme, while forms such as the ronda and the landscape poem are consigned to the status of "minor work." The *historieta* endures because of the gender roles that it enshrines: the naturally philandering male (really just a little boy looking for a mother); "*la otra,*" the other woman (sexually experienced and hungry for money, power, status) who lures him to his doom; the virginal country girl who remains true to her heart, solitary, and pure (our heroine—from a distance, please). This critical perspective goes on to argue that she becomes a virago-poet out of despair because the death of her only true love denies her the (male) child that will make her complete. Thus the current hierarchy, in which the poet of mourning, also a poet of frustrated maternity (in lullabies and school-based work, she strives to forget but really just looks for him in imaginary boy babies), is subsequently displaced into social conscience. As Madre de América she is a secularized version of the Madonna de la Misericordia (the Compassionate Madonna), who shelters the vulnerable, dispossessed, diminutive faithful. Further tragedy (why is it that men are always killing themselves around her?) impels her into a doddering old age; she is too sad, too devastated, ever to enjoy her international acclaim. Nothing lets a woman succeed like lack of success.

Making the sexually ambiguous Gabriela Mistral into a symbolic mother shores up the fragile foundations of masculinity and serves the patria whose schoolchildren she socializes (see Fiol-Matta). Her agonized mourning (if not repentance) crystallizes a postsexual version of *la otra,* replacing the embarrassingly sexualized one of "other woman," which may be omnipresent in popular culture but cannot be present at the level of quasi-official, national discourse. Turning her into a postsexual mother pushes aside the (scandalous at the time) way that her work lingers over the female body (in "Poesías de la Madre más triste") and the numerous ways that her figure attacks stereotypes of Chilean femininity. Her entry into national public discourse depends, all in all, on the maternalization of her canonized figure as a counter to the perceived pitfalls of "la idea de mujer infértil, solterona y lesbiana" (Raquel Olea, qtd. in Lanzarotti 31).

Alternative Versions of Honor: Speculating on Passion

When the local newspapers of Coquimbo and Elqui printed the young writer's introspective, pantheistic prose explorations that champion passionate solitude, Lucila Godoy found that public speech came with a price. Her alliances with "radical" politics, the poverty of her family, and her personal difficulties with local school authorities in the conservative provincial city of La Serena, all brought her formal schooling to an abrupt end, at age fifteen. The repercussions of the hostility that she encountered and the fact of having to work for a living become manifest in her prose from about 1908 onward. Her publications become more circumspect or strategic about her relation to the codes of decency and decorum that silenced women. In 1908 her most daring experimentation appears not in newspapers or in literary magazines but in her personal correspondence with an older admirer, tentatively identified as Alfredo Videla Pineda, a bachelor just past forty, heir to extensive and productive vineyards. Lucila Godoy is about seventeen years old when the correspondence begins.[5]

In a group of five letters (published in *Cartas de amor de Gabriela Mistral*), Lucila Godoy uses the occasion of writing letters to cast her correspondent in the role of dissolute, ardent, rich male admirer, and herself as the poor but honest country girl. When he demands a private meeting, she responds with descriptions of her solitary suffering and the assertion that writing letters constitutes the truest proof of a lover's sincerity. It's not his physical presence but his letters that she wants: they enable her to develop an intense, imaginary drama of love and honor in which she insists on her status as a third-party onlooker. Her role is detached, purely spectatorial, while his is "esa pasión loca y desbordante que muere con la ligereza con que nace. . . . mi amor es calmado, intenso, y noble; no hay en él ni falsedad ni perfidia" (Mistral, *Cartas de amor* 82; cited only by page number in the following discussion) [this mad and disordering passion that dies with the lightness with which it is born. . . . my love is calm, intense and noble, there is nothing of falsity or perfidy in it].

The fullest extension of the writer's self-consciously detached, yet obsessive, imaginings appears in the final letter of the correspondence, which the writer opens with an acknowledgment of the social differences between them and with her imagining the physical proximity of her rivals, as opposed to her absolute physical detachment:

Sabe en qué me pongo a pensar a veces? En que por los alrededores de su hacienda haya alguna aldeanita de esas cautivadoras que me esté robando sus miraditas tan preciosas para esta pobre mendiga! . . . el viento favorable me trae los acordes de la música lejana, de esa música de que Ud. goza todas las noches en el paseo lleno de damas entre las cuales hay una a quien Ud. quiere y que quizás sea más tarde la dueña de Mi Alfredo. ¿Para qué negarlo? (93)

[Know what I think of sometimes? About how close by your estate there would be some village girl, one of those captivating ones who is stealing from me those little glances that are so precious for this poor beggar! . . . coming my way, the wind brings me this music that you enjoy every night in the promenade full of ladies among whom there is one whom you love and who perhaps later will be my Alfredo's mistress. Why deny it?]

Concluding the imagined scenario, she asserts the supremacy of love as cruel master and indifferent idol which she devotedly serves:

El Amor cubre los infortunios más grandes con mantos de aurora y de flores. Bajo su imperio todo es bello. La tristeza es dulce, la queja es arrullo, la flagelación de la traición es caricia. Hasta la indiferencia del Ídolo hace amar más. (93)

[Love covers the greatest misfortunes with spreads of dawn and flowers. Under his empire all is beautiful. Sadness is sweet, complaint is a lullaby, the whipping of betrayal is caress. Even the indifference of the Idol makes one love more.]

For all her expressions of idolatry, she invokes the convention of "mi honor, la riqueza de la mujer pobre" (94) [my honor, the treasure of the poor woman] and argues for a code of guiltless suffering in which they both adhere to the decorum that the world requires, since "el mundo lo manda así, vivimos en él, y debemos respetar sus leyes aunque sean absurdos y ridiculeces" (94) [the world requires as much, and we live in the world and ought to respect its laws even though they are absurd and ridiculous]. She closes by contrasting his false rhetoric to her intensity and utter sincerity, observing that "el que ama no pide sacrificio, se sacrifica a sí mismo. Ese es amor; lo demás es mentira" (95) [the one who loves asks no sacrifice but self-sacrifice. This is love; the rest is a lie].

Writing personal letters provided valuable practice for developing an aesthetic of controlled, intense emotion. While a dissolute life might be expected, even required, of well-to-do, middle-aged men (her correspondents Videla and, later, the modernist poet Manuel Magallanes Moure are two cases in point), the world offered no such prospect to the seventeen-year-old girl writing these letters, who was supporting herself and her mother, and had been raised in an impoverished single-parent home, where the men were errant and often alcoholic. She uses the epistolary relationship to probe the bounds of decorum in developing that atmosphere of charged and repressed sexuality that later intrigued the ivory-tower aesthetes of Santiago, in the years leading up to 1920.

The literary activity of writing letters allowed her to experience vicariously the idea of dissolute romance as the road to ruin. She is, in effect, like a mass-market romance novelist, like a Corín Tellado, *una pornógrafa inocente* (an innocent pornographer). The third party writes, looking onto steamy sex scenes. Against a background of repression constituted by the writer's necessary physical distance (we rarely correspond with people we see daily), sexuality emerges despite itself, expressed as prohibition, deceit, voyeuristic desire to be the other woman, the one who openly expresses her lust, the one who controls the unfaithful man (see, for example, L. Godoy letter to Magallanes Moure, 20 May 1915, *Cartas de amor* 119–20). The writer uses the letters (to Videla, to Magallanes Moure) to practice what will become, over the next few years, her trademark narrative of frustrated sexuality, in which (someone else's) deceit and (still another's) betrayal versus (her own) purity (and sense of guilt) create ongoing unsatisfied desire. She becomes an expert in delineating the dramatic situations, characters, and locales of expression queered by an apparently unconfrontable, prohibited desire.

Whereas the later work of Gabriela Mistral (material composed and published after 1938) is both haunting and spare, the earlier work of Lucila Godoy/Gabriela Mistral is so lush as to verge on incoherence. That lushness to some extent reflects the poetic fashion of early twentieth-century Chile, where the excessiveness and extremity of emotion in her poetry alarmed many. When, for example, she declared in 1908 that she admired the (now canonical, once scandalous) modernist Rubén Darío and declared that the novelist Vargas Vila was her "Idol," one of earliest editors and supporters, Soto Ayala, published the statement along with her writing in his regional anthology *Literatura Coquimbana* (she was one of but two women included). Soto counseled her to forget Darío alto-gether: "Forget him, he is a monster" (prologue). Silent on the topic of the young poet's skill, he praised, instead, her work's affective intensity, indicating that it would find an audience among similarly frustrated kin-dred spirits:

Los que tengan muertas las esperanzas, los que sueñen con anhelos imposibles, los que alguna vez hayan llevado una historia escrita en el alma i algún retrato grabado en el corazón, los que en medio del destierro de la vida hayan percibido el perfume vago i arrobador de la pureza de una mujer sensible, apasionada, lean las prosas de Lucila Godoi. (Soto Ayala, *prologue*)

[Those for whom hope has died, those who dream of impossible longings, those whose soul and heart have once borne a tale written and some portrait engraved, those who amid life's exile have sensed the indefinite, rapture-inducing perfume of the purity of a woman who is feeling and impassioned, these people read the prose works of Lucila Godoy.]

The rhetoric of womanly purity and impassioned writing elevates the former because it makes possible the latter. The description of those simi-larly afflicted reads as Soto Ayala's coded acknowledgment (in the pro-logue to his anthology) that the poet articulates queer desire, as "impos-sible longings" in "life's exile." In this way, amid direct and indirect attacks on her writing, a rustic Gabriela comes forth, an upstart and outsider whose nonconformity and uncompromising attitudes brought her plenty of trouble in the church-dominated, class-conscious, provincial environ-ment of La Serena. Facing a false and constrictive social atmosphere, frus-trated with her immediate environment and the world, Gabriela Mistral's earliest publications convey struggle and a sense of tremendous discon-tent, a being at odds. Writing was at once a relief, a source of danger, and a tremendous effort of overtaking her own strange self.

En el ambiente de los liceos de las niñas

Entering the educational profession was crucial to Gabriela Mistral's in-tellectual development. Her older sister Emelina and her friend Fidelia Valdés Pereira, who both belonged to the first generation of women public school teachers in Chile, surely encouraged her to take this route. Public school teaching was the only profession open to women in rural areas, where the low wages, lodging included, were among the best a woman might hope for in Chile.

Encouraging women to work and live together allowed the state to max-imize each appointment and also to forestall the loneliness and isolation that such women would inevitably feel, assigned to provincial cities far from other friends and family. The young writer's initial appointments were to teach with her friend Fidelia Valdés Pereira: first they moved together to the rainy southern town of Traiguen; from there, a few months later, to the northern desert port of Antofagasta; and then, a year and a half later, to the city of Los Andes, outside Santiago, where the two remained until the writer's literary fame brought her an appointment to direct a school herself, in 1920. Like Valdés Pereira: and other school directors, Godoy/Mistral brought her staff, thus enabling her to continue collegial relationships and friendships over years, first with Laura Rodig and later with Palma Guillén.

Such an *ambiente,* of living and working in all-female groups in the schools and traveling, was as restrictive as it was liberating. The *liceos de las niñas* where Gabriela Mistral worked in Chile were more often than not ramshackle, poorly heated buildings with few texts or classroom supplies. In this environment she found herself amply rewarded (in paid publications, recognition, promotions) for writing uplifting, idealistic exhortations directed to her fellow schoolteachers, which theosophical magazines also printed. From the evidence of her correspondence in these years, she felt oppressed by the daily grind, isolated, lonely, with books, correspondence, and vacation in the dramatic rural landscapes nearby as her primary relief. She rarely dwells on the friendships of the women sharing her living quarters. With the survival of relatively few of the letters she wrote to close friends those seventy-five years ago and the writer's frequent references to the way that her mail was regularly stolen, opened, and read, it is difficult to say how much, if any, liberty of feeling the all-female world of the *liceos* might have permitted. One important liberty it did permit was the following forceful condemnation of the male-authored erotic and bellicose poetry of the time, a condemnation legitimated by the author's broader context of calling for more children's poetry, in a piece entitled "Cuentos: Oyendo los de kindergarten" (Cuentos: Listening to them in kindergarden):

Sobran los poetas que se deslién en poemas eróticos, sobran también los que hacen apoteosis de la espada y de la coraza, sobran los que lloran sus lepras íntimas revolcándose en el escepticismo. ¿Donde hay los poetas de los niños? (14 Jan. 1912; qtd. in Bahamonde 129)

[There are more than enough poets who sprawl out in erotic poetry, there are more than enough who do the apotheosis of sword and shield, there are more than enough who bewail their intimate leprosy, wallowing in skepticism. Where are the children's poets?]

Contending with Death: Alterity and Triangulated Desire in "El rival" (1911)

Strongly shaping Gabriela Mistral's development as a "*maestra*," a kind of guru combining spiritual and quasi-maternal authority, is her extensive and lasting involvement with alternative spirituality. Mistral began attending the local lodge of the international theosophy movement in about 1911.[6] Her engagement with theosophy supported her already manifest thematic preoccupations with love, destiny, death, and ascetic renunciation. As an intellectual movement organized around a publication program centered on esoteric spirituality, theosophy stressed the "spiritual plane" along with notions of fraternity promising to transcend the rigidly fixed divisions of gender, class, and ideology—divisions that Mistral met at every turn. The theosophists, moreover, seem to have had a high tolerance for personal eccentricity. Despite its U.S. origins, theosophy was by 1911 a truly international movement based in the effective exploitation of print media, including an ambitious publication program and lending libraries.[7] Its stated aim was to "transcend the cleavage between science and religion by a return to the concerns of an ancient wisdom-tradition, long forgotten" (Campbell 29).[8] It additionally drew on the nineteenth-century ideologies of individual genius and scientific progress. In Chile as elsewhere, this discourse appealed to idealistic internationalism, fascination with the power of the Masons, and the widespread legacy of interest in the occult.[9] Theosophy let individuals proclaim intellectual independence within a tradition of marginality and a loose bond of "fraternity" with others similarly interested in exploring "ancient wisdom." It enjoyed strong support among intellectuals living on the periphery of European influence—India, Russia, and the more European cities of Latin America—where the vogue continued well into the 1920s and 1930s.

Theosophy influenced Gabriela Mistral's attempt to imagine ways out of gender binaries, as is evident in a short story dealing with sex, death, and jealousy, which the Antofagasta *Mercurio* published as "El rival" in October of 1911.[10] Its narrative presents what will become a standard theme in Mistral's work: the description of how a special set of experiences leads to the individual's realization of having been marked by fate, set apart from others. It is the only instance in which she speaks from a male persona, through a male narrator named Gabriel, who discovers that his destiny involves desire spurred on and frustrated by the jealousy of an invisible, nonhuman rival: death as a personally malevolent force. "El rival" reflects nineteenth-century aesthetics, the story explicitly cites the stories of Poe and the verses of Baudelaire as analogues. In a monologue which the narrator begins as a way of explaining why he is old beyond his years and steers clear of the banter of love that delights the other young men, Gabriel describes how each of the three young women whom he has chastely loved has been snatched from him without warning, thwarting his desire. The first two were pure; the third one, quite the opposite; yet "El rival" wants each of them. Given that his invisible rival always prevents him from consummating his love, Gabriel concedes an honorable defeat, concluding that Death has marked him, that death is an active force, a jealous rival who has determined that he will enjoy neither love or marriage. Choosing celibacy, he seems old beyond his years, set apart from his less knowing peers, who blindly aspire to sexually active lives.

"El rival" is congruent with Mistral's later work in that the speaker experiences prohibited longings and discovers destiny in the renunciation of desire. Unique to "El rival," however, are the means by which the speaker arrives at this discovery; by trying to consummate his desire, he directly causes the deaths of the women he loves. As in Mistral's work generally, physical death, erotic love, and enforced celibacy are linked. Here, too, as throughout *Desolación,* desire in "El rival" is triangulated, involving a man, a woman, and a nebulous third party, elsewhere identified as *la otra,* here identified with jealous Death:

¡La muerte! Fue mi fantasma; la veía cerca de los míos, sarcástica y horrible, haciendo el vacío a mi alrededor, con la guadaña alzada sobre esas existencias jóvenes—almendras florecidas—que rodaron a su golpe. ("El rival," qtd. in Bahamonde 122)

[Death! She was my phantom; I saw her close to mine, sarcastic and horrible, leaving emptiness at my side, scythe raised over those young existences, flowering almond trees, that fell under her blow.]

This rival appears by synecdoche, as will later be the case with the unseen rival in Mistral's "Sonetos de la muerte," a similar narrative of carnal love cut short by death, where unspecified "malas manos" [evil hands] enter tragically and take away the (always unspecified) beloved's life (*Desolación, ternura* 29). The speaker in "El rival," who resolves to live without love, presents a conclusion reiterated in "Sonetos" as elsewhere in *Desolación* (e.g., "Íntima"): love purged of carnal desire outlasts death.

Women as Brothers among the Fraternal Theosophists

Although early twentieth-century Chile contained many utopian enthusiasms, the hodgepodge of theosophy, with its proclaimed compatibility with any of the world's leading religions, offered an umbrella for all, vegetarians and yogis, spiritualists, Tolstoyans, and antivivisectionists. Already inclined to internationalism and disinclined to dogma, Gabriela Mistral found that theosophy stimulated these and other interests, as explored in "El rival," all the while presenting unusual opportunities for women's intellectual development. In its specific openness to women, the "brotherhood" of theosophy stood apart from the other modes of postulating "fraternity."

Encouraging a certain independence of thought and self-development through literacy and taking a conciliatory attitude toward scientific modes of knowledge, theosophy had elements in common with the related early twentieth-century, women-directed organizations. Not much research on spiritualist clubs as enclaves for women has been done, although they seem to have existed in Argentina well into the 1920s (Masiello 177). In regard to gender roles, the writings of the theosophists suggest a greater flexibility in the theosophist lodges than in the culture at large. In part the flexibility resulted from the way that women such as Blavatsky and Besant disclaimed their power, presenting themselves not as leaders but as emissaries of the Masters. As single or widowed women, they pursued spiritual and philosophical interests that a male-dominated clergy regarded as superfluous to women's primarily domestic role.

While the literary texts of Helene P. Blavatsky and Annie Besant drew Gabriela Mistral's interest, seance attendance did not. When, for example, her correspondent Eugenio Labarca requested names of deceased spirits to contact, Gabriela Mistral was willing to give two names (of two women), but she went on to point out inconsistencies in the "messages" he had reported (Mistral, *Cartas a Eugenio Labarca* 45). Disembodied voices seem to have convinced the ingenuous Labarca, while Mistral's friends who belonged to the group known as Los Diez were not taken in. This brotherhood spoofed the overlapping languages of theosophy and Masonry as one of their favorite pastimes: each member was said to go through an initiation ceremony in which he pledged allegiance to the "older brother," whose identity no one knew (see Prado, Prado, and Ibáñez Santa María; Mistral, *En batalla*).[11]

The letters that Gabriela Mistral received from theosophists suggest that men in the movement regarded her as a "brother," that is, an honorary man. One lodge member took fraternity to the point of addressing her in the masculine when he wrote to request that she send poems for publication: "Dear Brother: . . . although I don't remember having had the pleasure of knowing you on the Physical Plane, I consider it my duty to put myself at your disposition. . . . We brothers of this lodge have managed to launch [a magazine]. . . . I hope you might find the necessary time to dedicate some lines to us for publication . . ." (Hamilton-Jones to Gabriela Mistral, 17 June 1915, qtd in *Boletín del Museo Gabriela Mistral* 5; hereafter cited as *BMGM*).

The brotherly language of theosophy allowed its members to articulate respect and admiration and to ask favors of "kin" they had never met. Apparently asexual and nonphysical, the metaphoric brotherhood allowed readers and writers to express as kinship that intimate identification that Mistral so often refers to, in the letters she sends to other, better-known writers at this time in her life. Writing to Amado Nervo, Eduardo Barrios, and Pedro Prado, her letters invoke intimacy while the brotherly ideal allows her to sidestep the uncomfortable and ambiguous element of sexual differentiation. She might use theosophy to let her hair down, but not quite; she, like Blavatsky, writes of "ecstasy" with no specific allusion to the female body.

For all its idealism of moving beyond the body, the language of theosophy rather prosaically acknowledges the earthly hierarchy. Striking up a correspondence with aristocratic writer Inés Echeverría de Larraín, who wrote as "Iris," Gabriela Mistral praises her and notes that she has "a luminous name that draws others" to her. The metaphor is precise, given the wealth and prestige associated with the surnames in question. Addressing the well-connected, independently wealthy poet Pedro Prado, for example, Gabriela Mistral terms him a "Rajah of the things of the Spirit" (letter to Pedro Prado, Dec. 1915, in Mistral, *En batalla* 31).

Yet as the name of Gabriela Mistral began to achieve a degree of renown in Chile, poets and editors correspondingly enlisted the language of spiritual kinship to address her as "a fraternal soul" whose serenity and inner peace inspired them. Writer and editor Luis Enrique Carrera, for instance, writes that he shares with her confidences about his inner spirit unknown even to his wife (letter, 20 Nov. 1915, qtd. in *BMGM* 5). Writer Eugenio Labarca presented himself as an admiring student (letter, 23 Feb. 1915, qtd. in *BMGM* 4), while poet Olga Azevedo went further, calling herself a disciple and Gabriela Mistral "Mi buena maestra" in thanking Mistral for having sponsored the publication of Azevedo's poetry in the magazine *Familia* (letter, 22 Sept. 1915, qtd. in *BMGM* 5).

Even those who did not share theosophical ideals recognized in Gabriela Mistral the essence of the "spiritual teacher." Thus the otherwise skeptical Chilean writer José Santos González Vera describes her in his memoirs, enumerating the troupe that descended on her during her regular visits to Santiago, circa 1916: "In the morning came Protestant ministers, retired and repentant military men, theosophists, women schoolteachers, salespersons, inventors, functionaries and strange types you would be afraid of, seeing them in the street. I never knew how she had met these people, or what she would say to them. It seems that even they didn't know what moved them to go see her" (209). Committed socialist, avowed atheist, González Vera nonetheless shared their fascination and included himself in this disparate crowd of followers, declaring her "an absolutely medicinal being" (209). Such language reveals how the epithet "maestra" and the input of theosophy presented Mistral with alternatives to the abject positions of the poor country girl and of the voyeur.

As a worldwide fraternity replete with queerness, transgendered identity, and the promise of intimacy, theosophy as Mistral and her correspondents practiced it sought to sidestep the uncomfortable element of sexual differentiation and to enter, through correspondence, the bohemian world that celebrated the artist as the chosen one, a being set apart. Mistral's poetry and prose poetry in *Desolación* spell this out further. In her poetry, the pronouns do not specify gender, however, the prose poetry borrows from theosophy the sense of an anthropomorphized world in which the earth, rocks, and trees are sensate and the artist/guru is beyond male or female. All these strategies frustrate attempts to identify the lover, or the speaker's gender, in poems such as "Extasis" and "Intima," which were written in around 1917 and collected in *Desolación*. These and other poems present a carefully constructed, highly fictional biomythography of love.

Most convoluted and involved in Mistral's poetic dramas of betrayal is the status of the speaking subject. The poet's seeming detachment and extreme vagueness about who else is involved are conveyed through inverted syntax, verbs without definite subjects or objects, and phrasing that refuses easy referentiality. The language twists and turns, heaping one possibility onto another, continually altering the subject. The ambiguity of her pronouns makes it nearly impossible to say, precisely, who does what to whom in the opening lines of a poem such as "El suplicio" (The entreaty, in *Desolación*). Here, the license to speak comes from the poet's visceral experience of bearing a dagger like a twenty-year pregnancy or secret wound. The dagger then gives way to "a verse cresting at high tide." The combined force of the high tide and the majesty (of the verse) makes the body (not named, but understood) "grow tired." Rather than addressing the deliberately ambiguous question of who or what buried the dagger in the flesh or who or what tires whom, and rather than naming the body, the poem casts the feeling of tiredness as the subject of the next line, leading up to the query, How is it that this (or any) mouth that has lied will now sing the detached truth of song? The impossibility of clear referentiality refuses any clear separation or delineation of grammatical subject from object, of speech from ocean, of boundaries on or possession of a body which speaks out of woundedness but may have lied. Such deflected expression of desire, of protest, of scarcely articulate emotion turned to verse, constantly presses on Gabriela Mistral's texts, edging on a huge unspeakable space, which the poet amplifies through twisting and erasures.

Despite self-censorship, and despite the fact that it is rarely studied today, *Desolación: Poemas* remains the strangest and most ambitious of the four volumes of poetry that Gabriela Mistral published during her lifetime. While it includes some of the didactic social conscience and Americanist work found in her other three collections, *Desolación* is distinctive in the sections "Dolor" and "Vida" and "Prosa," which catalogue the queerness of desire, impossible longings, prohibition, secret identities. The carefully coded, hyperbolic language abundantly typifies *modernismo* as the extension of symbolist *fin-de-siècle* decadence expressed in what Augusto Iglesias has called "intrasexualidad." [12] In *Desolación* the lavish poetics of *modernismo* are muted, even repressed, by the theosophist's rhetoric of disembodied longing on the part of masculinized women and feminized men.

"El" artista: Wounded by Beauty

Any attempt at writing a history of sexual sensibility expressed by women in the early twentieth century, in Latin America or Europe, would look to metaphors (recurring throughout *Desolación*) that pose the origins of speech in the quality of woundedness, that relate woundedness to the ability to apprehend beauty, that correlate versifying with violence. The artist transcends gender identification as male or female (for Mistral, in the ars poetica of the "Decálogo del artista"), presenting instead a special caste whose immersion in the life of the imagination is a sensory experience vastly superior to the grotesque impersonality of desire toward the woman. Opening the series "El arte" she states, "Una canción es una herida de amor que nos abrieron las cosas" (Mistral, *Desolación: Poemas* 203) [A song is a wound of love that opened things up to us]. The definition goes on to address the "hombre basto" (uncouth man) who, by contrast, finds that "sólo te turba un vientre de mujer, el montón de carne de la mujer" (203) [the only thing that arouses you is a woman's belly, the mount of woman's flesh]. In contrast with this characterization of individual desire, she depicts the artist's experience of desire as a shared wound to the spirit: "Nosotros vamos turbados, nosotros recibimos la lanzada de toda belleza del mundo, porque la noche estrellada nos fue amor tan agudo como un amor de carne" (203) [We are aroused, we receive the lance-wound of all the world's beauty, because the starry night was love to us, as sharp as carnal love].

Such stark oppositions are typical of modernist poetry, while the hyperbolic insistence on emotional suffering recalls the lesbian characters of early twentieth-century fiction, such as Radclyffe Hall's *The Well of Loneliness* and Djuna Barnes's *Nightwood,* which represent lesbians as misunderstood outsiders. As with the "invert" Stephen and the somnambulant Robin Vote, the speakers or characters in the aesthetic universe of Mistral's prose and narrative poetry represent a consciousness apart, distanced from, and incomprehensible to ordinary human beings. As in *Nightwood,* as in the poet H.D., the narrating or speaking voice is situated outside, looking in on, witnessing scenes of passion and betrayal.

While the outsider status is typical of modernist, symbolist, and romantic poets, specific to Mistral's work is the lingering over scenes of traumatic violence and personal loss, which her work frequently invokes in the context of questions of identity and sexuality. Biographical sources, such as Laura Rodig's subsequent memoir of her life with Gabriela Mistral (drawn heavily from the poet's notebooks of 1915–20), assign to the Chilean poet an intrinsic "genio violento" [violent nature] inherited from her father (283). The poet's youth was marked by suffering, struggle, perennial outsideness, which the external difficulties of her early life amply reinforced.[13] Gabriela Mistral apparently believed that her family of origin was marked, intergenerationally, by a violence that she herself replicated in a kind of cruel destiny.

Whatever the origins of Gabriela Mistral's linking of woundedness with speech, violence with the emergence of poetic identity, an outcome of these linkages is that she represents the self as so endlessly divided, so continually threatened by violence and its own excessiveness, as to make unconfrontable in *Desolación* the very lack of a safe haven from which to speak. Only close to the end of her life, in that most brilliant series entitled "Locas mujeres" (Mad women) in her final collection, *Lagar,* does the poet turn full attention to articulating the impossibility of a stable, unitary, fixed identity. Here, the condition of art begins each poem with the stripping down and shedding of all vestiges of identity, whether in the ballerina's dance of "losing as much as she had" (Mistral, *Poesías* 601) or in the systematic unlearning of love, in the opening of "La abandonada" (596). As in "La desasida," which opens "En el sueño yo no tenía / padre ni madre, gozos ni duelos" (604) [In dreams I have had no father or mother, joy or pain], the consciousness articulated in the series "Locas mujeres" is the consciousness of having sustained an absolute loss.

Lesbian Utopics: The Mother's Body

The poetics articulated in "Poesías de las madres" (earliest versions appeared in 1916, reprinted in *Desolación: Poemas*) move beyond the alternatives to heterosexuality presented in theosophy. The "Poesías" posit an

all-female, utopian world of bodily intimacy between women, distinct
from what she describes as the "brutality" of male sexual privilege. The
series hints at the possibility of erotic satisfaction. In contrast with the
generalized pantheism attributed to theosophy and in contrast with Mistral's adaptation of the prose poem for school-based work, the "Poesías
de las madres" individually and as a whole propose a specifically female
sensory experience of "infinite sweetness" that the poet associates with a
creativity antithetical to the patriarchal family, marriage, heterosexuality.
These and others of Mistral's prose parables use the veiled language of
semimystical speech for its similarity to the language of love, without what
the "Poesías" depict as heterosexuality's threat of male violence and demand for sexual favors. Mistral's seeming preoccupation with the theme
of motherhood and her evocations of gestation and the mother–infant relation show her claiming those aspects of the female body which least interested male writers of her day. Celebrating maternity is a pretext for an
eroticism concentrated on female sensory experience in ways utterly devoid of masculine influence. The poet demonstrates in these and other
poems an ongoing preoccupation with femininity as a visceral experience
of blood and breast, entrails, flesh, bone, and milk. Such vehement insistence on the physical and on desire as a wound, together with her concentrated attention to the physical traces of that wound in specifically feminine self-representations, recalls the stringent definition of the lesbian ("a
commitment of skin, blood, breast, and bone") that Catherine Stimpson
posits in "Zero-Degree Deviancy" (364), as well as Adrienne Rich's more
general "lesbian continuum . . . a range—through each woman's life and
throughout history—of woman-identified experience" ("Compulsory
Heterosexuality" 648). It is when Mistral evokes the body of the mother
that she is at her most utopian, constructing an autonomous identity that
is neither male nor female.

Mistral's utopianism is graphically centered on the pre-Oedipal celebra-
tion of the maternal body. Beginning with voyeuristic projections such as
"El niño solo," the language of the female body underlies her most characteristic vocabulary, in *Desolación*'s reiterated use of terms such as "entra-
ñas" [bowels, but also womb], "cuajo" [thickening] and "cuajar" [to produce a thickened liquid, esp. milk], and "el pezón de la rosa" [nipple-bud,
or the rose, which in Mistral often equals the nipple of the maternal
breast]. Underlying this network of allusions is a conception of the mother's language as primal play in the ultimate creative act, of creating the
world that surrounds the child. Thus in the prose poem entitled "Recuerdo
de la madre ausente" (A memory of the absent mother) (inscribed, "a mi
madre" and written in Mexico for publication on Mother's Day), a formula appears that recurs in many of the poet's earliest lullabies: "Los

versos no eran sino palabras juguetonas, pretextos para tus mimos" (*Lecturas para mujeres* 11) [The verses were nothing but playful words, pretexts for your caresses]. This language of utopian bliss, one almost says fusion, of the babe-with-mother recurs throughout Mistral's work (see Horan, *Gabriela Mistral* 145–71). Here, it is identified as the music of the spheres, and the mother, as "el primer músico" [the first musician] of the cradle song's "va-y-ven" (11), its go–and–come back, and by extension, any oscillating, rocking movement.

Writing, lingering about, surveying in graphic terms the maternal body allowed a woman of the early twentieth century to engage in a fantasy utterly taboo to men, in Latin America or anywhere. In writing about desire of and for the mother, Gabriela Mistral establishes a space from which she can write to and for women in ways that her male contemporaries cannot do. Her decision to write in the first person of desire for the maternal body stipulates a female-centered eroticism inimical to the bovarism of the time, that is, a male-centered eroticism in which the female serves only as the object of male desire. Her graphic descriptions of the humiliation suffered by pregnant women is where Mistral most explicitly rejects that male-centered eroticism, since it treats the pregnant female body as a sign of shame, to be hidden or discarded after male desire has been served. In the female-centered eroticism that Mistral proposes as an alternative, the hand discovers, explores the swelling breasts and belly. "Poesías de la madre" stress contact between women as physically intimate and full of meaning, covert understandings, sweet longings, and hope for the future, while human contact between men and women is described solely in terms of violence. Violence does not seem to enter the all-female world until much later in Mistral's work, as Molloy explores in her discussion of the poem "Electra en la niebla" (Electra in the fog) (Molloy 113).

The Queer Outside: "Motivos del barro" [Motifs in mud] and Other Explorations of the Natural World

In the prose of *Desolación,* Mistral is most explicit in the portrayal of desire when she projects human consciousness onto the olive grove, the rose, the tree, or the mud, using this "third" perspective to illustrate the projection of desire onto a specific individual as the harbinger of betrayal. This stance, which critic Alberto Sandoval-Sánchez and others in the feminist collection *Una palabra cómplice* accurately relate to voyeurism, emphasizes the speaker's or speakers' conscious psychic distance from and dissimilarity to those whom they watch. The representation of desire in terms of its thwarted effects on the natural and even inanimate world (the mud, the clay jug, the garden at Gethsemane, for example) marks a tendency to distance the speaking subject from desire. To speak from the consciousness of outsiders who, as voyeurs, aliens, look on the so-called normative human world, making, for example, the figure of Judas stand as the prototype for one who gives a kiss, is to point to the queerness, the otherness, of all desire.

The distancing of the speaking subject is a tactic for the representation of queer desire that Gabriela Mistral shared with other writers who similarly sought a language and refuge and philosophy of sexual dissidence. Others in the generation of Chilean writers to which Gabriela Mistral belonged similarly anthropomorphized the natural world. Mistral differs from her Chilean contemporaries in her concentration on suffering and in her possibly lesbian utopics of maternity. Her concentration on the natural world differs from Magallanes Moure and Pedro Prado in that her work's tortured expression of vehement desire, struggling toward articulation, is represented in terms of abjection, prohibition, longing, thwarted need. The poetic affinities of Gabriela Mistral lie closer to the less mainstream poets Amado Nervo and José Asunción Silva than to the tamer Prado and Magallanes. Like Nervo and Asunción Silva, she argues that love cannot be satisfied, because it involves the impossible bringing together of two distinct consciousnesses and is synonymous with suffering. That such love can be spoken only from outside, as a third-party onlooker, is a stance that Gabriela Mistral shares with her contemporaries among openly lesbian, English-language writers such as Djuna Barnes, in *Nightwood*.

One of prose poetry's great attractions to expressing sexual dissidence and positing alternative sexual identities resides in its allowance for ambiguities and slippage between subjects and objects of desire. Thus Gabriela Mistral's "Motivos del barro" (or, as in her manuscript draft's first title, "de las ánforas" [of the amphoras]) presents rocks and olive trees as constructing "el éxtasis" and "la pasión" in an onlooker's perspective that does not produce anything like a heterosexual text. Employing, as in "Poesías de las madres," a quasi-mystical, quasi-erotic language with an unspecified addressee, these prose poems recount quasi-allegorical stories of spent passion, that is, decadence. As in "El arte," Mistral combines the aesthetic impulse of the ars poetica with the kind of self-help literature that Poe might have written had he been surrounded by poets celebrating the countryside and had his income derived from generating morale among schoolteachers rather than from book reviewing. She takes what she has learned from Blavatsky, Besant, and Tagore, using the theosophical convention of the parable to speak from the position of an outsider, relaying truths about the nature of "thirst" (in "Cántaros de greda," *Desolación: Poemas* 222–23), which she safely encloses/encodes within the permissible context of "Poemas del hogar" (Poems of the home).

Comparing the writer's archival papers with her published texts and with other public expressions of eroticism at the time, it appears that she develops an aesthetics of distanced desire through a composing process that involved using the first person in early drafts to express erotic longing, then revising said texts into the third person prior to publication. This erasure or displacement of desire, part of a movement toward postsexuality, possibly arises in response to the circumstances in which she found herself: a vulnerable woman lacking family or marital connections, from the rural lower-middle class; an unmarried schoolteacher without a degree, living as an outsider in provincial cities with no word for privacy.[14] Although there is no presublimated, precensorship Mistral, the evidence of the manuscript drafts of her prose poetry suggests that the erasures and the accolades are utterly entwined, directly related to the increasing pressure to stand in definitive relation to the feminine, *la mujer chilena,* devoted to home and family. It cannot be stressed too much that she rejected this role and instead spent most of her adult life as an exile, rarely residing in one place for more than a few months at a time.

Mistral's self-censorship is manifest in two key practices. More obvious is (her?) erasure, by exclusion from publication, of phrases that reveal too much. More subtle is the recasting of materials written as letters in the first person, into more distant, seemingly allegorical, third-person fables of an anthropomorphized nature. Earlier drafts composed in 1918 through 1921—and here I caution that dates on the drafts I have examined sometimes appear altered in a hand other than Mistral's—are longer than the published versions and give more information about a speaker who is specifically human in the sensibility expressed. By contrast, the published versions reduce the degree of self-reference, producing a poetry more detached, more allegorical, less overtly erotic, ultimately less revealing of that favorite Mistral topos, the intimate wound.

With and through the perhaps complicitous erasure of directly expressed eroticism from Gabriela Mistral's work, she becomes the mother who, following the order of the symbolic, is always virgin, an empty and inviolable signifier that floats around discourses of national identity, marking the boundaries of nation and city, ambiguously inhabiting shared public spaces such as plazas and schools. My discussion of her early work has suggested a broader scenario underneath and previous to that erasure of desire. In learning to draw on a range of narrative strategies and situational self-representations for depicting the subjectivity of desire, Gabriela Mistral conveys in her writing the troubled and troubling character of erotic longing. Her struggle and achievement is in the attempt to replicate in language and feeling the continual slippage of the subject, the *vaivén* of

Eros, in the imagined mother, the landscape, and dramas of betrayal. Her elided pronouns and twisted syntax frustrate attempts to identify as masculine or feminine the gender, or subject position, of who desires whom. Her letters are open in stating her impatience with mediocrity and her rejection of the normal as insipid, mundane. Her frank preference for the language of emotional extremity stands in opposition to the normalizing narrative that critics developed when Gabriela Mistral's entry into that public sphere required that she be postsexualized.

Among the many ironies of Gabriela Mistral's fame is the fact that her celebrity is purchased at the price of her public silence about the very statements of erotic longing that made Chile's literary elite notice her in the first place. Conventional criticism has held that the writer's entry to fame dates from 1914, when she did not appear on stage to receive the first prize awared her "Sonetos de la muerte" in the contest known as Los Juegos Florales. The story goes that because the poet was modest and lacked the proper attire, she sat anonymously among the public in the balcony, above the president and his wife and assembled luminaries, listening to Víctor Domingo Silva declaim her verses. A more stringent condition in regard to her public speech has never been acknowledged in the accounts of this entry to fame: the Juegos Florales were designed half as a contest of poets and half as a beauty pageant. The winner among the poets was to write a poem to the young lady who was to be crowned queen of the pageant (María del Campo Letellier). Ever mindful of duty, Gabriela Mistral supplied the requisite verses in the following year. By withholding from the assembled public the spectacle of her own female body, however ill-attired, the poet sidestepped one kind of scrutiny and incited another, the perennial puzzle of her "real" identity.

To invoke the violent, even tortured, expression of desire manifest throughout Lucila Godoy's early work, to explore how the subject in Gabriela Mistral's poems speaks from a deeply ambiguous relation to erotic longing, we could do worse than return to the unresolved question posed in the penultimate line of her most famous poem: "Que no sé del amor, que no tuve piedad? / ¡Tú, que vas a juzgarme, lo comprendes, Señor!" ("Sonetos de la muerte," *Desolación, ternura* 29) [[You say] that I don't know of love, that I had no pity? / You, who will judge me, you understand it, Lord!]

Where heterosexist panic has jumped in to judge, it has nailed down and closed off the ambiguity of these lines, turning the open question into an answer involving love and pi(e)ty as devotion to memory. Yet if we return to the query itself, we can hear Gabriela Mistral's deflecting self-reference, offering art's impersonality as an alternative to human relationships' inevitably entangled jealousy, violence, and death. As she casts about to construct that alternative from the available materials, Gabriela

Mistral's endlessly revised, erased, thrown-away work brilliantly registers her discomfort with, and shedding of, the different garments that do not fit her.

Notes

1. On the erasures involved in the appropriation of Gabriela Mistral as an image synonymous with compromised femininity, see Ortega; and Trevizán. On Gabriela Mistral's relation to the ideology and iconography of maternity, see Molloy; Fiol-Matta; Horan ("Santa Maestra muerta"; "Matrilineage, Matrilanguage"; "Gabriela Mistral").

2. All translations from the original Spanish are my own. Variants in spelling and the use of accents all follow the cited source, without editorial corrections.

3. On the long battles over the education of women in Chile, see Santa Cruz et al.

4. The collection of poems and prose poetry entitled *Desolación* appears in a number of publications, among them: *Desolación: Poemas* and *Desolación, ternura, tala, lagar.*

5. The editor Fernández Larraín points out that Videla had a contradictory reputation: "hombre fino, de maneras exageradamente delicadas y 'femeniles,' que se contradicen con la fama que tenía de gran seductor de damas de la región y de otras que llegaban desde Santiago" (Mistral, *Cartas de amor* 22) [a refined man with exagerratedly delicate and "effeminate" manners, that are contradicted by his fame as a great seducer of ladies from the region and of other women who were arriving from Santiago].

6. Gabriela Mistral's inquiries into theosophy probably began during her 1911–12 residence in Antofagasta, where she met don Zacarías Gómez, a Spanish lawyer who was one of the city's leading citizens, and Carlos Parrau Escobar, the leader of the local lodge, Destellos. Both men loaned books by theosophist leader Madame Blavatsky to Mistral. The friendship with don Zacarías continued in exchanges of letters long after he had moved to Santiago and she had left Chile (Taylor 128; Bahamonde). The correspondence between don Zacarías and Gabriela Mistral may not survive. Taylor was able to examine it in part, and he indicates that, with the exception of a postcard from 1927, most of the letters were written from 1940 onward. Iglesias, Vargas Saavedra, and the poet's letters all offer additional valuable insights into how theosophy played a primary role in Gabriela Mistral's intellectual development from 1913 to 1918, as is clear from her correspondence, the testimony of her contemporaries, and her publications.

7. Theosophy had two principal cofounders. Russian medium and mystic Helene Petrovna Blavatsky, or H.P.B., as she preferred to be called, and Henry S. Olcott, a lawyer, journalist, and businessman with a strong interest in seances. Each took careful and calculated advantage of popular interest in spiritualism, science, and the East. Blavatsky, who had lived in Russia, Constantinople, Paris, Egypt, and perhaps Tibet, turned to Olcott not long after her move to New York. He had attracted her attention through biweekly reports on spiritualist phenomena for New York City newspapers. Curiosity about spiritualism drew followers at the start, even as the 1875 founding of the Theosophy Society turned that curiosity toward an interest in esoteric study.

8. Blavatsky, Olcott, and their successors construed theosophy as a channel for disseminating occult religious traditions. They cited Buddhist, Hindu, and Neo-platonic sources, often borrowing from Masonic doctrines. Compiled as "the wisdom of the ages," books such as Blavatsky's *Secret Doctrine* reflected and incited popular interest in Eastern religious traditions, working from unacknowledged sources, such as the novels of Bulwer-Lytton, Mackensie's *Masonic Cyclopaedia,* and Ennemoser's *History of Magic* (Campbell 33, 34, 211).

9. "Humanitarianismo antibélico, socialismo y anarquismo eran consignas propias de toda la juventud 'de ideas avanzadas' desde antes de 1920. . . . Del viejo radicalismo decimonónico subsiste aún el anticlericalismo y la denuncia contra los bienes de las Iglesia" (Góngora 110, 112). [Anti-war humanitarianism, socialism, and anarchism were the common order of all "forward-thinking" young people prior to 1920. . . . Of the old nineteenth-century radicalism, anti-clericalism and condemnation of the wealth of the church still persisted.]

10. Bahamonde 116–27 is the only source for "El rival."

11. The hilarity went public when Pedro Prado and Magallanes Moure published under a false, Arabic-sounding name a collection of pseudo-philosophical-spiritual verses that bore the photo of a Lebanese vendor from Santiago's Central Market. "Omar Emeth," the pseudonym of the Catholic cleric who was the official poetry and culture critic for *El Mercurio* was taken in, and wrote in praise of the book. That he was not let in on the hoax, but Gabriela Mistral was, shows something of the close connections that she maintained with the members of Los Diez. See Prado, Prado, and Ibáñez Santa María; and Mistral, *En batalla.*

12. For Iglesias's discussion of the "intrasexualidad literaria" of "la revolución modernista," see pp. 38–39 as well as his chapter "La Bohemia intelectual" (63–152).

13. Rodig's assertion of a rape—"A los siete años sostiene un choque físico y moral que no es posible describir en pocas líneas" (289) [At seven years of age she endured a physical and moral shock that is impossible to describe in a few lines]—is not the most compelling point to hunt for or to extract from the literature and archival material. More interesting in the context of Mistral's apprenticeship as a writer, when her writing is more experimental than at any other time in her life, is understanding how the poet's relationship to graphic violence, and particularly sexual violence, is intertwined with her dissent from heterosexual hegemony.

14. The letters that Gabriela Mistral/Lucila Godoy (she signs both ways in these years) sent to Magallanes Moure and to Isauro Santelices detail how her mail was routinely opened and read by third parties, as previously mentioned, and occasionally published, without her leave.

Works Cited

Bahamonde, Mario. *Gabriela Mistral en Antofagasta: Años de Forja y Valentía.* Santiago: Nascimiento, 1980.

Barnes, Djuna. *Nightwood.* Intro. by T. S. Eliot. New York: Harcourt Brace, 1937.

Bianchi, Soledad. "Ni santa ni divina." *Apsi* 418 (1992): 11–12.

Boletín del Museo Gabriela Mistral de Vicuña. No. 2 (1982) (Reprint of letter from theosophist Juan Enrique Lagarrigue to Gabriela Mistral, 10 Feb. 1913).

Boletín del Museo Gabriela Mistral de Vicuña. No. 4 (n.d.) (Reprints of letters from Eugenio Labarca, Manuel Magallanes Moure, Inés Echeverría de Larraín, Eduardo Barrios, and others).

Boletín del Museo Gabriela Mistral de Vicuña. No. 5 (1985). (Reprints of letters from Olga Azevedo to Gabriela Mistral, 22 Sept. 1915; Luis Enrique Carrera to Gabriela Mistral, 20 Nov. 1915 and n.d. 1916).

Campbell, Bruce F. *Ancient Wisdom Revived: A History of the Theosophical Movement.* Berkeley: U of California P, 1980.

Castro-Klarén, Sara, Sylvia Molloy, and Beatriz Sarlo, eds. *Women's Writing in Latin America: An Anthology.* Boulder: Westview, 1991.

Figueroa, Virgilio. *La Divina Gabriela.* Santiago: Impreso el Esfuerzo, 1933.

Fiol-Matta, Licia. "Gabriela Mistral, maestra de América." *¿Entiendes? Queer Readings, Hispanic Writings.* Ed. Emilie Bergmann and Paul Julian Smith. Durham: Duke UP, 1995. 201–29.

Franco, Jean. "Loca y no loca: La cultura popular en la obra de Gabriela Mistral." *Re-leer hoy a Gabriela Mistral: Mujer, historia y sociedad en América Latina.* Ed. Gaston Lillo and J. Guillermo Renart, with the collaboration of Naín Nómez. Ottawa and Santiago: Editorial de la Universidad de Santiago, 1997.

Gabriela Mistral en La Voz de Elqui. Santiago: Dirección de Bibliotecas, Archivos y Museos, 1992.

Góngora, Mario. *1925: Documentos de una crisis.* Santiago: Editorial Universitaria, 1992.

González Vera, José Santos. *Cuando era muchacho.* Santiago: Universitaria, 1968.

Guillén de Nicolau, Palma. Introdución. *Desolación, ternura, tala, lagar.* By Gabriela Mistral. México: Porrúa, 1986.

Hall, Radclyffe. *The Well of Loneliness.* With a commentary by Havelock Ellis. Garden City, N.Y.: Sun Dial, 1928.

Hopenhayn, Martín. *Ni apocalípticos ni integrados: Aventuras de la modernidad en América Latina.* Santiago and México: Fondo de Cultura Ecónomica, 1994.

Horan, Elizabeth Rosa. "Gabriela Mistral." *Latin American Writers on Gay and Lesbian Themes: A Bio-critical Sourcebook.* Ed. David William Foster. Westport, Conn.: Greenwood, 1994. 221–35.

Horan, Elizabeth Rosa. *Gabriela Mistral, an Artist and Her People.* Washington, D.C.: Organization of American States, 1994.

Horan, Elizabeth Rosa. "Matrilineage, Matrilanguage. Gabriela Mistral's Intimate Audience." *Revista Canadiense de Estudios Hispánicos* 14.3 (1990): 447–57. Rpt. in *Twentieth-Century Spanish American Literature to 1960.* Ed. David William Foster and Daniel Altamiranda. New York: Garland, 1997. 85–95.

Horan, Elizabeth Rosa. "Santa Maestra muerta: Body and Nation in Portraits of Gabriela Mistral." *Taller de Letras* 25 (1997): 21–43.

Iglesias, Augusto. *Gabriela Mistral y el modernismo en Chile: Ensayo de crítica subjetiva.* Santiago, 1949.

Lanzarotti, Susana. "Sospechosa para todos." *Apsi* 418 (1992): 30–33.

Martínez, Elena M. *Lesbian Voices from Latin America: Breaking Ground.* New York: Garland, 1996.

Masiello, Francine. *Between Civilization and Barbarism: Women, Nation and Literary Culture in Modern Argentina.* Lincoln: U of Nebraska P, 1992.

Mistral, Gabriela. *Cartas a Eugenio Labarca (1915–1916).* Intro. and notes by Raul Silva Castra. Santiago: Anales de la Universidad de Chile 13, 1957.

Mistral, Gabriela. *Cartas de amor de Gabriela Mistral.* Ed. Sergio Fernández Larraín. Santiago: Editorial Andrés Bello, 1978.

Mistral, Gabriela. *Desolación: Poemas.* New York: Instituto de las Españas, 1922.

Mistral, Gabriela. *Desolación, ternura, tala, lagar.* México: Porrúa, 1986.

Mistral, Gabriela. *En batalla de sencillez: Epistolario de Gabriela Mistral a Pedro Prado.* Ed. Luis Vargas Saavedra, M. Ester Martínez Sanz, and Regina Valdés Bowen. Santiago: Dolmen, 1992.

Mistral, Gabriela. *Epistolario de Gabriela Mistral y Eduardo Barrios.* Ed. Luis Vargas Saavedra. Santiago: Centro de Estudios de Literatura Chile, 1988.

Mistral, Gabriela. *Gabriela Mistral en La Voz de Elqui.* Research and recompilation by Pedro Pablo Zegers and Betty Jorquera Toro. Santiago: Dirección de Bibliotecas, Archivos y Museos, 1992.

Mistral, Gabriela. *Lecturas para mujeres.* 1924. México: Porrúa, 1974.

Mistral, Gabriela. *Poesías completas.* Madrid: Aguilar, 1958.

Molloy, Sylvia. "Female Textual Identities: The Strategies of Self-Figuration." *Women's Writing in Latin America: An Anthology.* Ed. Sara Castro-Klarén, Sylvia Molloy, and Beatriz Sarlo. Boulder: Westview, 1991. 107–24.

Nómez, Naín. "Gabriela Mistral y la poesía femenina de comienzos de siglo en Chile." *Re-leer hoy a Gabriela Mistral: Mujer historia y sociedad en América Latina.* Ed. Gastón Lillo and J. Guillermo Renart, with the collaboration of Naín Nómez. Ottawa and Santiago: Universitaria, 1997.

Olea, Raquel. "El lugar de Gabriela Mistral." *Una palabra cómplice: Encuentro con Gabriela Mistral.* Ed. Soledad Fariña and Raquel Olea. Collectivo Isis Internacional. Santiago: Casa de la mujer La Morada, Isis Internacional, 1990. 17–19.

Ortega, Eliana. "Amada amante: Discurso femenil de Gabriela Mistral." *Una palabra cómplice: Encuentro con Gabriela Mistral.* Ed. Soledad Fariña and Raquel Olea. Collectivo Isis Internacional. Santiago: Casa de la mujer La Morada, Isis Internacional, 1990. 41–45.

Pisano, Margarita. "Descubrir el gesto de Gabriela." *Una palabra cómplice: Encuentro con Gabriela Mistral.* Ed. Soledad Fariña and Raquel Olea. Collectivo Isis Internacional. Santiago: Casa de la mujer La Morada, Isis Internacional, 1990. 13–15.

Pizarro, Ana Mistral. *¿Qué modernidad? Re-leer hoy a Gabriela Mistral: Mujer, historia y sociedad en América Latina.* Ed. Gastón Lillo and J. Guillermo Renart, with the collaboration of Naín Nómez. Ottawa and Santiago: Universitaria, 1997.

Prado, Valeria Maino, Jorge Elizalde Prado, and Adolfo Ibañez Santa María, eds. *Los Diez en el arte chileno del siglo XX.* Santiago: Instituto Cultural de Providencia, 1976.

Pratt, Mary Louise. "Women, Literature and the National Brotherhood." *Women Culture and Politics in Latin America.* Ed. Seminar on Feminism and Culture in Latin America. Berkeley: U California P, 1990. 48–73.

Rich, Adrienne. "Compulsory Heterosexuality and Lesbian Existence." *Signs* 5.4 (1980): 631–60.

Rodig, Laura. "Presencia de Gabriela Mistral: Notas para un cuaderno de memorias." *Homenaje to Gabriela Mistral.* Special issue, *Anales de la Universidad de Chile* (Santiago) (1957): 282–92.

Rubio, Patricia. *Gabriela Mistral ante la crítica: Bibliografía anotada.* Santiago: Dirección de Archivos, Bibliotecas, y Museos, 1996.

Sandoval-Sánchez, Alberto. "Hacia una lectura del cuerpo de mujer." *Una palabra cómplice: Encuentro con Gabriela Mistral.* Ed. Soledad Fariña and Raquel Olea. Collectivo Isis Internacional. Santiago: Casa de la mujer La Morada, Isis Internacional, 1990. 47–57.

Santa Cruz, Lucía, Teresa Pereira, Isabel Zegers, and Valeria Maino. *Tres ensayos sobre la mujer chilena.* Santiago: Universitaria, 1978.

Soto Ayala, Luis, ed. *Literatura Coquimbana.* Santiago: n.p., 1908.

Stimpson, Catherine. "Zero-Degree Deviancy: The Lesbian Novel in English." *Critical Inquiry* 8.2 (1981): 363–79.

Taylor, Martin C. *Sensibilidad religiosa de Gabriela Mistral.* Trans. Pilar García Noreña. Madrid: Gredos, 1975.

Trevizán, Liliana. "Deshilando el mito de la maternidad." *Una palabra cómplice: Encuentro con Gabriela Mistral.* Ed. Soledad Fariña and Raquel Olea. Collectivo Isis Internacional. Santiago: Casa de la mujer La Morada, Isis Internacional, 1990. 27–35.

Vargas Saavedra, Luis. *El otro suicida de Gabriela Mistral.* Santiago: Universidad Católica, 1985.

Part 3

*Loca*ting Queer(s)

7

Chicanas in Love
Sandra Cisneros Talking Back and Alicia Gaspar de Alba "Giving Back the Wor[l]d"

Susana Chávez-Silverman

The subject is what speaks, writes, reads, and it is no more than that. Silence is death. Desire lives, then, in its inscription.
—Catherine Belsey, "Postmodern Love"

Black queer female sexualities . . . represent discursive and material terrains where there exists the possibility for the active production of speech, desire, and agency.
—Evelynn Hammonds, "Black (W)holes"

The power of the word and the pleasures of the female body are intimately related.
—Elaine Marks, quoted in Marilyn Farwell,
"Toward a Definition of Lesbian Literary Imagination"

Is it true, as Catherine Belsey has claimed recently, that "the postmodern condition brings with it an incredulity toward true love" ("Postmodern Love" 683)? I will not attempt to answer this question, dangerously loaded as it is with terminological—not to say philosophical—landmines: *the* postmodern, true, love. However, naïve or daring as it may seem, love is indeed my topic, love and women (overdetermined though this coupling may be), women in love, or, more precisely, women poets as they represent themselves in love. The postmodern Chicana writer, I will claim, does not tend to exhibit this incredulity toward true love. Of course, she is not alone, for, as Belsey reminds us (should we need reminding), "no amount of skepticism does away with desire" ("Postmodern Love" 683).

In this chapter, I explore the relationship between love and female agency in representations of subjectivity in the recent poetry of Chicana authors Sandra Cisneros and Alicia Gaspar de Alba. In earlier versions of this chapter, I posed the following couple of essentially rhetorical questions: Are women in love a fateful, ill-fated link in patriarchy's chain, irrevocably bound to, inevitably contained by, the master narrative even when—or, more insidiously still, precisely because—they attempt to position themselves against or outside the master's domain? Or is something else possible, in the oft-cited but still poignantly resonant words of Mexican poet Rosario Castellanos: "Otro modo de ser, más humano y libre" (28–29) [Another way to be human and free]? I confess I set Sandra Cisneros up as the "fall girl," her poetry constituting the unfortunately affirmative answer to the first question; Alicia Gaspar de Alba's writing, on the other hand, embodies the (positively coded) affirmative answer to the second question. A literary boxing match, with only one possible winner. Very binary. Not very postmodern. Subsequent reformulations of my argument have led, I hope, to a less hierarchizing, more subtle and complementary reading of both Cisneros's and Gaspar de Alba's poetry. I am attempting to take up, here, Chicana feminist scholar Chela Sandoval's challenge to U.S. third world feminists to "point out the differences that exist among all women not in order to fracture any hope of unity among women but to propose a new order—one that provides a new possibility for unity *without the erasure of differences*" (Sandoval, qtd. in Martin 283; emphasis mine). In addition, I have found Evelynn Hammonds's argument about the interdependency of black female sexuality and black *lesbian* sexuality compelling for my articulation of an analogous connectedness between Chicana sexuality and Chicana lesbian sexuality. "Theorizing about black lesbian sexuality," writes Hammonds, "is crucially dependent upon the existence of a conception of black women's sexuality in general. . . . we cannot understand [the one] without understanding it in relation to [the other]" (136).[1]

Sandra Cisneros was featured in 1995, along with Denise Chávez, Ana Castillo, and Julia Alvarez ("las girlfriends"), on the cover of *Vanity Fair.* Another indicator of mainstream success, she has also achieved literary "crossover" status, leaving Arte Público and Third Woman Presses, with whom she published *The House on Mango Street* and *My Wicked Wicked Ways,* respectively, for Random House and Knopf, who brought out *Woman Hollering Creek* and *Loose Woman.* Cisneros was perhaps best known (before winning the MacArthur "genius" award in 1995) as the creator of one of the most convincing child narrators in recent fiction, Esperanza from *Mango Street.* In her other works, however, the theme of women in love predominates.

Sandra Cisneros's self-presentation, both in ostensibly autobiographical formats and in her literary works, often manifests, at the same time, an avowedly feminist stance and what I call a self-tropicalizing tendency. Both can be seen in the following quotes from a March 1995 interview in *El Andar.* The interviewer asks Cisneros about possible criticisms of her (unflattering) portrayal of men, to which she responds: "Sometimes people

. . . say I have been real one-sided with the male characters, but I feel that there is much worse going on than what I've written about. . . . I think I have been rather lenient on them" (Craddock and Meléndez 16). Later, the interviewer comments on Cisneros's "evol[ution] into a more erotic poet," and she responds thus: "Well, Latinas are very sexual, that's something that makes us Latinas; we are really sexual and we are not afraid about that sexuality. . . . it's in our bodies. . . . it's in our colors, in the food. . . . Look at the way the earrings wiggle and jiggle. There's a wiggle in everything we do. . . . one of the things I look for as a writer is to discuss those things that are taboo subjects" (16). When the interviewer presses Cisneros on the reception of this "erotic" work by the "conservative Latino community," she disavows her just-invoked ethnic connection—an odd elision—claiming that she "mainly hang[s] around with a gay crowd . . . and artists" (19). I will only point to the disconcerting contradictions in Cisneros's linking of Latinas to a "wiggle" that she characterizes as at once essential to the culture as a whole and "taboo." The disturbingly essentializing claim to authenticity and representativeness implicit in her comments is then undermined by her peculiar disavowal of the "traditional" Latino sector.

The allure of the Latina wiggle is, undeniably, rather compelling, and not just in the dominant discourse. In the final paragraph of her book-length study, *Women Singing in the Snow: A Cultural Analysis of Chicana Literature,* preeminent Chicana scholar Tey Diana Rebolledo concludes:

If Chicanas can gain acceptance of being complex figures, of being good girls and more, they might be satisfied. . . . at the same time, the figure of the wicked woman, the troublemaker . . . is a very appealing one. It is an image that Chicana writers are not only willing to accept and to integrate, but one that they enthusiastically and passionately embrace. (206)

But of course, Chicanas *are* "good girls and more," in both the dominant and the traditional Chicano discourses, which always already allow the "hot tamale" or "luscious Latina" alongside the good mother/virgin. Cisneros's and Rebolledo's embrace, their self-tropicalizing recirculation of the dominant culture's images of Chicanas, must be seen as stereotypical. Lest we think this embrace an empowering move, let us recall the function of the stereotype according to the late art historian Craig Owens: "The stereotype . . . functions to reproduce ideological subjects that can be smoothly inserted into existing institutions of . . . sexual [and, I would add, racial and ethnic] identity. Stereotypes treat the body as an object to be held in position, subservience, submission; they disavow agency" (194). A glance at Cisneros's titles confirms her enthusiastic "embrace" of these hypereroticized, stereotypical images. Also, the frisson provoked by Cisneros's south-of-the-border brand of "wickedness" registers abundantly in the blurbs on the brilliantly colored, almost doggedly *multiculti* jacket on the hardcover edition of *Loose Woman.* "These poems are firecrackers and tequila," finds Native American Joy Harjo. "Fierce, intoxicating," from Cuban-born Cristina García; "sassy, tangy, intimate," says Dominican-born Julia Alvarez, who praises Cisneros's voice as "naughty with all we girls were taught not to say out loud—or even whisper."

Interesting to me, without tarrying to deconstruct the internalized racism in these comments, is comparing the self-tropicalizing, effusively eroticized praise of *Loose Woman* by mainstream heterosexual Latin American–born Latina authors, such as Alvarez and García, with the more muted comment by Chicana writer Ana Castillo, who has written and lived, variously, lesbian, bisexual, and straight subject positions. Castillo's blurb on the jacket, exquisitely lyrical, is itself a circular, playful metapoem, seeming to double back upon itself rather than referring to the same collection blurbed by Alvarez, García, and the others: "Some [poems] sheer jade and some for the jaded, a noose for the lover on the loose, a net for the next novio." Reassuringly normative after all—the non-gender-specific "lover" slides into "novio"—Castillo's praise nevertheless is strongest and most convincing (and convinced) when she leaves off the paean to heterosexual seduction scenarios and observes: "Sometimes they are simply love poems in wonderment of life and death. At all times, Sandra Cisneros has penned poetry of utterly divine language and imagery."

I do find a certain tension in *Loose Woman* between the speaker's "looseness"/"wickedness" and a lowering of her guard, rhetorically speaking, in terms of heterosexual politics, a shifting of focus from the would-be transgressive Chicana in love to a female speaker with a profound love of words. However, the former subject position predominates in Sandra Cisneros's poetry, both in *Loose Woman* and in her earlier collection, *My Wicked Wicked Ways.*[2] The following two texts exemplify Cisneros's poetic embodiment, in her most recent work, of the "wicked woman" and "troublemaker," espoused by Rebolledo as the images of complexity aspired to and "passionately embrace[d]" by contemporary Chicana writers (206).

In "You Bring Out the Mexican in Me" (4–6), *Loose Woman's* second text, notions of power and danger (nuclei of potential empowerment or containment in discursive constructions of sexuality) are relativized and inverted in relation to their meaning in dominant discourse, yet they are linked by the deployment of an uncritical, essentialist trope of "Mexicanness," represented variously as a "dark spiral," a howl, bile, and tequila-induced tears.

In the first stanza, the female speaker scripts love as "renuncia" [renunciation], but the traditional femaleness of this gesture is inverted by the performatively male actions carried out: a heavy drinking binge,[3] giving up promiscuity, allowing the house to become a sector domesticated by love. In the next two stanzas, the speaker begins to represent her loose or dangerous side, brought out by the love of the "you" the text addresses. The poem is structured as a series of parallel paradigmatic substitutions, sometimes nearly synonymous, other times antonymic, but all subsumed, in terms of history, geography, and popular culture, under the sign of "Mexicanness."

The third stanza represents the Mexican in the speaker by images of colonizers, a holocaust, the famous Mexico City earthquake in 1985, the nearby volcanoes, the recession, and *barbacoa taquitos.* Alice in Wonderland–like, the speaker's body has engulfed several cataclysmic historical events, which float free from their geohistorical contexts and are brought to bear as signifiers of the speaker's raging, out-of-control (Mexican) passion. The last couple of stanzas move into a more direct form of self-definition, using overdetermined icons of Mexican culture, both positive and negative—"the filth goddess Tlazoltéotl," Virgen Guadalupe, Coat-licue—from which the speaker derives (specifically female) power only to abdicate it, ironically, in the final stanza, in an apotheosis of "Mexicanness" signified by the intensified presence of Spanish—"*Quiero ser tuya. Only yours. Only you. / Quiero amarte. Atarte. Amarrarte.*" (6)—and by a way of loving which is at once self-abnegating and completely possessive. Significantly, here the speaker signals both her Mexicanness and its lack: "the way a Mexican woman loves" reveals the trace of performativity, of difference from itself, while the hyper-Mexicanness suggested in the Spanish—both phonetically and semantically—enacts the disavowal of this reading.

"Loose Woman" (112–15), the final, eponymous poem in this collection, again scripts the swaggering, "dangerously" powerful persona found in "You Bring Out the Mexican in Me," described earlier. Although not ostensibly about a woman in love, the text deploys gendered and sexualized imagery along a cross-cultural, transhistorical axis. The speaker recodes her identity as powerful and dangerous by conceding to an unnamed (but obviously patriarchal) third-person plural ("They") the truth in their naming of her. The terms these "they" throw at the speaker—beast, bitch, witch—are all firmly entrenched along the "*puta*" axis of the *virgen/ puta* binary, although the speaker's level of comfort and seamless self-identification vary according to the epithets.

In the third stanza, the speaker reveals her fixation on the lesbian as powerful, masculine, hypersexualized, and frightening, seamlessly overlapping with the dominant culture's image of the (butch) lesbian. Even as she appears to flirt, in an assertively nonhomophobic move, with the *semantic* possibilities of being a lesbian ("but I like the compliment"), the speaker hastily beats her (admittedly coy and ambiguous) retreat from this reality ("not necessarily").

Interestingly, in the fourth stanza, when the speaker opens her mouth to defend herself from the mob, what issues forth are not words but rather, disconcerting in this assumedly feminist reversal poem, images from fairy tales: diamonds and pearls, consumer goods from the province of fairy queens, or toads and serpents, seemingly related to a case of PMS. In the final stanza, the speaker "embraces," becomes fully present to, and claims the loose/wicked persona attributed to her by the patriarchy throughout the poem, admonishing the reader, "*¡Wáchale!*" and "I break things" (115).

Has she, in fact, really "broken" anything? In attempting to enact a reversal *from within* in *Loose Woman,* Cisneros replicates the "positive images" response (of black artists and cultural workers) critiqued by Cornel West, following Stuart Hall. West reminds us that there is no unmediated access to what "the real Black [or Chicano] community" is; he warns that this notion is "value-laden, socially loaded and ideologically-charged" (28). In attempting to empower this subject position positively, the "I" who speaks in Sandra Cisneros's *Loose Woman* seems naïvely unaware of the need, already clearly articulated by Gloria Anzaldúa in 1987 (and many other Chicana feminists, before and since), of "*unlearning* the puta/ virgen dichotomy" (*Borderlands* 84). A nonparodic recirculation—indeed, embodiment—of available stereotypes (slut, Scarlett O'Hara, Coatlicue, bitch, *perra,* lesbian, not to mention golden earrings, mangoes, incense galore) suggests the failure to recognize that looseness/wickedness is always already allowed to Chicanas. It simply constitutes the negative side of the *marianista-misoginista* binary of Hispanic culture and repeats stereotypes of wantonness overdetermined for Chicanas in the dominant Anglo culture as well. To reverse the valency without questioning/examining the nature of the underpinning structure is to risk inevitable containment.

We must remember, however, the tradition(s) from which Sandra Cisneros emerges.[4] Mestiza sexuality, in the Mexican and Chicano traditions, has been an oxymoron. From the disparaging, mysogynistic representation of woman's sexuality as "rajada" (27) [slash] in Octavio Paz's *El laberinto de la soledad* ([1950] 1959) through more recent, asexualized versions of the sainted mother in Chicano (male) narrative, the Chicana *as* sexual, present to herself and giving voice to her *own* sexuality, is a fairly recent phenomenon. In 1984, when the editors of *Third Woman* wanted to produce a Chicana/Latina lesbian issue, they found that "very few professional writers—be they creative or critical—have actively pursued a lesbian political identity" (Alarcón, Castillo, and Moraga 8). Although the situation has changed dramatically in the ensuing years, nevertheless in 1989, when *Third Woman: The Sexuality of Latinas* was published, Norma Alarcón, Ana Castillo, and Cherríe Moraga wrote in the introduction: "Our sexuality has been hidden, subverted, distorted within the 'sacred' walls of the 'familia'—be it myth or reality—and within the even more privatized walls of the bedroom . . . in the journey to the love of female self and each other we are ultimately forced to confront father, brother, and god (and mother as his agent)" (9).

And so, in 1994, the speaker of Sandra Cisneros's *Loose Woman* does indeed articulate a sexual voice, in open confrontation with father, brother, and god—and even with "mother," with the good girl in her self. Even if the subject position and sexuality of her poetic speaker ultimately are contained by the master narrative of heterosexual romance, we must recognize the importance, particularly within the phallocentric Chicano tradition, of Cisneros's *giving voice* to Chicana sexuality. It is *this* achievement—this *voz*—to which Julia Alvarez calls attention when she praises the poems of *Loose Woman* as "naughty with all we girls were taught not to say out loud—or even whisper."[5]

It is not the *presence* of signs of "looseness" in Sandra Cisneros's poetry that I find problematic. Before moving to a consideration of Alicia Gaspar de Alba's poetry, let me mention briefly the work of Latina lesbian poet-photographer Marcia Ochoa, who traffics in many of the same signs deployed by Cisneros in *Loose Woman,* to vastly different effect. As Yvonne Yarbro-Bejarano notes in a recent study, "Marcia Ochoa restructures [through photographic and verbal representation] a colonized reality [the female body] by rearranging its parts to create a different reality" (189). In an artist's statement Ochoa claims: "If I can't be Carmen Miranda, I can't be a Nazi dyke either—I'm too boy to be Latina, but I'm too Latina to be a boy" (qtd. in Yarbro-Bejarano 190). In this carefully calculated self-portrait, we can observe some of the same concepts and images which circulate in the Cisneros poem "You Bring Out the Mexican in Me," but with a difference. Whereas the Cisneros poem seems to rest content on an uncritical, fragmentary juxtaposition of images, such as Dolores del Río, Manifest Destiny, tequila, lace, and so on, Ochoa's statement layers images in a functional manner, purposefully disavowing, for example, the Carmen Miranda comparison that Cisneros's texts solicit. For Ochoa, Carmen Miranda is too Latina-femme; on the other hand, the traditional butch image is rejected for its excess Angloness: in other words, the butch in Ochoa complicates the Latina, and vice versa.

Without producing the closure implicit in an ethical adjudication between heterosexual and lesbian Chicana eroticism, I am interested in con-

trasting literary self-representations of Chicanas in love, looking for what
are, to me, the most compelling, counterhegemonic discursive instances—
locating texts, in other words, that enact the enticing promise of Cheryl
Clarke's lesbian poetics: "To imagine Black women's sexuality as a polymorphous erotic that does not exclude desire for men but also does not
privilege it. To imagine, without apology, voluptuous Black women's sexualities" (qtd. in Hammonds 139).

Many recent lesbian theorists caution against the tempting but facile
move to script "the lesbian" as essentially *anything.* "Lesbian bodies,"
writes Cathy Griggers, "are not essentially counterhegemonic sites of culture, as Wittig might like to theorize. The lesbian may not be a woman, as
[Wittig] argues . . . yet she is not entirely exterior to straight culture. . . .
lesbians are inside and outside, minority and majority, *at the same time"*
(129). Australian critic Annamarie Jagose, in her potently provocative recent study *Lesbian Utopics,* focuses on various textual attempts to theorize
a perfect lesbian space as altogether elsewhere, hence utopian (2) and concludes, following Foucault, that positing the lesbian as utopic, outside the
dominant conceptual framework, essentializes this category as transgressive or subversive while failing to recognize the category's implication
within the networks of power (9).

It is within this theoretical framework—acknowledging the tension between the temptation of the transgressive and the refusal to allow the figure of the lesbian to inhabit completely an essentialized exteriority to the
dominant discourse—that I read Alicia Gaspar de Alba's *Beggar on the
Córdoba Bridge* in *Three Times a Woman: Chicana Poetry.*[6] I read this me-
ticulously structured, steeped-in-paradox, four-part collection under the
sign of a voyage of discovery. Unlike the notion of "exiting," with which
Bonnie Zimmerman reactivates for the lesbian Bildungsroman the traditional Western trope of the voyage through the hostile heterosexual patriarchy to arrive eventually at the brave new world of lesbianism (Zimmerman 249), Gaspar de Alba's speaker is not going elsewhere, but rather
back to the *frontera,* which, through her journey, is reactualized as a hybrid, porous geosexual space, full of longing and pain.

Like musical movements, the four aptly titled sections of *Beggar on the
Córdoba Bridge* signal the speaker's odyssey through a brief heterosexual
marriage, a tentative initial sexual tryst with an anonymous Blonde, and
an affair with a closeted Latina, all recorded in poems in the second section, entitled "Bad Faith." Gaspar de Alba's move toward a "(sem)erotics,"
to use Elizabeth Meese's term—toward an explicit textualization of lesbian desire—begins with the poem "Dark Morning Husband" (21). This
four-stanza poem has a narrative structure: it moves temporally from
night toward dawn, spatially from outside to in, to outside, to in, to end,

literally, on the border between in and out, on the threshold, *en el umbral.* In terms of the textual voice, there is a move from initial visceral desire (expressed by the speaker to herself in the second person, as throughout the poem),

> You meet a woman on the street
> outside a gay bar. Blonde hair,
> open red shirt, nipples
> like tiny fists.
> She looks you over down
> the loose curve of shoulders
> arms and hips. Your massive thighs
> twitch in the dark.

through actualization of desire,

> Inside the red
> glare of the dance floor,
> she jams bone and muscle
> against your flesh, asks you
> for a light.

> You take the Blonde
> to her motel, watch her urinate,
> help her strip
> the blankets from the bed.
> She tastes of menthol
> and sour beer.

through an anagnorisis,

> She smells of secrets.
> Her odor clings to your finger-
> tips. You cannot lie.

which culminates, finally, in an explosion of rage at the threshold:

> She trembles at the way
> you smash your hands
> into the wall, bare your teeth.
> When you leave you kick
> the door.

The rage emanates from, but is unable yet to disavow productively, the inevitable capitulation to the heterosexual imperative:

> Somewhere,
> a dark morning husband
> waits for you to get home.

Why can't the speaker's rage smash *through* the wall, kick *down* the door? Why is her self articulated as monstrous, baring her teeth?[7] Why is the Blonde *qua* Blonde foregrounded, repeatedly inscribed with a capital *B*? Against whom is the speaker's rage directed: the Blonde? the "dark morning husband"? herself? These and other related questions are explored in several key poems of the collection.

"Leaving 'The Killing Fields'" (27), for example, is highly significant. In this text we learn that the "dark morning husband" of the earlier poem has been left, just as the speaker leaves the movie theater. The "leaving" metaphor also functions as a sign for the speaker's coming out:

> I leave the movie and the dog-eared
> shadows of trees, the afternoon
> light, the smell of popcorn
> remind me of you, white man
> stalking my dreams like Jack
> and his magic seeds. At night
> I hear helicopters pumping over
> the roof, radio waves, the click-
> click of telegrams on your pink
> tongue. Wherever you are,
> you must hear the same sounds,
> you must remember the trench
> we slept in, the hole that Alice
> found, the rabbit chasing her
> to a land far away from you.
> Remember the eggshells littered
> in the closet and my fingers
> cake-sweet with blood. The cock
> crowing in your belly warned you,
> the gray hairs showing on your head,
> the white space growing in our bed.
> Five years ago I left you
> wolfless: goodbye Peter, hello
> Rita Mae Brown.

The images used to characterize the former husband ("white man") develop a threatening, sinister, phallic portrait: he stalks her dreams; helicopters pump and telegrams "click-click . . . on [his] pink tongue," which seems, in this context, hardly sensual, instead grotesque, mechanical, and thrusting. The marital bed is represented as a battleground; it is a "trench," a "hole" from which the speaker ("Alice," with obvious echoes of Lewis Carroll; this is also the English version of the poet's own name) flees "to a land far away" from him. We glean other important details from this oddly dreamlike text. Ultimately the "white man," older and alone in what was once the marriage bed, seems not sinister but pathetic when the speaker leaves him "wolfless: goodbye Peter, hello / Rita Mae Brown," in an intertextual nod to her emergent lesbianism. In the final stanza, we learn that the husband was the speaker's only male lover:

> Today the memory of your body
> looms immense, a tree trunk
> sliding into the earth, into the black
> mud and the blood on the car seat.
> I took you between my thighs
> at sixteen, the only man
> who ever dropped his seeds there.
> No roots, Jack, no golden eggs.
> Just a slow chafing of thighs
> and the taste of popcorn.

The configuration of images here returns us to "Dark Morning Husband," the man's overdetermined whiteness correlating with the rage-inducing encounter with the "Blonde," the notion of leaving the husband "wolfless" resonating with the speaker's baring her teeth, wolflike, in the earlier poem. The sex act in this final stanza is demystified, a crass, hyperfunctional dropping of seeds, ultimately sterile in the reproductive sense ("no golden eggs") as well as in the erotic or emotional ("no roots") sense.[8] As "Leaving 'The Killing Fields'" remits the reader back to "Dark Morning Husband," so it also urges us forward, to "Bad Faith."

"Bad Faith" gives the title to the collection's second section; it is the third in a triptych of pivotal texts which deal specifically with ethnicity and sexuality. In "Dark Morning Husband" the speaker explores her lesbianism, but the encounter with the Blonde proves unsatisfactory. The lover's very "Blonde-ness," the closeted speaker's lesbian lust and the need to hide the encounter from her husband, her sense of the inauthenticity of the situation, all produce a physical rage in the speaker. The husband in "Leaving 'The Killing Fields'" is portrayed in a negative (although not completely unsympathetic) light because of his whiteness and maleness, both overdetermined. In "Bad Faith" (31), the physical signs of dissimulation—passing—are not what disturb the speaker about her closeted femme Latina lover:

> It's not that wild
> cinnamon lips, plumfrost
> cheekbones and henna high-
> lights upset me.

Rather, she laments the psychic energy her lover must expend daily to pass,

> But you come home
> bent, eyes and mouth
> smudged
> by the stories you have told all day:

and the untenable—invisible—position it puts her in,

> movies, Kahlúa crepes,
> Sundays at the mercado
> with a man who's really me.[9]

The speaker's coming out to herself is not imbued, as I've mentioned previously, with the sort of teleological value implicit in Bonnie Zimmerman's lesbianism-as-exit model. In fact, the nonlinear "mapping" (a psychic, ethnic, and sexual cartography) is implicitly critical, I would argue, of the tautological "journey home" of many autobiographic lesbian coming-out stories privileged by Anglo feminism. In the third section of *Beggar*, titled "Gitanerías," Gaspar de Alba displays an intimate understanding of flamenco music's *altibajos* (cadences), whose musical genre sign she deploys synesthetically to suggest her speaker's psychosexual *vaivenes* (fluctuations)—variations on flamenco's topnote of desire—in the section's subtitles, some of which are: "Frenesí," "Soledad," "Libertad," "Confusión," and "Pasión."

> . . . Someone tells me I am strangely
> aggressive today, and I say *yes, I'm practicing*
> *to be a vampire.*

> . . . we're too
> old for this furtive touching of hands.

> . . . She knows what they need, what
> she too would like to have.

> . . .
> the other two delve into each other's mouths
> as she fold herself into the firm triangle
> of breasts.

> . . . A womanhood as fresh and damp as these two
> flowers rooted in my heart. Perhaps one morning
> I will awaken to an insistent knocking. . . .

> . . . she is not the lady I want.
> I go back to the dark carpet and close my eyes,
> thirsting for her voice, letting myself bleed
> softly into the earth.

It could all be so simple, she thinks, . . .
. . .
. . . She will move only
when a brown hand grazes her thigh, and then she
will move forever.

(35–38)

These juxtaposed fragments from "Gitanerías" exemplify the sense of movement, of a journey back and forth through frustration, loneliness, voyeurism, flashes of rage, disavowal, and lust, during which the speaker arrives, finally, at an erotic epiphany which is also, implicitly, profoundly political: the representation of *Chicana* lesbian desire fulfilled, metonymically figured by the image of the brown woman's hand grazing the speaker's thigh. The difference here, in relation to the figurations of lesbian desire we have seen in the previous texts, is profound. Unlike the speaker's expression of her painfully closeted subjectivity in "Dark Morning Husband" and "Bad Faith," here she represents herself as an out lesbian, claiming the ex-centric (vampiric) aggressiveness which historically has encoded lesbianism. Her desired lover is also an out Chicana lesbian (she knocks on the door of the speaker's heart "insistent[ly]"; her "brown hand" is a political as well as an erotic emblem and ethnic marker), not like the passing Latina femme of "Bad Faith" or the menthol- and beer-tasting, illicit Blonde of "Dark Morning Husband." Indeed, the impact of "Gitanerías" is fully revealed only intertextually. The overarching bridge metaphor is particularly apt because, like the speaker who moves back and forth between and among two worlds when she crosses over the Córdoba Bridge connecting El Paso and Ciudad Juárez, the reader constructs meaning for the collection by weaving among and between the texts in a shuttlelike move that defers closure and privileges interconnectedness.

Although I will argue that Alicia Gaspar de Alba's poetics are ultimately too theoretically sophisticated to fall prey to the seductive utopianism inherent in much critical and creative work by lesbians and feminists of color, there is a sense in which the yearning for the "brown hand," as expressed in "Gitanerías," can *only* be utopian. It is not that Gaspar de Alba posits Chicana lesbianism as altogether outside patriarchy or outside the world. However, we must take note of the future and, especially, the conditional tenses piling up on each other in the juxtaposed lines I cited earlier: "would like," "perhaps one morning I will awaken," "*it could all be,*" "she will move." It is the poignant expression of *desire* for the Chicana lesbian that defers the brown woman as presence, for, as Catherine Belsey reminds us, "utopias represent objects of desire. . . . they also tend to indicate a place for passion within an alternative social order, and in utopian writing of the modern period it is possible to trace a deepening critique of

the increasing domestication of desire . . . and its confinement within the
nuclear family" (*Desire* 186).

I contend that Gaspar de Alba is well aware of the danger of containment inherent in *sustainedly* utopian figurations of lesbian desire. What
she does with the image of the brown hand, with the notion of Chicana
lesbian love, anticipates, I believe, Annemarie Jagose's critique of Gloria
Anzaldúa's deployment of the mestiza as *embodiment* of the border as
utopic site of cultural fusion and hybridity. As Jagose points out, "Despite
[*Borderlands/La frontera*'s] promotion of the *mestiza* as the site of conflu-
ence and intermixture . . . there is an undeniable sense in which the very
concept of the *mestiza* depends on concepts of diversity, distinction, and
difference" (156). Therefore, Jagose continues, "any prioritization of the
mestiza must not be due to her alleged ability to secure a space beyond
the border's adjudication of cultural difference but due to her foregrounding of the ambivalence that characterizes the operation of the border" (157). Alicia Gaspar de Alba defers closure at the individual and
iconically essentialist level of the brown woman's loving hand and moves
into the textualization of Chicana lesbian collectivity—in, not beyond,
the borderlands—in the final section, titled "Giving Back the World."
Here, the eponymous poem:

> Women, we crawl out of sleep with the night
> still heavy inside us. We glean the darkness
> of our lives from the people who loved us
> as children: Abuelitas teaching us to pray,
> Papás we remember in pictures, Tías and Tíos
> holding our hands at the matinee.
>
> Now, we are mothers or aunts, widows, teachers,
> or tortilleras, beggars gathered in a deep
> field of dreams. We offer our capacity
> to grow—like hair, like night. We root
> ourselves in the bedrock of our skin
> and suck on the blue milk of morning.
>
>   (50)

In this text, the speaker articulates her subjectivity within a plurality
which is inclusive, yet diverse—"women," whom the poem evokes in its
very first utterance. The first stanza grounds this subjectivity in tradition
and *familia.* However, lest this text be read as atavistic nostalgia for or
reinscription of "family values" *a lo Chicano,* the speaker emphasizes aspects of the culture that are to be remembered, incorporated, but put behind us: Abuelita taught us religion, and Papá is present only as the figu-

ration of an absence: in photos. The second stanza tells us to move on, to move *into* a world of women gathered together in "a deep field of dreams." And yet, this is *not* an end in itself, not *the* end, because the image of the field of dreams sends us irremediably back to the beginning. We return, through this leitmotiv, to the "body of dreams," the Río Grande, to the eroticized borderspace of the collection's opening poem, titled "La frontera."

In the opening section, also titled "La frontera," the speaker maps out her geocultural and familial history in poems about iconic Mexican and Chicano figures: *brujas, duendes, curanderas,* La Malinche, and La Llorona, her El Paso–Ciudad Juárez border childhood. Resonating now with the erotic and ideological coming (out) to consciousness chronicled in "Bad Faith" and "Gitanerías," which culminates in "Giving Back the World," the borderspace as resignified by Gaspar de Alba in *Beggar on the Córdoba Bridge* is what I call a *fronterótica.*[10]

> La frontera lies
> wide open, sleeping beauty.
> Her waist bends like the river
> bank around a flagpole.
> Her scent tangles in the arms
> of the mesquite. Her legs
> sink in the mud
> of two countries, both
> sides leaking sangre
> y sueños.
>   I come here
> mystified by the sleek Río Grande
> and its ripples and the moonlit curves
> of tumbleweeds, the silent lloronas,
> the children they lose.
> In that body of dreams,
> the Mexicans swim for years,
> their fine skins too tight to breathe.
> Yo también me he acostado con ella,
> crossed that cold bed, wading
> toward a hunched coyote.
>
>   (5)

Is this woman or river? Erotic reverie or anguished geopolitical lament? In Alicia Gaspar de Alba's postmodern *borderotics,* it is both/and, not either/or, as we can see in the polysemous final image of the coyote: timeless emblem of southwestern outlaw freedom or outlaw mercenary bordercrosser. In *Beggar on the Córdoba Bridge,* the figure of the Chicana lesbian, and, in a broader sense, the textualization of a *fronterótica*—by this I mean a theoretically sophisticated refiguration of both "the border" (vis-à-vis traditional Chicano renditions) and a specifically Chicana lesbian desire (vis-à-vis heterosexual Chicana eroticism and Anglo lesbian feminism)—which I claim as the collection's project, do not serve, in an Anzaldúan and ultimately recuperable, utopian sense, to heal the *brecha,* because Alicia Gaspar de Alba's poetics attempt not to foreclose but rather to foreground, in Annemarie Jagose's sense, the deep ambivalence, the differentiation and hybridity, of the border.

Let me conclude by returning to the issue with which I began this chapter: Chicanas in love and their fate. In Sandra Cisneros's *Loose Woman,* in all but a very few poems, such as "Bay Poem from Berkeley" (40) or the challenging, gorgeous "With Lorenzo at the Center of the Universe, el Zócalo, Mexico City" (60–63), the speaker merely inverts the valencies, attempting to ascribe a positive charge to stereotypical images and actions always already allowed women (especially Chicanas) in dominant heterosexist discourse. To her credit, like her sisters "las girlfriends" (Denise Chávez, Ana Castillo, Julia Alvarez) and others, Sandra Cisneros articulates, in the face of its persistent silencing and pathologizing, both in Chicano heterosexual and the dominant Anglo culture, a self-present, vibrant Chicana sexuality. However, I do not think it coincidental that Cisneros has been embraced by the literary mainstream in this country, for in *Loose Woman* particularly, she is giving back to the dominant culture something comfortable, something familiar: what they (think they) already know about Chicanas. For Alicia Gaspar de Alba, on the other hand, a Chicana in love is an unabashedly (brown) woman-loving woman. So, although her complex and lyrical *borderotics* is nourished by the shifting ground, the ambivalence, and hybridity of the *frontera,* and not by a dangerously utopic lesbian separatism, it is clear to me that—tropical-femme packaging notwithstanding—Gaspar de Alba's "crossing over" into mainstream success will take more than a wink and a wiggle.

Notes

This chapter is for my sister, Laura Chávez-Silverman, in whose East Village apartment I completed an earlier version. I would like to thank Florence Moorhead-Rosenberg, who was particularly helpful with the wording of my conclusion, and my colleague Margaret Waller, for her theoretical and stylistic queries and suggestions. A somewhat different version of this chapter appeared in *Chasqui: Revista de Literatura Latinoamericana* 27.1 (May 1998), and I am grateful to the editors for permission to reprint. Alicia Gaspar de Alba's poetry has been quoted with the permission of Bilingual Press/Editorial Bilingüe.

1. I owe to Evelynn Hammonds's incisive, elegant "Black (W)holes and the Geometry of Black Female Sexuality" a more productive way of reading Sandra Cisneros with (instead of merely against) Alicia Gaspar de Alba. My argument is indebted to her clear articulation, in "Black (W)holes," of the interconnectedness of representations of black female sexuality and black *lesbian* sexuality.

2. My critique of the sexual politics of Sandra Cisneros's poetry in no way is meant to imply a criticism of her literary accomplishments. I find her a prodigiously talented stylist, especially in prose. See my analysis of her short story "Eyes of Zapata" in "Inside the U.S. Latino Gender B(l)ender."

3. Although the representation of tears is usually encoded as feminine in Anglo culture, in my experience, this is less true within a Hispanic (I include Spain as well as Latin America and the U.S. Chicano-Latino) context; any lingering trace of the feminine resonating principally from the dominant culture is further attenuated by the overdetermined maleness of drinking (especially tequila) and the hangover.

4. I, as a biracial, non-Catholic who self-identifies as a Chicana, only partly inhabits this subject position; I would venture a guess that Cisneros's "bad girl" persona might seem more appealing, seem a more viable subversion of the hegemonic position assigned to woman, had I been raised exclusively within the Catholic, patriarchal, Hispanic paradigm.

5. Of course, Alvarez's comment presupposes a unitary Latina subject ("we girls"), flattening out racial, ethnic, national, class, religious, and sexual differences. But that is the subject for another study.

6. Just *how* compellingly antihegemonic a text it is is hard to predict from the Carmen Miranda–femme, hothouse-flower pink cover of the volume it's incongruously housed in, and from the volume's near-Commodores-sounding title, *Three Times a Woman.*

7. Note the similarity between this image of the painfully closeted lesbian as monstrous and Sandra Cisneros's use of the "beast" imagery to signify both patriarchy's naming of her *and* her claiming her self as bad girl. For Gaspar de Alba, the violent monster is a sign of inauthenticity, closetedness, whereas for Cisneros, the beast signifies positive, transgressive power.

8. It is interesting that although the speaker, in her remembered version of the sex act, acknowledges the man's phallic power (the memory of his body "looms immense," he is represented as a "tree trunk," he "dropped his seeds there"), the text functions as a subtle refusal of this power and of male privilege and even as a revisionary rewriting of heterosexual intercourse: "I *took* you between my thighs" and "No roots, Jack, no golden eggs," boasts the female speaker, undermining thus heterosexuality's male-dominant, compulsorily procreative paradigm.

9. Although there is no specific textual reference to the ethnicity of the lover in "Bad Faith," signs of her—and the speaker's—*latinidad* abound, for example: "Sundays at the mercado," and the exclamations of her co-workers, in Spanish: "*Qué suerte,* they moan . . ." (31).

10. I coined this term during the 1993 American Studies Association conven-

tion in Boston, in a discussion with Deena J. González and Alicia Gaspar de Alba. Readers may notice how melodious *borderotics* sounds in English too.

Works Cited

Alarcón, Norma, Ana Castillo, and Cherríe Moraga, eds. *Third Woman: The Sexuality of Latinas.* Vol. 4. Berkeley: Third Woman, 1989.

Anzaldúa, Gloria. *Borderlands/La frontera.* San Francisco: Spinsters/Aunt Lute, 1987.

Belsey, Catherine. *Desire: Love Stories in Western Culture.* Oxford: Blackwell, 1994.

Belsey, Catherine. "Postmodern Love: Questioning the Metaphysics of Desire." *New Literary History* 25.3 (summer 1994): 683–705.

Castellanos, Rosario. "Meditation on the Brink." *A Rosario Castellanos Reader.* Ed. Maureen Ahern. Austin: U of Texas P, 1988. 28–29.

Chávez-Silverman, Susana. "Inside the U.S. Latino Gender B(l)ender." *Tropicalizations: Transcultural Representations of Latinidad.* Ed. Frances R. Aparicio and Susana Chávez-Silverman. Hanover, N.H.: UP of New England, 1997. 101–18.

Cisneros, Sandra. *The House on Mango Street.* Houston: Arte Publico P, 1985.

Cisneros, Sandra. *Loose Woman.* New York: Knopf, 1994.

Cisneros, Sandra. *My Wicked Wicked Ways.* Bloomington, Ind., Third Woman P, 1987.

Cisneros, Sandra. *Woman Hollering Creek and Other Stories.* New York: Random House, 1991.

Craddock, Catherine, and Claudia Meléndez. "The Right to a Life of Letters: A Few Words with Sandra Cisneros." *El Andar* (Mar. 1995): 12–19.

Farwell, Marilyn R. "Toward a Definition of the Lesbian Literary Imagination." *Sexual Practice, Textual Theory: Lesbian Cultural Criticism.* Ed. Susan J. Wolfe and Julia Penelope. Oxford: Blackwell, 1993. 66–84.

Gaspar de Alba, Alicia, María Herrera-Sobek, and Demetria Martínez. *Three Times a Woman: Chicana Poetry.* Tempe, Ariz.: Bilingual Press, 1989.

Griggers, Cathy. "Lesbian Bodies in an Age of (Post)Mechanical Reproduction." *The Lesbian Postmodern.* Ed. Laura Doan. New York: Columbia UP, 1994. 118–33.

Hammonds, Evelynn. "Black (W)holes and the Geometry of Black Female Sexuality." *differences* 6.2–3 (1994): 126–45.

Jagose, Annamarie. *Lesbian Utopics.* New York: Routledge, 1994.

Jones, Ann Rosalind. "Writing the Body: Toward an Understanding of l'Ecriture féminine." *The New Feminist Criticism: Essays on Women, Literature, and Theory.* Ed. Elaine Showalter. New York: Pantheon, 1985. 361–77.

Martin, Biddy. "Lesbian Identity and Autobiographical Difference[s]." *The Lesbian and Gay Studies Reader.* Ed. Henry Abelove, Michèle Aina Barale, and David M. Halperin. New York: Routledge, 1993. 274–93.

Meese, Elizabeth. *(SEM)EROTICS: Theorizing Lesbian Writing.* New York: New York UP, 1992.

Owens, Craig. *Beyond Recognition: Representation, Power, and Culture.* Berkeley: U of California P, 1992.

Paz, Octavio. *El laberinto de la soledad.* Mexico City: Fondo de Cultura Económica, 1959.

Rebolledo, Tey Diana. *Women Singing in the Snow: A Cultural Analysis of Chicana Literature.* Tucson: U of Arizona P, 1995.

Sandoval, Chela. "Comment on Susan Krieger's 'Lesbian Identity and Community Recent Social Science Literature.'" *The Lesbian Issue: Essays from Signs.* Ed. Estelle B. Freedman, Barbara C. Gelp, Susan L. Johnson, and Kathleen M. Weston. Chicago: U of Chicago P, 1985. 242–44.

West, Cornel. "The New Cultural Politics of Difference." *Out There: Marginalization and Contemporary Cultures.* Ed. Russell Ferguson, Martha Gever, Trinh T. Minh-ha, and Cornel West. Cambridge, Mass.: MIT P, 1990. 19–36.

Yarbro-Bejarano, Yvonne. "The Lesbian Body in Latina Cultural Production." *¿Entiendes? Queer Readings, Hispanic Writings.* Ed. Emilie L. Bergmann and Paul Julian Smith. Durham: Duke UP, 1995. 181–97.

Zimmerman, Bonnie. "Exiting from Patriarchy: The Lesbian Novel of Development." *The Voyage In: Fictions of Female Development.* Ed. Elizabeth Abel, Marianne Hirsch, and Elizabeth Langland. Hanover, N.H.: UP of New England, 1983. 244–57.

8

Traveling Transgressions
Cubanidad in Performances by
Carmelita Tropicana and Marga Gómez

Yvonne Yarbro-Bejarano

In her study "Miranda's Diary," Coco Fusco reflects on her travels to Cuba since 1985. "Writing over" a male intellectual history that sought to recuperate the figure of Caliban in Shakespeare's *The Tempest*[1] as a Cuban American woman, Fusco reconfigures this key moment in Latin American theories of resistance by positioning Miranda's story in relation to the journeys of the daughters of exiles back to Cuba:

It was traveling to another place that allowed the original Miranda to understand her identity as different from the fiction that had been propagated by her symbolic father. The Mirandas of the present, myself among them, continue to undertake these journeys, straying far from the fictions of identity imparted to us by our symbolic fathers. (7)

My project here is to explore such transgressive travels (border-crossing, cross-dressing) in performance work by Carmelita Tropicana (the stage name of writer Alina Troyano) and Marga Gómez, specifically, the moments in which they actually embody the symbolic fathers of Cuban identity on stage. In *A Line around the Block,* Gómez plays her father, Willie Chevalier, a Cuban impresario of Harlem's Teatro Latino of days gone by. In *Milk of Amnesia,* Carmelita Tropicana plays Pingalito "the Cuban man" on stage, and a man who kills for love in the film *Carmelita Tropi-*

cana: Your Kunst *Is Your* Waffen (Your art is your weapon), directed by her sister Ela Troyano. Through its theatricality of difference, cross-dressing produces a "crisis of categories" (Garber 17), although, since "transvestite" is normatively male in usage, for Majorie Garber female-to-male cross-dressing is harder to codify and construct (102). The simultaneous performance of queer Latina bodies and Cuban men puts a particular spin on the gender critique of patriarchal patriotism found in Fusco's work.

Milk of Amnesia, among recent cultural interventions, seeks to articulate queer Cuban identities in a multiplicity of spaces formerly monopolized by hardened polarities defining the essence of authentic *cubanidad* (Cubanness) as either condemning or supporting socialist Cuba, with no space of critique, ambivalence, or nonhierarchic difference: the right-wing Miami- and New York–based exile community on one side and the Cuba- and U.S.-based Marxist pro-Cuba contingent on the other, both heterosexually defined. Gayness has often meant a literal or figurative voyage away from Cuban identity toward the whiteness of the openly gay U.S. community. The journeys undertaken by Marga Gómez and Alina Troyano/Carmelita Tropicana are transgressive in their queer configuration of an ambivalent Cuban/Latino identity, including ambivalence about Cuba, a taboo emotion on both sides of the Florida Straits.

In Marga Gómez, the symbolic father is also the biological father. *A Line around the Block* (1994) is the companion piece of the earlier *Memory Tricks* (1990), in which she performs her mother, a Puerto Rican showgirl and aspiring actress. By embodying a male member of the family, women in performance find a way to acknowledge a blood connection to a man without essentializing race as purely biological, in the view of Mimi Mc-Gurl. The use of a biological connection to play a male part retains the salience of "blood" while enabling a cross-gendered performance that demonstrates the detachment of identity, gender, and sexual roles from biology. The simultaneity in performance of queer Latino body and male persona allows us to look at two things at the same time, sustaining both critical distance and a re-creation of cultural identity.

Within the context of performance theories, *Milk of Amnesia, Carmelita Tropicana,* and *A Line around the Block* seem to be liminal in Richard Schechner's and Victor Turner's sense of performance sites as imaginative spaces in which social relations are both "played out" and transformed. Judith Butler has given new dimensions to the term "performative," expanding it from the Schechnerian model to point up the problem with the idea of transvestism as being necessarily subversive. Her caveat is that performance is also a reiteration of the normative, not always a liminal subversion. If performativity is the reiteration of a norm, or set of norms, that conceals the conventions of which it is a repetition, "a" performance, as Elin Diamond suggests, allows for the exposure and investigation of these conventions. "When performativity materializes as performance in that risky and dangerous negotiation between a doing . . . and a thing done . . . , between someone's body and the conventions of embodiment, we have access to cultural meanings and critique" (Introduction, 5). Performances are contested spaces, in which regulatory norms are both produced and challenged through enactment. The subversive effect is most likely to occur when the author/performer explicitly intends to transgress the normative in a critical way, as I argue in the case of Gómez and Troyano/Carmelita.

In the work of Alina Troyano/Carmelita Tropicana and Marga Gómez, outrageous humor and the materiality of the queer Latina body on stage destabilize both dominant and Latino notions of race and national identity and permit alternative imaginings to appear.[2] In kinship with Brechtian theories of performance ("Your *Kunst* is your *Waffen*"), Gómez's and Troyano/Carmelita's work provides for a distancing effect that makes these codes and markings visible.

But the negotiations between the two performers' bodies and the conventions of embodiment are not limited to the male characters they play. The first level of embodiment has to do with the performers' own stage personae. Marga Gómez's life and that of her parents have provided what she calls the "fodder" for her material for over fifteen years (Pérez and Uno 191). Her cheery opener in a "performance" within *Line*, "I'm Marga Gómez and I'll be your comic tonight," both draws and blurs the border between Marga Gómez and "Marga Gómez" in quotation marks, whose direct connection as stand-up comic with the audience in the present of the performance provides the through line for a series of "acts" in which she plays her mother, her father, a variety of other minor characters, both male and female, as well as herself at different ages in the past. These acts or performances are embedded in the overarching performance in which she plays herself in the present. Her stage performances, as well as the photographs that have appeared in the press, attest to her body's extraordinary capability of protean transformations, running the gamut from a femme persona to one more butch, for example, in pin-stripe suit with high tops. She plays "babes" like her mother, Daisy, and singing idol "Irma Pagán" (Iris Chacón), as well as male parts, such as her father, Rivera the reporter from *El Diario,* vocal Latino men on the street, and a policeman in Central Park who crashes her precious picnic time with her mother. Gómez links her physical malleability in embodying these characters to her sexuality, and vice versa; she reveals in *Marga Gómez Is Pretty,*

Witty and Gay (1991) that it was seeing lesbians in disguise on David Susskind's *Open End* show that made her want to be one (Pérez and Uno 196).

The persona Carmelita Tropicana was originally created as an extroverted alter ego enabling a more fearful Alina Troyano to perform (Román, "Carmelita"). The subsequent blurring of the lines between Alina Troyano and Carmelita Tropicana reveals how identity is layered and fragmented both on stage and off. Troyano represents the genesis of Carmelita Tropicana in *Milk of Amnesia* (1994). In fact, Carmelita Tropicana has been active in the East Village performance scene since the early 1980s, with her extravagant humor and fruity aesthetic (in both sartorial and sexual aspects). Embodying a Latina stereotype as a lesbian pushes the Latina stereotype as (hetero)sexual bombshell as well as the lesbian stereotype as butch. In her hyperfemininity, Carmelita Tropicana already suggests a kind of parodic drag performance, turning the male-gendered embodiments of *Milk of Amnesia* and *Carmelita Tropicana* into drag-on-drag metaperformances, in which the male roles are actually performed by Carmelita, not the actress playing Carmelita.

Layered over their self-performance as Latina lesbians, Gómez's and Carmelita's male role-playing conveys how cultural, racial, and national legacies impact these identities through the *mise en scène,* especially in *Line.* Watching both performers work, spectators derive pleasure in large part from their incredible artistry in making these characters rise up from their bodies with a minimum of props and changes in costume, voice, posture, and gesture. In spite of the power imbalances embedded in gender, in the maleness of the national subject, and in cross-gender performances throughout theater history, these performances delight because Marga Gómez and Carmelita Tropicana "do" their supposedly superior "others" so well. The notion of "doing" someone implies a degree of control and mastery over the one done, with connotations that slide between sexual topping and performative impersonation.

In their performance of Cuban men, Gómez and Carmelita focus on the visual elements of typical male clothing—personally idiosyncratic in the case of Willie Chevalier's captain's hat or symbolic of national identity in Pingalito's *guayabera* (a shirt with multiple pleats and pockets, typically white and worn by men)—including a hat, a cigar, and glasses. These men are aurally identifiable through an outrageous accent. The *teatro* scenes in *Line* are performed in Cuban-accented English by Gómez, who considers herself virtually monolingual in English. These "performances" within the performance that is *Line* would, of course, have been in Spanish in the actual *teatro.* This device signals the constructive nature of linguistic elements in her performance of *cubanidad.* Similarly, the reconstruction of Spanish in some of her characters' monologues, as heard and remembered by one who does not speak Spanish and has never been in Cuba, high-lights the capacity of performance for the imaginary crossing of national, cultural, and linguistic borders.

Just as Alina Troyano and Carmelita have become blended in reality, *Milk of Amnesia* distinguishes them only to blur the distinction. The stage is divided into two halves and furnished with a music stand, makeup, cos-tumes, and hats. The left, dimly lit, is the space of the autobiographical "writer" (Troyano). The right side, painted white and resembling a white cube, is the space of "performance" (of Carmelita and Pingalito). The writer communicates through taped voice-overs. This device of disem-bodying the writer, who supposedly created the character of Carmelita, appears to interrupt the porosity characteristic of the theater, in which spectators distinguish (or fail to distinguish) the character from the actor, both anchored in the same body. Yet the one time the writer is visible and speaking live, showing slides of her trip to Cuba, the images are projected on the half-painted wall traversing both spaces, underlying the performa-tive nature of both identities. As she says in an interview with David Ro-mán, "This staging forces the audience to confront the issue of multiple identities and perspectives" ("Carmelita" 91). The "writer" is as much a fiction as Carmelita is; there is no "real" Alina for Carmelita to refer back to, and Alina cannot point to Carmelita as a fiction separate from herself. *Milk of Amnesia* tells the story of the writer's and Carmelita's parallel journeys back to Cuba to cure their amnesia. Troyano lost her memory through cultural assimilation in the United States; Carmelita's amnesia is due to a head injury sustained while "chocolate pudding wrestling" (100). The title refers to how, in learning to drink the "Grade A pasteurized, homogenized" milk of the United States, the writer forgot "the sweet con-densed milk of Cuba," and with it, her Cuban identity, her *cubanidad* (95). The opening voice-over narrates the writer's arrival in the United States from Cuba at the age of seven. The process of gradually "forgetting to remember" her childhood home culminates in her resolve to "embrace America" after experiencing the shame of racial and cultural difference (95). Immediately afterward, Pingalito, described in the stage directions as "a cigar-chomping Cuban man," appears in the brightly lit cube (95). His name evokes the slang term for penis—"*pinga*"—but in the diminutive. He wears a white *guayabera,* black pants, white shoes, a hat, and glasses, which are held together at the bridge with tape. With one stroke this device references the economic hardships and scarcities of the "Special Period" in Cuba as well as an aesthetic of making due with limited resources, which underlines class dimensions of the U.S. art world. With resourceful-ness, ingenuity, and humor, even the most costly medium can be exploited, as Harry Gamboa, Jr., has phrased it, "for less than ten dollars" (28).

Besides constructing a transnational Cuban identity for Pingalito through linguistic devices, Carmelita/Troyano also signals Pingalito's cultural hybridity through music: he makes his entrance to the tune "Patricia," a million-seller "swing" by Dámaso Pérez Prado that was part of the U.S. mambo craze in the 1950s. As Gustavo Pérez Firmat has pointed out:

Although some of its roots are Cuban, the mambo's sound emerged only in contact with North American music, moreover, it spread to Latin America and the United States from recordings made in Mexico City. . . . Like Ricky [Ricardo], the mambo is no less American than Cuban, and it was never as popular in Cuba as it has been in the United States. . . . As a bicultural creation with divided roots and multiple allegiances, the mambo has always been Cuban American. (80)

Pingalito is "located" in ambiguous relation to Cuba in the play, through his accent, the music that identifies him binationally, and the mixture of "tradition" and "critique" in his presentation of Cuban identity. He is determined to cure Carmelita's memory loss through his own unique methodologies. He relates how he attempted to re-create her childhood memory of car sickness by making the hospital bed go up and down while smoking a cigar. The discrepancy between his desire to help and the potentially destructive consequences of his actions captures the simultaneous critique and connections to the "man of the race" (not to mention the sexual overtones of the bed's gyrations). "A doctor comes in and says I gotta go. Something about my cigar and an oxygen tank" (*Milk of Amnesia* 95). Since Carmelita is 150 percent Cuban, Pingalito's next tactic is to regale the audience with facts about Cuba, taken from a paper place mat from Las Lilas, a popular restaurant for the middle-class Cuban exile community in Miami. The sexual overtones of the bed's gyrations continue as his praise for the Cuban landscape quickly lisps into praise of the human landscape in the form of the Tropicana showgirls ("big breasts, big legs" [96]). Besides highlighting the sexism inherent in this construction of Cuban masculinity, the bit evokes the male monopoly of the subject of national identity that constructs the nation as female. But Pingalito takes exception to the claim that three-fourths of all Cubans are white of Spanish descent by cracking, "And a lot of these three-fourths have a very dark suntan all year around" (96). He affirms that when he is asked about his racial heritage, he answers "dark and proud" (96). His sexism distances him from Carmelita, whereas his critique of the racism of the middle-class exile community aligns him with her. Finally, he recites the "Ode to the Cuban Man," a send-up of the stereotypical machismo, cultural privilege, and sexism of the archetypal Cuban man, and sings a "romantic" love song, "Burbujas de amor" (Bubbles of love). In spite of the aspects of Cuban identity he accesses for the writer, especially certain poetic and musical traditions, Pingalito is not sufficient or adequate to cure either Carmelita or the writer of her amnesia.

Having just exposed the fiction of masculine *cubanidad,* the writer turns to the topics of American identity and how, as a lesbian-desiring subject, she didn't dare compare the two cultures as different kinds of "fruit" in her school essay. "I didn't want them thinking I wasn't normal" (98). Pingalito, with his relentlessly heterosexist perspective, fails in his attempt at a cure, in part because he does not address aspects of identity and experience that are Cubana and lesbian. The genesis of Carmelita at this point in the narrative parallels the visual image of the actress's stage transformation from Pingalito into Carmelita, who emerges in the dual yet connected spheres of performance and sexuality. "*Pingalito exits. An audiotape with the writer's voice comes on while the actress is seen changing costume from male to female*" (98). The critique of racism, reoriented to U.S. culture, reminds us that Pingalito accesses both a construction and a critique of racialized identity for the writer. Troyano's early attraction to the theater was squelched by a teacher's racist comment about the Puerto Rican Traveling Theater Company. Carmelita can do what Troyano is afraid to do: perform, but also publicly claim (and perform) her lesbian identity. "But it wasn't me. I couldn't stand in front of an audience, wear sequined gowns, tell jokes. But she could. . . . She was a fruit and wasn't afraid to admit it" (98–99). Through this dual conduit of performance *and* sexuality, Carmelita becomes Troyano's link to the past, to memory and to a recuperated *cubanidad,* signaled in the reconfiguration of Pingalito's object of desire, the Tropicana showgirls, as Latina lesbian-desiring subject, Carmelita Tropicana. Carmelita Tropicana sports a hat made of helium balloons that have been connected to her brain in an attempt to recover her memory. "This is linked to my libido (pointing to a highly inflated balloon). When I think of Soraya, my nurse, giving me a sponge bath . . . it (balloon pops) pops uncontrollably" (99).

Carmelita's amnesia is resolved in part through CUMAAs, or collective unconscious memory appropriation attacks. In one attack, Carmelita appropriates the memories of a conquistador's horse who witnessed the death of countless Indians. Another CUMAA embodies a pig being raised in a Havana apartment because of radical food shortages in what is called the Special Period, a situation deriving from the dissolution of the Soviet Union and the continuing U.S. embargo. He, too, was deprived of his mother's sweet milk, and when his throat is slit, Carmelita remembers a childhood tonsillectomy and is cured. José Muñoz had studied humorous Cuban performance styles that mediate between identification with and disavowal of dominant cultural formations precisely through these kinds of "disorderly connections" (see "Fácil"). The identity Carmelita Tropicana recuperates is not pure but that of the diasporic border, or hybrid, subject:

> I remember
> Que soy de allá
> Que soy de aquí
> Un pie en new York (a foot in new York)
> Un pie en La Habana (a foot in Havana)
> And when I put a foot in Berlin (cuando pongo pata en Berlin)
> I remember
> That I am from there
> That I am from here
> I am called
> A lesbische Cubanerin
> A woman of color aquí
> Culturally fragmented
> Sexually intersected
> But I don't esplit
> I am fluid and interconnected.
>
> (*Milk of Amnesia* 109)

Although Carmelita's journey is complete, her amnesia banished in the realization of her subjectivity ("I can drink two kinds of milk. The sweet condensed milk of Cuba and the pasteurized homo kind from America," 110), the writer is left with more questions than answers. The persistence of her ambivalence is marked by her appropriation of the play's refrain, "No es fácil" [It's not easy], the understatement used by Cubans to describe the hardships of the Special Period, to her own issues of transnational identity, which she affirms is not about a competition (Cuba vs. the United States) but is a matter of shifting positionality. But the end of the play belongs to Carmelita and the space of the performance within which ambivalence can cede to political optimism. She celebrates the recovery of her memory in a poem and tells the audience about the embargo through a song ("A song tells it best") that envisions political efficacy as a tolerance of nonhierarchic difference ("Todos por lo mismo"):

> Everybody for the same thing
> Between the pages of colonialism
> Capitalists, homosexuals, atheists, spiritualists
> Moralists
> Everybody for the same thing.
>
> (110–11)

Pingalito's parallel poem and song at the beginning point to the flickering dyamic of sameness and difference. Musical and poetic traditions link the new queer subjects of a transnational *cubanidad* to the symbolic fathers, but with different lyrics and different orientations.

The desire both to identify with and to disavow *cubanidad* in this and all the texts I discuss here has been theorized by Muñoz as "disidentifica-tion": "a performative mode of tactical recognition that various minorit-arian subjects employ in an effort to resist the oppressive and normalizing discourse of dominant ideology" ("White" 83). In his study of Vaginal Davis, Muñoz explains how the performer wanted to identify with the black power movement, but could not entirely because it did not speak to his queer identity. His performative option, then, was to "disidentify" with the movement by espousing Angela Davis instead of the Black Panthers (84). Similarly, Gómez and Troyano/Carmelita perform strategies of dis-identifying with the Cuban Revolution by queering it.

Milk of Amnesia chronicles the daughter's departure from Cuba and her transgressive return, fraught with repercussions on both the personal-familial and the political levels. In the film *Carmelita Tropicana,* the two-way traffic between New York and Cuba travels down a telephone line or occurs in the narrative space of the imagination. The narrative movement begins on stage, with a performance by Carmelita Tropicana, and takes us to the street, where she is mugged at the door of her apartment. Inside, a phone call informs her, after years of silence from her family, that she has a little brother. On the street again, she meets her Latina lover, and they take part in an action defending a clinic against antiabortion demon-strators. After a scuffle, she finds herself in a jail cell with her lover, her sister (an upwardly mobile type, who is horrified by Carmelita's politics), and the white woman who mugged her the night before. The four over-come their differences through a series of performances in the jail cell. Their release leads to the white woman's utopian rehabilitation and even-tual death from AIDS, and the film ends with Carmelita Tropicana on stage once more paying tribute to her memory, with the newly discovered younger brother in the audience.

The jail performances contest the symbolic fathers' fictions of Cuban identity, especially the imaginative return to Cuba by the daughters. Again, the mode of reconfiguration is one of excess and "disorderly connections," in which norms regulating a variety of identities, including that of "lesbian of color," are cited and parodied. In the first performance, Carmelita and her lover sing the hilarious theme song of their lesbian-of-color radical action group. The performance of their unity along political, sexual, and racial lines unites the disgusted spectators, Carmelita's sister and the white woman, across their differences, accomplished largely by the white woman voicing her response in Spanish ("Dos locas"). This leads to her own story of being taken in as *familia* while in prison by a group of Latinas called Las Zandungueras. This construction of alternative families elicits the second performance, staged as a black-and-white movie within the movie, as Carmelita reveals a family secret to her sister that their great aunt Cuca was killed by a man, for love. The black-and-white sequence, a mini–drag performance with Carmelita playing the assassin and the white woman playing the part of their great aunt's father, evokes a Cuban era recently on view in Aramis perfume ads for a cologne called "Havana," showing a white-suited, 1940s-style gentleman on a colonial balcony in the old city. This "misty old Cuba before Fidel" of the recent Cuba merchandising as fad, is, as Juli Reynolds points out, intimately linked to what the "post-socialist Cuba bankers and realtors are waiting for" (9). What disarticulates the scene in *Carmelita Tropicana* from this construction of Cuba is the dual referencing of the fabulous Latin American "*cine de oro*" of past eras and the family's own material history. The sequence evokes and avoids a romanticizing nostalgia by its skewed camera angles, discordant soundtrack, drag performance, and its critique of the potentially fatal consequences to women of a certain brand of romantic love, popularized in Latin American film and popular music.

Alternating with the menacing attentions of the murderous suitor to one daughter the father listens to her sister play the piano in what appears to be his almost erotic paroxysm of musical appreciation but turns out to be a heart attack. In this scenario of paternal alienation, the murder occurs at the father's deathbed. Carmelita's sister's response—"I didn't know"—marks the space of performance as one of familial estrangement as well as reconnection in the exposure of patriarchal secrets, like the newly discovered brother. It is also a space for cross-racial and -sexual understanding. After pondering Cuca's fate and the fate of all women, they perform the song "Prisioneras de amor" (Prisoners of love) in full (and, of course, matching) costume. The camp performance of this *ranchera* both sends up and appropriates certain musical traditions, as in *Milk of Amnesia,* parodying the kind of romantic love critiqued in the black-and-white sequence by performing it with a vengeance while having a lot of fun. At the same time, heterosexual desire gets recirculated among women cross-racially and cross-sexually in a tribute to the beloved lesbian idol of Mexican song, Chabela Vargas.

Ela Troyano, the director and Alina Troyano/Carmelita Tropicana's sister, has remarked that the film presents a "day in the life" of Carmelita. Although the film is intended as fiction and not documentary, much that happens in it is from "real life," including the sudden discovery of the eight-year-old brother, Cuca's death (who was actually their grandmother's fourth sister), and Carmelita's mugging. Reality is even more drastic than fiction, for Troyano/Carmelita has actually been mugged three times, not once. This interpenetration of art and life (who got mugged, Carmelita Tropicana or Alina Troyano?) in filming what is for them normal and mundane translates aesthetically into a subversive transgression of conventions, a "disorderly" aesthetic that presents an alternative to the exile community's attempts to construct a "pure" identity, while managing to make a serious statement about women in prison with AIDS, just as Carmelita's excesses in *Milk of Amnesia* do not merely coexist with but also provide the fuel for an antiembargo political position. Citing but mixing different genres and forms, *Carmelita Tropicana* practices the notion of "media ju-jitsu," theorized by Ella Shohat and Robert Stam in their discussion of syncretic strategies and aesthetics of resistance in the cinema (328–31). Through the use of hybrid motifs, the Troyano's film appropriates dominant discourses against domination.

The most sustained challenge to the symbolic fathers' fiction of identity takes place in the context of *familia.* The critique of Cuban masculinity in the black-and-white sequence and the symbolic deposing of the patriarch unite the sisters/women across their sexual, racial, and political differences and consolidate the notion of alternative *familia* sent up by the lesbian-of-color action group and posited by Las Zandungueras. The inclusion of the white woman in these alternative structures debiologizes family and disrupts the binary oppositions upon which monolithic representations of racial and national identities depend. The film takes advantage of the risk such discursive systems run, which must come into contact with the abjected and excluded term in order to reinforce their differences. The desire to bring opposites together in order to reinforce the barriers that separate them into cohesive, pure or "authentic" groups opens the door to the potential blurring or transgressing of these boundaries. This contact, which is both necessary and threatening, provides the potential for multiple readings whose meanings cannot be controlled, destabilizing the hierarchic positioning of the terms of the oppositions as well as the separateness of the categories. This is accomplished in the film *Carmelita Tropicana* by performance that bring together male and female, straight and queer, Latina/o and white. The film further disrupts these binaries by introducing a third term. For example, the relentless U.S./Cuba opposition is opened up by the introduction of Germany in *Milk of Amnesia*. "And when I put a foot in Berlin . . . / I am called / A lesbische Cubanerin" (109). The inclusion of an identity as "lesbische Cubanerin" destabilizes the binational dynamic of her "soy de allá / soy de aquí" (109). The displacement of ethnic unity in the family's identity, begun in the space of performance in jail, culminates in the Asian face of the little brother in the audience at the end.

Sorting out family is also at the heart of Marga Gómez's *A Line around the Block* and its companion piece about her mother, *Memory Tricks.*

These two pieces emerged from Gómez's desire to "explore the complexities of assimilation and sexual identity" (Pérez and Uno 191), worked out on the personal-familial level, both on stage and in relationships: "I do what I do because of my parents" (191). In between these two shows, Gómez created and performed *Marga Gómez Is Pretty, Witty and Gay,* giving her a chance to flaunt her gay credentials in the faces of those who would have been uncomfortable with greater emphasis on lesbianism as part of her mainstream success as well as in the faces of detractors in the gay community for whom *Memory Tricks* was not "gay" enough (192). *Pretty, Witty and Gay* sends up lesbian identity and culture with equal glee but is not as revelatory as one might expect. As the writer suggests, "My deeper truths are in between the lines of my parents' stories" (192). As in Troyano/Carmelita's work, the personal and familial intertwine with larger political issues of race and nation. Her nostalgic gaze toward the past of her parents' heyday as stars in the Latino scene is tempered by the knowledge that "the present and the future offer more for someone of my ethnic background and sexual orientation" (191).

Memory Tricks also sorts out the maternal fictions of identity concerning femininity and sexuality and the desire for racial and cultural assimilation. Motivated by her mother's Alzheimer's, Gómez found that doing the show dissolved her resentment toward her mother around these issues. In *Memory Tricks,* "Marga Gómez" reveals that from her mother she learned "how to cut a deal." Asked to say which parent she prefers, the daughter chooses the mother, leveraging a deal for a picnic with just the two of them in Central Park to fulfill her longings to mimic a white, middle-class family not in show business. Her mother undercuts this deal, first by taking so long to get ready that by the time they get to the park it is almost dark, and then by allowing a policeman to join them. "Marga Gómez" sends up her mother's desire for her own and her daughter's assimilation, her own plastic surgery so she could have a Caucasian nose (like Michael Jackson's), dyeing Marga's hair red so her daughter can fit into a white neighborhood after the divorce from Gómez's father, and calling Elke Somers a role model for Latinas.

Gómez's budding lesbian sexuality alienates her from her mother's hyperfemininity; she contrasts her mother's low-cut dresses with her "own look," which her mother never liked. One of the funniest bits in the show is when the mother attempts to teach little Marga about fashion—how to hold a pocketbook and especially how to walk. The play recaptures the moment she "did it" as a moment of approval from and intimacy with the mother. For her prayer that she never be like her mother, "Marga Gómez" appropriates the mother's refrain that the daughter's need to be with her mother never changes. In fact, she has inherited some of her mother's traits: she sings like her, overreacts like her, and sounds like her when she hears herself asking for help in the role of helpless femininity.

She distances herself from this construction of femininity, but the most delicious irony of the piece is that she "does" her mother to perfection, including the famous pocketbook stance and the walk. As in the ways Gómez relates to her mother in *Memory Tricks,* her marginalized ethnicity, sexuality, and gender also provide points of identification with and distance from her father as heterosexual male, performer, and Cuban. Marginalization from the mainstream on the grounds of ethnicity and sexuality blends in her identification with her father as a performer.

Like *Milk of Amnesia, A Line around the Block* is filled with references to Cuban and Latin American culture, yet unlike in the former piece, the daughter never travels back to Cuba in the latter, and none of the action is set on the island. *A Line around the Block* does record Willie Chevalier's trajectories from Cuba to the United States and from fame to failure through markers of *cubanidad*—his masculinity, defined in opposition to beautiful women as objects of desire, and his passion for superstrong coffee and the theater—while locating him exclusively in the New York milieu of Latino show business. As in *Stella Manhattan,* a Brazilian gay novel by Silviano Santiago that transpires entirely in New York, in *Line* Gómez's performance of a Cuban character defined by his *cubanidad,* yet removed geographically from Cuba, interrupts the Cuba/U.S. polarity by establishing a transnational Cuban identity. Like Pingalito and Carmelita, Willie Chevalier is aurally marked as binationally Cuban through his heavy accent and is linked to his "roots," which manifest themselves in anti-Castro rituals. Marga Gómez uses humor to distance herself from that milieu of the New York exile community that equates "authentic" *cubanidad* with anti-Castro sentiments.

Marga Gómez's travels away from paternal fictions of identity are internal: within her psyche, within the borders of the United States, her geographic travels include movements between New York City and the suburbs after her parents' divorce. While the piece captures her disappointment with Willie Chevalier in his fathering role and in aspects of his Cuban masculinity, Marga Gómez never loses her admiration for him as a performer. *A Line around the Block* recaptures their excitement surrounding the opening of Willie Chevalier's new Teatro in Harlem in a moment in which the *teatro* scene and her father's career initiate their decline. Marga Gómez's performance of her father through his stage persona as Willie Chevalier allows both the adulation and the ragged edges to show. The day of opening night, too nervous to stay home, Willie Chevalier takes her to the beach, an outing that parallels the picnic in Central

Park with the mother in *Memory Tricks.* Both outings frustrate Marga
Gómez's desire to be what she perceives as a normal all-American family.
The beach is merely an extension of the urban wasteland, with syringes
lying alongside seashells. Because she has no bathing suit, Willie Chevalier
gives her one of the costumes from the show to wear. Her inappropriate
clothing (recalling her mother's inappropriate picnic outfit in *Memory
Tricks*) brings forth humiliating catcalls from men on the beach. Clothing
marks their difference from ideal American identity as well as the internal
tensions between father and daughter along the axes of *cubanidad* and the
sexual body. Marga Gómez describes the father's old bathing suit, the
same old stretched-out trunks he brought from Cuba, and how she looked
up them and saw his balls. The play's most pointed critique of the father
centers on these intersections that put gendered, raced, and sexed bodies
into play, as when she witnesses her father's jealousy and violence toward
his girlfriend Carmen. The rift produced by this incident propels Marga
Gómez on her journey away from New York and the father.

Whereas her summer journeys toward the Cuban father and New York
inscribe her admiration for him, her definitive move to San Francisco
traces the extent of her alienation. Marga Gómez describes life with her
mother in the suburbs after the divorce as a kind of hiatus, but she finally
comes back to life in the gay mecca of the United States. At the same
time, she seeks fame as a performer in San Francisco, just like Willie Chevalier. Marga Gómez's self-performance in her new environment continues
to blend and traverse ethnic and sexual categories: upon arriving in San
Francisco, she goes to the Castro because she thinks that's where the Cubans must be; instead, she finds a new kind of community.

Marga Gómez's most radical journey away from the fictions of identity
imparted by the symbolic father involves her lesbian identity. Even before
the geographic distancing, symbolized by the roles of San Francisco and
New York, Marga Gómez infuses the beloved milieu of the *teatros* with
lesbian desire. Helping Willie Chevalier tape up an ad for opening night,
she keeps missing her cues when he mentions Irma Pagán (a send-up of
Iris Chacón), (hetero)sex symbol. In a move similar to Troyano/Carmeli-
ta's retooling of the Latina (hetero)stereotype, Marga Gómez "does" Irma
Pagán traveling with her "personal secretary," Leonela. Performing Irma
Pagán's seductive, breathy style, Marga Gómez has her call out Leonela's
name at the height of her sexual gyrations. The heterosexuality of the sex
symbol is radically decentered as both object of Marga Gómez's desire
and desiring-lesbian subject. Willie Chevalier warns his daughter away
from Irma Pagán by saying she's a communist, coding homophobia through
a Cuban identity constructed as inherently anti-communist. When Marga

meets Irma backstage, she stays within this encryption, presenting an alternative to anti-Castro *cubanidad* through lesbian sexuality by declaring her desire to be a communist as well.

The ultimate irony of these companion pieces is that although Marga Gómez worried about becoming like her mother, she turns out to be more like her father, a "funny and charming man on stage, but moody and melancholy in private" (Pérez and Uno 192). These parallels are most closely drawn through performance. As a performer of Latino ancestry, she is like him, as a Latina lesbian performer, she is unlike him. This dynamic of sameness and difference through ethnicity, performance, and sexuality is communicated in part through the metaperformances referred to earlier. *Line around the Block* consists of a series of onstage acts or performances that alternate between domestic scenes involving Willie Chevalier and Marga Gómez in the past and scenes of Marga Gómez interacting with the audience in the present. In his act "Los trece minutos," advertising El Pico coffee, Willie Chevalier performs from the coffin, as a dead man. But Willie Chevalier is really always "on," even in the scenes of domestic intimacy—as in his stories about cooking chicken and killing Nazis during the war or about how his diet was determined by his limited English vocabulary when he first came to the United States—that further extend the stages of performance. At the end of the play, Marga Gómez performs his deterioration, both physical and professional, as a coke addict waiting tables and entertaining in a dive. Marga Gómez, ensconced in her career in San Francisco as "exotic comic" (a reference to both ethnicity through her mother as exotic dancer and her marginalization as a lesbian performer), reconnects with her father only after he is diagnosed with cancer.

After his death, the parallels and divergences between the two continue to be played out in the sphere of performance. Gómez's embodiment of both Cuban father and queer Latina *as performers* facilitates an understanding of identities that does not hinge on biology. The daughter has turned out to be like the father after all, but in the imaginative reconfiguration made possible by her performance of him, he has also become more like her. This move is accomplished through the presence or absence of a (male) gendered physical attribute: the moustache. Introducing Marga Gómez on the opening night of his *teatro* as an extension of himself minus the moustache, Willie Chevalier maintains his position of (male) superiority (no moustache as lack). Yet at the end of *A Line around the Block,* he comes down from heaven to close the show, declaring, "I shaved my mustache. Now I look just like Marga" (33). By stressing his resemblance to herself, Marga Gómez takes the space of the stage to enact her father's acknowledgment of her power as a (female, queer) performer. Willie Chevalier's transformation occurs at the site of *A Line around the Block*'s sharpest critique, Cuban heteromasculinity. He is still cracking jokes that emphasize his self-identification with this hypermasculinity (since he went to heaven, the Virgin Mary is called simply Mary), but he is now more polymorphously perverse, as in his reference to fucking both women and men, at least once, in heaven. "All the women in heaven are beautiful and they always . . . say yes. . . . So do the men. . . . But don't get me wrong I'm muy macho, yo soy un hombre heterosexual. . . . You'll never catch me fucking a guy except maybe one time, just to try, what the hell I'm in heaven" (33).

In her analysis of women's performance, Elin Diamond explores the refunctioning of catharsis in Karen Finley's embodiment of the trauma of social being. According to Diamond, Finley works the Western metaphysical link between the female body on one hand and nature, matter, and substance on the other through the focus on her gaping mouth and by covering her body "with symbolic defilement" ("Shudder" 164–65). Although Finley's performances and the ones I have been talking about today share the "explicit protest against racism, sexism and homophobia" (Diamond, "Shudder" 165), Finley's aesthetics of abjection through her deployment of the female body on stage could not be further from the representational strategies of Carmelita Tropicana and Marga Gómez. There is an implicit reference to Finley in Carmelita's loss of memory due to a head injury while chocolate pudding wrestling (Diamond reminds us that what Finley smears on herself is chocolate pudding, not shit, because "this is true performance, not true psychosis" ["Shudder" 165]). In *A Line around the Block,* Marga Gómez relates how she got carried away her first time on stage at her father's *teatro,* tossing bags of El Pico *café* into the audience: "One woman rose up victorious clutching her torn bag of Pico, coffee smeared all over her face, bare arms, and white dress—like Karen Finley" (4). Such references gesture toward connections with this tradition of performance art while foregrounding a totally different aesthetic based on humor and disorder rather than on anguish and agony. In performance, excess and hyperbole can challenge normative discourses with forceful efficacy. Their *Kunst* is indeed their *Waffen,* and this artistic weapon is laughter. The works of Alina Troyano/Carmelita Tropicana and Marga Gómez, with their outrageous humor and the materiality of their queer Latina bodies on stage, destabilize both dominant and Latino notions of race and national identity and permit alternative imaginings and embodiments to appear.

Notes

1. See, for example, Roberto Fernández Retamar's *Calibán.*
2. For an analysis of queer/Latino performance in the context of AIDS, see David Román's *Acts of Intervention.*

Works Cited

Butler, Judith. *Bodies That Matter: On the Discursive Limits of "Sex."* New York: Routledge, 1993.

Carmelita Tropicana: Your Kunst *Is Your* Waffen. Screenplay by Alina Troyano. Dir. Ela Troyano. Du Art, 1974.

Diamond, Elin. Introduction. *Performance and Cultural Politics.* Ed. Elin Diamond. New York: Routledge, 1996. 1–12.

Diamond, Elin. "The Shudder of Catharsis in Twentieth-Century Performance." *Performativity and Performance.* Ed. Andrew Parker and Eve Kosofsky Sedgwick. London: Routledge, 1995. 152–72.

Fernández Retamar, Roberto. *Calibán.* 2d ed. Mexico City: Editorial Diogenes, 1974.

Fusco, Coco. "El diario de Miranda/Miranda's Diary." *English Is Broken Here: Notes on Cultural Fusion in the Americas.* New York: New Press, 1995. 3–20.

Gamboa, Harry, Jr. "Interview: Gronk and Gamboa." *Urban Exile: Collected Writings of Harry Gamboa, Jr.* Ed. Chon A. Noriega. Minneapolis: U of Minnesota P, 1998. 27–31.

Garber, Marjorie. *Vested Interests: Cross-Dressing and Cultural Anxiety.* New York: Harper Perennial, 1993.

Gómez, Marga. *A Line around the Block.* First performance 1994, San Francisco. (Excerpt in K. A. Pérez and R. Uno, eds. *Contemporary Plays by Women of Color.* New York: Routledge, 1996. 197–98.)

Gómez, Marga. *Marga Gómez Is Pretty, Witty and Gay.* First performance 1991, San Francisco. (Excerpt in K. A. Pérez and R. Uno, eds., *Contemporary Plays by Women of Color.* New York: Routledge, 1996. 195–97.)

Gómez, Marga. *Memory Tricks.* First performance 1990, San Francisco. (Excerpt in K. A. Pérez and R. Uno, eds. *Contemporary Plays by Women of Color.* New York: Routledge, 1996. 194–95.)

hooks, bell. *Black Looks: Race and Representation.* Boston: South End Press, 1992.

McGurl, Mimi. University oral exam. Drama Department, Stanford University, spring 1996.

Muñoz, José Esteban. "No es fácil. Notes on the Negotiation of Cubanidad and Exilic Memory in Carmelita Tropicana's *Milk of Amnesia." Drama Review* 39.3 (fall 1995): 76–82.

Muñoz, José Esteban. "'The White to Be Angry': Vaginal Davis's Terrorist Drag." *Social Text* 52/53, 15. 3–4 (fall/winter 1997): 80–103.

Pérez, Kathy A., and Roberta Uno, eds. *Contemporary Plays by Women of Color.* New York: Routledge, 1996.

Pérez Firmat, Gustavo. *Life on the Hyphen: The Cuban-American Way.* Austin: U of Texas P, 1994.

Reynolds, Juli. "Cuba." *El Andar* 6.7 (Jan. 1996): 8–9.

Román, David. *Acts of Intervention.* Bloomington: Indiana UP, 1998.

Román, David. "Carmelita Tropicana Unplugged." *Drama Review* 39.3 (fall 1995): 83–93.

Santiago, Silviano. *Stella Manhattan.* Trans. George Yúdice. Durham: Duke UP, 1994.

Schechner, Richard. *Performance Theory.* New York: Routledge, 1988.

Shohat, Ella, and Robert Stam. *Unthinking Eurocentrism: Multiculturalism and the Media.* New York: Routledge, 1994.

Troyano, Alina. *Milk of Amnesia. Drama Review* 39.3 (fall 1995): 94–111.

Troyano, Ela. Presentation on her work. El Frente: A Conference on U.S. Latina Feminisms. Cornell University, Oct. 1995.

Turner, Victor. *The Anthropology of Performance.* New York: PAJ Publications, 1986.

9

Evita Perón, Juan José Sebreli, and Gender

David William Foster

Una mujer decente es la que se lleva al mundo de los machos por delante. [A decent woman is one who rides roughshod over machos.]
> —Attributed to Eva Duarte de Perón by Abel Posse, *La pasión según Eva*

"Si Evita viviera, sería tortillera" [If Evita were still alive, she'd be a dyke]. With this play on the 1970s rallying cry of the guerrilla movement of the Argentine Left—"Si Evita viviera, sería montonera" [If Evita were still alive, she'd be a Montonera][1]—the late 1980s fledgling gay movement, which was made possible only by postdictatorship redemocratization and Argentina's abiding, unflagging determination to be *absolument moderne,* attempted to claim Eva Duarte de Perón as a potent symbol. For fifty years, Evita has served as a symbol of social liberation under a host of different political banners. For example, the Left used her during the 1960s and 1970s as a way to assert its identity both against and within Peronismo. Perón energetically moved to squelch the leftist component of Peronismo once he returned to power. Yet, taking a cue from Evita's successful efforts in 1947 to gain the vote for Argentine women, feminist movements both within and outside Latin America have accorded her prototypic status (see *Eva Perón*; Hodges).

It should be noted that there is no evidence that Evita ever showed any interest or participated in homosexual circles, aside from the inevitable contact with gays and lesbians in the entertainment world of 1930s Argentina, which enjoyed a relatively relaxed moral climate.[2] Indeed, it seems probable that she was basically asexual in her private life, ripe gossip to the contrary. But as a gay symbol, Evita joins the ranks of other famous women of power who have been notorious "fag hags": Imelda Marcos, Madame Chiang, and a host of divas (Maria Callas being perhaps the most famous) and Hollywood grand dames (including Mae West, Tallulah Bankhead, Barbara Stanwyck, and Joan Crawford). (Today such women are less likely to be dames than "personalities": e.g., Elizabeth Taylor, Barbra Streisand, Madonna, and Roseanne.)

In his 1995 novel *Santa Evita,* undoubtedly the best fictional treatment of Eva Perón to date, Tomás Eloy Martínez has several pages on Evita and gays, including the following passage:

Quienes mejor han entendido la yunta histórica de amor y muerte son los homosexuales. Todos se imaginan fornicando locamente con Evita. La chupan, la resucitan, la entierran, se la entierran, la idolatran. Son Ella, Ella hasta la extenuación. (199)

[Homosexuals have best understood the historical yoking of love and death. They have all imagined themselves fornicating madly with Evita. They suck her, they resuscitate her, they bury her, they idolize her. They are She, She to the point of extenuation.]

This passage is typical of the almost delirious texture of Martínez's account, where fact and fiction, sober analysis and grotesque fugues, turn around the obsessive fetish that Eva Perón's body becomes for all concerned, but most especially for the military government that overthrew her husband. Anxious to prevent the perfectly embalmed body from becoming an object of veneration by the supporters of the ousted president but refusing to destroy it (according to Martínez, out of conservative Catholic sentiment), the regime is faced with the dilemma of what exactly to do with the body.

Although there are other sources of information about this necrophiliac tale (including a fine essay by V. S. Naipaul [1981]), no one has told it with Martínez's degree of black humor. As part of his narration, Martínez creates a whole network of pseudoaccurate and specious bibliographic sources. It is therefore unlikely that his information about gay interest in Evita Perón (and even here it is unclear how a desire to have sex with her body can itself be described as gay) has any documentary validity, although it may correspond to a valid cultural interpretation. For example, although Martínez's references to Copi's play are accurate (see below), my guess is that his references to Néstor Perlongher are invented. (On the other hand, the title of Perlongher's poem "El cadáver de la nación" [1989] is subsequently attributed to an unidentified ex-president's assessment of the long shadow cast by her body over recent Argentine history.)

Another recent book to underscore both the strength and the complex nature of the symbol of Eva Perón is Alicia Dujovne Ortiz's *Eva Perón:*

La biografía (1995). Dujovne Ortiz, who originally published her book in French, is the daughter of leftist Argentine Jewish intellectuals and the niece of the important social essayist Raul Scalabrini Ortiz. *Eva Perón* is in many ways a straightforward biography, complete with published and unpublished documentary sources. However, it is unique in other regards. In the first place, Dujovne Ortiz comes to the conclusion that, had Evita lived, she would have ended up affiliating herself with the Left, which explains why someone of the author's background may have been interested in writing about her in the first place. Yet Dujovne Ortiz also makes it clear that, fifty years after the inaugural moves of Peronismo and over forty years since the death of Evita, one can no longer invest in either the myths of Eva Duarte as a whore or Evita Perón as a saint. Taking her cue from the American anthropologist Julie Taylor's widely influential work on Eva Perón as a socially symbolic figure, Dujovne Ortiz is interested in providing as balanced and detailed an account of the complexities of Perón's character as is possible. Although she does seem at times to fall under the sway of the soap-opera motifs that have always provided the master narratives of Evita's life, Dujovne Ortiz is primarily concerned with the "Rashomon effect": the belief that historical truth is elusive if not nonexistent and that the narrator's real task is to create a mosaic of possible meanings that constitute ever-shifting reality effects. The result is a work of highly original observations and at times brilliant insights, particularly when the author demonstrates her thorough mastery of feminist ideological principles that other writers have been unable to utilize. This is most apparent in two major subthemes: the analysis of the construction of Evita's persona through dress; and the analysis of a woman's body in a perpetually delicate state of health, which prefigured her terminal cancer. In the context of masculinist principles of control, as exemplified by Perón as the Macho Triumphant, Dujovne Ortiz's analysis is particularly eloquent and effective.

Evita's basic allure has undoubtedly been that of the strong woman able to accrue power. This results in a portrait of a woman who defies macho-dominated society, often by assuming the macho's own trappings of power. Nevertheless, the woman does not become the macho but rather displaces him through the deconstructive gestures of a skillfully crafted presence. Such a presence calls into question the "naturalness" of the masculinist pose and at the same time underscores how power and presence are complex constructions that entail equally complex performances (I am evoking here the form of analysis of gender identity pursued by Judith Butler [1990]). The rags-to-riches tale of someone like Evita is homologous with a program of personal construction—the body and sexual identity as works in progress—that is central to so much of what is attributed to gay sensibility. And the parvenu as display text is coterminous with drag (the latter understood not just as ostentatious cross-dressing but as any form of dress) and related phenomena, representing structures of dissident articulation: bodily adornments, body language, affective speech, narrative discourse, and spatial placement, all as "perversions" of the putatively and ideologically enforced "natural."

Moreover, the excesses of the self-constructed woman become part of a powerful semiosis. These excesses do not necessarily imply abuses of power, although they can involve, as in the case of La Señora, legendary stories told in disgust by her detractors but with awe by her supporters. Rather, these excesses have to do with patterns of overdetermination in the process of signifying femininity or the power of the feminine. Just as Evita found it necessary to overstate her newfound position and wealth, so may the sexual outsider find it necessary or advantageous to overstate difference, dissidence, and deviance (which is in great part the signifying power of the screaming queen). Finally, the circumstantial aporia and tropes in the behavior of the powerful woman—in the case of Evita, her famous rages, her strategic lapses into barroom and brothel language, her refusal to adhere to time-honored protocol—legitimate defiance in the face of the norm and the normal, providing yet other opportunities for an enhanced elaboration of symbolic presence.

I do not mean to imply that there are easy and evident continuities between Evita and the libertarian and gay rights movements or between Evita the power queen and gay sensibility. Rather, what I mean to underscore is how the surpluses of meaning generated by a public persona like Evita lend themselves to multiple appropriations, of which Evita as *tortillera* (dyke) is only one. This appropriation may appall traditional Peronistas, who had no ideological component championing a restructuring of sexuality beyond the vote for women and a concomitant greater role for women in the Peronista political process (which, to be sure, necessarily brought with it redefinitions of sexual roles, although apparently never as part of any conscious political process; indeed, Evita's public declarations consistently maintained that suffrage for women meant the opportunity to enhance male-centered politics such as those manifested in General Perón's programs). I know of no research on how marginalized groups other than ethnic groups (notably the Jews) interacted with Peronismo. Nonetheless, it is safe to assume that the masculinism of the military establishment, which was always Perón's basic point of reference, and the generally homophobic climate of Argentina offered little room for sexual dissidence, just as, in the end, they really made little room for feminism understood in any way other than as power for the president's wife in her role as an adjunct of his programs. Any other serious feminist dimensions follow from historical assessments of the implications of Eva Duarte de Perón's political participation rather than from programmatic proposals formulated by her or her circle.

The alliance between the historical and the iconographic Evita and the gay movement—and it remains to be sorted out if Evita is a more powerful image for certain gay males, for whom the powerful woman is meaningful, or for lesbians, who may appreciate her defiance of masculinist privilege—is equally a matter of interpretive projections. It is not so much a question of what Evita might have signified had she lived on into the 1980s, or even had she been a power figure in that decade, as it is a question of what her position in the hypermasculinist, homophobic context of the 1940s and 1950s might be taken to mean.

Finally, Evita's operatic/soap-opera death, her cancer, her forced renunciation of the vice-presidential candidacy in Juan Perón's second bid for the presidency, the pathetic valor of her appearance at his reinauguration, and the grand theatrics of her state funeral and subsequent veneration by a regime desperate to shore itself up against its inevitable decline (leading to the widespread belief that Perón could not function without Evita) are all the stuff of gay tragedy, whether as the kitsch of the theater of the ridiculous (one can only surmise why major performance artists like Enrique Pinti and Antonio Gasalla have yet to mine this rich lode) or as actually bespeaking the inevitable death of hyperfeminine beauty and all that it metonymizes for sexual dissidence.

It is perhaps not surprising that there has not been much in the way of rich cultural production on Evita, although the bibliography of historical and political assessments of Eva Duarte de Perón abounds with contrasting interpretive opinions (especially if one takes into account material published outside Argentina and scholarship free of the sectarian debate grounded in the immediate humus of the national political process, which has included both the demonization and the mythicization of Peronismo). A legacy of partisan poetry endures, as well as Nacha Guevara's rock opera *Eva,* a rather grimly messy attempt to counteract the offhanded fictions of Lloyd Webber and Rice's *Evita.* Yet the absence of any performance of *Evita* in Argentina (although "Don't Cry for Me, Argentina" [sung in Spanish as "No llores por mí, Argentina"] was a popular song hit) speaks eloquently to the virtual taboo in Argentine culture regarding narrative, theatrical, or filmic interpretations (other than partisan documentaries) of Evita. Abel Posse's *La pasión según Evita* (The passion according to Evita), an account of Evita's last year of life as culled from documentary sources, is indicative of the abiding problem of writing fiction in the context of intransigent sectarian politics. Posse, not surprisingly although rather disappointingly, provides an essentially dithyrambic portrait of Evita, which fails to reach the core of her subjectivity or to place her in any unsuperficial way with respect to sociohistorical coordinates. The book is interesting, but no significant new insights are provided beyond those of Posse's cited documentary sources.

Posse's book is made possible, one assumes, by the new face of Peronismo in Argentina.[3] Menem has been widely recognized, and widely denounced, for having substantially modified the nature of Peronismo, most specifically by eliminating the imperative social conflict (often interpreted as social resentment), trade-union domination, and welfare bureaucracy (see, for example, Galasso). For many, this means that there is nothing Peronista (or Justicialista) left in Peronismo—except perhaps for its principal exponents' lower-middle-class and immigrant social origins—and that contemporary Peronismo is only an appropriation of liberalism (see Posse's tirade against the "new" Peronismo, 276–77). Menem would insist that his neoliberalist administration is popular because his policies ultimately benefit the broad electorate that supported his party. And one might also characterize Menem as following in the best Peronista tradition because of his artful ability to govern so often by virtual fiat. What all of this has meant is a radical revision of the icons of Peronismo. It is probably unnecessary to determine if this radical revision has been required for the formulation of Menem's unique definition of Peronismo or if that uniqueness has rendered many of the icons meaningless or incoherent.

One such icon is that of Evita (see Geltman; Taylor; Goldar 63–71). Evita remains one of the most effective Peronista images, and examples abound of the government's support for her continuing importance among Argentines. Nevertheless, when one recalls the potent uses of her symbolism in the context of the relegitimation of Peronismo in the early 1970s and the return of Perón in 1973, current images of Evita are pale indeed. When Perón's third wife became president in 1974, it was customary both to comment on how far short she fell of Evita's model and to observe that she was in a sense usurping a position that should have been Evita's: María Isabel (a.k.a. Isabelita) Martínez became president upon Perón's death because she was able to be a vice-presidential candidate in 1973, whereas Evita had been kept by the military from a similar position on the Peronista ticket in 1950. The attenuation of the Evitine iconography provides a major context for Posse's novel, both in the sense of giving it resonance—its basically hagiographic portrait of Evita, a renewal of the legend for a new generation, and the pathos of the painful agony of her declining health—and in the sense of allowing it to have narrative significance outside the official version of Peronismo. Evita's agony is shown to parallel significantly the decline of the Peronista experiment, and Perón's appearances in the novel hardly rise above his portrayal as a military hack and a boorish buffoon, which only serves to reconfirm the belief that Peronista mythopoesis gives credit either to Perón or to Evita, but never to both in a balanced fashion.

Perhaps the most fascinating cultural interpretation of Evita is Copi's 1969 play *Eva Perón*. Although he wrote most of his works, principally novels and plays, in French, Copi (1941–87) was Argentine (his real name was Raúl Damonte). Only a scant amount of his dramatic production has been translated into Spanish (see Wetsel). There was a 1994 Spanish-language production of *Eva Perón* in San Juan, Puerto Rico, directed by Rafael Acevedo; the play was reproduced in the 1992–93 season in Paris under the direction of Laurent Pelly.[4] In the play's original productions, Copi is reputed to have played the part of Eva Perón, and his drag interpretation was abetted by his public homosexuality. Like Posse's novel,[5] Copi's play focuses on Evita's final days.[6] But unlike Posse's, Copi's play stresses her rage: rage against the power structure that denies her and that blocks her desires, rage over her disease (which is also given sociopolitical meanings), and rage over her realization that she will be monumentalized, turned into a public icon to serve the interests of others.

The first word of Evita's opening is "Shit!" (Copi, *Plays* 9; this word becomes a veritable motif). The play closes with Perón's words of beatification: "Eva Perón, ladies and gentlemen, is more alive now than ever before" (35). Perón's words are doubly ironic, because they allude not only to how mythicization makes one larger than life but also to how, in the play, the character of Eva Perón has absconded with the numbers of her secret bank accounts, leaving her nurse to take her place on the deathbed. It is Evita as survivor whom Copi wishes to enshrine (clearly, Evita the martyr is the one who interests Posse), and it is this Evita, in all her creatural presence and her bodily materiality, who is the drag queen's unholy icon and who has nothing to do with the worn political pieties of Perón himself. "Don't talk such fucking rubbish" (30), she tells him at one point, and she tells her brother (who in the play is named Ibiza): "You left me all alone to sink into the depths of my cancer. You're a pair [Ibiza and Perón] of skunks. . . . You watched me die like an animal at the slaughter house" (32).[7]

Copi's play is wickedly anti-Peronista. Copi was from a diplomatic family who left Argentina because of Perón; one of his first books, *¿A dónde va Perón? De Berlín a Wall Street* (1955), was a denunciation of Peronismo. While he was uninterested in buying into the Santa Evita myth that Peronismo has repeatedly staged so well, Copi was attempting to represent Eva Perón's oppositional character and her ability to prevail against the three "patriarchal" figures in the play: Perón, her brother, and her mother.

In this sense, Copi's characterization of Eva Duarte is in line with my characterization of the ways in which she would interest a gay audience.

In contrast with Copi's play, Juan José Sebreli's *Eva Perón: ¿Aventurera o militante?* (Eva Perón: Adventuress or militant?) is a much more sober (and regrettably unfunny) effort to establish distance between Evita and Peronismo. This book, which has been issued in numerous editions and widely cited, is the first to be written from a markedly leftist perspective. It seeks to find in Evita's public persona a defense of Marxist ideals that would be radically at variance with the Peronista establishment, which, as has been firmly established, repudiated Marxism and leftist ideologies in general and persecuted their adherents in Argentina as *apatridas* (persons without a country; i.e., anti-Argentines). In this sense, Sebreli's book anticipates the leftist appropriation of Evita by the Montoneros and other radical movements of the late 1960s and early 1970s, with, as previously stated, their apogee coming in their collaboration with institutional Peronismo in Perón's return to power in 1973.[8]

Sebreli (b. 1930), Argentina's major extra-academic sociologist, has produced an extensive body of research, mostly in the form of interpretive essays and characterized by the absence of the sort of original statistical evidence that typically accompanies the academic exercise of sociology. His writings have centered on three main themes: the Argentine oligarchy (Sebreli, *La saga*); the Marxist interpretation of cultural phenomena, including popular culture (Sebreli, *Martínez Estrada; Buenos Aires; Eva Perón; Fútbol y masas*)[9] and the exploration of homoeroticism. The latter has been more of an implied subtext in Sebreli's writing. It emerges explicitly, albeit guardedly, in his examination of the homosociality of soccer (Sebreli, *Fútbol y masas* 93–98). This theme should be examined in full detail in Sebreli's much promised but as yet unpublished book on homosexuality in Argentina.

Eva Perón: ¿Aventurera o militante? was written under the aegis of the intellectual Left of the postwar years. The intellectual Left exercised a considerable impact in Argentina during a time when opposition to Perón and general economic prosperity combined to renew fulsomely the commitment of Argentine writers and artists to European, especially French, culture. Victoria Ocampo's literary and intellectual review, *Sur* (South) (first published in the 1930s), devoted considerable space to Spanish translations of the best of postwar writing in Europe and the United States. The publication of these translations was intended to counteract the official culture of Peronismo, which had come to prevail in many public and private sectors (particularly in university-sponsored and commercial publishing). *Sur* also had its own publishing imprint, which brought out an extensive list of non-Peronista writers and book-length translations from English and French: a typical publication was the 1956 translation by Jorge Luis Borges of Virginia Woolf's *A Room of One's Own.*

Sebreli served for a time as an assiduous contributor to *Sur,* and in 1953 he published in its pages a classic existential interpretation of Roberto Arlt (1900–1942), one of a number of important Argentine authors who were rediscovered by the Left in the 1960s. (Sebreli also collaborated with *Contorno,* the major leftist intellectual review in Argentina during the period 1953–59, and in a 1956 issue dedicated to Peronismo he made statements in defense of certain aspects of the movement [see Katra, *Contorno* 76–79].) To be sure, *Sur* was hardly a left-wing journal. Ocampo's cultural ties were with the old oligarchy, which was one of the major objects of scorn of the Peronista regime, and Sebreli was subsequently to break with Ocampo and to criticize her and the journal openly (King 156–57). But in the way in which difficult times make for strange bedfellows, *Sur* involved the participation of Argentine writers whose affinities lay more with the postwar Left, and the magazine saw fit to oppose Peronismo with texts by Sartre and company in the name of a serious cultural tradition.

Eva Perón: ¿Aventurera o militante? contains specific acknowledgments of the French Left. It is dedicated to Simone de Beauvoir, one of the foremothers of contemporary feminism (thereby suggesting from the outset Evita's affiliation with feminism), and it opens with a long epigraph, quoted in Spanish, from Sartre's text published in English as *Critique of Dialectical Reason,* a passage that speaks of the dynamic and dialectic relationship between the individual and the social group: "Hay que ir más lejos y considerar en cada caso el papel del individuo en el acontecimiento histórico" (9) [One must go farther and consider in each case the rule of the individual in historic events] (my translation from Sebreli's Spanish).[10] This epigraph makes it clear that Sebreli wishes to examine Evita from an existential perspective; that he wishes to place her in a social context with which she was involved in a single process of mutual and reciprocal determination of meaning; and that, by virtue of the implications of Sebreli's choosing to analyze her life in the first place, Evita may be viewed as complying favorably with Sartre's understanding of historical agency.

Thirty years later in *Los deseos imaginarios,* Sebreli would revise his interpretation of Evita, moving more into line with the interpretation of her as embodying fascist characteristics. However, in the 1950s, in the period of transition between Evita's death and the collapse of Perón's second Evita-less government, then the military takeover of 1955, Sebreli was able to frame Evita as a revolutionary figure. He significantly re-echoes this position in the fourth, expanded, edition of *Eva Perón: ¿Aventurera o militante?* published in 1971, precisely the period in which the urban guerrilla movement emerged. That movement would claim Evita as one of its icons, using the aforementioned slogan, "Si Evita viviera, sería montonera." (A few years later, in 1978, Andrew Lloyd Webber and Tim Rice depicted this left-wing identification of Evita by pairing her in a dialectic relationship with Che Guevara [1928–67], thus lending their rock opera *Evita* significant additional meaning. Noting, however, that Che Guevara had no known contact with Evita, both the radical Left and traditional Peronistas have focused on this conjunction as a grand metonym of the serious historical inaccuracies that plague the work—a master example of the impossibility of adequate interpretations by foreigners of Argentine social history.)

Sebreli quickly establishes the parameters of his interpretation of Evita's militancy, and it becomes obvious that his subtitle is purely rhetorical:

Su breve vida, su espectacular conversión, su acción desenfrenada, las circunstancias dramáticas de su muerte han devenido una leyenda, haciendo de ella una heroína romántica. (*Eva Perón* 11)

[Her brief life, her spectacular conversion, her unchecked actions, the dramatic circumstances of her death have become a legend and turned her into a romantic heroine.]

This quotation is marked by two intersecting discursive strategies: the utilization of unanalyzed assumptions (expressed in either adjectives or adjectival phrases such as "espectacular" and "heroína romántica"); and an *accumulatio* that establishes a network of qualities for Evita which, rather than synthesizing the militancy of her life, provide it with the dimensions of operatic pathos. One will recall that the pathetic functions to a large degree through the deployment of unanalyzed assumptions about human behavior, such as one finds typically in the soap opera. Indeed, I would argue that the quality of Sebreli's interpretation of Evita which evokes gay sensibility is that she is construed as an operatic persona, as a Camille or a Manon struck down while almost a child, after a heroic and romantic struggle during a febrile emotional period. In order to pursue this theatrical casting of Evita, Sebreli must necessarily compromise with the sober historical agency that Sartre has in mind. After all, Eva Perón as an individual whose life is marked by a "*conversión*" can hardly be equated with one of Sartre's paradigmatic dark angels—for example, Jean Genet, who for a long time was for Sartre the embodiment of the existential hero, precisely because of his strenuous acts of separation from social institutions (in contrast with Evita, whose existence was solely defined through interactions with social institutions).

Sebreli makes it clear that Evita is a heroine in the way in which she struggled to prevail against the forces in which she was caught up. In this sense, the meaning of her life is more operatically pathetic than that of the tragic hero of existentialism, whose struggle is to disengage from established institutions. By all accounts, Evita struggled *against* conventional social norms, *against* the institutions of class structure, and *against* the processes of social marginalization. Yet there is, with the exception of the alienation imposed by the intense pain of her final agony, a paucity of evidence for the willed, sustained disengagement that one associates with the classic existential paradigm.

This mismatch between canonical existentialism and Sebreli's operatic interpretation of Evita does not make all that much difference, not because it is important whether or not Argentine thinkers capture exactly the conceptual framework of their French models, but rather because their interface creates fields of interpretation that are more interesting (at least today) than any strict intellectual accuracy. This issue could be fruitfully explored with regard to the general relationship between Argentine and foreign models. And it should be raised with respect to other major cultural analyses of the day, such as Adolfo Prieto's monograph on Borges, *Borges y la nueva generación* (Borges and the new generation), a text that also reflected the influence of French existentialism (it was the first monograph to be published on Borges and one of the opening salvos in the parricidal criticism of Borges that prevailed at least until his death in 1986).

It would seem reasonable to be less interested in the rigor of Sebreli's existentialist line of thought than in his use of it to legitimate an interpretation of Evita that is, from the opening characterization of her life, marked more by the narrative schemata of grand opera than by those of the "stranger": Evita may have been an outcast, but she was not an outlaw, especially when one accepts the proposition that the black legend of her fabled rise to fame through diligent prostitution and shrewd courtesanship is mostly nothing but the nasty fabrication of her enemies on numerous fronts (presumably even within macho Peronismo). Of course, in order to demonstrate the authenticity (this is a key word, certainly) of Evita's personal commitment to militancy—a militancy that derived from her personal story, and not from any role imposed on her by a Peronismo that was, in any event, insensitive to the specific dimensions of social activism embodied by her—Sebreli must emphasize those interpretational strategies that separate her from the Peronista apparatus and that ground her activism in other spheres.

In the former case, this means repudiating her affiliation with the Peronista machine:

Tampoco es admisible . . . una variante de interpretación antiperonista que muestra a Eva Perón como un mero producto mecánico de la máquina de Estado, el aparato político y la propaganda masiva. (*Eva Perón* 17)

[Equally inadmissible is . . . a variant of the anti-Peronista interpretation that depicts Eva Perón as a mere mechanical product of the machine of the state, the political apparatus, and the massive political propaganda.]

Regarding the latter case, Sebreli easily bases his interpretation on the rich lore of Evita's background of social, cultural, and economic deprivation. Such a background was hardly unique for the time, but was nevertheless one from which she was able to draw inspiration, so to speak, in her exercise of individual power. Posse, who cites Sebreli in his bibliography, pursues the same line of narrative exposition; this is confirmed by Perón's virtual absence from the novel or his appearance only in passing, in buffoonish poses.

It should be noted that, while I have continued to use "Evita" to evoke not so much the historical figure as the cultural icon, Sebreli rarely uses the familiar diminutive, which was exploited so effectively by Peronista propaganda in the 1950s and again in the 1970s and by certain left-wing ideologues of the late 1960s and 1970s. Rather, Sebreli prefers the more neutral and presumably more respectful "Eva Perón," both in the title of his book and in the body of his text (this is also true of Posse, whose novel is titled *La pasión según Eva*). It is interesting to speculate why Sebreli would not have preferred "Eva Duarte" or "Eva Duarte de Perón." Although the former was not her legal name, it would have underscored better her pre-Peronista roots; the latter, which sequentially articulates her origins and her separable relationship with Perón, would have evoked her legal status as Perón's wife.[11] I suspect that Sebreli prefers "Eva Perón" to refer to her problematic relationship to Peronismo and eschews "Eva Duarte de Perón" as cumbersomely resounding the society pages of the oligarchy. Rather, as suggested by the icon of her exclusively personal name, "Eva Perón," Evita is

creación y creadora a la vez, producto y a la vez productora, reflejo y reflejante, punto de llegada y punto de partida, [quien] padece la historia y a la vez la elige. (*Eva Perón* 20)

[Both creation and creator, product and producer at the same time, reflected image and that which reflects, goal and source, she suffers history and at the same time she chooses it.]

This formulation echoes both the existential concepts of a forged self-identity and the subsequent gay adherence to constructionist principles.

Such adherence means, among other things, that one's identity—which is not just sexual, since it is important to disavow the identification of individuals in terms of some kind of magnified sexual disposition—is a project of constant elaboration.

The recurring grounding of Evita in the overarching narratives of opera is particularly evident when Sebreli begins to sum up her character in the concluding chapter, "Lo vivo y lo muerto" (What is alive and what is dead), when once again the myth of Evita must be rejected in order to achieve a proper historicization of Eva Perón, a historical romantic heroine:

El mito de Evita [*sic*] como expresión simbólica de los anhelos de justicia e igualdad de las mujeres y los trabajadores argentinos, solo a medias realizados en la realidad, y a la vez como expresión del temor por la pérdida de sus privilegios por parte de las clases burguesas, fue como tal un mito de carácter dinámico, creador y progresivo, estaba dirigido hacia el futuro y no hacia el pasado, como los mitos regresivos. . . .
La característica del mito regresivo es el eterno retorno al pasado y la negación del tiempo histórico, del progreso. La muerte de Eva Perón fue una contingencia histórica, pero tal vez coincidió con una necesidad que su ciclo estaba cumplido: no nos podemos imaginar a una Evita envejeciendo en la inacción del destierro. La muerte de Evita viene a coincidir con el fin del poder del ala plebeya del peronismo. . . .
Es por ello que entre las masas populares, se repetía insistentemente en el 55: "Si Evita viviera esto no hubiera pasado." Se intuía vagamente que la caída del peronismo se debía antes que nada al freno puesto por el propio Perón a la clase obrera, a la que Evita representaba dentro del gobierno, más que al propio Perón. (*Eva Perón* 109–10)

[The myth of Evita as a symbolic expression of the desire for justice and equality of Argentine women and workers, in reality only halfway achieved, and at the same time as an expression of fear over the loss of their privileges on the part of the bourgeoisie, was something like a myth with a dynamic, creative, progressive character, [and] was oriented toward the future and not the past, as are regressive myths. . . .
The characteristic of regressive myth is the eternal return to the past and the negation of historical time, of progress. The death of Eva Perón was a historical contingency, but perhaps it coincided with a necessity that its cycle was complete: we cannot imagine an Evita growing old in the inactivity of exile. Evita's death comes to coincide with the end of power for the plebeian wing of Peronismo. . . .
It is for this reason that among the popular classes, one finds the phrase endlessly repeated in 1955: "If Evita were still alive, this would not have happened." There was the vague intuition that the fall of Peronismo owed itself more than anything to the brake applied by Perón himself on the working class, which Evita represented within the government more than Perón himself.]

At this point, one could well ask to what extent Sebreli has been successful in establishing a distance between Perón/Peronismo and Evita and to what extent he has displaced Evita in favor of Eva Perón. Sebreli does consistently argue for the proper historicization of Evita and the demonstration that her character formation and her conduct in power responded to concrete sociohistorical circumstances. He also argues that she was neither an adjunct to Perón's ideology—its more "human" face—nor the consequence of some telluric process, which seems to lie at the root of her quasi canonization that exceeds the boundaries of Peronismo itself. But I would also submit that, while Sebreli is consistent in his evocation of the existentialist concept of the dialectic relationship between individuals and their sociohistorical circumstance, such that the predicates "made" and "making" work in both directions at once, the grandeur that his study confers upon Evita strains the parameters of history by reaching toward the ahistorically operatic, the Evita who is somehow "larger than history."

This perception is necessary in order to account for the surplus of meanings that as early as the mid-1950s had begun to accrue to her. And these are, in turn, excesses that are juxtaposed to the masculinism of Perón and Peronismo, such that they inexorably point out its inadequacies, its flaws, and finally its failures. These are Sebreli's concluding comments, and it is significant to note that, in this 1971 edition, he has added a specific reference to Che Guevara, who was murdered in captivity by the Bolivian police in 1967:

Contra las necrofilias de ciertos peronistas que reclaman la momia de Evita para convertirla en un objeto mágico de adoración mística, prefiero que la tumba de Evita siga abierta y que su fantasma siga perturbando las conciencias. Los héroes que de una u otra manera mueren por la libertad de los pueblos de América Latina no tienen sepultura; los cadáveres de Evita y del Che no tienen descanso ni han comenzado a modelarse sus estatuas. Profanar el tabú, desacralizar el mito, tanto en su versión angélica como diabólica, develando el verdadero significado histórico de Evita, haciendo aflorar a la conciencia el secreto de su poder que una severa censura interna y externa nos impone ocultar, es una de las maneras—la que corresponde al escritor más que al político—de contribuir al esclarecimiento de la concienca de la clase trabajadora y de las mujeres argentinas, o por lo menos de sus posibles dirigentes, de los cuadros, de quienes depende que la transformación social del país, el cambio histórico, deje de ser un mito nostálgico en el que se proyectan las esperanzas y los sueños más ardientes de una gran parte del pueblo. (*Eva Perón* 113)

[In opposition to the necrophilias of certain Peronists who were demanding Evita's mummy in order to turn it into a magical object of mystic adoration, I would prefer that Evita's tomb remain open and that her phantom continue to upset people's consciences. Those heroes who in one way or another die for the liberty of Latin American people have no burial; the bodies of Evita and Che [Guevara] have no rest, nor have their statues begun to be molded. To defile the taboo, to desecrate the myth, in its angelic version as much as in its diabolic one, revealing the true historical meaning of Evita and causing to come to the surface of consciousness the secret of her power, which a severe internal and external censorship requires us to hide, is one of the ways—which belong more to the writer than to the politician—to contribute to the clarification of the conscience of the working class and Argentine women, or at least of their possible leaders, of their cadres, on whom it depends that the social transformation of the country, historical change, cease to be a nostalgic myth in which the most burning hopes and dreams of a large part of the people are projected.]

I have quoted so extensively from the conclusion of the 1971 edition, with its added reference to Che, because it demonstrates that over fifteen years after the original publication of *Eva Perón,* Sebreli is still committed to propagating the excesses of meaning attributed to her figure, whereby a very emotional understanding of historical meaning is juxtaposed to the futility of both "angelic" and "diabolic" myths surrounding her. However, by 1983, Sebreli, with the publication of *Los deseos imaginarios del peronismo* (The imaginary desires of Peronismo), definitively liquidates any belief in a positive political meaning for Eva Perón, ascribing his earlier enthusiasms to

la rebelión juvenil típicamente pequeñoburguesa contra las convenciones y tabúes de la familia y sociedad, el deseo bohemio de *épater le bourgeois.* (12)

[the typically petit bourgeois youthful rebellion against the conventions and taboos of family and society, the Bohemian desire to startle those who are bourgeois.]

Furthermore, he confesses that he has been moved especially by his literary commitments:

No pudiendo tampoco sustraerme a las influencias literarias, identifiqué a Evita con el bastardo sartreano, ese personaje a quien la condena de la sociedad transforma en censor implacable de la misma. . . . [La] exaltación lírica de la juventud, la borrachera heroica de un joven, si por añadidura es intelectual de izquierda, no se detiene ante los triviales hechos cotidianos. (13)

[Since I am also unable to withdraw myself from literary influences, I identified Evita with the Sartrean bastard, that character whom society's condemnation transforms into the implacable censor of itself. . . . The lyrical exaltation of youth, the heroic drunkenness of a young man, if he is in addition a left-wing intellectual, cannot be stopped by trivial daily facts.]

Thus, Sebreli falls into line with current historical assessments of Peronismo that resist any attachment of socialist meaning either to Peronismo or to the biography of Evita, and Eva Perón is barely mentioned in the remaining two hundred pages of the book. Indeed, as Francesca Miller has argued, it is difficult to attach even much of a feminist meaning to Evita: "Eva Perón had little or no interest in or understanding of women's rights, and she expressed disdain for feminists as 'women who did not know how to be women'" (123).

What Sebreli provides in *Los deseos imaginarios* is a minute analysis of the irrefutable fascist underpinnings of Peronismo and the conclusion that Evita was simply an integral, if flamboyant, component of its propaganda apparatus (see Ciria 305–7). Sebreli is still unable or unwilling to step back and analyze the cultural meanings of Evita apart from Peronismo, to return to his interpretation of her as an operatic heroine, and to discuss why the excesses of her public persona may have had cultural meanings impinging on issues of masculinity other than those that (rather uncomfortably) conform to his idea of the Sartrean bastard. Nor, as he proceeds to reinterpret her as a weft in the fabric of Peronista fascism, is he interested in the still vibrant connotations she evokes in Argentina. It is simply not enough to dismiss her as part and parcel of a set of "deseos imaginarios" (imaginary desires). In the best of the Argentine Lacanian tradition, imaginary desires have potent, unsuperfluous meanings, which, as a Peronista like Menem realizes, include, yet cannot be reduced to, the meanings of exhausted political systems.

"Si Evita viviera, sería tortillera" [If Evita were still alive, she'd be a dyke]. Both Katra ("Eva Perón: Popular ♥ueen") and I ("Narrative Persona") have examined the relationship between Evita and Argentine popular culture, but no one has yet connected her with issues like gay sensibility, sexual dissidence, and masculine subjectivity. The studies of her participation in popular culture begin to build a bridge toward the notion of "queering culture," as in Alexander Doty's sense in *Making Things Perfectly Queer,* which examines how mass culture necessarily escapes the sharp boundaries of the stable signifiers of compulsory heterosexuality. Yet it can come as no surprise that Sebreli, committed to homosexual issues either as the young bohemian rebel who wrote *Eva Perón: ¿Aventurera o militante?* or as the jaded social analyst of *Los deseos imaginarios,* declines the opportunity to place the figure of Eva Perón in larger cultural contexts, which might involve dissident sexual identities.

In characterizing the extremely difficult history of homosexual liberation in Argentina, Zelmar Acevedo, in fifteen pages of chronicle, mentions no names of individuals involved with movements, publications, or cultural acts. The stakes are too high. Of course, Sebreli might find it outrageous to establish links between Evita and gay sensibility, for there can be no question that the homophobia of the Peronista movement, with its military roots, played a role in an appalling historical record of homophobia in Argentina. But the excesses of meaning surrounding Evita Perón do exist, and Sebreli's interpretation of them in the framework of the Sartrean bastard is only one approach. Though Sebreli may no longer be interested in Evita as a militant, he was in the mid-1950s, and his book exercised a considerable amount of influence at that time and subsequently. Sebreli's book stood alone, because although many other books about Evita were published in Argentina after her death, they were all hagiographic, and none attempted to establish larger historical, social, and cultural connections (indeed, the very goal of hagiography is to define the uniqueness of the individual). But when *Eva Perón* is read today from the point of view of new cultural parameters in Argentina and an emerging interest in sexual dissidence, the coincidences among the gay slogan, the meanings of Evita as a popular-culture icon, and the excesses of meaning that derive from her characterization by Sebreli as, alternately, a Sartrean bastard or a romantic-operatic heroine point toward the possibility of a productive queer reading.

Notes

This chapter previously appeared in David William Foster's *Sexual Textualities: Essays on Queer/ing Latin American Writing,* chapter 2. Copyright © 1997 by the University of Texas Press. Used with the permission of the University of Texas Press.

1. A Montonera is a member of the urban guerrilla group of the late 1960s and early 1970s that took its name from a group of pro-independence irregulars who were active in the mountains of rural Argentina during the early nineteenth century.

All translations from the original Spanish are my own.

2. Eva Perón appears briefly in the second part of Jaime Chavarri's movie *Las cosas del querer* (1995), where she is depicted as having rescued the Spanish flamenco singer and dancer Miguel Molina in a scandal involving public indecency (i.e., homosexuality). Although Miguel Molina, who died recently, did end up in Argentina after being "encouraged" to leave Franco's Spain, it seems unlikely that Evita was ever his benefactress in any run-in with the law. But, historical accuracy aside, the important thing is that the film attributes this role to her.

Perhaps the best-known connection between Eva Perón and the Buenos Aires gay demimonde was Paco Jamandreu, Evita's principal dress designer in Argentina. He speaks of his personal relationship with her in *Evita fuera del balcón* (1981). His personal memoirs, *La cabeza contra el suelo* (1975), which present a frank discussion of his homosexuality, contain numerous references to her. The only reference to Eva's knowledge of Jamandreu's personal life occurs in a passage describing her sighting of him in the street at three in the morning. Directing her chauffeur to stop the car, she confronts him: "—¡Mira que no cambias! ¡Las tres de la mañana! ¡Yirando!" (80). ["You never change! Three o'clock in the morning! Working the streets!"]

However, in *Evita fuera del balcón,* Jamandreu speaks of Evita's reaction to an inaugural party held in 1945 in his new design study. The morning after the party, Eva Duarte, still only one actress among many competing for attention, calls to thank him for his invitation:

—Muy linda tu fiesta, pendejo! ¡Progresás, eh! Todo muy lindo, encantadora la gente. . . . Pero cuanta mariquita, querido! No te fayó una, eh? Bueno, son la sal de la vida, ahora me doy cuenta que yo me estoy metiendo demasiado en el vinagre de la vida. Voy a empezar a salir más. Cuando hagas otro party invítame. (unpaginated)

["Your party was great, kiddo! You're making progress, no! Everything was very lovely, and the people where charming. . . . But what a lot of fags, darling! They were sure all there, right? Of course, they are the salt of life, and I can see I'm really beginning to get into the thick of things. I'm going to start going out more. Next time you have a party, be sure to invite me."]

No matter how much Jamandreu may be exaggerating Evita's interest in his circle of friends, one can assume his admiration for her has kept him from outright fabrication.

Little material is currently available on the history of homosexuality in Argentina. Although Guy makes some references to it, she is principally interested in the record for women (she refers briefly to Eva Perón's alleged experiences as a prostitute and only in passing to the relationship between prostitutes and Evita's work for women's rights in the creation of a broad base of Peronista loyalists [207–8]). Jorge Salessi has begun to construct such a history in several recent articles ("Tango"; "Argentine Dissemination").

In another dimension, a South African transvestite and political commentator, Evita Bezuidenhout, has assumed a persona built around the figure of Eva Perón. I have not been able to obtain a copy of Bezuidenhout's book, *A Part Hate, a Part Love: The Legend of Evita Bezuidenhout* (ca. 1994).

3. Posse serves as Menem's ambassador to the Czech Republic.

4. Note also should be taken of the recent play *Evita y Victoria* by Mónica Ottino, directed by Oscar Barney Finn; the Victoria of the title is Victoria Ocampo, Eva Perón's paradigmatic nemesis. One intriguing interpretation of the play is that, in the second act, when the model of personal antagonism of the first act is overcome, a homosocial female bonding takes place that, within the Adrienne Rich tradition, could be called lesbian.

5. It can be assumed that Posse was familiar with Copi's work. The first Argentine monograph on Copi was published by César Aira in 1991, although Posse does not cite this work in his bibliography.

6. The Argentine novelist Ernesto Schóó published a very informative note on Copi in 1995, in which he discusses Copi's homosexuality; he makes no mention, however, of Copi's play about Eva Perón.

7. This is undoubtedly a reference to one of the founding fictional texts of Argentine literature, Esteban Echeverría's short story "El matadero" (which was written around 1840 but not published until 1871, after his death). Noted for its images

of social violence in the context of Argentina's first dictatorship; "El matadero" concludes with the death of a young man at the hands of the political opposition.

8. After assuming office in 1973, Perón immediately distanced himself from the Left, which was subsequently dismantled, first by official ostracism and then by a war of extermination: the *guerra sucia,* begun after the military's return to power in 1976.

9. Sebreli's text *Martínez Estrada* concerns one of the first individuals of the Argentine intellectual elite to defend the Cuban revolution. His *Buenos Aires,* one of the most reprinted sociology texts in Argentina, is a probing examination of the profound changes in Argentine social life wrought by the Peronista experiment.

10. It is necessary to go further and consider in each case the role of the individual in historical events.

11. It was a separable relationship to the extent that, although divorce was never a real possibility, widows either lost the *de* association upon the death of their spouses or became *viuda de;* the patronymics, bestowed upon them at birth, remain inseparable (certainly an ironic attribution in the case of Eva, since Duarte is her unmarried mother's name).

Works Cited

Acevedo, Zelmar. *Homosexualidad: Hacia la destrucción de los mitos.* Buenos Aires: Ediciones del Ser, 1985.

Aira, César. *Copi.* Buenos Aires: Beatriz Viterbo Editora, 1991.

Butler, Judith. *Gender Trouble: Feminism and the Subversion of Identity.* New York: Routledge, 1990.

Ciria, Alberto. *Política y cultura popular: La Argentina peronista 1946–1955.* Buenos Aires: Ediciones de la Flor, 1983.

Copi. *¿A dónde va Perón? De Berlín a Wall Street.* Montevideo: Ediciones de la Resistencia Revolucionaria, 1955.

Copi. *Plays.* Trans. Anni Lee Taylor. London: John Calder, 1976.

Doty, Alexander. *Making Things Perfectly Queer: Interpreting Mass Culture.* Minneapolis: U of Minnesota P, 1993.

Dujovne Ortiz, Alicia. *Eva Perón: La biografía.* Buenos Aires: Aguilar, 1995.

Echeverría, Esteban. "El matadero." *Revista del Río de la Plata* 1.4 (1871): 556–85. Trans. Angel Flores as "The Slaughterhouse" (*Adam* 179 [1948]: 5–13).

Eva Perón. Cuadernos de crisis. 7. Buenos Aires: Editorial del Noroeste, 1974.

Evita: The Legend of Eva Perón (1919–1952). By Andrew Lloyd Webber, lyricist, and Tim Rice, composer. New York: Avon Books, 1979.

Foster, David William. "Narrative Persona in Evita Perón's *La razón de mi vida.*" *Alternative Voices in the Contemporary Latin American Narrative.* Columbia: U of Missouri P, 1985. 45–59.

Galasso, Norberto. *De Perón a Menem: El peronismo en la encrucijada.* Buenos Aires: Ediciones de Pensamiento Nacional, 1990.

Geltman, Pedro. "Mito, símbolos y héroes en el peronismo." *El peronismo.* Buenos Aires: Carlos Pérez Editor, 1969. 109–37.

Goldar, Ernesto. *El peronismo en la literatura argentina.* Buenos Aires: Editorial Freeland, 1971.

Guy, Donna J. *Sex and Danger in Buenos Aires: Prostitution, Family, and Nation in Argentina.* Lincoln: U of Nebraska P, 1991.

Hodges, Donald C. *Argentina, 1943–1976: The National Revolution and Resistance.* Albuquerque: U of New Mexico P, 1976.

Jamandreu, Paco. *La cabeza contra el suelo: Memorias.* Buenos Aires: Ediciones de la Flor, 1975.

Jamandreu, Paco. *Evita fuera del balcón.* Buenos Aires: Ediciones del Libro Abierto, 1981.

Katra, William H. *Contorno: Literary Engagement in Post-Peronist Argentina.* Madison, N.J.: Fairleigh Dickinson UP, 1988.

Katra, William H. "Eva Perón: Media Queen of the Peronista Working Class." *Revista/Review Interamericana* 11 (1981): 238–51.

Katra, William. "Eva Perón: Popular ♥ueen of Hearts." *Latin American Digest* 14.2 (1980): 6–7, 19–20.

King, John. *Sur: A Study of the Argentine Literary Journal and Its Role in the Development of Culture, 1931–1970.* Cambridge: Cambridge UP, 1986.

Martínez, Tomás Eloy. *Santa Evita.* Buenos Aires: Editorial Sudamericana, 1995.

Miller, Francesca. *Latin American Women and the Search for Social Justice.* Hanover, N.H.: UP of New England, 1991.

Naipaul, V. S. "The Return of Eva Perón." *The Return of Eva Perón with the Killings in Trinidad.* New York: Vintage Books, 1981. 99–181.

Ottino, Mónica. *Evita y Victoria: Comedia patriótica en tres actos.* Buenos Aires: Grupo Latinoamericano.

Perlongher, Néstor. "El cadáver de la nación." *Hule.* Buenos Aires: Ediciones Último Reino, 1989. 68–75.

Posse, Abel. *La pasión según Eva.* Buenos Aires: Emecé Editores, 1994.

Prieto, Adolfo. *Borges y la nueva generación.* Buenos Aires: Letras Universitarias, 1954.

Salessi, Jorge. "The Argentine Dissemination of Homosexuality, 1890–1914." *¿Entiendes? Queer Readings, Hispanic Writings.* Ed. Emilie L. Bergmann and Paul Julian Smith. Durham: Duke UP, 1995. 49–91.

Salessi, Jorge. "Tango, nacionalismo y sexualidad: Buenos Aires, 1880–1914." *Hispamérica* 60 (1991): 33–53.

Schóó, Ernesto. "Copi: El autor de la vida es un tango." *El Cronista Cultural* (11 Aug. 1995): 1–2.

Sebreli, Juan José. *Buenos Aires: Vida cotidiana y alienación.* 1964. 15th ed. Buenos Aires: Ediciones Siglo Veinte, 1979.

Sebreli, Juan José. *Los deseos imaginarios del peronismo.* 1983. 4th ed. Buenos Aires: Editorial Legasa, 1984.

Sebreli, Juan José. *Eva Perón: ¿Aventurera o militante?* [1954?] 4th ed., ampl. Buenos Aires: Editorial La Pleyade, 1971.

Sebreli, Juan José. *Fútbol y masas.* Buenos Aires: Editorial Galerna, [1981?].

Sebreli, Juan José. "Inocencia y culpabilidad de Roberto Arlt." *Sur* 223 (1953): 109–19.

Sebreli, Juan José. *Martínez Estrada: Una rebelión inútil.* Buenos Aires: Palestra, 1960.

Sebreli, Juan José. *La saga de los Anchorena.* Buenos Aires: Sudamericana, 1986.

Sebreli, Juan José. "Testimonio [sobre el peronismo]." *Contorno* 7–8 (1956): 45–49.

Sur (Buenos Aires). Published 1931–70.

Taylor, J. M. *Eva Perón: The Myths of a Woman.* Chicago: U of Chicago P, 1979.

Wetsel, David. "Copi." *Latin American Writers on Gay and Lesbian Themes: A Biocritical Sourcebook.* Ed. David William Foster. Westport, Conn.: Greenwood P, 1994. 116–21.

Woolf, Virginia. *Un cuarto propio.* Trans. Jorge Luis Borges. Buenos Aires: Sur, 1956.

10

Queer Cortázar and the *Lectora Macho*

Rosemary Geisdorfer Feal

The title of this chapter suggests that Julio Cortázar merits a place among the ranks of "queer" writers in Latin America or that at least his works deserve a queer reading. I haven't settled on this interpretive mode with ease. In fact, I'd call the analysis I want to do here quite unsettling, especially coming from a feminist critic who has felt viscerally that Cortázar's treatment of sexuality may be called sadistic, sexist, misogynistic, and worse. I remember having flung a Cortázar book or two against my study wall in outrage over the humiliations of la Maga in *Rayuela* (Hopscotch), the wife abuse in "El río" (The river), the sick mind of the rapist in "Anillo de Moebius" (published in English as "Moebius Strip"). But as I thought about Cortázar over the years since I first encountered his fiction, I became increasingly convinced that only a "perverse" or "queer" reading could reveal the complex dynamics of desire in his work and address the sadomasochistic pleasures of his texts. Such a reading could therefore place Cortázar among those who have delved into explorations of marginalized sexualities and provide a critical framework to counter reductionisms such as the ones that compelled me to slam his (book) spine to the wall.[1]

Queer theory is often spoken of in the singular, as a kind of condensation or amalgamation of the multiple approaches available under its umbrella.² According to Biddy Martin, queer theory "seeks to complicate hegemonic assumptions about the continuities between anatomical sex, social gender, gender identity, sexual identity, sexual object choice, and sexual practice" (105). Yet we might understand "queer" not only as limited to analyses that focus on gay, lesbian, or bisexualities but also as a risky category that, in Elizabeth Grosz's words, "is capable of accommodating . . . many of the most blatant and extreme forms of heterosexual and patriarchal power games, which are, in a certain sense, queer, persecuted, ostracized" (224). Although Grosz implicitly objects to any strategy that fails to differentiate "good" queers from "bad," that indiscretion is precisely the appeal of queer as an interpretive mode for dealing with Cortázar. "Gay" or "lesbian" literary criticism would have little to say about an author who does not identify as a gay writer and whose works in general focus on heterosexualities (insofar as conduct goes). Queer criticism, however, can take stock of how "outlaw" sexualities (and I include fantasies as a necessary component thereof) function in a text, even though any attempt to coalign the range of expressions that queer sexualities encompass will be a theoretically fraught enterprise.

For some help with this problem I want to turn to Gayle Rubin's signal study, "Thinking Sex: Notes for a Radical Theory of the Politics of Sexuality." Rubin diagrams the sexual value system as a large circle containing a smaller circle drawn within. The charmed inner circle consists of sanctioned conduct: "Sexuality that is to be viewed as 'good,' 'normal' and 'natural' should ideally be heterosexual, marital, monogamous, reproductive, non-commercial . . . coupled, relational, within the same generation, and occur at home" (280). The outer limits of the circle are "bad, abnormal, unnatural, and damned sexuality: homosexual, unmarried, promiscuous, non-procreative, commercial, alone or in groups, casual, cross-generational, in public, pornography, with manufactured objects, sado-masochistic" (281). While Rubin demonstrates how gays and lesbians have been particularly victimized by this repressive structure, she deliberately brings into alignment a range of persecuted sexual practices to demonstrate the need for a radical theory of sexuality that today we might call queer. I should mention two points that complicate the applicability of this sociological analysis to the literary context. First, in fiction we need not concern ourselves with the expressions of sexuality as lived realities, although we may wish to speak of the relation between literary fantasies and the material world in which human exchanges take place. Second, Rubin is speaking of consensual sexuality, whereas some of Cortázar's queerness centers on language that, if translated to a sociological venue and carried out as acts, would lie outside either circle. Yet despite these limitations, I contend that Julio Cortázar's imaginings of outer-circle sexualities (and those beyond) are best looked at for their queer potential to elucidate the codes or effects through which gender is made manifest.

My first analytic approach to gender and sexuality in Cortázar was quite rigid, following Freud in his "Instincts and Their Vicissitudes" (1915), in which he claimed that our mental life as a whole is governed by three polarities, expressed in the following antitheses: subject/object, pleasure/pain, active/passive. It struck me that Julio Cortázar's short fiction is infused with the same three polarities, or positions, which become activated both within the text and in relation to readers. His best-known "*microcuento*" (ministory) is paradigmatic of these polarities. As always with Cortázar, the torture and its demand for readerly surrender begins as soon as one enters his fictions. And what better place to begin than at the end: the end of a path through a woods, a walk through the rooms of a house, an encounter with a reader comfortably seated in a green velvet armchair. This character in Cortázar's "Continuidad de los parques" (Continuity of the parks) may be said to undergo a transition from passive reader-in-the-text to imagined murder victim in the mind of the active, collaborative implied reader. The man in the armchair thus embodies one kind of receptor, who stands—or sits, rather—in antithesis to the active, narrating subject. This reader-in-the-text is male, yet his role is prototypically feminine in the way that Cortázar frequently constructs it: passive, subordinated, silent, violated, objectified, dead. I want to argue that "feminine" is therefore not conflated with "female" for the Argentine writer; it is instead a reversible, mobilizing polarity in a sadomasochistic dynamic.[3] If this is so, the dynamic would allow us to uncover some alternative enactments of feminine-masculine in Cortázar's works and to study those unsettling subject positions that have left characters and readers alike stranded on the border between pleasure and pain. That's the pleasure of the Cortázar text, or so we have been told: it hurts so good that we beg to be hit again; we long to become the "battered reader" that Sara Castro-Klarén has identified: "Every time the reader lets down his guard . . . the author, that is the authority, the entity in command . . . slaps the reader's face and forces him to follow and accept the inexorable denouement of the story as demanded by the obsessive game played by the writing subject" (66).[4] To understand what would make such pleasures possible, we need to look at gender and sexual difference through language and narrative structure, which, after all, serve as the fist that delivers the technical knockout in Cortázar's works.

Who is in the green velvet chair? Is it the notorious *lector hembra* (translated as "female reader," but note that "*lector*" is a masculine noun), passive, pleasure-seeking, and perverse: "Gozaba del placer casi perverso de irse desgajando línea a línea de lo que lo rodeaba" (*Los relatos* 2: 7) [He was enjoying the almost perverse pleasure of breaking away line by line from what was around him]?[5] If he represents passivity, then the inscribed reader in Cortázar's "Continuidad de los parques" does not inevitably get his in the end, as so many critics would like to think. Jonathan Tittler has argued that to conflate the reader in the green velvet chair with the victim of the love triangle, that is, the protagonist of the book being read *by* the man in the armchair, is to act as a passive reader, one who is submerged in an illusion (173).[6] Yet at the same time, to ignore the continuity of the two stories, the narrative twist, is also to miss the point, to miss the "hit." If we place ourselves imaginarily in the green armchair, we might fear for our lives, which is part of the fun of that story. But if we resist identification and become the collaborative, active coauthors, ironically, we still fall into a passive role in the sense that the author has set us up: we were meant to arrive.

To "get" the story is therefore both to collaborate and to be "gotten." Herein lies the sadomasochistic dynamic so pervasive on the structural and content level of so many of Cortázar's stories. As Freud explains, sadomasochism entails a change of object (passive to active) while the aim remains the same (to torture, to be tortured); further, "the masochist also enjoys the *act* of torturing when this is being applied to himself" whereas the sadist derives pleasure from "inflicting pain upon others, through his identification of himself with the suffering object" (77, 79).[7] This interrelated sadomasochistic play in the text is what makes the *lector hembra,* the masculine subject modified by a feminizing adjective, stand in antithesis to what I want to call the *lectora macho,* the phallic feminine subject who is not named as such but whose functions in Cortázar's fiction certainly allow us to lift the textual veil and find "her." The masochist may be aligned with the passive *hembra,* the sadist with the active *macho,* but, as Freud demonstrated, the two poles are inextricably bound to each other, and cross-identifications are necessary for their stasis.

The conventional scheme set up by Cortázar himself in *Rayuela* pits the *lector hembra* against the reader of higher moral order, the *lector cómplice* (complicitous reader). As Debra Castillo notes, the female-gendered composite, *lector hembra,* is a "symbol of negativity, of all that is wrong with traditional texts and traditional readings of those texts. . . . Loved and hated, desired and despised, his/her superficiality permits *el lector hembra* to escape from the commitment . . . to serious prose typical of the highly touted *lector cómplice*" (48). Castillo goes on to make a compelling case for a subversive *lectora hembra* within the framework of strategic superficiality in writers such as Rosario Castellanos. The *lectora macho* that I am identifying in Cortázar's short fiction is a queer reading subject (within or beyond the narrative) who surpasses the Freudian binary of active/passive or escapes his category of the masculine woman. Instead, the *lectora macho* is perverse, not because "she" finds pleasure in submerging herself in the fiction like the *lector hembra,* but because "she" gets off on the gender and sex games that Cortázar plays, and "she" delights in twisting the heterotropes, striking back at the battering text.[8]

The role of queer readers in and outside the text may be illustrated through an analysis of Julio Cortázar's "Historia con migalas" (published in English as "Story with Spiders"), originally appearing in *Queremos tanto a Glenda* (1981) (published in English as *We Love Glenda So Much*).[9] Brilliant in its use of grammatical gender in the Spanish language, the "hit" of the story is totally eclipsed in the English translation. The narrative voice is conveyed through the first-person plural of the verb forms: "Llegamos a las dos de la tarde al bungalow" (*Los relatos* 2: 24) ["We arrived at the bungalow at two in the afternoon" (*We Love* 17)]; "Anoche, mientras guardábamos la ropa y ordenábamos las provisiones compradas en Saint-Pierre, oímos las voces de quienes ocupan la otra ala del bungalow" (*Los relatos* 2: 24) ["Last night, while we were putting our clothes away and lining up the groceries bought in Saint-Pierre, we could hear the voices of the people in the other wing of the bungalow" (*We Love* 18)]. The one or two adjectives used to describe the "we" are neuter: "Dejamos irse las horas en el agua o la arena, incapaces de otra cosa" (*Los relatos* 2: 25) ["We let the hours pass in the water or on the sand, incapable of anything else" (*We Love* 19)]. It appears that this couple has escaped to a Caribbean island at Christmastime, following an event they seek to forget, which took place at "la granja de Erik" ["Erik's farm"] near Delft and involves a man named Michael. The actions of the couple are conveyed in unison, as if one consciousness were telling the story for both in what Doris Sommer calls a "grotesque double first person" (252–53): "Nos mecemos en las mecedoras y fumamos en la oscuridad" (*Los relatos* 2: 28) ["We rock in the rocking chairs and smoke in the darkness" (*We Love* 22)]; "Buscábamos la soledad pero ahora pensamos en lo que sería la noche aquí si realmente no hubiera nadie en el otro lado" (*Los relatos* 2: 28) ["We were looking for solitude but now we're thinking about what night would be like here if there really weren't anybody on the other side" (*We Love* 22)].

Although the couple tries to block out the episode at Erik's farm, they recount flashes of memory.

Curiosamente no nos afecta pensar en Michael, en el pozo de la granja de Erik, cosas ya clausuradas; casi nunca hablamos de ellas o de las precedentes aunque sabemos que pueden volver a la palabra sin hacernos daño, al fin y al cabo el placer y la delicia vinieron de ellas, y la noche de la granja valió el precio que estamos pagando, pero a la vez sentimos que todo eso está demasiado próximo todavía, los detalles, Michael desnudo bajo la luna. (*Los relatos* 2: 27)

[Curiously, it doesn't affect us to think about Michael, about the well on Erik's farm, things all closed up now; we almost never talk about them or about what preceded them even though we know they can be mentioned without doing us any harm. After all, pleasure and delight came from them, and the night on the farm was worth the price we're paying, but at the same time we feel all that is still too close, the details. Michael naked in the moonlight.] (*We Love* 21)

Pleasure, delight, pursuit, a naked man beneath the moon about to meet his death: this familiar-sounding tale evokes Diana, the moon goddess, and Actaeon, her victim. At this point I can no longer save the surprise at the end of "Historia con migalas" because the rest of my analysis hinges on it. The couple goes over to the bungalow next door in search of the man whose voice they have heard:

A la hora de dormir nos habíamos puesto como siempre los camisones; ahora los dejamos caer como manchas blancas y gelatinosas en el piso, desnudas vamos hacia la puerta y salimos al jardín. . . . No hay luz adentro cuando entramos juntas; es la primera vez en mucho tiempo que nos apoyamos la una en la otra para andar. (*Los relatos* 2: 33)

[At bedtime we'd put on our nightshirts as usual; now we let them drop like white, gelatinous splotches onto the floor, naked, we go toward the door and out into the garden. . . . There's no light inside when we go in together; it's the first time in a long while that we lean on each other in order to walk.] (*We Love* 28–29)

The English translation contains no explanation of this grammatical precision of feminine gender ("desnudas," feminine plural ["naked"]) that holds the potential to challenge our previous conception of the characters.

With the surprise ending in mind, let's go back. The narrative presentation of the couple tells us nothing of their gender, up until the final paragraph. We could operate under heteronormativity and presume that this pair, composed of two people who know each other well, who seem bored with their routine, who eat, sleep, sunbathe at the beach, and even think or dream in linked ways, are husband and wife, escaping some terrible incident back in Delft. In fact, I want to argue that this heterosexist presumption is what Cortázar plays with here, and the narrative knockout at the end "hits" someone only if he or she sits in the green velvet heterosexist chair. The queer reading position (the *lectora macho*) can imagine the lesbian subtext of the story, in anticipation or retrospection, beginning with the first line, "Llegamos a las dos de la tarde . . ." ["We arrived at . . . two in the afternoon"], which, stripped of the preposition (the very letter *a* that is lacking in the rest of the story), becomes "llegamos las dos" [the two of us arrived], with the feminine article "las." The homoerotic dimension is communicated through all kinds of twinnings and pairings: there

is the couple in the adjoining bungalow, two women whom the narrators
hear and believe to be the same two women they see on the beach: "Les
imaginamos secretariados o escuelas de párvulos en Detroit, en Nebraska" (*Los relatos* 2: 26) ["We imagine them to be secretaries or elemen-
tary school teachers from Detroit, from Nebraska" (*We Love* 19)]. Like
the narrators, these women move in unison: "Las vemos entrar juntas al
mar, alejarse deportivamente" (*Los relatos* 2: 26) ["We watch them go into
the sea together, go off sportingly" (*We Love* 19)]. But these "schoolteachers of America"—the term applied to Gabriela Mistral, one of Latin
America's greatest queer subjects (see Horan, this volume)—turn out to
share a bed: "Dormían ahí, en la gran cama de sábanas con flores amari-
llas. Las dos. Y se hablaban, se hablaban antes de dormir. Se hablaban
tanto antes de dormir" (*Los relatos* 2: 31). ["They slept there, in the big
bed with sheets with yellow flowers. The two of them. And they talked,
they talked before going to sleep. They talked so much before sleeping"
(*We Love* 26).] These two women live in ways that are typical of partners,
and as such they become mirror reflections, projections, or continuities of
the narrators, transformed into nice midwestern lesbian teachers or secretaries: "Continuidad de las parcas."[10]

Cortázar's lesbian subjects in "Historia con migalas" represent two extremes: the midwestern schoolteacher types, seemingly innocuous and
ordinary, and the vampire spiderwomen to whom the "we" of the story
corresponds. Between pairs the differences seem great, which makes
the mirrorlike duplication primarily structural (each female couple in a
double-bedded bungalow). One of the uncanny features of "Historia con
migalas" is that Cortázar makes no distinctions *within* the couples, an
effect that produces interchangeability. The similarities within each pair
suggest an old stereotype, which the psychopathological model of female
homosexuality imposed, wherein all lesbians are said to function in a
twinned, narcissistic relation. Teresa de Lauretis, in fact, contests this very
model when she bases her book about lesbian sexuality and perverse desire on the notion that it takes *two* distinct women to make a lesbian out
of *one*.[11] The trope of lesbian mankillers or vampires also strikes a stereotypical note in the story. Cortázar thus recirculates some cut-out characters in his surprise lesbians, whose appearance as such is codified definitively only with the adjective "desnudas" ["naked"]. The mark of gender
also reveals the mark of sex in this case: the women are stripped bare of
their neuter adjective cloaks *and* their nightshirts.

To add to the queerness of this story, Cortázar plays with the grammatical gender of the animals that surround the visitors to the tropics (gender
here also overlaps with the category of sex). There are the usual "perros"
(dogs, masculine) "pájaros" (birds, masculine), "cabras" (goats, feminine),

and "lagartijas" (lizards, feminine). But then one begins to notice things like the "mosquitos" (mosquitos, masculine), which by the end of the story have become "moscas" (flies, feminine).[12] The narrators, of course, are related to the "migalas" of the title—spiders, a psychoanalytic symbol for the phallic woman, Cortázar's *lectora macho*. Then there are "una gata mansa y pedigüeña, otra negra más salvaje pero igualmente hambrienta" (*Los relatos* 2: 25) ["a tame and mendicant female cat, another black one, wilder but just as hungry" (*We Love* 18)]; these female cats are obviously to be connected to the pairs of women as well. Of the many noises they hear, the plural narrative voice notes "el amor lacinante de los gatos" (*Los relatos* 2: 29) ["the shrill lovemaking of cats [masculine]" (*We Love* 24)], but on another night they hear "el coro de perros . . . y en la maleza el amor de las gatas lacera el aire" (*Los relatos* 2: 32) ["the chorus of dogs [masculine] . . . and in the underbrush the lovemaking of cats [feminine] tears the air" (*We Love* 26)]. Now, just what are those *gatas* rolling around in bed with?[13] By deploying the same feline noun, the same sexual activity, but changing the gender from masculine to feminine, Cortázar destabilizes the whole sexual economy and implies two sets of queer possibilities: "*gatos,*" understood as exclusively male (and we think of the Michael-Erik pair here, and the referents in the story to gay male writers such as Capote and Cavafy), and "*gatas,*" the sex of which can only be exclusively female. For that matter, the narrating couple, revealed to be two women by the use of gender in the story's last line, could have just as plausibly been a pair of gay males, given the queer economy deployed here. The Spanish language, however, would have no simple device by which to denote double maleness in a couple's constitution. The masculine plural used for a mixed couple would effectively preclude the kind of game Cortázar has played here with female subjects, and heteronormativity would make the ambiguities of gender or of sexual orientation unlikely to be communicated without supporting devices (names, anatomy, and so on).[14]

What disrupts the queer symmetries in "Historia con migalas" is the nocturnal presence of a male voice in the adjoining bungalow. When the narrators first perceive it, they are deeply disturbed. Then they become obsessed with listening for that sound, yet they witness no signs of a male at times other than night. The first mention of this change could be interpreted as if one of the midwestern women had taken on the voice of a man: "Las voces del otro lado del bungalow habían pasado del susurro a algunas frases claramente audibles aunque el sentido se nos escapara. Pero no era el sentido el que nos atrajo . . . sino que una de las voces era una voz de hombre" (*Los relatos* 2: 27). ["The voices from the other side of the bungalow had gone from whispering to a few clearly audible phrases, even

if their meaning escaped us. But it wasn't the meaning that attracted us
. . . but that one of the voices was that of a man" (*We Love* 21).] Another
queer encoding, a possible reference to butch-femme roles, is "una gata
mansa y . . . otra . . . más salvaje" [a tame female cat and another wilder
one]. The narrators certainly don't seem to think so; they take the male-
pitched voice literally and match audible gender to visible sex: where is
he? No cars, no traces of a "real man" having been to the bungalow. After
the (presumed to be) North American women leave, the narrators lie in
wait to see what will happen that night. Sure enough, in typical Cortázar
style, we are told, "No nos desconcierta demasiado la breve, seca tos que
viene del otro bungalow, su tono inconfundiblemente masculino" (*Los relatos* 2: 33) ["We're not disconcerted too much by the short, dry cough
that comes from the other side of the bungalow, its tone unmistakably
masculine" (*We Love* 28)]. When last I taught this story, I asked the class,
"Whose voice *is* that in the bungalow next door?" "Cortázar!" blurted
out a sophisticated graduate student who might otherwise have restrained
herself. But it's neither far-fetched nor naïve to conflate the author and
the voice within the text. On one level, we could say that Cortázar projects
himself through the disembodied voice into that double bed for women,
thereby disrupting the lesbian self-enclosure, the strictly female world,
which by implication shuts out men—or, worse, does away with them, a
literary fantasy that performs an exaggerated act of exclusion. And the
coughing male is related to Michael, the victim of these women: "Michael
volvió a la granja de Erik . . . como ha vuelto el visitante de las mucha-
chas" (*Los relatos* 2: 33) ["Michael too went back to Erik's farm . . . just
as the girls' visitor has come back" (*We Love* 28)]. The story ends with the
naked women entering the adjoining bungalow, presumably to kill the man
who lies in what is the duplication of their own bed, a scene in which
sexuality is also implicated. To return to an earlier quote: "Al fin y al cabo
el placer y la delicia vinieron de ellas" (*Los relatos* 2: 27) ["After all, pleasure and delight came from them" (*We Love* 21)]—"ellas" is now taken to
refer to the women, not "las cosas" [the things].

There is more to say about the symbolic value of grammatical gender
in this story. Another queer writer, Arthur Rimbaud, imagined it over a
century ago in his poem "Voyelles," written in 1872:

> A noir, E blanc, I rouge, U vert, O bleu: voyelles,
> Je dirai quelque jour vos naissances latentes:
> A, noir corset velu des mouches éclatantes
> Qui bombinent autour des puanteurs cruelles
>   (*Oeuvres* 110)

[A black, E white, I red, U green, O blue: vowels,
Someday I will say your latent births:
A, black hairy corset of glittering flies
that buzz around cruel stenches]

A: the origin, the feminine *la,* the abject, *la mosca, la araña,* the fetish, the phallic *O* with a tail, but also the grammatical gender associated with the masculine sex organ: *la polla, la verga, la picha.*[15]
And here's Rimbaud on the *O:*

O, suprême Clairon plein des strideurs étranges,
Silences traversés des Mondes et des Anges:
—O l'Oméga, rayon violet de Ses Yeux!

(*Oeuvres* 360)

[O, supreme trumpet full of strange stridences
Traversed silences of Worlds and Angels
O the Omega, purple ray of His Eyes!]

Omega: the great *O,* the masculine *lo,* the light of the beloved's eyes, the halo in the sky, the anus, the circle, but also the hole, the zero, the void, the vagina, and perhaps the most popular curse word in the Spanish language: *coño* with two *O*'s. Once again it is the dynamic movement within a category (here, the *a* and the *o*) that sets up the kinds of polarities to which Freud refers. The *a* and the *o* as grammatical markers of gender are not opposed only from without; they also encode the differences within themselves, thereby undoing the binaries that have traditionally served to uphold sexual difference.

Cortázar's "Historia con migalas" averts the gaze from the *a*/*o* of grammatical gender until the very end, when the narrative curtain is lifted to reveal two women. The fetish operates only when it is veiled, and the powerful symbolism of feminine and masculine gender is mobilized through its having been studiously avoided throughout the story. Cortázar has thus imagined a queer lipogram (a text written so as to avoid one or more letters, an effect often achieved by choosing a single vowel). This is a deconstruction of absence or lack—*lipo*—through overdetermination or a distracting presence. A lipogram points to a void through its insistent use of disguise. A closet for the forbidden letter. "The *a* of différance," says Derrida, "is not heard; it remains silent, secret, and discreet, like a tomb" (4).

If you think I'm *rizando el rizo* (curling the curl) of the tail on the letter *a*—si creen que estoy de coña[16]—then it might serve well to elaborate on Derrida's concept of *différance.* "*Différance*" with an *a* sounds just like "*différence*" with an *e,* but the Derridean term "designates both a 'passive' difference already in place as the condition of signification and an act of differing which produces differences," in Jonathan Culler's words (97). According to Derrida, *différance* is the "systematic play of differences, of traces of differences, of the spacing by which elements relate to one another. This spacing is the production, simultaneously active and passive (the *a* of *différance* indicates this indecision as regards activity and passivity, that which cannot yet be governed and organized by that opposition" (Culler 97). Seen through the lens of *différance,* Cortázar's gender game does not correspond to some rigid opposition of active/passive, masculine/ feminine, heterosexual/homosexual, but is itself a production, or performance, of the gaps or spaces that allow differences to operate. The ungovernability of Cortázar's short fiction is, in fact, one of its uncanny features, and its liminality resists and subverts—but never relinquishes—those Freudian binaries with which I started my thinking on these dynamics.

If we've caught Cortázar in some narrative trap in "Historia con migalas," it's in part because he's been expecting us; "habíamos jugado el mismo juego" [we'd played the same game], as the male-entrapping ghost of a woman says to Jacobo in "Reunión con un círculo rojo" (published in English as "Encounter within a Red Circle").[17] As Sara Castro-Klarén notes, Cortázar "deploys his writing as a game of entrapment," and the search for the reader is therefore a "hunt" (69). Somebody is always the metaphoric top in Cortázar's stories, and usually it is the narrative voice itself that triumphs rather violently. But frequently the position of "top" is taken up by the *lectora macho:* the lesbian vampire types like in "Historia con migalas" on the internal level of the story, or the reader who turns the text into a "battered book" by giving it a fling. The transition from "battered reader" to "battering reader," from *lector hembra* to *lectora macho,* does not, of course, take place along strict male–female sex roles, as my argument has sought to demonstrate. What is missing from my account here is a deeper look at the ways in which Cortázar co-opts the reader into this sadomasochistic dynamic. While that discussion would take me far afield of the more limited use of "queer" that I have adopted for this study, I nevertheless want to make mention of its main thrust. Put simply: Cortázar sets up the narrative structure so that the victimized woman acquires power and agency and either executes a revenge on the male protagonist or otherwise achieves her own ends. The narrating subject in many of his stories forces the reader to enter the consciousness of victim turned victimizer, or aggrieved turned avenged, or battered turned batterer. We are therefore invited to access, that is, to understand, a female narrative voice that claims to have discovered sexual pleasure as a result of a rape ("Anillo de Moebius" ["Moebius Strip"]), one that goes from witness of torture to torturer herself ("Recortes de prensa" ["Press Clippings"]), or one that alternates between administering maternallike care and inflicting sadistic, even lethal, treatment on her young male patient ("La señorita Cora" [Miss Cora]).[18] Suffice it to say that the S/M structure of all these stories is charged with a sexual dimension, either explicitly, as in "Anillo de Moebius," or more subtly, as in the encoding of nurse–patient sex games in "La señorita Cora."

Pat Califia, modern champion of lesbian S/M and other outer-circle sexualities, says in one of her self-revelations, "I have never asked a submissive to do something I haven't done or couldn't do" (158). Queer Cortázar plays the same consensual S/M game with his readers and even with his critics. Perhaps you remember (or can imagine) the photograph of don Julio, the gentle giant, as he mock strangles the diminutive Evelyn Picón Garfield, in front of the ruins of the Marquis de Sade's castle in Lacoste, France.[19] There she is, going under for him, in a performance of male dominance and female submission, not unlike the position he invites readers to assume with relation to his texts: "Cuello de gatit[a]."[20] Subject/object, pleasure/pain, active/passive. But in Cortázar, these polarities are not fixed according to gender; they are, as I have shown, the signs through which gender can be made to perform. As Shoshana Felman notes, male self-identity, and "the mastery to which it lays claim, turns out to be a sexual as well as a political fantasy, subverted by the dynamics of bisexuality and by the rhetorical reversibility of masculine and feminine" (qtd. in Culler 171). And, we should add, subverted also by the dynamics of lesbian sexuality and the rhetorical reversibility of masculine as active and feminine as passive. I hope I have also argued convincingly that queer theory and performativity have a place among readers' responses to Cortázar's works, since he was, through his textual practices, one of the first writers to instantiate the modern notion of "gender fuck." Queer theory has been particularly useful to show how Cortázar's literary imagination undoes some of the old dichotomies: gay/straight, perverse/normal, pain/pleasure. Claiming a queer sensitivity for Cortázar certainly entails risk and ambiguity, and it demands precision, even caution. Or, in the Derridean manner, we could just call our critical enterprise, with the purloined letter *O,* "Continuidad de los parcos."[21]

Notes

1. An examination of "reader rage" as I experienced it might be akin to countertransference analysis as the vocabulary of psychoanalysis understands it. The text (analysand) projects its unconscious material onto the analyst, whose own psyche interacts and responds; a deep look at these dynamics can uncover and name the conflicts that manifest symptomatically.

2. For a discussion of queer theory and its relation to "Hispanism," see my "Queer Theory, Sexuality, and Women's Writing from Latin America."

3. This is a good place to remind ourselves that Freud did not always construe "passive" with the female sex or gender role. His discussions of passivity even include remarks to the effect that the relation between femininity and passivity is an arbitrary one. Nevertheless, Freud's basic position is that passivity and normal femininity coincide. For a good discussion of these issues, see "Freud, Sexuality, and Perversion" in de Lauretis.

4. Carlos Alonso's elegant statement on "the death of the author" articulates a philosophical framework in which we may place the reader's submissions and triumphs: "The moment of greatest critical rigor and understanding into a text coincides with the realization that we are somehow expendable, that if we thought that we were uncovering the text's self-mystification we were in effect the ones truly mystified. . . . The death that we confidently read in the text as that of the author is also our own as supposed masters of our discourse on that same text. We too, die a little with each critical act—figuratively speaking, of course" (69).

5. All English translations from the original language are my own unless otherwise noted.

6. Tittler also remarks: "Insistir . . . que el sillón verde en la última escena es el mismo sillón verde del lector ficticio, es obedecer ese mismo hábito de leer que se está interrogando" (172) [To insist . . . that the green armchair in the last scene is the same green armchair of the fictitious reader is to obey the very reading habit that is being interrogated].

7. The older term "*algolagnia*" seems in some ways preferable to "sadomasochism." "*Algolagnia,*" from the Greek, combines "pain" and "lust" as a psychiatric term to mean "finding pleasure in inflicting or enduring pain." The composite "sadomasochism" has deeper literary resonances in its evocation of Sade and Sacher-Masoch, but it separates the sadist from the masochist, at least linguistically. "*Algolagnia*" more eloquently conveys the mutuality involved in painful pleasure-giving and -taking, which undergirds the Cortázar reading process as I view it.

8. Cortázar claims that as a reader, he is humble, never aggressive: "Yo como lector no tengo nunca una actitud agresiva que parecería a priori ser el signo de la virilidad, del machismo. . . . cuando yo abro un libro lo abro como puedo abrir un paquete de chocolate, o entrar en el cine, o llegar por primera vez a la cama de una mujer que deseo" ("Julio Cortázar, lector" 20). [As a reader I never have an aggressive attitude that would a priori seem to be the sign of virility, of machismo. . . . when I open a book I open it like I could open a box of chocolates, or go into a movie theater, or get into bed for the first time with a woman I desire.] Yet Cortázar's definition of aggressive is the critical reader who anticipates that the book will be bad. The aggression I am discussing in the *lectora macho* would be an active, enjoyable engagement with the text, not unlike the pleasures that Cortázar describes when he opens a book: a good eat, a good flick, a good lay.

9. Although "Historia con migalas" originally appeared in the collection *Queremos tanto a Glenda,* in this chapter I am quoting from its later publication in *Los relatos,* vol. 2. The accompanying English translations are quoted from *We Love Glenda So Much.*

10. My pun literally means "Continuity of the Parcae." The Parcae are the three

Fates. As for continuities, Doris Sommer suggests a parallel between "Historia con migalas" and "Lacan's discussion of the pathological Papin sisters who were inseparable to the point of being unable to distinguish one from the other. When their shared identity was threatened by an outsider, in the form of another female couple, their response was violent murder" (253).

11. See also Noreen O'Connor and Joanna Ryan for an excellent discussion of the psychopathological model.

12. Both *"mosquito"* and *"mosca"* etymologically derive from the Latin *"musca"* (fly).

13. I am making playful reference to the well-known conversation between Amber Hollibaugh and Cherríe Moraga, "What We're Rolling around in Bed With: Sexual Silences in Feminism."

14. Actually, the use of gender with regard to sex and sexual orientation is more complicated in Spanish. For example, gay males who assume a female gender role may have feminine adjectives applied to them. And we recall the transvestite Manuela in José Donoso's *El lugar sin límites* (Hell has no limits), who always referred to herself as "una," and is described by the narrative voice in the feminine as well.

15. These are all slang or vulgar terms in Spanish, roughly equivalent to "prick," "dick," and so on.

16. *Estar de coña* means something like "to be kidding" in the sense of "jerking someone around." *Coña* is the feminine of *coño,* "cunt."

17. "Reunión con un círculo rojo" appears in *Los relatos,* vol. 1, "Encounter within a Red Circle" appears in *We Love Glenda So Much.* This is one of the dozens of stories by Cortázar that reverses the polarities of victim/aggressor. Jacobo thinks he is saving this woman from death at the hands of some vampire types who are waiters in a restaurant where she was dining, when in reality she has already passed from the world of mortals and ends up leading him back to the restaurant (and to his demise). There are two women characters, doubles of each other: the hapless "Jenny," who tries to save Jacobo but in fact ushers him back into danger, and the sinister waitress, who was expecting his return.

18. "Anillo de Moebius," "Recortes de prensa," and "La señorita Cora" appear in *Los relatos,* vols. 3, 4, and 2, respectively; "Moebius Strip" and "Press Clippings" appear in *We Love Glenda So Much.*

19. This photograph can be found in *Review of Contemporary Fiction* 3.3 (1983): 4.

20. I refer to a story by Cortázar, in English publication entitled "Throat of a Black Kitten" (see *We Love Glenda so Much*); in the original Spanish, "Cuello de gatito negro," with the masculine gender (see *Los relatos,* vol. 2).

21. The adjective *"parco"* (used here as a plural masculine noun) means "moderate" or "sparing."

Works Cited

Alonso, Carlos. "Julio Cortázar: The Death of the Author." *Revista de Estudios Hispánicos* 21.2 (1987): 61–71.
Califia, Pat. *Public Sex: The Culture of Radical Sex.* Pittsburgh: Cleis P, 1994.

Castillo, Debra A. *Talking Back: Toward a Latin American Feminist Literary Criticism.* Ithaca: Cornell UP, 1992.

Castro-Klarén, Sara. "Desire: The Author and the Reader in Cortázar's Narrative." *Review of Contemporary Fiction* 3.3 (1983): 65–71.

Cortázar, Julio. *Hopscotch.* Trans. Gregory Rabassa. New York: Avon, 1966.

Cortázar, Julio. "Julio Cortázar, lector: Conversación con Julio Cortázar." With Sara Castro-Klarén. *Cuadernos Hispanoamericanos* 364–66 (1980): 11–36.

Cortázar, Julio. *Queremos tanto a Glenda y otros relatos.* Madrid: Alfaguara, 1981.

Cortázar, Julio. *Rayuela.* 1963. Barcelona: Bruguera, 1979.

Cortázar, Julio. *Los relatos.* 4 vols. Madrid: Alianza, 1991.

Cortázar, Julio. *We Love Glenda So Much and A Change of Light.* Trans. Gregory Rabassa. New York: Vintage/Random House, 1984.

Culler, Jonathan. *On Deconstruction: Theory and Criticism after Structuralism.* Ithaca: Cornell UP, 1982.

de Lauretis, Teresa. *The Practice of Love: Lesbian Sexuality and Perverse Desire.* Bloomington: Indiana UP, 1994.

Derrida, Jacques. "Différance." *Margins of Philosophy.* Chicago: U of Chicago P, 1982. 1–27.

Feal, Rosemary Geisdorfer. "Queer Theory, Sexuality, and Women's Writing from Latin America." *Intertexts* 1 (1997): 51–62.

Felman, Shoshana. "Rereading Femininity." *Yale French Studies* 62 (1981): 19–44.

Freud, Sigmund. "Instincts and Their Vicissitudes." 1915. *A General Selection from the Works of Sigmund Freud.* 1937. Ed. John Rickman. Garden City, N.Y.: Doubleday, 1957. 70–86.

Grosz, Elizabeth. "Bodies and Pleasures in Queer Theory." *Who Can Speak: Authority and Critical Identity.* Ed. Judith Roof and Robin Wiegman. Urbana: U of Illinois P, 1995. 221–30.

Hollibaugh, Amber, and Cherríe Moraga. "What We're Rolling around in Bed With: Sexual Silences in Feminism." *Powers of Desire: The Politics of Sexuality.* Ed. Ann Snitow, Christine Stansell, and Sharon Thompson. New York: Monthly Review P, 1983. 394–405.

Martin, Biddy. "Sexualities without Genders and Other Queer Utopias." *Diacritics* 24.2–3 (1994): 104–21.

O'Connor, Noreen, and Joanna Ryan. *Wild Desires and Mistaken Identities: Lesbianism and Psychoanalysis.* New York: Columbia UP, 1993.

Rimbaud, Arthur. *Oeuvres.* Ed. Suzanne Bernard. Paris: Garnier, 1960.

Rubin, Gayle. "Thinking Sex: Notes for a Radical Theory of the Politics of Sexuality." *Pleasure and Danger: Exploring Female Sexuality.* Ed. Carole S. Vance. Boston: Routledge, 1984. 267–319.

Sommer, Doris. "A Nowhere for Us: The Promising Pronouns in Cortázar's 'Utopian' Stories." *Discurso Literario* 4.1 (1986): 231–63.

Tittler, Jonathan. "La continuidad en 'Continuidad de los parques.'" *Crítica Hispánica* 6.2 (1984): 167–74.

Part 4

Living/Writing Queer: An Open Book

11

Looking Queer in the Autobiography of Terenci Moix

Robert Richmond Ellis

When Terenci Moix was fourteen years old, he witnessed for the first time an act of civil disobedience. As he was about to purchase a copy of *La Vanguardia* from a kiosk on the Paralelo of Barcelona, a throng of Catalán dissidents suddenly burst down the street, shouting and seizing newspapers. At the time, he was completely unaware of the historical significance of the incident, and as the police began to club and arrest the protestors, he felt a profound sense of relief. And with good reason too. After all, poor Norma Shearer had been led off to the guillotine by a similar sort of mob in the film *Marie Antoinette.* According to his autobiographical volumes, *El cine de los sábados* (The Saturday matinee) and *El beso de Peter Pan* (The kiss of Peter Pan), Hollywood cinema (and to a lesser degree radio, comics, and film in general) determined his childhood vision of the world and himself and constituted him as "la perfecta imagen del jovencito colonizado" (*El beso* 299) [the perfect image of the colonized little lad].[1] This cinematic colonization preceded his birth (his mother supposedly went into labor during a screening of *Gaslight*), fixing the parameters of his alienation as a gay youth and simultaneously establishing the context for his eventual act of defiance as an openly gay writer and autobiographer. For the young Moix, however, cinema was not an instrument of social control (or "mass culture" as propounded by the Frankfurt School) but rather, as Michael Denning writes with regard to the term "popular

257

culture," "a contested terrain" (253). During his formative years Moix in fact both passively internalized and, through the prism of his burgeoning homoerotic desire, actively refocused the heterosexual (and heterosexist) lens of Hollywood cinema. Moix, like Puig, ultimately "retrieves and refashions works made for indoctrination and manipulation" (181), as Frances Wyers writes of the collaborative efforts of the readers of Puig's *El beso de la mujer araña*. Moix's autobiography thus offers insight into the interconnectedness of popular culture and gay self-representation, positing gay sexuality not as an essence but as a gaze through which the ostensibly natural constructions of heterosexual ideology are denaturalized and rendered queer.

Hollywood Cinema and the Queer Gaze

Gaze theory, as advanced by film scholars, has for the most part been grounded in gender (as opposed to the power structures of Foucauldian analysis) and articulated through the psychoanalytic paradigms of Freud and Lacan. In the 1975 landmark essay, "Visual Pleasure and Narrative Cinema," Laura Mulvey set the terms of debate for a whole generation of psychoanalytic film critics by arguing that Hollywood cinema aims precisely to satisfy the unconscious desire of heterosexual males. Though she allowed for female pleasure through identification with the male perspective, Mulvey remained focused on how cinematic narrative structures the experience of the spectator. More recent film theorists, while often retaining the psychoanalytic framework of Mulvey, have attempted to address lesbian and gay-male spectatorship through a reexamination and reconfiguration of spectator agency. Steven Drukman, for example, delineates a formula for a gay-male gaze whereby "the object of scopophilic pleasure is the man and the subject of ego-identification is . . . in constant flux between the woman and the man" (84–85).[2] Whereas such a distinction destabilizes the position of the viewer and loosens the gaze from the gridlock of monolithic gender identities, the object of desire remains fixed. In contrast with Drukman's "gay gaze," a "queer gaze" subverts the identities of not only the spectators but their objects as well. As Caroline Evans and Lorraine Gamman suggest, it even challenges the essentialist idea that "relations of looking are determined by the biological sex of the individual/s you choose to fornicate with, more than any other social relations (such as those associated with ethnic or class subjectivities)" (40).

In elucidating the theory of homographesis, Lee Edelman situates the discussion of the gaze and cinematic spectatorship in a historical context, noting the intriguing fact that modern homosexuality, as articulated in late nineteenth-century medical and legal treatises, and the technology capable of making cinema a major cultural force were both produced at the same moment in the development of industrial capitalism (200). The early discourses of homosexuality, like the patriarchal ideology operative in traditional, mainstream films, sought to affirm heterosexual masculinity as the universal male nature by representing the male homosexual as psychologically and socially deviant. Yet cinema as a medium implicitly questions the naturalness of heterosexual masculinity by reversing "the culturally determined meanings and relations of looking and being looked at" (Edelman 200). Through film, the male body is given as an object to be seen. What is more, masculinity is transformed from a supposed essence into an appearance to the extent that it is performed. Steven Cohan and Ina Rae Hark thus write:

> The male's seeming exemption from visual representation may work very hard to preserve the cultural fiction that masculinity is not a social construction, but American movies have always served as one of the primary sites through which the culture, in the process of promulgating that fiction, has also exposed its workings as a mythology. (3)

As Hark further clarifies, the spectacularization of the male is frequently coded in films as unnatural (152). Cinema nevertheless remains a site where the constructedness of gender identity is made explicit.

The notion of a natural masculinity, which simply is and need not appear in order to be, is destabilized through the act of representation fundamental to all the performing arts. This destabilization is intensified by a feminization as well as an overmasculinization of the male role. As Lacan contends, "In the human being, virile display itself appears as feminine" (85; also qtd. in Edelman 208). Gay and lesbian actors, moreover, frequently leave a mark on the cinematic product (Dyer, "Entertainment" 278); and the masculine posturing of such performers as James Dean in *Giant* is so highly stylized that it becomes a camp parody of masculinity (Dyer, "Rock" 28). Not only is masculine identity performed in popular cinema, but also when posited as an object of desire through the gaze of a gay-male viewer, the subject/object binary of the ostensibly masculine, heterosexual character and feminine, homosexual viewer is inverted. It is through cinema viewing that homoerotic desire is in fact often articulated. Edelman writes:

> The cinema affords the gay male spectator an opportunity to focus on the issue of bodiliness and ways of wearing the body precisely because the image on the screen is disembodied and fragmented. It allows, that is, for the intense scrutiny of the body as such—and from close up—without fear of being seen in the guilty enterprise of looking. (271, n. 21)

As Judith Mayne urges us to remember, however, this "'safe zone' in which homosexual as well as heterosexual desires can be fantasized and acted out" is not indicative of "an innate capacity to 'read against the grain,' but rather of the way in which desire and pleasure in the cinema may well function to problematize the categories of heterosexual versus homosexual" (97).

According to *El beso de Peter Pan*, the adolescent Ramón[3] experienced concrete, erotic desire while watching performances by Steve Reeves and other male actors. He furthermore attempted to emulate what he perceived to be gay-inclined males in such characters as Cal Trask, played by James Dean in *East of Eden* (141). After seeing this particular film, he openly declared his hatred for his father, whose ritual remark at Sunday dinner, "Preferiría tener un hijo muerto antes que maricón" (142) [I would rather have a dead son than a queer one], revealed to him the latent violence of heterosexual patriarchy.[4] Ironically, though not surprisingly, it was through the overtly heterosexist cinema of Hollywood, imposed on Spain by the cultural colonialism of the United States, that he managed to resist indigenous heterosexism. As Dyer points out, several major American actors of the 1950s, including James Dean, Montgomery Clift, and Sal Mineo, were not only "to some degree or other, gay" but also "fit a certain stereotype of the gay man—sad, neurotic, confused, . . . physically slight, with intense eyes and pretty faces" ("Rock" 28); and along with Tony Curtis, Tab Hunter, and Marlon Brando, they formed part of the gay iconography of the period.[5] In one piece of youthful writing, Ramón even imagines starring in a film as the son of Rock Hudson in a script written expressly for the two of them by John Steinbeck. He thereby establishes a symbolic connection with a real gay man through and in spite of his heterosexual representation on the screen. While this might be taken as an affirmation on his part of a transnational and transcultural gay-male identity, what his text demonstrates, as Mayne writes with regard to lesbian and gay spectatorship in general, is "how going to the movies *situates* gay/lesbian desire in specific ways" (166; emphasis mine).

Peter Pan Moix: Lost Boy and Fairy

Moix makes much of the fact that crucial events of his life, including the beginning of his mother's labor and his own first sexual encounter, actually took place in movie houses. He maintains that his personal identity (and specifically his sexuality) is inseparable from the images he saw projected onto the screen during childhood and adolescence. In analyzing the first volume of memoirs, *El cine de los sábados,* Paul Julian Smith thus writes that for Moix "desire must be projected before it can be felt (and projected onto the widest possible screen)" (48). He further clarifies that to the extent that Moix conceives of the self as fundamentally cinematic, and hence as flat, he avoids the probing of identity and of a tormented sexuality so typical of traditional gay autobiographers. It is Smith's contention that "if the limits of the cinema screen are identical with those of the world (if subjectivity is a purely aesthetic category), then there can remain no ground at all on which to take up an ethical position" (52). In *El beso de Peter Pan,* nevertheless, Moix begins to stake out such a space. He continues to view himself as a product of cinematic culture, yet he specifically re-represents the film narratives of his youth, the most significant of which is *Peter Pan.* In so doing he does not posit an inherent gay identity but contests the ideology of identity on which heterosexual hegemony is founded. *El beso de Peter Pan* is therefore a moral and political gesture. As the opening scene reveals, it is also a fairy tale of gay-male love.

Cuando Peter Pan me besó en una pérgola de los jardines de Nunca Jamás tuve miedo de que su amor fuese flor de un día y decidí apropiarme de su puñal para obligarle a recurrir a mí en momentos de peligro. Pero el héroe me aseguró que tal precaución era innecesaria porque nunca nos separaríamos. A guisa de confirmación nos hicimos unos cortes en las muñecas y mezclamos nuestra sangre y por eso conozco que por mis venas corre el polvillo de estrellas que sólo tienen los niños eternos. (29)

[When Peter Pan kissed me in a pergola of the gardens of Neverland, I was afraid that his love might be a one-day flower, and I decided to seize his dagger in order to force him to return to me in moments of danger. But the hero assured me that such a precaution was unnecessary because we would never be parted. By way of confirmation we made cuts in our wrists and mixed our blood, and therefore I know that through my veins flows the stardust that only eternal children have.]

In this passage Moix rescripts the conventional Peter Pan narrative. Whereas in most renditions Peter avoids his sexuality, preferring, for example, that Wendy play the part of little mother instead of mistress or wife, in *El beso de Peter Pan* he makes his initial appearance as a lover, and a gay one at that. In keeping with the masculinity of the Walt Disney character, he comes equipped with a weapon of violence.[6] At the outset Ramón is passive; the image of masculinity emerges from the screen and awakens him with a kiss. Yet when this Sleeping Beauty comes to life, he attempts to take control of his situation, going first for the knife—and years later for the autobiographer's pen. What he seeks is not only love but also safety from violence. To achieve it, he must appropriate the phallic weapon (and with it the heterosexist apparatus of Hollywood cinema) and convert it into an instrument of male reciprocity. Ramón and Peter consequently engage in an act of blood brotherhood, but rather than blood itself, it is the stardust of the dream factory that constitutes their commonality.[7] This ersatz essence binds Ramón to the dominant culture of Hollywood while instilling in him the illusion that he might fly away like a fairy. In re-representing the Peter Pan movie, Moix thus highlights its intrinsic fakeness, and in the process deessentializes both his own and Peter's sexuality through a camp performance whose ultimate aim is freedom.

Though Ramón occasionally engages in "camp behavior" by explicitly imitating the feminine, he is more apt to adopt what Moe Meyer calls a "camp-eye" (13) or what Dyer describes as a "camp attitude" (*The Matter of Images* 42) vis-à-vis the dominant culture. Dyer elucidates the concept of camp attitude:

There is a difference between camp behaviour and a camp attitude. The latter implies an ironic stance towards official or mainstream images or representations. Camp in this sense is profoundly denaturalizing. Far from expressing a sense of what is natural, it constantly draws attention to the artifices attendant on the construction of images of what is natural. (*The Matter of Images* 42)

Drukman nuances the point by arguing that camp is not the same as the gay gaze, but instead "a primary hue through which the gay gaze is filtered" (87). As such it is an instrument that helps recast the subject/object binary of heterosexual masculinity and lightens the dynamic of scopophilia altogether:

Like a rose-tinted pair of glasses kept in the breast pocket of the gay male spectator, camp is ever handy, but used more for cosmetic reasons than for clarity of vision. In other words, camp allows for a more seamless shifting (between object of scopophilia and subject of ego-identification) for the gay gaze. Rose-tinted lenses blur the rigid constraints of "straight" heterosexual narrative, making it easier on the eyes. (Drukman 88)

In camping *Peter Pan,* Moix actually seizes on ambiguities already present in the original text. Peter is in fact an androgynous character, usually played by a woman and distinguished by what Jacqueline Rose describes as a "swaggering effeminacy" (xiii). He first appeared in J. M. Barrie's *The Little White Bird,* which according to Rose is charged with the erotic desire of a man for a little boy. Subsequent theatric and cinematic productions of the Peter Pan narrative have endeavored "to wipe out the residual signs of the disturbance out of which it was produced" (Rose 5).[8] Yet an "unsettling of gender identities" (Rose xiii) remains, and in a 1991 version staged at London's Drill Hall, Peter is played as a lesbian in disguise (ix), and the famous call for audience participation—"clap your hands if you believe in fairies"—is cast in an explicitly queer context (xiii). Moix's reading of Peter draws specifically on the paradox of "a little boy who flies away because he does not want to grow up" (Rose 26), that is, a child who must abandon the protective sphere of the childhood nursery (and in the process steal other children) in order to remain an eternal child. As a youth, Ramón himself inhabits a hostile world (better a dead son than a queer one), and his escape involves an effort not only to retain his childhood identity but also to forge a refuge from an alien adult society. The space for this refuge is provided by Hollywood, but unlike the Neverland of Disney and of most previous adaptations of *Peter Pan,* his enchanted isle of lost boys and fairies is imagined as a distinctively homoerotic utopia.

As Dyer maintains, the Hollywood construction of utopia is clearly a problematic enterprise, since "to draw attention to the gap between what is and what could be, is, ideologically speaking, playing with fire" ("Entertainment" 279). Although most mainstream Hollywood productions try to work through the contradictions raised by utopian representations "in such a way as to 'manage' them, to make them seem to disappear[,] they don't always succeed" (279). This is clearly the case with Neverland. Through the use of temporal negation, Neverland is posited as a place without time.[9] It is dehistoricized, like the mythical child of the adult imagination or, for that matter, gay and lesbian culture in general under patriarchy. For Ramón, however, it is also the realm of a boy unlike any other boy, who excites his homoerotic desire while holding forth the promise of an idyllic space in which love between men is possible. For this reason his Neverland is not a static and timeless entity but the site on which sexuality is produced and queer praxis temporalized.

That notwithstanding, Ramón's first real sexual encounter, which occurs in the Cine Cervantes of Barcelona during a screening of the film version of *Aïda* with Sophia Loren, is altogether different from the imaginary affair with Peter Pan depicted at the outset of *El beso de Peter Pan.* As the scene of jealousy between Aïda and Amneris unfolds, Ramón feels a hand unzip his pants and begin to masturbate him. He continues to sit passively with his eyes riveted to the screen, and in the moment of climax witnesses a subliminal penetration as the victorious soldiers of Radamés, having returned from the Nubian campaign, make their triumphal entry into the city of Memphis. From his adult perspective, the cacophony of emotions experienced in the moment ("placer," "necesidad urgente de llorar," "voluntad de echar a correr, de liberarme y al mismo tiempo de sucumbir" [100] [pleasure, urgent need to cry, desire to start running, to free myself and at the same time to succumb]) are overshadowed and enveloped by the absurd artificiality of the film:

No podía pedirse mayor acumulación de falsedades: Sofía Loren embetunada para parecer princesa etíope y expresando sus cuitas con la voz prestada de la Tebaldi, mientras la Simionato cedía la suya a Lois Maxwell, disfrazada de hija de los faraones sin anunciar que, con los años, acabaría haciendo de permanente secretaria de James Bond. (101)

[One could not ask for a greater accumulation of falsities: Sophia Loren in black-face in order to look like an Ethiopian princess and telling her troubles with the dubbed voice of Tebaldi, while Simionato relinquished hers to Lois Maxwell, disguised as the daughter of the pharaohs, without revealing that over the years she would end up playing the permanent secretary of James Bond.]

The young Ramón nevertheless sees himself diametrically opposed to the stars of *Aïda*. Whereas they are endowed with glamorous bodies and grand passions, he is an awkward and unattractive adolescent being fondled by a middle-aged man. His drama, moreover, takes place in silence and darkness, and though he might turn to face the figure at his side, he remains transfixed by the overarching narrative of *Aïda*. As autobiographer, Moix exposes both the unnaturalness of the film and the incongruity of the events on the screen as well as in the darkened rows of a cinema called Cervantes: "Más adelante encontré divertido contar que la primera vez que me metieron mano fue en un cine con nombre de escritor manco" (101) [Later I found it amusing to tell that the first time someone put his hand in my pants was in a theater named after a one-handed writer]. In rereading the episode he hence conflates both "low" (popular cinematic) and "high" (operatic and, by implication, Cervantine) culture.[10] More important, he makes the public space of cultural representation (the movie house as opposed to the private sphere of the "closet") the locus of the expression of a marginalized sexuality. As an adolescent, Ramón attempts to escape the homoeroticism of the Cine Cervantes by running out the door of the theater. Eventually, however, he achieves a veritable "coming-out" when he learns to perform his sexuality as a "counteract" to the dominant representations he observes.

Although Ramón initially flees the world of gay sexuality, several gay males play a decisive role in his adolescent development. The most influential of these is Roberto.[11] As competing students in an acting school, they first see each other as rivals, but a friendship develops when they accidentally meet at a screening of *Ben-Hur*. Although Ramón remained alienated from his sexual partner in the Cine Cervantes, he and Roberto manage to dissociate themselves from the discourse of the film and establish a complicity as gay viewers. Roberto initiates the operation through ironic comments and gestures. Ramón responds with uncontrollable laughter:

A mi lado, Roberto tenía el rostro exacto de la inocencia. Su fingida gravedad acentuaba mi diversión mientras la altisonante música de Miklos Rosza proclamaba que nos hallábamos ante un momento sublime de la historia de la humanidad. Acababa de nacer el Mesías. Lástima que yo no paraba de reír. (*El beso* 338)

[At my side, Roberto had the perfect face of innocence. His feigned seriousness accentuated my amusement while the high-sounding music of Miklos Rosza proclaimed that we were witnessing a sublime moment in the history of humanity. The Messiah had just been born. Too bad I couldn't stop laughing.]

In this way Ramón mocks the aesthetics of the film as well as the values that it professes. He laughs at the representation of the Nativity, thereby rejecting the official religion of his culture and expressing delight at the "advent" of Roberto in his life and the "birth" of their friendship. Through an act of play, he and Roberto thus achieve a temporary space of their own within the domain of the movie house and in opposition to the representation on the screen.[12]

At the conclusion of *Ben-Hur,* as Roberto and Ramón leave the cinema, Roberto begins to question the ostensible heterosexuality of the characters, Ben-Hur and Messala, and argues that the two are actually bound by a homoerotic passion. Ramón is caught off guard by his argument and insists that the meaning of their relationship is to be found in the conflict between Jewish nationalism and Roman imperialism. Yet according to Roberto, they are lovers: "'Por eso le da a Mesala esa rabieta. . . . A nadie le da una rabieta tan gorda por cosas del nacionalismo ese. Tiene que haber una pasión'" (*El beso* 340). ["That's why Messala has that fit. . . . No one throws such a hissy fit because of that nationalism stuff. There has to be passion."] He further contends that essential scenes of love between Ben-Hur and Messala have been cut and that, as it stands, the film makes no sense.[13] In reading the film in this way, Roberto not only indulges in a homoerotic fantasy but also reveals an intuition of how heterosexuality and homosexuality are interconnected and how an affirmation of the former is predicated on and even requires an implicit affirmation of the latter.

Ramón and Roberto become inseparable friends, and Roberto eventually suggests that they imitate the relationship of Messala and Ben-Hur as he has interpreted it. Although Ramón is cognizant of his own homoerotic desire, he tries at this point to assert a heterosexual identity, and when Roberto announces that he will willingly adopt a feminine role in order to comply with Ramón's feigned machismo, the latter ascribes to him the negative stereotype of "las mariconas más detestadas" (*El beso* 380) [the most detested little faggots]. Ironically, whereas Roberto strives to rescript the heterosexist cinema of Hollywood and in so doing create a positive gay relationship, Ramón unwittingly plays the part of censor, restraining his homoerotic desire and rigorously enforcing the literal interpretation of the cinematic fictions that dominated his early years. Soon afterward, he admits to himself his desire for Roberto, but before he can win him back, Roberto takes a different lover. As a consequence, Ramón experiences a nervous collapse. His mother sends him to a psychiatrist, who treats him with disgust and contempt, as well as to a series of faith healers, all of whom fail to "cure" him of his homosexuality or relieve him of his psychological and physical malaise. Only gradually does he recover from the loss of Roberto as a lover (the two actually remain friends for years, until the latter's death from AIDS), realizing that his unhappiness resulted not from his sexual desire per se but from his inability to rescript his life in accordance with Roberto's queer reading of the movies.

As autobiographer, Moix in fact comes to blame Peter Pan for Ramón's failed relationship with Roberto (*El beso* 412). Though Peter continues to elicit Ramón's homoerotic desire, in the final analysis he holds Ramón captive, charming him with seductive images but obstructing reciprocity with real boys his age—"los niños que Peter Pan ató a la butaca de un cine de barrio para que se les llenasen los ojos con imágenes destinadas a no abandonarles jamás" (416) [the boys that Peter Pan tied to the seat of a neighborhood cinema in order to fill their eyes with images destined never to abandon them]. Peter haunts Ramón's every fantasy, appearing in the guises of lover, friend, and even progenitor, and in the end subsuming the entire second-hand repertoire of popular imagery that Ramón recycles in order to reproduce himself. In nightly rituals of masturbation, he conjures forth images of Peter, whose kiss leaves on his lips a wound "que sólo otros labios más maduros podrían cerrar" (390) [that only other more mature lips could heal]. As a result, his homoerotic desire short-circuits, and all that remains is the detritus of Hollywood. In a particularly graphic passage Moix depicts his childhood persona as "el último aborto de las brujas que, en un aquelarre insensato, jodieron con Peter Pan" (303) [the final abortion of the witches who, in a senseless witches' sabbath, screwed with Peter Pan]. The agent here is, of course, Ramón himself in the vortex of his fantasies. What is significant is that in each of his avatars, Peter Pan continues to reveal a homoeroticism representative of Ramón's sexuality. Moix finally suggests that Ramón and Peter are one and the same ("acaso [su] beso fuese el mío propio" [390] [perhaps his kiss was my very own]), and as imaginary gay clones Ramón carries the blood of Peter Pan not only in his veins but also "hasta el fondo de su ano" (454) [to the end of his anus]. Ultimately, however, "Peter Pan Moix" disappears when the young adult fully expresses his sexuality. For this reason the child eludes the mature life-writer as the impossible other of all autobiographical praxes.

Si(gh)ting Neverland

In the "Epílogo en Nunca Jamás" (Epilogue in Neverland) that follows the narration of adolescence, Moix orchestrates a complex scenario in which the adult autobiographer (Terenci) confronts the figures of Peter Pan, Ramón, and the alter ego that he has attempted to forge throughout his writing career. This last persona, El Niño del Invierno (the winter boy), first appears in the prologue to *El beso de Peter Pan,* when Terenci visits the site in Paris (the second floor of a bookshop inhabited by expatriate youths) where his final transition from childhood to adulthood occurred in what he describes as the glorious year of 1963. El Niño del Invierno is identified with winter to the extent that the youthful Moix sought to escape the fullness of life through his cultivation of the imaginary. Yet he is not the Ramón of the past, but is instead a product of the writer's imagination and, along with Terenci, a fictional representation of the writing self. Whereas El Niño del Invierno is implicitly present whenever Moix reflects on the past, Ramón remains inaccessible, not only because he has ceased to exist but also because his existence was ultimately articulated through a fantasy that the adult can no longer sustain.

Moix writes that one day while in Paris, Ramón attends a screening of the film *All about Eve* (which he describes as "el apasionamiento de los cinéfilos y el delirio de las mariquitas adeptas al culto de Bette" [*El beso* 471–72] [the passion of cinephiles and the rapture of the little fairies that followed the cult of Bette]), and as he is leaving the cinema of Chaillot, whom should he encounter but El Niño Eterno (the eternal boy), Peter Pan. The two initiate an animated discussion of the movie. Peter criticizes its aesthetics, and Ramón wonders if he has turned Marxist:

Sólo faltaría que se arrancara con un discurso sobre Brecht o Piscator. Pero no eran aquéllas sus intenciones. Por el contrario, estaba en onda de seductor. (472)

[The only thing left was for him to break into a speech on Brecht or Piscator. But those weren't his intentions. On the contrary, he was out to pick someone up.]

Ramón agrees to his overtures, if only to convince him that Mankiewicz is a great director. (As with Roberto, a homoerotic relationship is constructed in reference to a mainstream Hollywood film.) When they reach the bookshop where he sleeps, Ramón shows Peter an old edition of the work of J. M. Barrie, whom Peter labels "puritan" for having failed to tell the truth about his relationship with Captain Hook and the displeasure the latter felt when Peter chose to escape to Shangri-la with Kim of India. His was, in fact, a tale of homoerotic love, as Roberto knew to be the case with *Ben-Hur.* Before Peter and Ramón ascend to the upstairs room, the fairy tale is thus revealed as such.[14]

When they reach the next floor, however, an unexpected visitor awaits them: El Niño del Invierno. In a sense this is the moment when the narrative of the past is completed and childhood ends. Peter informs Ramón that El Niño del Invierno is not yet born, since some ten years will elapse before Moix begins to create him through his writing. Then Terenci himself enters, and he and Ramón gaze into each other's eyes. Again it is Peter who clarifies for Ramón the identity of the new visitor: "'Ese tío eres tú'" (*El beso* 475) ["That guy's you"]. Ramón is saddened by the vision of what he will become, and rather than merge with his image, he refuses the implicit narcissism of the adult autobiographer and pleads with Peter to take him away. Suddenly, "Peter Pan levantaba el vuelo, con el joven Ramón aferrado a sus muslos" (*El beso* 475) [Peter Pan took flight with the young Ramón clinging to his thighs], and the two fly off over the rooftops of Paris, carrying with them the entire cast of actors and characters that populated Moix's youth, including Michael Strogoff, the Little Lord, the body of Steve Reeves, and the face of Lillian Gish. Afterward, Terenci remains alone with El Niño del Invierno, pondering the past that he has managed to evoke throughout his writing but whose freshness and insolence ("el descaro primordial que fue el verdadero origen de la vida" [476] [the primordial effrontery that was the true origin of life]) he has failed to recover.

Moix's closing comments function as a gloss to the epilogue but leave unresolved the ambiguity of his quadripartite self-representation, which ultimately finds meaning in the spatial configuration of the scenario. Two interior spaces are posited—the cinema and the bookshop. These are the physical sites wherein culture is represented and where Ramón performs the primary activities (watching and reading) out of which his childhood self is constituted. Ramón is made by what he sees and reads, but through it (and specifically through the image of Peter Pan) he also attempts to make himself. The inevitable conflict (between Ramón and Peter and in the final analysis between Ramón and himself as both a passive and active agent of identity) is temporarily suspended when a third space is delineated in the intermediate zone separating the cinema from the bookshop.

In the opening sentence of the epilogue, Moix writes: "Ramón Moix Meseguer descubrió su juventud en uno de esos *quais* de París" (*El beso* 463) [Ramón Moix Meseguer discovered his youth on one of those quays of Paris]. This discovery occurs within neither the movie house nor the bookshop but outside, on the streets of the city and at the edge of the river. To accomplish it, Ramón must first "come out" of the cinema and assume his sexuality. (On previous occasions such a move involved a flight from his sexuality, as in the Cine Cervantes episode and even with Roberto.) While he and Peter make their way through the open space of the

city, they themselves begin to project their images: "Continuaron conver-
sando por las viejas calles, reflejándose en los charcos de la lluvia reciente"
(473) [They continued talking through the old streets, casting their reflection in the puddles from the recent rain]. Through the repetition of their
steps, moreover, they actually stretch space out ("paseando, paseando"
[473] [walking, walking]), increasing their distance from the cinema and
the bookshop and momentarily transforming their marginal social position into a point of centrality. When they arrive at the quay beneath the
bookshop, Peter "quiso detenerse junto al Sena para contemplar el reflejo
de Notre Dame en sus aguas cabrilleantes" (473) [wanted to stop next to
the Seine so as to contemplate the reflection of Notre Dame in its twin-
kling waters], but in response, "Ramón le dijo que la iglesia se veía mucho
mejor desde el sofá situado junto a la ventana" (473) [Ramón told him
that the church could be seen much better from the sofa next to the win-
dow]. Through this decisive statement, Ramón "picks up" Peter Pan.
Though as a result the child will presently be "picked up" and carried
away forever, Ramón clearly becomes the agent of seduction of the companion at his side. He then takes him, via the bookshelves on the first
floor, to the sofa in a corner of the upstairs room, which he claims as his
"absoluta propiedad" (473) [absolute property].

In reaching this goal, Ramón completes a long trajectory, not only from
the cinema of Chaillot through the streets of Paris, but from that more
distant movie house in Barcelona where his mother's labor first began,
across the years of childhood and adolescence. Now it is he who waves his
wand over Neverland, breathing new life into the lost boys and fairies of
the enchanted isle. Perhaps in this moment he makes love for the first time
to a real man, dispelling the child and his imaginary lover and living once
and for all the youth he was denied and that he denied himself.[15] Perhaps
he fancies himself free at last from the idols of the imagination and capable of forging his own destiny in the world. In either case, however, he remains bound to the text—whether as Ramón, el Niño del Invierno, Terenci,
or Peter Pan himself—and the seeming rupture that occurs in the epilogue between child and adult, text and life, and cinema and self (in spatial terms, the opening of an intermediate zone as the locus of freedom) is
itself a fiction. As Moix has earlier admitted, he is not the author of his
life, and in opposition to the realist illusion, he declares: "En literatura,
como en la vida, el protagonista nace, pero no se hace" (294) [In literature,
as in life, the protagonist is born, but he doesn't make himself].

Despite the dream of freedom, the autobiographical persona in all his
incarnations remains overdetermined by the discourse of film. At one
point death appears as the real through which the kaleidoscopic imagery
of life will eventually be darkened and consumed. But death is also articu-

lated through movie scripts. In meditating on the passing of family and friends, Moix evokes the quintessential representation of the Grim Reaper ("empuñando la guadaña y el reloj de arena" [*El beso* 444] [brandishing the scythe and the hourglass]) from the final scene of Bergman's *The Seventh Seal,* envisioning himself as a latter-day Blanche DuBois in the age of AIDS, dependent for solace on "la amabilidad de [sus] cadáveres" (439) [the kindness of his cadavers]. Even AIDS is a means of enacting a previously scripted identity, and in recalling the death of the poet Jaime Gil de Biedma, Moix goes so far as to transform the disease into a final gesture of camp performance: "Se iría al otro mundo reteniendo como letanía última la inmortal proclama: «He necesitado muchos hombres en mi vida para llamarme Shanghai Lili»" (439) [He would depart for the other world keeping as his ultimate litany the immortal proclamation: "I have needed many men in my life in order to call myself Shanghai Lili"]. He thus continues to transcribe the cinematic texts through which his world has been mediated. He does not create images (as Rose has demonstrated in the case of Peter Pan, it is unlikely that any individual actually does) but instead casts his gaze on the ready-made images of his cultural milieu. In so doing he refocuses them, constituting himself not as the hero (Peter Pan Moix after all disappears before the end of the performance) but as a lens through which the imaginary is reorganized and re-represented. *El beso de Peter Pan* is therefore bound to its culture, but, like little Ramón dangling from the legs of Peter Pan, the text deflects its course, revealing an alternate perspective on the world and in the process rendering the image of Moix's own experience as a gay adolescent in postwar, Francoist Spain.

Notes

This chapter previously appeared in *The Hispanic Homograph: Gay Self-Representation in Contemporary Spanish Autobiography,* 90–105. Copyright © 1997 by the Board of Trustees of the University of Illinois. Used with the permission of the University of Illinois Press.

1. *El cine de los sábados* covers the period of Moix's childhood, whereas *El beso de Peter Pan* focuses on his adolescent years up to the age of twenty-one. The first volume shares its title with a poem by the Spanish poet and autobiographer Antonio Martínez Sarrión (*El beso* 52). In the second, Moix not only evokes the title of *El beso de la mujer araña* (published in English as *Kiss of the Spider Woman*), but like Puig he uses the image of the kiss to elucidate the relationship of popular cinema to the gay-male spectator. In an introductory note to *El beso de Peter Pan,* Moix announces three future installments of his autobiography: *La edad de un sueño «pop»* (The age of a pop dream), *El misterio del amor* (The mystery of love),

and *Entrada de artistas* (Entrance of artists). All five will fall under the general title, *El Peso de la Paja* (The Weight of Straw), the name of the plaza in Barcelona where his childhood home was located.

All translations are mine.

2. The term "gay gaze" first appeared in "When the Gaze Is Gay," the title of a section of *Film Comment* devoted to the representation of gays and lesbians in Hollywood cinema.

3. Moix was in fact born "Ramón Moix Meseguer" and uses "Terenci Moix" as a pen name. I will follow his practice of referring to his childhood and adolescent personae as Ramón.

4. According to Vito Russo, the film *Rebel without a Cause* depicts a quasi homosexual in the character played by Sal Mineo (109). Moix found this film less appealing than *East of Eden* because of its violence. He indicates, moreover, that it was withheld for several years from the Spanish screen by censors who feared its deleterious effects on Spanish youth (*El beso* 141). In his case, however, the seemingly more innocent *East of Eden* was to have a far greater impact.

5. Moix discusses at some length the film *Tea and Sympathy*. When he saw it as an adolescent, he viewed the character Tom as gay and identified with him, only to feel betrayed when he was "cured" of his "affliction" through a sexual experience with an older woman (*El beso* 166–67). Vito Russo explains that the film did not explicitly deal with gay sexuality, since, given the restrictions of the Production Code, in effect at the time, homoeroticism could not be represented and hence did not officially exist. Rather, it portrays Tom as a "sissy," though, as Russo writes, "*Tea and Sympathy* . . . confirms what the creators and portrayers of sissies have always sought to deny, that the iconography for sissies and for sexual deviates is the same and that the one has come to *mean* the other" (113). Thus, though early Hollywood films were ostensibly silent with regard to gay sexuality, they nevertheless sought to contain and ultimately eliminate it.

6. It seems likely, given the description of Peter Pan in *El beso de Peter Pan,* that Moix first encountered the character in the Disney film. This version of the Peter Pan narrative in fact highlights his masculinity while presenting the female characters in an exaggeratedly sexist light. Tinkerbell, for example, is so jealous of Wendy that she attempts to kill her. The response of the mermaids is similar. Peter, in contrast, is uninterested in the love of women, and his primary passion remains his unexplained rivalry with Captain Hook.

7. For a discussion of blood brotherhood as it relates to gay sexuality in Christian European history, see Boswell.

8. As Rose clarifies, the concept of origins is particularly problematical in the case of Peter Pan. Although the character first appeared in *The Little White Bird,* a theatrical version of his adventures was produced twenty-four years before Barrie actually wrote the play. What is considered the children's classic hence depends on a number of writers, and according to Rose the subsequent reworkings of the text are as significant as the ostensible source.

9. The name of this utopia is ambiguous. In Spanish, Nunca Jamás suggests a place that once existed but that has forever ceased to be, that is, the land of "never-

more." In English three designations are used: Neverland, Never-Never Land, and Never-Never-Never Land. The first and the third signify timelessness. The second, through the use of the double negation, indicates a place that has always existed (never never = ever) but that has heretofore been invisible. Moix renders it visible precisely through his queer gaze.

10. The culture of Moix's youth was limited primarily to popular cinema, movie magazines, and comic books. As a sort of autodidact (when he was thirteen his parents decided that he should attend a trade school rather than pursue an academic degree in preparation for the university), he eventually acquired "high" literary and cinematic tastes. It is through his reading of "low culture," however, that he expresses his greatest creativity. This, in keeping with the analysis of John Fiske, might be explained at least in part by the very shallowness of low-culture texts: "Conventionality and superficiality not only keep production costs down, they also open the text up to productive reading strategies" (Fiske 109). A high-culture text, on the other hand, often requires readers to decipher rather than generate meanings and can even work "to exclude those who have not the cultural competence [the undereducated Ramón] (or the motivation) to decode it on its own terms" (109).

11. Moix sees his uncle Cornelio (a pseudonym surely attributed to him by Ramón in an effort to equate him with the actor Cornel Wilde) and his lover Alberto as positive, gay role models. Of his childhood friends, El Niño Rico (the rich boy) was significant insofar as he was the first to ascribe to Ramón the label "maricón" when the latter tentatively expressed his affection for him. The word fell on Ramón like a curse and a mark of shame, and it is with irony and bitterness that Moix describes in *El cine de los sábados* his surprise upon discovering years later that El Niño Rico was himself actually gay.

12. Elsewhere, Moix insists: "YO NO HABÍA TENIDO INFANCIA" (*El cine* 305) [I never had a childhood]. Nevertheless, in this and other moments with Roberto he reveals the spontaneity and exhilaration of a child, engaging in a playful behavior that is not an apprenticeship for adulthood but an affirmation of freedom and an act of rebellion. His conception of play is in fact suggestive of Nietzsche's "gay science" and Sartre's rejection of the "spirit of seriousness."

13. Gore Vidal scripted and Willy Wyler directed this version of *Ben-Hur*. In his memoirs, Vidal explains at some length how he chose to read the original text as a tale of homoerotic love and how this might have negatively affected Wyler's career (301–7). His comments to Wyler and Sam Zimbalist regarding the relationship of Ben-Hur and Messala were in fact surprisingly similar to those of Roberto to Ramón. Vidal recalls: "I . . . told them that Ben Hur and Messala had been boyhood lovers. But Ben Hur, under the fierce Palestinian sun and its jealous god, has turned straight as a die while Messala, the decadent gentile, had remained in love with Ben and wanted to take up where they had left off" (304). (Russo also cites this conversation [76].) Despite significant cultural differences, Vidal and Roberto thus queer the narrative in the same way.

14. This magical space is reminiscent of the rooms of both Melquíades in *Cien años de soledad* (published in English as *One Hundred Years of Solitude*) and Carmen Martín Gaite in *El cuarto de atrás* (published in English as *The Back Room*),

in that it is posited as the site wherein the text is generated. It also evokes the room in the pawnbroker's shop in *Fanny and Alexander* where the young Bergman discovers his own alter ego and the source of his creative genius.

15. It should be noted that Ramón had several sexual experiences during adolescence, but like the encounter in the Cine Cervantes, none was particularly fulfilling.

Works Cited

Barrie, J. M. *The Little White Bird.* London: Hodder and Stoughton, 1902.

Boswell, John. *Same-Sex Unions in Premodern Europe.* New York: Villard, 1994.

Cohan, Steven, and Ina Rae Hark. Introduction. *Screening the Male: Exploring Masculinities in Hollywood Cinema.* Ed. Steven Cohan and Ina Rae Hark. New York: Routledge, 1993. 1–8.

Denning, Michael. "The End of Mass Culture." *Modernity and Mass Culture.* Ed. James Naremore and Patrick Brantlinger. Bloomington: Indiana UP, 1991. 253–68.

Drukman, Steven. "The Gay Gaze, or Why I Want My MTV." *A Queer Romance: Lesbians, Gay Men and Popular Culture.* Ed. Paul Burston and Colin Richardson. New York: Routledge, 1995. 81–95.

Dyer, Richard. "Entertainment and Utopia." *The Cultural Studies Reader.* Ed. Simon During. New York: Routledge, 1993. 271–83.

Dyer, Richard. *The Matter of Images: Essays on Representations.* New York: Routledge, 1993.

Dyer, Richard. "Rock—the Last Guy You'd Have Figured?" *You Tarzan: Masculinity, Movies and Men.* Ed. Pat Kirkham and Janet Thumim. New York: St. Martin's, 1993. 27–34.

Edelman, Lee. *Homographesis: Essays in Gay Literary and Cultural Theory.* New York: Routledge, 1994.

Evans, Caroline, and Lorraine Gamman. "The Gaze Revisited, or Reviewing Queer Viewing." *A Queer Romance: Lesbians, Gay Men and Popular Culture.* Ed. Paul Burston and Colin Richardson. New York: Routledge, 1995. 13–56.

Fiske, John. "Popular Discrimination." *Modernity and Mass Culture.* Ed. James Naremore and Patrick Brantlinger. Bloomington: Indiana UP, 1991. 103–16.

García Márquez, Gabriel. *Cien años de soledad.* Buenos Aires: Sudamericana, 1967.

Hark, Ina Rae. "Animals or Romans: Looking at Masculinity in *Spartacus.*" *Screening the Male: Exploring Masculinities in Hollywood Cinema.* Ed. Steven Cohan and Ina Rae Hark. New York: Routledge, 1993. 151–72.

Lacan, Jacques. "The Meaning of the Phallus." *Feminine Sexuality: Jacques Lacan and the école freudienne.* Ed. Juliet Mitchell and Jacqueline Rose. Trans. Jacqueline Rose. New York: Norton, 1982. 74–85.

Martín Gaite, Carmen. *El cuarto de atrás.* Barcelona: Destino, 1978.

Martínez Sarrión, Antonio. *El centro inaccesible (Poesía 1967–1980).* Prologue by Jenaro Talens. Madrid: Hiperión, 1981.

Mayne, Judith. *Cinema and Spectatorship.* New York: Routledge, 1993.

Meyer, Moe. "Introduction: Reclaiming the Discourse of Camp." *The Politics and Poetics of Camp.* Ed. Moe Meyer. New York: Routledge, 1994. 1–22.

Moix, Terenci. *El beso de Peter Pan.* Vol. 2 of *El Peso de la Paja: Memorias.* Barcelona: Plaza y Janés, 1993.

Moix, Terenci. *El cine de los sábados.* Vol. 1 of *El Peso de la Paja: Memorias.* Barcelona: Plaza y Janés, 1990.

Mulvey, Laura. "Visual Pleasure and Narrative Cinema." *Screen* 16.3 (1975): 6–18.

Puig, Manuel. *El beso de la mujer araña.* Barcelona: Seix Barral, 1976.

Rose, Jacqueline. *The Case of Peter Pan or the Impossibility of Children's Fiction.* Philadelphia: U of Pennsylvania P, 1992.

Russo, Vito. *The Celluloid Closet: Homosexuality in the Movies.* New York: Harper and Row, 1981.

Smith, Paul Julian. *Laws of Desire: Questions of Homosexuality in Spanish Writing and Film 1960–1990.* Oxford: Clarendon, 1992.

Vidal, Gore. *Palimpsest: A Memoir.* New York: Random House, 1995.

"When the Gaze Is Gay." Spec. section in *Film Comment* 22.2 (1986): 31–50.

Wyers (Weber), Frances. "Manuel Puig at the Movies." *Hispanic Review* 49.2 (1981): 163–81.

12

Lesbianism, Female Homosociality, and the Maternal Imaginary in Montserrat Roig's *L'hora violeta*

Emilie L. Bergmann

Toward the end of Montserrat Roig's *El temps de les cireres* (1977), the protagonist Natàlia discovers upon returning from exile that her father has been dressing in women's clothes since the death of her mother. Her widowed aunt Patrícia Miralpeix spends her evenings drinking and retelling the discovery of her husband's lifelong homosexual relationship. The only confidante with whom Patrícia can share her disappointment is the Andalusian maid. Finally, Natàlia's sister-in-law Sílvia hosts a Tupperware party that turns into a lesbian orgy. The narrative perspective on masculine transvestism and homosexuality in *El temps de les cireres* is sympathetic. Natàlia understands that her father has fetishized the feminine only because he loved her mother so completely, and it is the compulsory heterosexuality and marriage dictated by the social conservatism of the Catalan bourgeoisie that caused her aunt Patrícia's unhappiness.

Lesbianism in *El temps de les cireres* is quite another matter. It is represented as a grotesque parody of heterosexuality, in which bourgeois women act out the sadomasochistic roles and abjection of female sexuality that they learned in childhood from the nuns in Catholic schools during the Franco dictatorship. Natàlia is not a guest at Sílvia's party—she is an unmarried, sexually liberated professional photographer with better things to do with her time—but she and her friend Norma take up the question of lesbianism as a key feminist issue in *L'hora violeta* (1980), the next novel in Roig's trilogy. Here, lesbianism is represented as an alternative that only militant separatists could enjoy or as a marginalized occasion for physical pleasure that offers no escape from heterosexist patterns of objectification. None of Roig's main characters has a sexual relationship with another woman, although Natàlia recalls that her lover Jordi once said, half joking, that she is in love with Norma (72), and this recollection brings with it Natàlia's disapproving memory of an "adolescent" attachment between Norma and her friend Mar. Natàlia, addressing her thoughts to Jordi, distances herself from "that kind of friendship":

"Quan la Norma va trobar la Mar semblava com si hagués recuperat l'adolescència. I ja saps, Jordi, que jo no comparteixo aquesta mena d'amistats. Ella ho deu intuir perquè fuig de mi. La Norma i la Mar es van tallar els cabells de la mateixa manera, estil patge, i anaven vestides igual. Dues gotes d'aigua. La veritat és que no sé on començava la Norma i on acabava la Mar. Feien petits xiscles pel carrer, anaven agafades de la mà com dues col·legiales." (72)

["When Norma met Mar it seemed as if she had returned to adolescence. And you already know, Jordi, that I don't get involved in that kind of friendship. She must have guessed that because she avoided me. Norma and Mar cut their hair the same way, in a pageboy, and dressed exactly alike. Two peas in a pod. The truth is that I don't know where Norma began and Mar stopped. They let out little shrieks as they walked down the street, they walked hand in hand like two schoolgirls."][1]

It is easy to see in this disavowal an example of what Patricia Juliana Smith terms "lesbian panic," the "disruptive action or reaction that occurs when a character—or conceivably, an author—is either unable or unwilling to confront or reveal her own lesbianism or lesbian desire." It might be more appropriate, however, to use the term "anxiety" rather than Smith's "panic," since Natàlia does not engage in the "emotional or physical harm to herself or others" typical of characters in novels that use lesbian panic as a narrative strategy (Smith, "And I Wondered" 568). Natàlia's disavowal notwithstanding, her exploration of relationships between women in *L'hora violeta* threatens to displace heterosexual authority as it foregrounds feminine sexuality in the narrative. Smith cites Rachel Blau DuPlessis's analysis of alternatives to the traditional romance plot in novels by modernist women writers and challenges to "the individual quest and couple formation" (DuPlessis xi, qtd. in Smith, "And I Wondered" 576–77). Marilyn Farwell, in *Heterosexual Plots and Lesbian Narratives* explores definitions of "lesbian texts" in terms of two generational poles. "Traditional lesbian theory validates traditional narrative structures like quest stories and detective fiction as potentially lesbian; postmodernist theory valorizes only the nonlinear disruption of the 'master plot'" (12). My analysis of the

interweaving of voices throughout Roig's trilogy and the dialogical structures of *L'hora violeta* in particular views them as alternatives to the "individual quest," while the depiction of the women characters' relationships
with men and with each other contributes to a destabilization of the heterosexual couple as a basis for female identity.[2]

Throughout the novel, Roig's characters struggle with their heterosexual
desire, their fears, their dependency, and their autonomy in feminist terms.
Roig's approach to "lesbianism" is not as a universal of feminine sexuality
but as the politicized discourse of sexuality in the 1970s that she witnessed,
and she inscribes it in the novel's historical perspective on love, friendship,
femininity, masculinity, and the mother–daughter relationship.[3] The characters struggle to come to terms with both lesbian and mother–daughter
relationships, and both are represented as impossibly elusive. What is significant in this novel of the *transición* is Roig's resistance to what Teresa
de Lauretis calls "the seductions of lesbianism," that is, the confusion of
lesbian sexuality and desire with the maternal imaginary, a confusion that
leads to the "assimilation of feminism to lesbianism," which de Lauretis
views as a "liability" of the paternal-phallocentric structure of Kristeva's
thought (184).[4] In "Freud's Mnemonic Screen Memories and Feminist
Nostalgia," an essay first published in 1987, Mary Jacobus questions what
she calls the "implicit psychic utopianism" underlying the feminist concept of the pre-Oedipal, prelinguistic relationship with the body of the
mother as a universal "memory." Jacobus critiques feminist uses of the
myth of Persephone as an act of "re-membering," that is, reconstituting
the physical and psychic wholeness of the mother–daughter bond (16).[5]
As central as the theme of memory is in Roig's fiction, and as central as
the quest for the maternal is to her characters in *L'hora violeta,* these characters do not endorse this interpretation. Instead, they come to recognize
that wholeness will not be achieved through a fantasized utopian harmony
among generations of women but through struggle, dialogue, difference,
and loss.

This deconstruction of a feminist myth in Jacobus's theoretical essay
has a great deal to do with Montserrat Roig's engagement with French
feminism of the late 1970s in *L'hora violeta.* The plot of *L'hora violeta*
centers on the quest for the mother. But the mother is not sought by the
daughter in order to reunite with her as nurturer, instead, the daughter's
quest is to reconstitute her mother's pre–Civil War friendship with a politically and sexually daring young woman and to understand the relationships among women in her own time. What Roig depicts is the historically
situated discourse of political lesbianism in French and Catalan feminist
intellectual circles in the late 1970s.[6] The heterosexual female characters'

personal response to this theoretical discourse is inextricable from their conflicted relationships with men and their ambivalent feelings toward their mothers.

Roig's trilogy focuses on three generations of women in the fictional Ventura, Miralpeix, and Claret families and places women's lives at the center of a historical process. These novels narrate the awakening of feminist consciousness in the political context of three key moments in Catalan history: the political upheavals at the turn of the century, the Second Republic and the Civil War, and political organizing on the Left against the Franco dictatorship and during the transition to democracy in the 1960s and 1970s. The first two novels, *Ramona, adéu* (1972) and *El temps de les cireres,* are haunted by the lack of communication between sexually liberated women of the late 1960s and 1970s and their mothers, whose adulthood was shaped by the liberation of the Second Republic, the Civil War, and postwar repression.[7] *L'hora violeta* is also an attempt to bridge that generation gap through fiction, but there are significant differences the quest is cast as metafiction, involving not only "La novel·la de l'hora violeta," written by one character at the request of another, but also interior monologue, diaries, letters, and fragments of dialogue remembered differently by each character. The three protagonists, who also provide first- and third-person narratives, are three women unconnected by family ties and roughly of the same generation: Natàlia, Norma, and Agnès. All three are university-educated and hold jobs outside the home. Natàlia is a professional photographer, Norma is a journalist, and Agnès works in child care. Although all three have slept with the same man, Jordi, a Communist Party leader, Roig leaves undeveloped the implicit homosocial triangulation. Natàlia and Norma, the characters most often in dialogue, do not regard each other as rivals for Jordi. A third-person narrative of Agnès's hatred for Natàlia keeps the most powerful rivalry at a distance. Jordi is in the process of breaking up with Natàlia after a six-year relationship and is about to return to Agnès, the mother of his two sons, if only because, as Natàlia suggests in her letter to Norma, Agnès will be more complacent about the relationship he is developing with another, younger woman. A gratifying scene in the final section of the novel, "L'hora oberta," reveals that in Jordi's absence the long-suffering Agnès has learned to do without him, rejecting the role of Penelope (Bellver, "Montserrat Roig and the Penelope Syndrome"; Davies 61–62, 64). Norma, whose close relationship with Natàlia is key to the structure of the novel, is involved with a married Englishman, Alfred, and is in the process of a separation from her husband, Ferrán, another Communist Party member. All three express their (hetero)sexual desires openly, but their newly liberated sexuality is always contextualized in the political history and gender politics of the *transición.*

Two of the women characters are not only daughters but also mothers. The focus, however, is on Agnès's relationship with her two young sons; Norma's son plays a minor role as interlocutor as she tells a story, and her daughter is hardly mentioned.[8]

Profound ambivalence shapes not only the daughter's perception of the mother's body in *L'hora violeta* but also the mother's perception of her own body as sensual, perverse, and abjected. Agnès enjoys allowing her two young sons to treat her body as a plaything, with little Adriá, already able to speak, sucking at her nipples, which he describes as strawberry candies. She is aware that their father, Jordi, doesn't approve, but he only visits on weekends. These mornings with her sons are the only times she experiences her body as pleasurable, in contrast with her recurrent nightmares about snakes and her sensations of grittiness on her skin and cottony dryness in her mouth. There is, however, another disconcerting image that is emblematic of the abjection of the feminine in the first, long section of the novel, "L'hora perduda." In the third-person narratives of Agnès's relationship and breakup with Jordi (with whom Natàlia is now breaking up), she describes his reaction to an intriguing design on her pink dress. "I es va posar el vestit rosa per tot això, perquè sabia que, a ell, li agradava el vestit que fa una flor menuda, com de satalia. Mira, feia en Jordi, si t'hi acostes no són roses sinó formigues" (34). [She put on the pink dress because she knew he liked it, the dress with the design of tiny flowers, like wild roses. "Look," said Jordi, "if you get close they're not roses but ants."] Agnès's recurring memory of this image signals a profound ambivalence regarding both love and motherhood. Through the association of this emblem with Agnès, the experience of idyllic first impression and then horror upon closer inspection is distanced from the mother who is at the center of this novel: Natàlia's mother, Judit, who inspires both pity and horror, but also a memory of great sensual power.

The central project of *L'hora violeta* is Natàlia's challenge to her friend Norma, not only a journalist but also a novelist and historian, to write about the relationship between two women of the previous generation: her mother, Judit, and her mother's friend Kati. Norma remembers her telephone conversation with Natàlia: "'M'agradaria que escribissis alguna cosa sobre la mamá y la Kati. De la mateixa manera que ho faries sobre tu i sobre mi'" (11). ["I'd like you to write something about my mother and Kati. The same way that you'd write about you and me."] Later, in the letter that accompanies her mother's diaries, Natàlia adds another, heterosexual, relationship to deflect attention from the homosocial parallel established on the first page of the novel. Thinking of Judit and Kati, and—she adds as if in an obligatory heterosexual afterthought—Kati and Patrick, Natàlia says she thinks of herself and Norma (18).

In the first long section of the novel, titled "L'hora perduda" (The lost hour), in which the narrative alternates between Natàlia and Agnès, Natàlia reminisces, writing a letter she may or may not send to her lover, Jordi, with whom she is in the process of breaking up. For Jordi, Natàlia provides another view of the writing project she has given Norma. She distinguishes the work of imagination, projection, and memory, which characterize what she terms "writing," from the chronological, factual discourse of history. "El temps dins de la memòria no té res a veure amb el temps de la història. . . . L'ordre de la imaginació s'escapa a totes les dades, a tots els fets. Aquesta és la revenja de la literatura contra la Història" (89). [Time within memory has nothing to do with historical time. . . . The order of the imagination escapes all data, all facts. This is the revenge of literature against History.] Here in "L'hora perduda," Natàlia tells Jordi that she wants Norma to write as a "cronista" [historian], not as an "escriptora" [novelist], but confesses that she has perversely withheld some of the pieces of the puzzle. She wants to keep the "narració íntima," the "imaginació" to herself. Precisely what that intimate history composed by memory and imagination may be, and why it and not "History" requires those missing pieces, is not made explicit.

In the letter to Norma that accompanies her notes and Judit's diaries, Natàlia frames her request somewhat differently. She is handing the work of fiction over to her friend because she is only a photographer, although her letter to Jordi belies this claim. Natàlia also expresses fear that her "implication" in the story—she mentions her jealousy that a Judit existed who was not her mother—might incline her to "lie" about Judit and Kati. But she makes two affirmations in this epistolary frame of the novel that are later qualified and blurred in the following four sections. First, she says she believes that her mother and Kati loved each other. "Es van fer mentre es van estimar, n'estic segura. I, quan es trencà la relació per la mort de la Kati, va perdre un bon tros d'ella mateixa" (15). [They existed while they loved each other, of that I am certain. And when the relationship was broken off by Kati's death [by suicide], Judit lost a part of herself.][9] Equally important, in the course of three paragraphs, Natàlia widens her focus from the intimate portrait of two women to the view of a busy space populated by husbands, children, and male lovers. From the close-up of Judit and Kati's love, imagined as intense and eternal, Natàlia draws back to include Kati's brief, passionate relationship with her lover Patrick, but she contrasts the mutuality of Judit and Kati's love with the love her father, Joan Miralpeix, felt for his wife, a love that she cannot quite imagine her mother could have reciprocated (18).

Later in the novel, however, Norma recalls how Natàlia refused to impose her interpretation, although it was clear that she has already thought about the possible relationships between Judit and her daring, liberated friend Kati, whom she mourned throughout her life after Kati's suicide in 1942:

La Norma li demanava dades de la relació entre la Judit i la Kati. Era amor? Era amistad? Va ser la síntesi de totes dues coses?
  —Això és cosa teva —responia la Natàlia
  —Però, com puc inventar-me una relació així si no n'he viscuda cap de semblant?
  —És que has de viure tot el que escrius? —feia la Natàlia—. Vols ser tots els personatges alhora? (200)

[Norma asked her for information about the relationship between Judit and Kati. Was it love? Was it friendship? Was it a synthesis of both?
  "It's up to you," answered Natàlia
  "But, how can I invent such a relationship if I've never experienced anything like it?"
  "Do you have to experience everything you write about?" said Natàlia. "Do you want to be all the characters at once?"]

There is another way to read this passage, not as a dialogue about Norma's writing project, but as a dialogue about Roig's project of writing about women's lives and relationships. How can Roig, or Norma, write about love between women if she's never experienced it? But hasn't she already written about other experiences of generations of women and men far more distinct from her own? Norma, like Roig herself in the late 1970s, has just finished a historical study of Catalan prisoners in Nazi concentration camps,[10] and her awareness of what cannot be written or known by those who did not witness it has not discouraged Norma from writing.

Roig's characters may claim never to have experienced love between women, whether a passionate female friendship or a full-blooded lesbian relationship, but Roig and her readers already had ample opportunity to read about fictional lesbian relationships. *L'hora violeta* appeared only two years after two landmark lesbian narratives: Esther Tusquets's *El mismo mar de todos los veranos* (The same sea every summer, 1978) and Carme Riera's short story "Te deix, amor, la mar com a penyora" (I leave you, love, the sea as a token, 1975). There are significant differences between the women characters' relationships in Roig's novel on one hand and those in Tusquets's and Riera's fictions on the other, apart from the obvious physicality of the homoeroticism in the latter two. The relationships in these two works are between women teachers and their students, one in university and the other in high school, and are thus marked by significant inequalities of age and social position. Both intergenerational relationships are framed in terms of a utopian reunion with the body of the mother, both literally and in the figure of the sea, a framing of the relationship that dooms it on the terra firma of adult realities. Tusquets associates the lesbian relationship with childhood fantasies, the myth of Peter Pan, and the protagonist's unsatisfied need for a nurturing mother. When "Wendy" grows up, she leaves homosexuality behind and returns to the normative, hypocritical marriage required by her social milieu. Roig's three main characters, Norma, Natàlia, and Agnès, are adult women, and the two women whose prewar relationship has captured Natàlia's imagination, Judit and Kati, are equals. Unlike the lesbian lovers in Tusquets's and Riera's narratives, Roig's female characters are never immersed in the feminine to the exclusion of struggles with the men in their lives.

In contrast with the lesbian relationships that shape the narrative in Tusquets's *El mismo mar* and Riera's story "Te deix, amor, la mar com a penyora," albeit encoded in the latter to be revealed as a lesson in reading against the heterosexual grain, the confrontations with lesbianism throughout the text of *L'hora violeta* exclude it as a possibility for the characters in the novel. In discussing the encodings of lesbianism written in "invisible ink" in Riera's story "Te deix, amor," Brad Epps describes lesbianism in Hispanic letters as "all but lost ghostwritten, as it were, in invisible ink. Its appearance is almost always a pledge to disappearance, its presence, an artful testimony to its absence" (317). Epps cites Elizabeth Meese: "'Lesbian' is a word written in invisible ink, readable when held up to a flame and self-consuming. . . . An unwriting goes on as quickly as the inscription takes (its) place" (Meese 18, qtd. in Epps 338). This "unwriting" is also an accurate characterization of the self-consuming inscriptions of lesbianism throughout the text of *L'hora violeta,* although the erasure is accomplished through different strategies.

The writing project at the center of *L'hora violeta* is motivated by the fantasy of the mother's voice and also by the desire to capture in writing a relationship that Natàlia and Norma imagine as perfect: all-consuming, eternal, and doomed by its wartime circumstances. Norma's aspiration to put the pieces back together, an aspiration that is radically reconceptualized by the end of the novel, evokes the "oneness of mother and child" figured in Julia Kristeva's theory of the *chora.*[11] Natàlia's relationship with Judit, on the other hand, was far from perfect: she hated her mute, paralyzed mother during her life and did not return from exile in England when Judit died. In "The Fantasy of the Maternal Voice," Kaja Silverman makes a key observation about Kristeva's representation of the child's linguistic "mastery" as a "victory" over the mother (Kristeva, "Place Names" 289). "The child's discursive exteriority—its emergence from the maternal enclosure—can be established only by placing the mother herself inside that enclosure, by relegating her to the interior of the *chora,* or—

what is the same thing—by stripping her of all linguistic capabilities" (Silverman 105). This is precisely what Roig did with Natàlia's mother, Judit, in *El temps de les cireres,* and she takes up this mother–daughter plot again in *L'hora violeta.* In her youth Judit was a gifted pianist trained for the concert stage, but she was defeated by the weakness of her own body and the perceived necessity of making a choice between career and family for the sake of her health. As the outcome of the war became all too evident, Kati proposed that she and Judit run away together, but Judit, lacking Kati's appetite for adventure, chose to stay with her children where her husband Joan would be able to find them. Within three years, Kati committed suicide. Like the Catalan bourgeoisie in a figurative sense under the Franco dictatorship, Judit literally became paralyzed and mute during the last decade of her life.

Kati had encouraged Judit's dreams of composing her own music: "alguna melodia nova, que ningú no hagués sentit mai" (134) [a new melody, that no one would have ever heard before] *L'hora violeta,* as well as Roig's last two novels, *L'òpera quotidiana* and *La veu melodiosa* with the musical references in their titles, might be read as versions of that music, a fiction "available to the writing consciousness not through memory but through [the daughter's] fantasy and projection," as Marianne Hirsch describes it in her study of the "mother–daughter plot" (138). Hirsch finds that the mother "may have to be eliminated as subject and maintained in the position of object of a 'sustained quest'" that is pursued by the daughter "only with extreme ambivalence toward the mother" (138). Natàlia hated Judit while she was alive, only now that she has been dead for several years is it possible to pursue, by proxy, the unanswered questions of her life.

Although she entrusts her friend Norma with the delicate task of recovering or creating the fantasy and projection of her mother's relationship with Kati, Natàlia's conflicted feelings of admiration and distrust toward Norma surface in the long letter in which she directs her thoughts to Jordi in "L'hora perduda." Norma is almost ten years younger, and Natàlia envies her energy and self-confidence. She criticizes her and associates her with the powerful archetypal figure of the witch. Not only does Roig's character share a name with the heroine of Bellini's opera *Norma,* alone in her rural retreat, she experiences a welcome catharsis, suggestive of autoeroticism, as she listens to a version sung by a great Catalan soprano: "Posà un disc, la *Norma* de Bellini, sota la dutxa seguia la *Casta Diva* cantada per la Montserrat Caballé. Quan de temps feia que no plorava sota la dutxa?" (230). [She put on a record, Bellini's *Norma,* in the shower she listened to "Casta diva" sung by Montserrat Caballé. How long had it been since she'd cried in the shower?][12]

It is no coincidence that *Norma* is one of the very rare operas that involve a passionate commitment between women "surpassing the love of men" while it also makes possible Norma's redemptive sacrifice as an "icon of [national] resistance" (Smith, "O Patria Mia" 100; see also Wood 38–39). In Bellini's operatic re-creation of history, Norma is a Druid priestess of the Gauls, oppressed by their Roman overlords. Catherine Clément calls the setting "the Moon Age" and cites Michelet's *La sorcière* to characterize the "fierce, feminine resistances" represented by Norma's pagan religious power (101–2).[13] The like-voice duet "Mira O Norma" is a declaration of the young priestess Adalgisa's eternal loyalty to chief priestess Norma and her indifference to the Roman proconsul, who was preparing to leave Norma and take Adalgisa away with him. Adalgisa proposes that she and Norma run away and live together in hiding, not unlike Kati begging her friend Judit to accompany her into exile to escape the repressive dictatorship that will destroy them both. Bellini's Norma surprises the faithless Roman proconsul by sacrificing herself rather than revealing Adalgisa's disloyalty to her people. In addition to this striking representation of female friendship, Bellini uses an ancient people's struggle against Rome to dramatize the nineteenth-century Italian project of nation-building (Smith, "O Patria Mia" 98), to which Roig thus alludes in a context of Catalonian autonomy in the period of the *transición*. *L'hora violeta,* published in Catalan in 1980, represents the struggles of a histori-cal moment in Catalonian feminism, inextricable from the political struggles of the Left as it emerged from the dictatorship.

In addition to the allusion to Bellini's *Norma* and Norma's writing proj-ect about relationships between women, lesbian and "queer" sexualities are encoded in the title and the epigraph from T. S. Eliot's *Waste Land,* quoted in English. The prophetic and hermaphroditic figure of Tiresias points to the activity of writing in the in-between of gender and to the writing of history, characterized as much by blindness as by insight:

> At the violet hour, when the eyes and back
> Turn upward from the desk, when the human engine waits
> Like a taxi throbbing waiting,
> I, Tiresias, though blind, throbbing between two lives,
> Old man with wrinkled female breasts, can see
> At the violet hour . . .
>
> (lines 215–20)

Much in the novel, including the relationship of the epigraph with the narrative, however, is as elusive as the moment that distinguishes day from night.

The discourse of the novel deploys powerful encodings of love between women, vacillating between names for the relationship between Judit and

Kati: love? friendship? Lesbianism is allowed to speak its name directly several times in the novel, but not between the main characters. In each case it is associated with the marginal: lesbians and the women who suggest lesbianism as a possibility are foreign or they are militant separatists, Natàlia has a homoerotic experience only in a dream, and Norma has sex with a woman and her male lover after smoking marijuana. Natàlia recalls a conversation in which Norma cited Doris Lessing as having said that women are either lesbians or embittered and resentful. She imagines an epitaph for struggling heterosexual feminists like Natàlia and herself: "Aquí jau una ressentida i amargada que no va gosar de ser lesbiana" (50) [Here lies a resentful, embittered woman who didn't have the courage to be a lesbian].[14] The conversation ends with Norma's assertion that she values friendship over health, happiness, and love.

Natàlia recalls a dinner at the home of a Catalan publisher honoring a French writer of children's literature. The French writer, the publisher, and a poet defend lesbianism as the only alternative to the unequal power relationships between men and women, and when Norma demurs, insisting that all men are not alike, the Frenchwoman disagrees:

"No m'ho crec, va fer la francesa, un home, a la llarga, sempre et desvetllarà el seu *ego,* hi sortirá la vanitat ferida, t'exigeix que li valoris la iniciativa o la força. Se sent incòmode, si només li reclames tendresa." (64)

["I don't believe that," said the Frenchwoman, "with a man, in the long run, his ego always takes over, his wounded vanity comes to the surface, and he demands that you value his initiative or his strength. He feels uncomfortable if all you ask from him is tenderness."]

Norma, unwilling to give up, points out the essentialism of the Frenchwoman's position, asking if she really wants to claim that gendered categories of personality traits are anything other than a cultural invention. Although Natàlia says she felt uncomfortable, she also recalls how the argument dissolved into laughter and affectionate hugs and how free she felt to express her playfulness in a context in which there was nothing to win or lose. Later that night, in bed with Jordi, Natàlia is haunted by the Frenchwoman's skeptical response to Norma's insistence that she had found tenderness in some men.

The cover of the original Catalan edition of *L'hora violeta* offers a key to perceiving the physical and emotional relationships between men and women in the novel. It does not match the color named in the title, instead, it reproduces an etching by Joan Ponç in the colors of the Senyera, a yellow background with a fragmented and grotesquely positioned woman's body drawn in deep red.[15] Since some of Roig's key essays contemplate the resonance of images in historical memory,[16] it can be assumed that this and other images in the text of the novel will be significant. The fragmented female body frames feminine desire within a feminist discourse that protests against gender inequality while insisting upon heterosexuality as a choice worthy of a serious feminist in a feminist context that casts that choice in serious doubt. This insistence upon heterosexuality presents some problems similar to those confronted by Doris Lessing's protagonist Anna Wulf as she "seeks to define herself as a heterosexual woman outside the structures of institutional heterosexuality" (Smith, "And I Wondered" 577).

The key description of the fragmented female body appears just after the dinner-party conversation about lesbianism. Natàlia has come home to find Jordi asleep in her bed and remembers her sense of pride. "Vaig sentir un secret orgull, com si m'haguessin atorgat el títol de campiona" (65) [I felt a secret pride, as if they had awarded me the first prize]. Now that she and Jordi are breaking up, the irony of this memory surfaces in the narration. But in Natàlia's remembered struggle to repress her alienation and participate in sexual pleasure, there is another level of irony and contradiction in the split subjectivity and fragmentation of her body that Natàlia perceived even in the midst of lovemaking. At first she sees Jordi, asleep, curled like a fetus. But as he awakens he embraces her violently and she distances herself, observing from the other side of the room "com en Jordi Soteres feia l'amor amb la Natàlia Miralpiex" (66) [how Jordi Soteres made love with Natàlia Miralpeix]. She sees herself from the perspective of a girl standing in the corner, just as Natàlia the photographer is accustomed to positioning herself as voyeur:

La noia que observava l'escena des del racó va recordar a la Natàlia la conversa de la nit, a casa de l'editora. Li va recordar el que havia dit la francesa, un home vol que li valoris la virilitat, la força. I tot el meu cos es va dividir en trossos, les mans anaven per un cantó, la vagina per un altre, l'esquena s'escampava en diverses particules, el ventre s'estavellava, res no es recomponia. Com si s'hagués escampat en un cosmos immens i no hi hagués manera de compondre les peces una altra vegada. (66)

[The girl who observed the scene from the corner reminded Natàlia of the conversation that evening at the publisher's house. She reminded her of what the Frenchwoman had said, that a man wants you to value [confirm] his virility, his strength. And my body was separated into pieces, the hands in one place, the vagina in another, the spine was shattered into thousands of particles, the belly was blown apart, nothing could be put back together. As if it had been dispersed in an enormous cosmos and there was no way to bring the pieces back together again.]

Norma connects another alienating, conflictive heterosexual moment with the dinner party. Recalling moments in which she failed at love, she thinks that she envies lesbians, in the most abstract sense. She recalls the conversation in simpler, more passionate terms, without the humor of Na-tàlia's recollection. The Frenchwoman sounds much more dogmatic, even defensive: "'Nosaltres tenim molts avantatges sobre les dones heterosexu-als. No hem d'establir cap mena d'aliança amb l'enemic que és l'home. El nostre és exclusivament un món de dones i ens hi sentim molt a gust'" (202). ["We have a lot of advantages over heterosexual women. We don't have to make alliances with men, who are the enemy. We have an exclu-sively female world, and we are very happy there."] Norma recalls that she and Natàlia agreed that they "opposed" the idea of "love between women" (202). But the context in which Norma recalls the dinner party and consid-ers her need to include men in her everyday life and relationships is a scene in which she has just hung up on her married English lover, Alfred, and then remembers a moment in which she refused to allow sexual desire to obliterate her assertion of personal autonomy. When Alfred, approach-ing sexual climax, shouted, "'Ara ets meva, ets meva'" (203) ["Now you're mine, mine"], she replied that she would never belong to anyone, nor would she be cast as a sexual object. And now she says that she does not regret that confrontation.

The heterosexual desire of Agnès and Natàlia in numerous other epi-sodes is represented as insatiable, but Jordi is not blamed for their dissat-isfaction. This is clearly a novel of the late 1970s: the female characters struggle to conceal their desire for commitment from their male lovers in a political and cultural context dominated by masculinity and heterosexu-ality. Roig's characters struggle for autonomy against their traditional so-cial roles rather than against individual men. Nonetheless, readers who have already met Jordi in *El temps de les cireres* may not be convinced by Natàlia's representations of him as innocent, honest, self-sacrificing, and courageous.[17] Frustrating as Natàlia's and Agnès's relationships with Jordi and Norma's marriage to Ferrán have been, they anticipate and engage in heterosexual activity with an enthusiasm that may be attributed in part to the sexual "*destape*" (taking the lid off) of the first years of the post-Franco period. While Agnès's obsessive fear is that she may appear "des-perate," repeating her abandoned mother's humiliation, it is hard to resist labeling the detailed sexual narratives not so much as desperate but as protesting too much, as exaggerated efforts to affirm the characters' exclu-sive heterosexual desire. Roig's characters Natàlia, Agnès, and Norma re-call their own sexual experiences in graphic terms, but it is important to note that Kati's graphic language about lovemaking in her letters to her lover Patrick in the metafictional "La novel·la de l'hora violeta" is a voy-euristic invention of Norma at the insistence of her friend Natàlia. This metafictional relationship mirrors the homoerotic dimensions of the rela-tionship between the reader's and the narrator's sexual imagination.

It is also significant that Judit in *El temps de les cireres* was sexually

knowledgeable before her marriage.[18] In "La novel·la de l'hora violeta"
Norma writes that only Judit's friend Kati had the intimate knowledge of
how this had happened. The idealistic Ignasi, with whom Judit had an
affair in the earlier novel, was unable to bear the consequences of his own
cowardice and committed suicide, and in Norma's "La novel·la de l'hora
violeta," Kati tells Judit what happened to Ignasi. Thus Norma imagines
a triangular relationship in which Kati is Ignasi's rival for Judit's admiration, while she shares with Ignasi not only intimate sexual knowledge
about Judit and a "perfect," uncompromising relationship with her but
also, ultimately, the suicidal outcome of Ignasi's uncompromising idealism. Judit dispelled her husband's fear of impotence before their marriage
in a delicately narrated scene in *El temps de les cireres,* but it is Kati's
sexual aggressiveness with her Irish militiaman Patrick that is the focus of
Norma's imagination in "La novel·la de l'hora violeta." This shift in focus
has the effect of insulating Judit from the voyeuristic gaze of the writer,
who creates an erotic fantasy for Judit's daughter, a fiction about the
mother's best friend, whom Natàlia hardly knew. Thus the erotic in *L'hora
violeta* is kept at a safe remove from the mother herself, about whom the
daughter already has such conflicted emotions.

There are, however, powerful depictions of affection between Judit and
Kati in "La novel·la de l'hora violeta." Norma invents the first conversation in which Judit and Kati are alone, much the way such a meeting is
narrated in romantic fiction when a man recognizes that he has fallen in
love with a woman he has seen before and not noticed: the way the light
falls on her face, the meaningful conversation that shows Judit's quiet
courage and Kati's daring, and, as night begins to fall, an evening stroll
through the city. "La Kati s'adonà que parlaven com mai no ho havien
fet. Mirà la Judit I pensà que li agradava el seu rostre, tenia una mirada
febrosa, estraya però intensa" (130). [Kati noticed that they were talking
as they never had before. She looked at Judit and thought that she liked
her face. She had a feverish look, strange but intense.] Later, after Kati
has fallen in love with Patrick and he has been killed at the Ebro, Kati
sees that the republic is about to fall. She and Judit are sitting with their
arms around each other in her sister-in-law Patricia's garden. Kati breaks
a long silence and asks, "'Per què no ens n'anem ben lluny?'" (142). ["Why
don't we just go somewhere far away?"] Judit answers that she has to wait
for her husband. Kati is certain that she will not be able to bear what is
about to happen and runs out of the garden, but she does not leave Barcelona. When Judit decides to stop writing in her diary on 1 November 1950,
eight years after Kati's death, she says she can sometimes hear Kati's soul
promising her that she'll come back, that neither war nor oppressive laws
can separate them. "'Seré riu i platja, códol i tronc. Omple la casa del meu

fantasma, Judit, omple-la del meu record. . . . No em treguis de tu, Judit, amor de la meva vida, amor de la meva mort'" (144). ["I will be river and beach, pebble and tree. Fill the house with my spirit, Judit, fill it with my memory. . . . Don't leave me, Judit, love of my life, love of my death."] Judit wonders if she has invented Kati, but she vows never to let go of her memory. Norma gives the doubly metafictional Kati the last word on her relationship with Judit. "La novel·la de l'hora violeta" ends with a line that could be Norma's as well as Judit's: "Prou, s'ha acabat. Ja no escriuré més. Continuaré" (144). [Enough, it's over. I won't write any more. I'll go on.]

In "La novel·la de l'hora violeta," Norma creates a narrative of "perfect," nonsexual, but all-consuming, female friendship. In contrast, lesbian sexuality is experienced by Norma and Natàlia on the margins of everyday life. It is not in waking experience but on the level of dream that lesbian desire is recognized and consummated by Natàlia. Roig locates the erotic in the cultural discourse of the authoritarian state with a hysterically parodic twist and a disturbing reflection on the potential for objectification of women in lesbian eroticism:

He tingut un somni m'estava ajaguda en una platja i el vent de garbí em bressolava amb calidesa Al meu costat, una noia de llarga cabellera i de pell de préssec em besava el cos. El recorria amb lentitud. Damunt les nostres pells, gotetes de salobre. Vam fer l'amor mentre les ones ens acariciaven els peus. Semblàvem un anunci de la televisió. Però el fet és que jo me la passava bé M'havien posat a mà tots els ressorts de la bellesa, o sigui la naturalesa en calma, amb el rerafons del mar com a símbol d'alliberament, i una dona perfecta. Sexe i natura. O, en realitat, una mateixa cosa I jo feia l'amor amb tot plegat. Tot d'una, en Franco emergia com un Neptú furós i rabent de dins les aigües. Semblava un profeta bíblic a punt de proferir-nos el pitjor dels anatemes. Ens vam separar esglaiades. Bé, era jo qui em separava, l'altra no hi era com a subjecte. (91)

[I dreamt that I was lying on a beach, and the southwest wind was cradling me warmly. Next to me, a girl with long hair and skin like a peach was kissing my body. She traced its contours slowly. On our skin, droplets of saltwater. We made love while the waves caressed our feet. We looked like an advertisement on television. But the fact is that I enjoyed it. I had within my reach all the aspects of beauty: nature at rest, with the backdrop of the sea as a symbol of freedom, and a perfect woman. Sex and nature. Or, in reality, the same thing. And I made love with all of that. Suddenly, Franco emerged from the water like a furious Neptune. He looked like a biblical prophet about to strike us with the worst of curses. We separated from each other in terror. Well, I was the one who drew back, because the other woman wasn't there as a subject.]

The problem of objectification also arises in Norma's fleeting, anonymous homoerotic experiment with two strangers, a woman and a man, perceived as a physical experience with no relevance to her feminist politics or her core sexuality. Her husband and two children are away, and she picks up two hippie hitchhikers, whom she is not likely to see again "Va pensar, coneixeré gent nova, em servirá d'experiencia. . . . És una nova experiencia, es repetia" (206). [She thought, I'll meet new people, it will provide me with experience. . . . It will be a new experience, she repeated to herself.] They barely speak at dinner, they smoke marijuana in silence, and at first she feels only fatigue and a dulling of the senses "Acariciá els pits de la dona amb curiositat, per a sentir el que sentien els homes. Però acabà per esclatar el desig quan la dona li besà el sexe. Un desig molt fort, punyent. I tinguè por" (206). [She caressed the woman's breasts with curiosity, to feel what men feel. But desire finally exploded when the woman kissed her sex. A very strong, piercing desire. And she was frightened.] Roig's characters in *L'hora violeta* marginalize their homoerotic experience, but it is not as troubling as the drunken, sadomasochistic orgy in *El temps de les cireres* that displays abjection of female sexuality in the punitive educational "formation" of bourgeois women.

As Christina Dupláa notes in her study of "la voz testimonial," in Roig's work *L'hora violeta,* with its multiple voices addressing central questions of feminism, "podría ser calificado de *híbrido* entre novela y ensayo por las reflexiones teóricas que allí se apuntan sobre feminismo y literatura" (118) [could be categorized as a hybrid between novel and essay for its theoretical considerations regarding feminism and literature]. In Roig's trilogy of the Miralpeix, Claret, and Ventura families, *L'hora violeta* is the most actively engaged in feminist ideological debates specific to the historical context of Roig's time and place, including those regarding lesbianism. And yet the first section of the novel is framed in "universals," traditional icons of spectacular feminine sexual power and patient fidelity. The former is figured in Calypso and Circe, the latter in Penelope in the *Odyssey,* which Natàlia Miralpeix is reading on a Mediterranean island in the first section of the novel. Myth and history, desire and social constraints, political and personal are interwoven in the novel, but there is also the aspect of *testimonio* in the ideological discussions between Natàlia and Norma. This novel, like all Roig's novels, essays, and historical writing, is rooted in its time and place.[19] Thus it is productive to read the novel as a feminist memoir in which Norma and Natàlia's dialogues record the feminist discourse of Roig's generation of politically engaged women.

In her memoir, *Family Frames: Photography, Narrative and Postmemory* (1997), feminist critic Marianne Hirsch expands the concept of postmemory beyond its original concept in relation to children of Holocaust survivors. She explains, "Postmemory characterizes the experience of those who grow up dominated by narratives that preceded their birth, whose own belated stories are evacuated by the stories of the previous generation shaped by traumatic events that can be neither understood nor re-created" (qtd. in Miller 1000). Roig's historical study *Els catalans als camps nazis,* published three years before *L'hora violeta* and dominating Norma's sense of memory and writing, brings together two twentieth-century forms of postmemory that affect the notions of history and subjectivity for a generation that was born after they occurred: the Holocaust and the Spanish Civil War. Roig's trilogy belongs among the recent explosion in retrospective writing by feminists following almost four decades later in the footsteps of Simone de Beauvoir's *Memoirs of a Dutiful Daughter.*[20] Although critics have made a convincing case against misreading *L'hora violeta* as a coherent autobiographical account, the novel incorporates unmistakable details of Roig's feminist interviews and literary projects. The section titled "L'hora perduda" narrates the conflicts among Natàlia's membership in the Communist Party, her awareness of comrades' perception of her, and her growing feminist consciousness in her conversations with Norma. Natàlia, in her forties in this novel set in late 1970s, can look back ironically on what she has learned and what issues are still unresolved, as many U.S. feminists now in their forties, fifties, and sixties are now doing. The novel is an ideal genre in which to engage the reader in questioning false answers and imagining possibilities.

Roig's novel has something else in common with the recent U.S. boom in feminist memoirs, succinctly stated in the title of Susan Suleiman's *Budapest Diary: In Search of the Motherbook.* Suleiman's subtitle uses a literal translation of the Hungarian bureaucratic term "motherbook," which refers to the official collection of records of the lives of individuals in relation to the state. The term has a particular eloquence for the current interest in recovering the traces of their mother's lives that will allow women to understand and re-create those lives. Dupláa describes the diaries, letters, and oral histories in Roig's "novelas testimoniales" as "artefactos arqueológicos que sirven para dar luz a una cultura femenina abandonada" (122) [archeological artifacts that shed light on an abandoned feminine culture]. Nancy K. Miller, a scholar as well as another memoirist, writes that "for most daughters, the mother is the one with whom we struggle in order to be born, through or against whom we figure out what we might become" (999). Miller observes that despite the greatest scruples, "there's no way to traffic with the dead without opening the box of family secrets," which is particularly apt in the case of Natàlia, handing her mother's letters and diaries to a friend. It is the attempt to find or create the motherbook, to bring together these unlikely terms, "motherhood" and "writing"—not just the voice or language, but the authority conferred by the form of a book rather than scattered diaries or letters—that drove

Roig's quest as a writer, as a mother and a daughter, and as one of the very few self-identified feminists in Spain.

In the third section of the novel, "L'hora dispersa" (The scattered hour), Roig provides a view of the process of weaving together memory, awareness, and background sounds in Norma's writing process, which is, of course, her own. For her depiction of the married Irishman Patrick, Norma draws upon her memory of Alfred, her own married English lover. In the first long section of the novel, "L'hora perduda," Roig writes about her characters' fictionalized interviews with famous women writers, fairly transparent vignettes of well-known writers including Mercè Rodoreda, whose statements about women would be familiar to Roig's Catalan and Castilian readers. But in the third section, "L'hora dispersa," she creates a more subtle homage to women writers, a testimony not only of women she has met but also of those whose work has shaped her own, in particular Virginia Woolf, Mercè Rodoreda, Simone de Beauvoir, and Doris Lessing (Davies 54). And she writes about a "madwoman in the attic," whom Norma does not have the courage to recognize and rescue. As Norma tries to write about Judit and Kati, her concentration is interrupted by the screams of an inmate protesting the terrible conditions in a neighboring home for elderly women, a nod to Charlotte Brontë and to Sandra Gilbert and Susan Gubar's *The Madwoman in the Attic.* As Catherine Davies points out, for all her political commitment and her moral high ground, Norma admits that she is capable of callousness, using recordings of Mozart to drown out the woman's tormented screaming instead of investigating the institutional abuses as a journalist (Davies 64). But I would also attribute this disruptive voice to Norma's awareness of what is repressed, that is, what is silenced and unwelcome although clearly not unspeakable.

The conflicts, contradictions, and inextricable links between the political and the personal—journalism and historical writing on one hand and fiction on the other—are the fabric of *L'hora violeta,* which Catherine Bellver has compared to Penelope's tapestry ("Montserrat Roig and the Penelope Syndrome"). Read with the other two novels in the trilogy, *L'hora violeta* leaves unresolved the possibility of narrating, much less understanding fully, the lives and experience of others. A concentration camp survivor tells Norma, "The truth will never be known," even as he hands her all his records, his meticulous lists of names and dates. All three novels are marked by dates that create a context for Castilian and Catalonian readers. The themes of the opening section of the novel are inevitably mediated by historical circumstance, especially those so often regarded as universal love and motherhood.

The harmonious wholeness that Norma claims she is trying to recover or create, bringing together all the disparate pieces, may be read as the fantasy of lesbian sexuality as a mother-and-child reunion. After she stops writing "La novel·la de l'hora violeta," Norma continues to think about the project in the section titled "L'hora dispersa." The last few pages of this section were published in Angeles Encinar's collection *Cuentos de este siglo* (1995) as the story "Madre, no entiendo a los salmones." This passage is emblematic of the novel we have in our hands and constitutes the writing Norma/Roig believed she could not accomplish, a heteroglossic narrative that encompasses an apparently incompatible range of ideological and emotional struggles existing in relationships of unequal power. It does not represent the "perfect" friendship between Judit and Kati that Norma attempted to recover in writing, but rather the uneven, unstable relationships of which women's everyday lives are woven. Several threads of Roig's/Norma's literary imagination are interwoven in this story, which includes a dialogue between Norma and her son about the mysterious, sometimes tragic migration of salmon, a metaphor for political dissidents swimming against the current of history and risking destruction. Norma remembers walking alongside a dying "ex-deportado," a Catalan survivor of a Nazi concentration camp, in a memorial procession in a Paris cemetery honoring Spanish Republicans, while thinking about her lover Alfred and imagining her friend Natàlia's feminist critiques (210–13). *L'hora violeta* is a feminist memoir that insists upon including men in its representation of feminism and women in its representation of the political disaster of the Civil War, the dictatorship, and the political commitment of the postwar generation during the *transición*.

The lyricism and the dissonance of the closing passage of the third section of the novel, "L'hora dispersa," could be the music Judit never wrote, infused with Norma's political and historical consciousness. Norma, reflecting upon her novel, dreams of writing something that would include all she has seen, heard, and thought, all the contradictions, the rational and the irrational, brought together in a harmonic work. As she carries out Natàlia's quest, Norma learns that her writing will not transcend difference, it will not put all the pieces back together in a seamless whole. Rather, it must confront and include loss, conflict, incompleteness, suffering, and death:

Les peces s'havien dispersat, era cert, però amb la paraula les tornaria a ajuntar. . . . Tot es recompondria, però no de manera pacífica. Sinó a través de la lluita. La lluita per a convertir en un de sol l'amor col·lectiu y l'amor individual.

I potser ara podria escriure fins al fons la història de la Judit I de la Kati. Potser. (231)

[The pieces had been scattered, that was certain, but with words she could bring them together. . . . Everything would be put together again, but not in a peaceful way; rather, it would be through struggle. The struggle to convert collective love and individual love into a single love. Then perhaps she might be able to write the story of Judit and Kati. Perhaps.]

Notes

1. Catalan citations are from Roig, *L'hora violeta* (1980) and are cited only by page number. English translations are mine.

2. Smith discusses Virginia Woolf's *Mrs. Dalloway,* Muriel Spark's *The Prime of Miss Jean Brodie,* Doris Lessing's *The Golden Notebook,* Elizabeth Bowen's *The Little Girls,* and several more recent novels by British women writers. She observes that "the panic evoked by the presence of the lesbian or even the perception of lesbianism has long functioned as a pervasive narrative strategy in literature representing women's lives and consciousnesses" ("And I Wondered" 571).

3. Ramón Buckley locates a significant shift in Roig's relationship to Kristeva's feminist theory in her last two novels, *L'opera quotidiana* and *La veu melodiosa,* in which Roig devotes more attention to questions of gender involving male characters, seen from a feminine perspective (130). I would contend that this shift is already evident in *L'hora violeta,* in which Norma, clearly the author's alter ego, expresses her reluctance to write about the familiar issue of the masculine domination of bourgeois women's lives in the *Eixample* after her work with Catalan men who survived Nazi concentration camps.

4. De Lauretis's clarification of key aspects of Kaja Silverman's analysis of Kristeva's "homosexual-maternal" is crucial to my reading of Roig's novel. De Lauretis points out how Kristeva's concept of the "homosexual-maternal" can be and has been misinterpreted to imply "that connections between women in feminism hinge on an erotic attachment . . . carried over, in the female subject, from the 'passion' for the mother that she felt during the years of the Oedipus complex," a "logic" that would make all feminists "either lesbians or consistently bisexual" (183). She points out that Silverman's project in *The Acoustic Mirror* "is to provide a *revised* account of female subjectivity, and one that would be *inclusive of all women*" (183) rather than one that would reproduce traditional psychoanalytic theories of female homosexual object-choice, assimilating feminism to lesbianism and equating "'lesbian loves' to 'the embrace of the baby and its nourishing mother'" (184). The discussions among women in *L'hora violeta* engage some of the theoretical problems addressed in both studies, never losing sight of differences and conflicts among women. Roig's characters resist the "popular feminist fantasy which *projects onto female sexuality certain features of an idealized feminist sociality*" (de Lauretis 185; emphasis in original). This is, however, not to say that Roig foregrounds lesbianism in *L'hora violeta* for her characters, lesbianism is a marginalized discourse that must be addressed in their explorations of feminist issues, and their sexual liberation consists in acknowledging their heterosexual desire.

5. Jacobus's essay focuses specifically upon Adrienne Rich's influential book on motherhood, *Of Woman Born,* and the poem "Transcendental Etude," from *The Dream of a Common Language,* critiquing the positing of lesbian love in the poem as resolving the "history of bodily expropriation underwritten by the mythic moth-

er's mourning for her lost daughter and the daughter's mourning for the loss of her nurturing mother" (16).

6. In her discussion of Roig's "rebellion" against "the reduction of woman to an ideological construction and against the homogenizing and dogmatic tendency" of the critique of her work by Lidia Falcón and other feminists in the 1970s, Isolina Ballesteros cites Catherine Bellver's analysis of *L'hora violeta.* Roig's characters "'sense that feminism has neither reconciled women's need for autonomy with their desire for love nor taken into account the possibility of intense and total love between a woman and a man'" (Ballesteros 120; Bellver, "Montserrat Roig and the Penelope Syndrome" 119, cited in Ballesteros 120). Ballesteros discusses the maternal role but does not examine in detail Agnès's ambivalence toward motherhood, neither Bellver nor Ballesteros addresses the question of lesbianism in the novel.

7. For a discussion of political history in the feminine voice in *Ramona, adéu,* see Janzon's "Contested Historiography." For a discussion of *El temps de les cireres,* see my forthcoming article, "Mothers, Daughters and the Mother Tongue."

8. Roig's interview with Geraldine Nichols includes a brief discussion of her relationship with her two sons (Nichols 166–67).

9. Here, I follow Enrique Sordo's Castilian translation of this passage, which renders "Es van fer" as "Existieron" (Roig, *La hora violeta* 17).

10. Roig, *Els catalans als camps nazis* (1977).

11. Silverman discusses three of Kristeva's key essays, "Motherhood According to Giovanni Bellini," "Place Names," and "Stabat Mater," in relation to her formulation of the *chora* as associated with the mother and the prehistory of the subject, "figuring the oneness of mother and child" (Silverman 102). See also Silverman's discussion of Julia Kristeva's denial of the eroticism of the mother–daughter relationship in her theory of the "homosexual-maternal facet" (Kristeva, "Motherhood," qtd. in Silverman 108–11); and de Lauretis's critique, cited in n. 4 above.

12. Since Maria Callas was known for her performance as Norma, and the fantasies of one of Roig's characters in *L'òpera quotidiana* (1982) involve Callas's performance of *La Traviata,* it is significant that Roig chooses for her character Norma a more contemporary performance by a Catalan soprano.

13. Marilyn Farwell in *Heterosexual Plots and Lesbian Narratives* referring to a specific performance of the duet, "Mira O Norma," by Marilyn Horne and Joan Sutherland, suggests that it "appears to position [Norma and Adalgisa] as lovers rather than rivals." Farwell finds that this aria is as close as any moment in opera can be to one of "primary intensity" between women (3).

14. The allusion is to *The Golden Notebook,* in which Anna Wulf writes, "I was stuck fast in an emotion common to women of our time, that can turn them bitter, or Lesbian, or solitary" (480). The Catalan *"gosar"* is equivalent to the Castilian *"atreverse"* rather than to the false cognate *"gozar."*

15. This disturbing figure has been replaced on the cover of the current Catalan edition by a headless female nude from a painting by Max Ernst.

16. See, for example, Roig's essays on memory and the visual, "Els ulls de la ment" and "Davant la catedral d'Estrasburg," in *Digues que me'estimes encara que sigui mentida* 99–109.

17. Christina Dupláa characterizes him as "un ser indeciso y un tanto frívolo en relación con su comportamiento con Agnès y Natàlia" (120) [an indecisive and somewhat frivolous being in relation to his behavior toward Agnès and Natàlia].

18. In her discussion of Natàlia's father Joan's fetishization of feminine clothing and Natàlia's mother's collection of dolls and hunting horns, referred to as "fetitxes" in *El temps de les cireres,* Catherine Davies observes that "female fetishism is associated in psychoanalysis with female homosexuality; that is, a woman disavows her own castration and becomes the phallus. Judit takes the sexual initiative in her relationship with Joan, and her ambiguous relationship with Kati is the pivot point of both this novel and, more overtly, the next. Thus, there seems to be a suggestion of role reversal with a demasculated Joan absorbed in a phallic Judit" (49). Davies does not, however, support this plausible but sketchy psychoanalytic approach with regard to *L'hora violeta.*

19. See Dupláa, as well as Bellver, "Montserrat Roig: A Feminine Perspective"; Tsuchiya; and Davies.

20. In her review article in *Signs,* Nancy K. Miller discusses a selection of recent texts by U.S. feminists from diverse ethnic backgrounds. Carolyn Heilbrun's biography of Gloria Steinem, *Education of a Woman;* Shirley Geok-lin Lim's *Among the White Moon Faces. An Asian-American Memoir of Homelands;* Jane Tompkins's *A Life in School;* Meena Alexander's *Fault Lines;* and Patricia Williams's *The Alchemy of Race and Rights: Diary of a Law Professor.*

Works Cited

Ballesteros, Isolina. "The Feminism (Anti-Feminism) According to Montserrat Roig." *Catalan Review* 7.2 (1993). 117–28.

Beauvoir, Simone de. *Memoirs of a Dutiful Daughter.* Trans. James Kirkup. Cleveland: World Publishing, 1959. Originally published as *Mémoires d'une jeune fille raugée,* 1959.

Bellver, Catherine. "Monserrat Roig: A Feminine Perspective and a Journalistic Slant." *Feminine Concerns in Contemporary Spanish Fiction by Women.* Ed. Roberto C. Manteiga, Carolyn Galerstein and Kathleen McNerney. Potomac, Md.: Scripta Humanistica, 1988. 152–68.

Bellver, Catherine. "Montserrat Roig and the Penelope Syndrome." *Anales de Literatura Española Contemporánea* 12 (1987): 111–21.

Bergmann, Emilie. "Mothers, Daughters and the Mother Tongue: Martín Gaite's *El cuarto de atrás* and Montserrat Roig's *El temps de les cireres." Comparative Literature, Linguistics and Culture: An Iberian Dialogue.* Ed. Dru Dougherty and Milton Azevedo. University of California, International and Area Studies, forthcoming. 1–16.

Buckley, Ramón. "Montserrat Roig: The Dialectics of Castration." *Catalan Review* 7.2 (1993): 129–36.

Clément, Catherine. *Opera or the Undoing of Women.* Trans. Betsy Wing. Foreword by Susan McClary. Minneapolis: U of Minnesota P, 1988.

Davies, Catherine. *Contemporary Feminist Fiction in Spain: The Work of Montserrat Roig and Rosa Montero.* Providence, R.I.: Berg, 1994.

de Lauretis, Teresa. *The Practice of Love: Lesbian Sexuality and Perverse Desire.* Bloomington: Indiana UP, 1994.

Dupláa, Christina. *La voz testimonial en Montserrat Roig. Estudio cultural de los textos.* Barcelona: Icaria/Antrazyt, 1996.

DuPlessis, Rachel Blau. *Writing Beyond the Ending: Narrative Strategies of Twentieth-Century Women Writers.* Bloomington: Indiana UP, 1985.

Encinar, Angeles. *Cuentos de este siglo: 30 narradoras españolas contemporáneas.* Barcelona: Editorial Lumen, 1995.

Epps, Brad. "Virtual Sexuality, Lesbianism, Loss, and Deliverance in Carme Riera's 'Te deix, amor, la mar com a penyora.'" *¿Entiendes? Queer Readings, Hispanic Writings.* Ed. Emilie L. Bergmann and Paul Julian Smith. Durham: Duke UP, 1995. 317–45.

Farwell, Marilyn. *Heterosexual Plots and Lesbian Narratives.* New York: New York UP, 1996.

Gilbert, Sandra M., and Susan Gubar. *The Madwoman in the Attic: The Woman Writer and the Nineteenth-Century Literary Imagination.* New Haven: Yale UP, 1979.

Hirsch, Marianne. *Family Frames: Photography, Narrative, and Postmemory.* Cambridge, Mass.: Harvard UP, 1997.

Hirsch, Marianne. *The Mother/Daughter Plot: Narrative, Psychoanalysis, Feminism.* Bloomington: Indiana UP, 1989.

Jacobus, Mary. "Freud's Mnemonic: Screen Memories and Feminist Nostalgia." *First Things: The Maternal Imaginary in Literature, Art, and Psychoanalysis.* New York: Routledge, 1995. 1–22.

Janzon, Anjouli. "Contested Historiography: Women Writers of Spain and the Former German Democratic Republic." Diss. University of California, Berkeley, 1998.

Kristeva, Julia. "Motherhood According to Giovanni Bellini." *Desire in Language: A Semiotic Approach to Literature and Art.* Ed. Leon S. Roudiez. Trans. Thomas Gora, Alice Jardine, and Leon S. Roudiez. New York: Columbia UP, 1980. 237–70.

Kristeva, Julia. "Place Names." *Desire in Language: A Semiotic Approach to Literature and Art.* Ed. Leon S. Roudiez. Trans. Thomas Gora, Alice Jardine, and Leon S. Roudiez. New York: Columbia UP, 1980. 271–94.

Kristeva, Julia. "Stabat Mater." *The Kristeva Reader.* Ed. Toril Moi. Trans. Leon S. Roudiez. Oxford: Basil Blackwell, 1986. 160–86.

Lessing, Doris. *The Golden Notebook.* 1962. New York: Ballantine, 1968.

Meese, Elizabeth A. *(SEM)EROTICS: Theorizing Lesbian Writing.* New York: New York UP, 1992.

Miller, Nancy K. "Public Statements, Private Lives: Academic Memoirs for the Nineties." *Signs* 22.4 (summer 1997): 981–1016.

Nichols, Geraldine Cleary. *Escribir, espacio propio: Laforet, Matute, Moix, Tusquets, Riera y Roig por sí mismas.* Minneapolis: Institute for the Study of Ideologies and Literature, 1989.

Rich, Adrienne. *The Dream of a Common Language: Poems, 1974–1977.* New York: Norton, 1978.

Rich, Adrienne. *Of Woman Born: Motherhood as Experience and Institution.* 1st ed. New York: Norton, 1976.

Riera, Carme. "Te deix, amor, la mar com a penyora." *Te deix, amore, la mar com a penyora.* Barcelona: Laia, 1975. 15–32.

Roig, Montserrat. *Els catalans als camps nazis.* Barcelona: Edicions 62, 1977.

Roig, Montserrat. *Digues que m'estimes encara que sigui mentida: Sobre el plaer solitari d'escriure i el vici compartit de llegir.* Barcelona: Edicions 62, 1991.

Roig, Montserrat. *L'hora violeta.* Barcelona: Edicions 62, 1980.

Roig, Montserrat. *La hora violeta.* Trans. Enrique Sordo. Barcelona: Argos Vergara, 1981.

Roig, Montserrat. *L'òpera quotidiana.* Barcelona: Planeta, 1983.

Roig, Montserrat. *Ramona, adéu.* Barcelona: Edicions 62, 1972.

Roig, Montserrat. *Ramona, adiós.* Barcelona: Editorial Argos Vergara, 1980.

Roig, Montserrat. *El temps de les cireres.* Barcelona: Edicions 62, 1977.

Roig, Montserrat. *Tiempo de cerezas.* Barcelona: Argos Vergara S. A., 1978.

Roig, Montserrat. *La veu melodiosa.* Barcelona: Edicions 62, 1987.

Silverman, Kaja. *The Acoustic Mirror: The Female Voice in Psychoanalysis and Cinema.* Bloomington: Indiana UP, 1988.

Smith, Patricia Juliana. "'And I Wondered If She Might Kiss Me.' Lesbian Panic as Narrative Strategy in British Women's Fictions." *Modern Fiction Studies* 41.3–4 (1995): 567–607.

Smith, Patricia Juliana. "'O Patria Mia': Female Homosociality and the Gendered Nation in Bellini's *Norma* and Verdi's *Aïda.*" *The Work of Opera: Genre, Nationhood, and Sexual Difference.* Ed. Richard Dellamora and Daniel Fischlin. New York: Columbia UP, 1997. 93–114.

Suleiman, Susan Rubin. *Budapest Diary: In Search of the Motherbook.* Lincoln: U of Nebraska P, 1996.

Tsuchiya, Akiko. "Montserrat Roig's *La ópera cotidiana* as Historical Metafiction." *Anales de Literatura Española Contemporánea* 15 (1990): 145–59.

Tusquets, Esther. *El mismo mar de todos los veranos.* Barcelona: Editorial Lumen, 1978.

Wing, Helen. "Deviance and Legitimation. Archetypal Traps in Roig's *La hora violeta. Bulletin of Hispanic Studies* 72 (1995): 87–96.

Wood, Elizabeth. "Sapphonics." *Queering the Pitch: The New Gay and Lesbian Musicology.* Ed. Philip Brett, Elizabeth Wood, and Gary Thomas. New York: Routledge, 1994. 27–66.

13

Arenas's *Antes que anochezca*
Autobiography of a Gay Cuban Dissident

Emilio Bejel

Obsession with homosexuality is never simply an obsession with homosexuality alone. This is very obvious upon a critical reading of Reinaldo Arenas's *Antes que anochezca* (1992) (published in English as *Before Night Falls*), an autobiography in which homosexual desire and political power are furiously interwoven. As a text which draws its creativity from its very paradoxes, as well as from an absence of authority, Arenas's work emerges as a struggle among a wide range of conflicting and contradictory forces. This struggle goes far beyond the rebelliousness of a gay man who dedicated his literary production to the indignant avengement of the harassment he suffered at the hands of the Cuban political system. To view Arenas's work exclusively in this light would be to reduce it to just another example of discourse produced by a soldier of the cold war. I am convinced that this autobiography is more than that—much more. A critical reading of *Antes que anochezca* reveals its complexity and leads to a questioning of how the problem of autobiographical writing relates to the struggle between desire and power, as well as between dissidence and transgression.

In December of 1990, Reinaldo Arenas committed suicide in New York City to end his suffering from AIDS. Although only forty-seven years old at the time of his death, Arenas left a truly impressive literary output, consisting of eleven novels, several collections of short stories, a poetic trilogy, six plays, various essays, and his autobiography.[1] It would not be an exaggeration to say that, in a sense, all his works are autobiographical and that his life was a continuous attempt to write its own story, as is perhaps the case in the life of all writers, or indeed, of everyone.

The protagonist of *Antes que anochezca* first emerges while narrating the story of his unfortunate life to come: his mother was "tricked" by a man promising marriage only to abandon her with a child with whom he never again concerned himself. This picaresque narrator-protagonist tells of his childhood in his grandparents' dilapidated house and of his poor family—all peasants from an isolated region in the east of Cuba. This family instilled in the child a deep hatred for his father, even to the point of teaching him a song with obvious Oedipal overtones in which a child kills his father to avenge his mother's suffering. The absence of the father coupled with the violence with which its symbolism is established is the first and most fundamental crisis of authority in the text. The family itself, including the mother, seems to despise this "child of sin." But this same scorn, neglect, and at times verbal abuse open up a space for creative escape, according to the protagonist. "Mi existencia ni siquiera estaba justificada y a nadie le interesaba; eso me ofrecía un enorme margen para escaparme" (*Antes* 22).[2] ["My existence was not even justified, nobody cared. This gave me an incredible opportunity to escape" (*Before* 5).] On the basis of his description, we may ask ourselves: Is Arenas's work, especially his autobiography, a means of self-justification in the midst of these feelings of abandonment? Is this self-justification unique to Arenas, or is it simply a variation of something that always occurs, particularly when a writer narrates his own story?

It is evident that throughout the text a complete theory of creativity and sexuality is being developed; this theory responds to a creative paradox (creative in the sense that it becomes a dramatic means of supplementing the text). Also evident is a constant denunciation of the abuses of power brought on by institutionalized machismo along with other forms of political and social control that limit and attempt to annihilate creativity and sexuality.[3] The limitations imposed by this power have had terrible consequences for Cuban society and, in reality, all societies. Yet, as the narrator-protagonist confesses, it was precisely because of this denigration and familial oppression that he was able to obtain "an incredible opportunity to escape." This escape is not limited to a simple withdrawal from society, but also gives rise to an uncontrollable desire to create: the boy is compelled to compose the gaudy operatic songs which form part of his first shows and which he belts out at the top of his lungs in the open countryside, alone and far from his family.

If we take into account the creative delirium of the narrator-protagonist in *Antes que anochezca,* as well as his obsession with producing shows, which is due, at least in part, to the lack of attention and the frequent abuse shown him by his family, we can arrive at the tentative conclusion that the theory of desire and power implicit in his work is similar to that of Freud.[4] Seen in this light, power is a force external to desire, and it produces a hydraulic effect in which the "brute force" of desire (the libido), upon being sublimated, emerges as the creative force of "civilization." Nevertheless, the theory proposed by Arenas's work seems more utopian than Freudian, since time and again it insists that desire is a polymorphic force, instinctive and natural, that can express itself freely only in a universe where power has disappeared. Thus, in Arenas, power is not only external to desire but also completely pernicious to it. What the protagonist seeks is the total absence of rules, a utopia where desire can express itself in a limitless world. This fiercely utopian ideology, implicit in *Antes que anochezca,* appears to disregard the close interdependence of power and desire. As Foucault has observed, desire is conditioned by power; without power, desire would lack meaning and expression.[5] In opposition to this idea, Arenas's text presents us with a narrator-protagonist who constantly describes himself as an individual in crisis, a crisis that is almost exclusively the result of external limitations produced by three interwoven forces: the *machista* tradition, the family as a representative of tradition, and the state. The union of these three forces creates a castrating limitation of the individual, who demands only that they let him live. According to the logic of the text, this implies that he must be liberated from all rules and restrictions, since for him all truly authentic life "es enemiga de todo dogma e hipocresía política" (*Antes* 15) ["opposes all dogma and political hypocrisy" (*Before* xvii)].

In a number of ways, the implications of desire in *Antes que anochezca* are related to another dilemma: the opposition between the rural and the urban. Just as desire is implied to be an instinctive and presocial force leading to a utopia unregulated by power, the countryside is often perceived as something "natural," where the forces of nature are conducive to a polymorphic sexuality without rules or dogmas. And yet it is precisely in this opposition between city and country that we find one of the most complex paradoxes of the text. On the one hand, the narration constantly dwells upon the unfortunate isolation of the countryside and the oppression experienced by the protagonist-narrator during his childhood at his grandparents' country home. But on the other hand, the countryside is emphatically proposed as a place of promiscuous "natural" freedom, where everything (or almost everything) is permitted, including bestiality, incest, homosexuality, and bisexuality. In other words, the country is a polymorphic sexual space, of which Arenas writes:

Es falsa esa teoría sostenida por algunos acerca de la inocencia sexual de los campesinos; en los medios campesinos hay una fuerza erótica que, generalmente, supera todos los prejuicios, represiones y castigos. Esa fuerza, la fuerza de la naturaleza, se impone. (*Antes* 40)

[There is no truth to the theory, held by some, about the sexual innocence of peasants. In the country, sexual energy generally overcomes all prejudice, repression, and punishment. That force, the force of nature, dominates.] (*Before* 19)

He continues:

Creo que en el campo son pocos los hombres que no han tenido relaciones con otros hombres; en ellos los deseos del cuerpo están por encima de todos los sentimientos machistas que nuestros padres se encargaron de inculcarnos. (*Antes* 40)

[In the country, I think, it is a rare man who has not had sexual relations with another man. Physical desire overpowers whatever feelings of machismo our fathers take upon themselves to instill in us.] (*Before* 19)

All these statements can be seen as the confessions of a gay peasant who becomes a writer, allowing him to give voice to his sexual identity and to tell the "truth" about his life, condition, and social milieu.

Nevertheless, these statements exhibit a conceptual complexity rife with paradox. First of all, although it may be that these affirmations have a high degree of validity in terms of actual practice in the Cuban countryside, the text confuses the concept of nature with that of brute force, equating desire with a kind of naked pleasure (naked in the sense of being stripped of all socializing processes). Within this frame of logic, to live in the countryside is to be close to nature, which is considered a pure erotic force conducive to a polymorphic sexuality. This vision of "the natural" does not recognize that so-called nature is already an interpretation (always ideologically charged) of a certain environment. It refuses to acknowledge that environment as a phenomenon filtered by acculturated human consciousness, radically different from brute force or naked pleasure. Yet the paradoxes inherent in the opposition between the rural and the urban do not stop there. The protagonist-narrator of *Antes que anochezca* relates how, after his first sexual experiences and especially after his first homosexual experience, he was filled with feelings of guilt. The free and polymorphic eroticism that the protagonist-narrator sees in the countryside (as a product of being close to nature) appears to contradict the feelings of guilt that the boy feels, since guilt is always the product of an intense process of socialization. This concept of eroticism also contradicts the abusive oppression to which he is subjected by his grandfather as well as his entire family. If it is true that the Cuban peasant is sexually voluptuous, this is not necessarily because of a closeness to nature or because of "the natural" being in and of itself an issue that is unquestionable. Intense homoerotic activity and guilt seem to go hand in hand in these accounts of the countryside. In men of the countryside, we are told, "los deseos del cuerpo están por encima de todos los sentimientos machistas que nuestros padres se encargaron de inculcarnos" (*Antes* 40) ["physical desire overpowers whatever feelings of machismo our fathers take upon themselves to instill in us" (*Before* 19)]. However, if these parents (I think that Arenas meant "parents" and not "fathers," as Koch translates the word) are also peasants, is it not paradoxical to say on the one hand that the force of nature overcomes the socialization of the peasants, while on the other insisting that the parents, who are also peasants, inculcate "*machista* sentiments" in their children? It is unlikely that a community of puritans will, simply by virtue of living in the middle of the countryside, stop being puritanical. If we accept the accounts offered in Arenas's text, the concept of nature is a complex and specific process of socialization that simultaneously produces homoerotic activity and guilt in the Cuban situation. Furthermore, the idea of the countryside as a happy place, harmonious and free of prejudice, is clearly a pastoral idealization. The calamities suffered by the boy during his childhood in the countryside can hardly be described as happy, free, or harmonious. Indeed, the need to escape in order to produce his deliriously creative experiments arises from the repressiveness of the social milieu, which he feels from his very early childhood. The paradox of the countryside in this text can be summarized as follows: on the one hand the countryside is a place of freedom and natural sexual activity without complications, yet on the other it is a repressive and terrible place of intolerable scarcity.

The other pole of the city/country binomial poses a similar paradox. The representation of the city in *Antes que anochezca* is plagued with conceptual tensions. The protagonist-narrator experiences his first change in environment as a teenager, when economic difficulties force his grandfather to sell his land and the entire family must move to the provincial town of Holguín, which the protagonist-narrator sees in an entirely negative light. The text informs us that the sale of the land and the subsequent move were necessitated by the worsening economic conditions experienced by peasants under the Batista government. In reality, this was not a situation exclusive to Cuba, but rather a socioeconomic phenomenon of global proportions: the massive immigration from country to city (with the corresponding transformation of the peasant into urban worker). Having told of this change from village to town, the protagonist-narrator reflects, with an obviously idealized nostalgia, on the country house he left behind:

Sin duda, en aquella casa de yagua y guano, donde tanta hambre habíamos pasado, también habíamos vivido los mejores momentos de nuestra vida; terminaba tal vez una época de absoluta miseria y aislamiento, pero también de un encanto, una expansión, un misterio y una libertad, que ya no íbamos a encontrar en ninguna parte. (*Antes* 55)

[In that hut with its thatched roof, where we had suffered so much hunger, we had no doubt also lived the best moments of our lives. This was perhaps the end of our period of absolute poverty and isolation, but also the end of a kind of enchantment, exultation, mystery, and freedom that we would never find again.] (*Before* 33)

So, in spite of the calamities of his childhood in the country, once distanced from that environment the protagonist-narrator idealizes (at least partly) his childhood in the countryside through a nostalgic filtering of the past.

It is interesting to note that the protagonist-narrator names three principal factors as the possible source of his creativity in the countryside: the abuse and lack of affection from his family, the erotic indiscrimination of nature, and the peasant mythology (generally represented by the grandmother). In Holguín, however, the creative influences on the future writer are much more urban. What the protagonist-narrator sees as his possible influences in this provincial town during the 1950s are radio soap operas and movies (almost all from the United States or Mexico). All this was happening during his adolescence, at about the age of thirteen. In Holguín, the protagonist's sexuality was ambiguous; although he had discovered his homosexual inclinations at the age of six while watching some naked boys bathing in a river, his erotic experiences were almost all heterosexual: he had girlfriends and on one occasion went to a brothel, where he had his first heterosexual relation, with a prostitute. In terms of creativity and sexuality, the protagonist-narrator gives an almost entirely negative interpretation of his life in Holguín: the move to the city did not bring with it more sexual freedom, and although he was writing novels, they were, in his opinion, very bad and tacky. For these reasons the town of Holguín is an intermediate step of sorts between country and city. The great urban revelation will occur in Havana.

Most of *Antes que anochezca* is dedicated to the protagonist's life in Havana as well as his life after the triumph of the revolution. This should not be surprising, since all revolutions invite self-analysis in terms of coping with before and after. The capital city, Havana, is portrayed paradoxically in the text: on the one hand it represents liberation from the limitations of the countryside and the provincial town, while on the other it is the very place where the protagonist encounters his worst enemy, the Cuban state, in all its proximity and ferocity. Thus every stage in the narrator-protagonist's life becomes a step from one oppression to another. Rather than a story of progressive liberation, the text narrates a process of increasing, ever-worsening oppression, including the protagonist's life in New York, where he suffers the physical horrors and social alienation of AIDS.[6] According to this account, the city (specifically Havana) is in some respects more permissive, allowing the protagonist to engage in entirely anonymous homosexual activity, yet in another sense it is in the city where the great battle between desire and power takes place. This battle, as the story would like to convince us, is a result of the encounter between the marginalized sexuality of a creative and rebellious gay man and the coercive power of the state, which, in the end, persecutes and finally incarcerates him. This coercive power is symbolized in the text by the figure of Fidel Castro, the supreme, *macho* Father who ought to be eliminated but toward whom the protagonist simultaneously demonstrates obsessive feelings of hatred and concealed attraction.[7]

As previously stated, the sublimation of desire, according to the psychoanalytic model, is the foundation for the production of the creativity of civilization. In *Antes que anochezca,* however, creativity, far from being a sublimation of sexuality, is rather its ally. It is a question of a utopian universe wherein creativity is almost synonymous with a limitless sexuality. Yet there is something more at play here: this place without limits is often found in a world where life and death nearly converge. The forces of sexuality seek to attain life with such extreme delirium that sexuality overflows and ends up pouring into death. Moreover, it is the phantom of death that incites and hastens creativity. Arenas always lived as if a merciless clock were constantly reminding him that he must furiously create before death arrived, before night fell. For Arenas, writing is a question of obsessive creativity always situated between Eros and Thanatos. This living in the "in-between" zone is characteristic of all the works of Arenas, not just his autobiography. He lives not only between life and death but also between light and darkness, between country and city, between sanity and insanity, between the search for truth and the absolute disdain for all reality, between realistic detail and fantastic hyperbole, and between the struggle for liberation and suicide (or suicide as liberation). As with all autobiography, *Antes que anochezca* is an obsession to remain alive, to give semblance to that which is no more, and this aspect is dramatically accentuated by Arenas. This is why Paul de Man said that the predominant rhetorical figure of all autobiography is *prosopopeia,* the figure of speech that gives voice and face to the dead or the voiceless.[8] (It is pertinent to note that *Webster's* dictionary defines "prosopopeia" as "a figure in rhetoric by which things are represented as persons, or by which things inanimate are spoken of as animated beings, or by which an absent person is introduced as speaking, or a deceased person is represented as alive and present.")[9]

The text of *Antes que anochezca* informs us that there is a double meaning to its title: at first, when the autobiography was begun (after the protagonist's escape to Lenin Park in Havana), it meant writing before nightfall, when darkness no longer permitted him to see; now, in the present enunciation of the text, it signifies the hurried need to finish writing before his imminent death from AIDS. Although the figure of death in Arenas's work is more dramatic than in other autobiographies, in reality autobiography always deals with a life that disfigures itself through the process of writing: writing as the death of life and at the same time as the uncontrollable desire to preserve it.[10] To write about something alive implies a substitution of the life being described by the life that is being written, and therefore the moment of writing acquires its reality only when the life described is no longer present. For this reason the title of Arenas's work could apply to all autobiographies, because all are obsessed with the moment "before night falls," before death arrives. Or perhaps the contrary is true; perhaps this and all other autobiographies ought to be titled "after night fell," since from the point of view of the reader, life that becomes writing (the *bio* that becomes *graphia*) is read when only the latter prevails.

More than anything else, the autobiography of Reinaldo Arenas is concerned with the struggle between homoerotic desire and political power and with all the complexities and interdependencies these terms imply. This struggle, as was previously stated, is charged with a complex paradoxical tension. Confronted with this problematic struggle, we may ask: Why is there such a detailed confession of sexual experiences? To whom is the text directed? Is there an authority figure in this text, despite its strong refusal to respond to any authority? All autobiography appears to be a kind of confession aspiring to self-reparation and self-justification; it is rather like saying: "You failed to acknowledge me and I will tell you who I am so that you will recognize my value as a unique individual" (Moreiras 131). If we continue with this line of thought, it is obvious that Arenas's confession in his autobiography is an issue of self-reparation in the face of the fundamental vacuum represented by his marginalized sexuality, which is seen by Cuban society (and many other societies for that matter) as a serious breach of socially acceptable behavior. *Antes que anochezca,* like most of Arenas's other works, is in a sense a monumental coming out of the closet, but a coming out that always ends up in another terrible situation. It is also an endless and frustrated demand for recognition from someone—from an ideal reader or an ideal father.

The story tells of innumerable sexual experiences of every kind: besides those relating to incest and bestiality, so numerous and prodigious are the homosexual encounters that the protagonist himself says that by the beginning of the 1970s he estimates having had sexual relations with some five thousand men. In addition to questioning the truth of this hyperbole, I would also underscore here the degree of rupture that such spectacular marginalized sexual activity signifies, as well as the obsession with recounting it in such detail. In effect, these revelations can be interpreted in many ways: as a way of enlightening the reader, as an insult to the establishment, as a cunning bid for recognition, as a declaration of the "naturalness" of this kind of sexuality, as an expression of disdain for and aggressiveness toward potential readers, and also as an expression of self-hatred.

It is interesting to note that in *Antes que anochezca* the narrator-protagonist dedicates his life to rebelling against the *machista* power structure with the goal, explicit or implicit, of liberating himself from that power. In fact, one could say that this is the central theme of the text. Nevertheless, and in spite of the centrality of this insistence, the protagonist declares his uncontrollable attraction to, his tremendous desire to have sexual relations with, a "real man"—with a *macho*. In fact, the narration speaks disparagingly of gay men who have sexual relations with other gay men, referring to them as "locas" [fags], a very insulting and denigrating term in Latin American culture. For the narrator-protagonist, attraction between two gay men is simply incomprehensible. This expression of desire is key to understanding the complexity of the desire–power relationship, since, while fighting against *machismo* as public enemy number one, he also feels the desire to have sexual relations with a *macho,* the prototypical representative of the oppressive system, something basically the same as the paradoxical love–hate relationship with the figure of Fidel Castro. This is an obvious case of the internalization of power in desire, the interdependence of the roles that power plays in regard to desire: it oppresses desire and at the same time is an integral part of the object of desire. Needless to say, Arenas's internalization of power corresponds to the specific social conditions under which he grew up. In Cuban society, homoerotic relationships are often based on the masculine/feminine binary, and Arenas was unable to free himself from this mold.

Arenas's prodigious description, great detail, and voluminous number of examples of sexual encounters, with people both known and unknown, provoke yet another interpretation of his hyperbole. All these descriptions give the impression that Arenas was compensating for, and perhaps at the same time avenging, a guilt of monumental proportions by means of a compulsive confession that attempts to fill an apparently bottomless void. This is the void upon which the textuality of *Antes que anochezca* is founded and in which homosexuality can be seen as a breach of the rules of the establishment, but which can also be interpreted in Lacanian psychoanalytic terms. Since the search for the total object of desire is an impossible goal and in this text there is such a tremendous vacuum of authority, it is necessary for the human subject, in order to enter into some form of sociability or accepted language, to abandon somehow his aspiration of absolute grandeur, that is to say, the all-encompassing object of desire. This renunciation of absolute grandeur is strongly resisted by the protagonist of *Antes que anochezca*. In other words, the protagonist shows great difficulty in renouncing his narcissistic fantasy, the aspiration of the Imaginary absolute object of desire. In Arenas's text we are dealing with a human subject who refuses to accept that desire is only partial and imperfect; as a subject he has difficulty participating in the Symbolic social exchange. Therefore, in order to attempt to "solve" this dilemma and to attempt participation in the Symbolic social order, the subject must seek some kind of tradition that inscribes him into a type of language or socialization.[11] This is why Arenas's entire autobiography (and, in the end, all autobiography) is a retrospective construction of an absolute idealization that never existed, but without which the human subject cannot continue to live and cannot continue to write. Moreover, this writing or living can be achieved only through the metonymic pursuit of partial objects of desire.

In Arenas's text there is an extreme dramatization of a crisis of authority, but it is precisely this very crisis that makes the text not only possible but also particularly fascinating. However, if we are to have a text at all, this crisis of authority cannot be absolute. All discourse must have at least some form of ideological sender—a representative of a kind of authority that permits entry into language. The visible sender of *Antes que anochezca* is the image of Cuban writer Virgilio Piñera, whom Arenas elevates as his symbolic hero, as the symbol of some form of law, or as a substitute for the "original" absent Father. Yet, the figure of Virgilio Piñera as sender or bearer of (literary) tradition is rather problematic, because he is elevated to this role precisely for having been perceived by Arenas as the dissident writer par excellence, as the maximum representative of transgression. Therefore, the figure of Virgilio Piñera leads to what is called a composition in abyss. The symbolic figure of Virgilio Piñera can send only two messages to Arenas: to write, and to transgress (or to write transgressing). The message of transgression conveys another form of void, or crisis, whose meaning can be interpreted as *the very limit of modernity:* Arenas idealized the figure of Piñera because he imagined him to embody literary rebellion, representing the art of constant rupture and tireless artistic dissidence. This is the limit of the art of modernity: an art based on the constant breaking of tradition or on a tradition of constant breaking and rupture.[12] It is for this reason that the art implied in *Antes que anochezca* points to the typical crisis of modernity and, accordingly, to the possibility of the postmodern.

All this explains the obsession in this text with literary work, with the compulsion to write, and to write about the process of writing. In a way, this is the only message that can be viewed as affirmative. There is no doubt that in Arenas's text, as in the autobiographies of so many other writers, a great deal of self-justification stems from the prestige of being a writer. It is the equivalent of saying: "Since the readers of this autobiography may not be aware of who I am and why I did what I did, I will tell them who I am: I am a gay man of peasant origin who possesses the courage (the boldness, the authenticity, the sincerity) to tell them all the details I can remember of my sexual and political adventures; but furthermore, I am a writer, extremely dedicated to my literary production, even in the most terrible and sublime moments." Literary work is the center of self-justification in the difficult life of this persecuted gay man. In this sense, it is interesting that literary work justifies the life of the protagonist, just as the life of the protagonist justifies the literary work (in the sense of "real" facts that can be proven). It is as though his work and life were interwoven and interdependent: the literary work is both inside and outside the protagonist's life, just as the protagonist's life is inside and outside the literary work. Thus we return to the same basic paradox: life, in order to justify itself, must write itself. Yet to write about something alive is in a certain sense to kill it, since it is written about when life is already absent.

Antes que anochezca frequently concerns itself with the narrator-protagonist's literary production and with how his manuscripts were written, then lost or confiscated by the Cuban authorities, only to be recovered and lost yet again. Even the autobiography itself was written, as we are told by the text, on more than one occasion. In fact, the "final version"—the one we read today—wasn't *written* in the literal sense but, rather, was tape recorded by Arenas, so that some friends could then posthumously transcribe and publish it (see Hasson). According to the narration, the narrator-protagonist first began to write his autobiography as a fugitive from justice. It is perhaps in this section that the most extraordinary events are related. The adventures and misadventures of the protagonist of *Antes que anochezca* appear to take on special significance and dramatic effect in the sections that tell of his persecutions, arrests, escapes, rearrests, and reescapes in his struggle against Cuban political power. So prodigious are these adventures that at least the more outstanding of them deserve mention and some measure of interpretation.

According to the text, the greatest persecution began in the summer of 1973 on the beach at Guanabo, where Arenas and a friend named Coco Salá (who accompanied him on many of his homoerotic adventures) had sex with some teenagers. These teenagers robbed Reinaldo and Coco of their belongings, and Coco called the police. The teenagers were detained, but they accused Reinaldo and Coco of being "maricones" [fags] who tried to fondle them. As a result, the accusers became the accused. Both men were arrested, Reinaldo was found guilty in court of "perverting minors," yet Coco was not even formally accused in court. Reinaldo, free on bail, began a series of attempts to leave the country and go anywhere, by any means possible. The text states that he asked his friends in Paris for a plastic life raft, a fake passport, and underwater gear. Despite being free on bail, Reinaldo was rearrested. In prison again, he managed to escape by diving into the ocean while the guards were on a coffee break and then swimming a number of kilometers to a beach far from the prison. The truth or falsehood of all these accounts cannot be completely proven or disproven, but this amazing story is only the beginning of an almost interminable series of extraordinary escape adventures. In the midst of so many calamities, Arenas decided in a moment of desperation to kill himself by slitting his wrists with some shards of glass. After losing consciousness, he miraculously awoke some hours later, hungry and with the blood on his wrists clotted. After this he traveled to Oriente Province (several hundred kilometers from Havana) in order to try escaping via the U.S. naval base at Guantánamo. Unsuccessful in this endeavor, he went to Holguín, where his mother and other members of his family were living and where everyone, or almost everyone, and especially his aunt Ofelia, as the text informs us, hated him and wanted to see him recaptured. From Holguín, Reinaldo took a train with his mother to Havana, where he was once again arrested and once again managed to trick the authorities, showing them a false ID card.

Of all the adventures and escapes in this section of the autobiography, perhaps one of the most interesting (from various points of view, including that of the preeminently romantic adventure) occurred in Lenin Park, on the outskirts of Havana, where the protagonist took refuge during his never-ending escape. Although this section is titled simply "The Escape" ("La fuga" in the original Spanish) it could just as well have been called "The Phantom of the Park" (or perhaps "The Phantom of Lenin," if taken in the political sense), because it recounts the fugitive life of the protagonist in an extremely marginalized situation (he lived in hiding in the park for several days or weeks). From this hideout, or underworld, he sent signs of his presence to representatives of the establishment in order to confuse or surprise them with his abilities as a fugitive. In fact, the narration tells us that while Reinaldo was hiding in the park, he arranged for friends in Europe to send telegrams to Cuba, to important figures of the Cuban regime, informing them that he was already out of the country. The symbolism of the Lenin Park adventures can be read romantically (in the Promethean sense of the term)[13] because of the intricate relation of frustrated and unattained love, a love mainly for the text he is writing, his autobiography, which he began to compose at that time. It is also romantic because the romantic hero sends forth ambiguous signals from a hidden, marginalized, and nocturnal world to the established world that persecutes him, which in psychoanalytic terms would be something like the return of the repressed. Furthermore, in Lenin Park, Reinaldo compulsively reads the *Iliad,* a book brought by a friend during one of his clandestine visits to the park. It would not be an exaggeration to see the fugitive's reading of this classic book as symbolic of a self-justification of the "other life," that is, the life that Arenas is narrating, one which has so many things in common with that of the hero of the *Iliad.*[14]

The implicit questioning of the validity of this self-reflexive writing coincides with the questioning of the national discourse (and therefore of one of the most important modern master narratives), because throughout the entire text the concept of nationality as proposed by Cuban socialism is questioned, and a "new" nationalism is set forth that is based upon "rescuing" the lost history, or stories, of marginality—in this case, of sexual marginality. Although nationalism in itself is not rejected as a principle, despotism is furiously denounced, specifically the despotic *machismo* so prevalent in the formation of nationalism (especially in the nationalism of socialist Cuba). Although Arenas began to publish in the 1960s, his posthumous autobiography has given him a much wider visibility in the non-Spanish-speaking world, especially in the United States. The translation of this autobiography into English has introduced Arenas to many English-speaking readers, in particular, gay readers in the United States, as one might expect. Undoubtedly, the undermining of modern master narratives in postmodern societies, with their well-known space for marginal discourse, has made room for this dissident and transgressive text.

Everything thus far has led up to the idea that Arenas's autobiography exists in a space created by a crisis of authority, a crisis that manifests itself on the personal, social, and institutional levels. On the personal level there is a crisis in relation to the Father figure, and on the social and institutional levels, one finds the absence of established models of both conduct and government. This discourse is radically dissident and transgressive from both ethical and political perspectives, but not in terms of aesthetics (at least not intentionally so). A struggle between marginal sex-ual desire and political power exists in *Antes que anochezca,* which implies an ideology in which desire is an instinctive and natural force whose ulti-mate aspiration is to liberate itself from all forces of power. In other words, there is an implicit desire in this text, perceived as a presocial force, whose fullest expression is achieved only when all the pressures of power are absent. In accordance with this position, it is in "pure desire" that the individual's true authenticity resides, and this individuality expresses itself through writing. Moreover, the autobiographical persona of *Antes que ano-chezca* seeks to convey the extraliterary truth of his life, something that the reader must believe as an established historical fact. All this means that, although in other works Arenas stylistically implies a decentraliza-tion of subjectivity and a questioning of the realist mimesis or representa-tion, in *Antes que anochezca* he returns to realism, at least on the level of the ideology proposed in the text.[15] It is not a text that questions subjectiv-ity and mimetic representation, but rather a text that obviously, because of the nature of autobiographical writing, insists on an extraliterary *truth.* So in this autobiography there is an approach toward an ethical rather than an aesthetic transgression—toward a position closer to that of Gide than that of Wilde,[16] closer to the testimonial novel than to the textuality of Lezama Lima or Sarduy.[17] To do otherwise would require a rejection of the principles of naturalness and reality themselves.

In *Antes que anochezca* there is a search for *the truth,* something which, as Nietzsche reminds us, is the ultimate basis of Western metaphysics.[18] Nevertheless, and in spite of the proposed ideology of the text, Arenas's text contains elements that undermine (perhaps unintentionally) its im-plicit realism, inasmuch as the extreme hyperboles undermine the basis of the realist discourse. For this reason *Antes que anochezca,* on the one hand, takes part in the basic discourse of modernity—in its desperate search for authenticity, freedom, posterity, and history—and, on the other hand, offers exaggerations and extreme sexual transgressions that open up a space pointing to a postmodern condition. Perhaps it is not, after all, sexual transgression that is the greatest rupture in *Antes que anochezca,* but rather its constant hyperbole, its drawing near to falsehood and lies (the exaggerations of the text are often hard to believe). The liar is so dangerous because he undermines not only conventional morals but also the foundation that sustains such morality: "the truth," which is the episte-mological legitimization of "the real." Reality, thus devalued and demysti-fied by the loss of the true, is forced to imitate art, which is rhetorically associated with appearance, style, and falsehood. *Antes que anochezca* is a text that represents a rhetorical struggle between *prosopopeia,* the figure that gives voice and face to the dead and the absent, and *hyperbole,* the figure that undermines the prosopopeia by means of exaggeration. A face is given and simultaneously taken away as the narrator-protagonist desperately attempts to survive in his own writing—a survival that is betrayed over and over again by the very act of writing itself. All these furious paradoxical tensions make *Antes que anochezca* one of the most dramatic and compelling autobiographies ever produced in Latin America.

Notes

Another version of this chapter has been published as *"Antes que anochezca:* Autobiografía de un disidente cubano homosexual," *Hispamérica* 25.74 (1996): 29–45.

1. For an article that gives a general view of Arenas's entire literary production, see Ette. Eduardo Béjar, in his excellent book *La textualidad de Reinaldo Arenas,* explains the philosophical importance of Arenas's works.

2. In this chapter, I have first quoted from the original Spanish edition, cited as *Antes,* then, following in brackets, from Dolores Koch's English translation, *Before Night Falls (A Memoir),* cited as *Before.*

3. Almost the entire autobiography points to the struggle between power (family, society, and state) and desire, which, according to Arenas, is a presocial force that is associated with sexuality and creativity.

4. For a study of the Freudian concept of desire and the Lacanian version of it, see Ragland-Sullivan, especially chapters 2 and 5.

5. See Foucault's *History of Sexuality.*

6. For a theory of *coming out of the closet,* see Sedgwick. In her insightful and influential work, Sedgwick explains how and why each coming out of the closet is often a new form of entering another closet. My own view regarding Arenas's coming out follows some of Sedgwick's suggestions.

7. After I finished writing this chapter, I read Brad Epps's magnificent study in which he shows a fascinating relationship between the figures of Reinaldo Arenas and Fidel Castro (see "Proper Conduct").

8. For a study of prosopopeia as the dominant autobiographical rhetorical figure, see Paul de Man's classic essay "Autobiography as De-Facement."

9. *Webster's New Universal Unabridged Dictionary,* 2d ed., s.v. "prosopopeia."

10. For a study of these ideas, besides de Man's article, see Moreiras.

11. For an explanation of this idea, see Ragland-Sullivan, especially chapters 2 and 5.

12. This idea is often associated with Octavio Paz's *Los hijos del limo.*

13. See Bloom (whose article was first published in the *Yale Review* 63.4 [summer 1969]). In his article, Bloom explains how the initial phase of the romantic quest was basically Promethean (Prometheus was the god of the unfulfilled promise). In the Promethean romantic phase, the poet is the hero of an endless iconoclastic rebellion that always ends in an unfulfilled situation. Also, for Bloom, as well as for Paul de Man and others, romanticism is a cultural movement that ex-

tends from the end of the eighteenth century to the present. These critics believe that all efforts to truly overcome the basic romantic premises or objectives have failed.

14. For a study of the importance of classical texts in Spanish American autobiography, see Molloy.

15. I want to emphasize that several of Arenas's texts previous to his autobiography constitute, as is well known, radical questionings of the realist foundation. Nevertheless, *Antes que anochezca* is a different kind of text in this respect. His objective seems to be more ethical than aesthetic.

16. For a comparison between Gide's and Wilde's ethical and aesthetic positions, see Dollimore.

17. I have studied the antirealist aesthetics of José Lezama Lima. See my *José Lezama Lima: Poet of the Image.*

18. See Clark.

Works Cited

Arenas, Reinaldo. *Antes que anochezca (Autobiografía).* Barcelona: Tusquets Editores, 1992.

Arenas, Reinaldo. *Before Night Falls (A Memoir).* Trans. Dolores M. Koch. New York: Penguin, 1993.

Béjar, Eduardo. *La textualidad de Reinaldo Arenas: Juegos de la escritura posmoderna.* Madrid: Editorial Playor, 1987.

Bejel, Emilio. *Jóse Lezama Lima: Poet of the Image.* Gainesville: U of Florida P, 1990.

Bloom, Harold. "The Internalization of the Quest-Romance." *Romanticism and Consciousness. Essays in Criticism.* Ed. Harold Bloom. New York: Norton, 1970. 3–24.

Clark, Maudemarie. *Nietzsche on Truth and Philosophy.* Cambridge: Cambridge UP, 1991.

de Man, Paul. "Autobiography as De-Facement." *Modern Language Notes* 94 (1979): 919–30.

Dollimore, Jonathan. *Sexual Dissidence: Augustine to Wilde, Freud to Foucault.* Oxford: Clarendon, 1991.

Epps, Brad. "Proper Conduct: Reinaldo Arenas, Fidel Castro, and the Politics of Homosexuality." *Journal of the History of Sexuality* 6.6 (1995): 231–83.

Ette, Ottmar. "La obra de Reinaldo Arenas." *La escritura de la memoria: Reinaldo Arenas: Textos, estudios y documentación.* Ed. Ottmar Ette. Frankfurt am Main: Vervuert, 1991. 95–138.

Foucault, Michel. *The History of Sexuality.* Vol 1: *An Introduction.* Trans. Robert Hurley. New York: Vintage Books, 1980.

Hasson, Liliane. "*Antes que anochezca (Autobiografía):* Una lectura distinta de la obra de Reinaldo Arenas." *La escritura de la memoria: Reinaldo Arenas: Textos, estudios, y documentación.* Ed. Ottmar Ette. Frankfurt am Main: Vervuert, 1991. 165–73.

Molloy, Sylvia. *At Face Value: Autobiographical Writing in Spanish America.* Cambridge: Cambridge UP, 1991.

Moreiras, Alberto. "Autobiografía: Pensador firmado (Nietzsche y Derrida)." *Anthropos* 29 (December 1991): 129–36.

Paz, Octavio. *Los hijos del limo.* Barcelona: Seix Barral, 1974.

Ragland-Sullivan, Ellie. *Jacques Lacan and the Philosophy of Psychoanalysis.* Urbana and Chicago: U of Illinois P, 1986.

Sedgwick, Eve Kosofsky. *Epistemology of the Closet.* Berkeley and Los Angeles: U of California P, 1990.

Contributors
Index

Contributors

EMILIO BEJEL is professor of Spanish American literature at the University of Colorado at Boulder. Born in Cuba, he received his Ph.D. from Florida State University in 1970. He has published several books on literary and cultural studies of Spain and Spanish America, mainly Cuba. Among his critical books are *José Lezama Lima: Poet of the Image* (U of Florida P, 1990); *Literatura de Nuestra América* (Editorial de la Universidad Veracruzana, 1982), and *Escribir en Cuba* (Editorial de la Universidad de Puerto Rico, 1991). He has published several poetry collections of his own, two of which are *Casas deshabitadas* (Editorial Corripio, 1989) and *El libro regalado* (Ediciones Libertarias, 1994). His main research at the present is on the relationship between the categories of homosexuality and Cuban nationalism. On this topic he has a forthcoming book entitled *Gay Cuban Nation: Readings on Representations of Cuban Nationalisms and Homosexualities.*

EMILIE L. BERGMANN is professor of Spanish at the University of California, Berkeley, specializing in gender studies in early modern Hispanic literature. She coedited ¿Entiendes? *Queer Readings, Hispanic Writings* (Duke UP, 1995), is a coauthor of *Women, Culture, and Politics in Latin America* (U of California P, 1990), and has published on gender and sexuality in the theater of Lope de Vega and the poetry of Sor Juana Inés de la Cruz and on the representations of the maternal in early modern and twentieth-century Spanish writing.

SUSANA CHÁVEZ-SILVERMAN is associate professor of Spanish and chair of the Latin American Studies Program at Pomona College. She is coeditor, with Frances Aparicio, of the book *Tropicalizations: Transcultural Representations of Latinidad* (UP of New England, 1997) and the author of studies on gender, sexuality, and queer theory in Latin American and U.S.

Latino/a writing and culture. Her current project is a book entitled *Desire In/Verse Readings in Argentine Women's Poetry from Pizarnik through the Millennium.*

ROBERT RICHMOND ELLIS is professor of Spanish at Occidental College. He is currently completing a book on representations of homoeroticism, gender, and race in Latin American autobiography. His major publications include *The Hispanic Homograph: Gay Self-Representation in Contemporary Spanish Autobiography* (U of Illinois P, 1997); *San Juan de la Cruz: Mysticism and Sartrean Existentialism* (Peter Lang, 1992); and *The Tragic Pursuit of Being: Unamuno and Sartre* (U of Alabama P, 1988).

ROSEMARY GEISDORFER FEAL is professor of modern languages and literatures and director of the graduate program in Spanish at the State University of New York at Buffalo. She specializes in Caribbean and South American literature and literary theory, including Afro-Hispanic studies, feminist criticism, and queer theory. Feal is an associate editor of the *Afro-Hispanic Review.* She is the author of *Novel Lives: The Fictional Autobiographies of Guillermo Cabrera Infante and Mario Vargas Llosa* (University of North Carolina Studies in the Romance Languages and Literatures, 1986) and co-author of *Painting on the Page: Interartistic Approaches to Modern Hispanic Texts* (State U of New York P, 1995). Feal's latest research focuses on women's erotic writing *en español.*

DAVID WILLIAM FOSTER is chair of the Department of Languages and Literatures and Regents' Professor of Spanish, humanities, and women's studies at Arizona State University. His research interests focus on urban culture in Latin America, with emphasis on issues of gender construction and sexual identity, as well as Jewish culture. He has written extensively on Argentine narrative and theater, and he has held Fulbright teaching appointments in Argentina, Brazil, and Uruguay. He has also served as an Inter-American Development Bank professor in Chile. Among his most recent publications are *Sexual Textualities: Essays on Queer/ing Latin American Writing* (U of Texas P, 1997); *Violence in Argentine Literature: Cultural Responses to Tyranny* (U of Missouri P, 1995); and *Latin American Writers on Gay and Lesbian Themes: A Bio-Critical Sourcebook* (Greenwood P, 1994), which he edited. Foster is also the translator of novels by Enrique Medina, Aristeo Brito, Miguel Méndez-M., and Ana María Shúa. In 1989, he was named the graduate college's outstanding graduate mentor, and in 1994 he was named the researcher of the year by the Alumni Association.

LIBRADA HERNÁNDEZ is assistant professor of Spanish at Los Angeles Valley College in California. She graduated from the University of California, Los Angeles, in Hispanic studies and works in nineteenth-century peninsular literature. Among her interests are women writers of the nineteenth century and contemporary Cuban American women writers. Her essays have appeared in various journals, including *Letras Peninsulares, Letras Femeninas, Hispanic Review, Revista Hispánica Moderna,* and *Review of the Americas.*

ELIZABETH ROSA HORAN's book, *Gabriela Mistral: An Artist and Her People* (Organization of American States, 1994), was awarded first prize in the Gabriela Mistral Centenary Contest, sponsored by the Organization of American States and the Chilean Government. Her essays on Gabriela Mistral, Carmen Lyra, Sor Juana Inés de la Cruz, Emily Dickinson, Jewish women writers, lullabies, and literary theory have appeared in a range of journals and edited collections. Currently she is completing a biography of Gabriela Mistral and is employed as associate professor of English, women's studies, and humanities at Arizona State University, where she directs the Comparative Studies in Literature Program.

ROBERT MCKEE IRWIN is a visiting assistant professor of Latin American literature at Tulane University. His publications include the anthology *Hispanisms and Homosexuality* (Duke UP, 1998), which he coedited with Sylvia Molloy. His essays have appeared in various publications in the United States and Mexico, including *Revista Iberoamericana* and the *Universidad Nacional Autonoma de Mexico's Literatura Mexicana.* He is currently working on his doctoral dissertation, which treats the notions and rhetoric of masculinity in Mexico from the nineteenth century through the 1950s.

CARMEN TISNADO is assistant professor of Spanish at Franklin & Marshall College in Pennsylvania. She has published articles on narrative from Argentina, Uruguay, and Peru, dealing with the representation of censorship, dictatorship, torture, and exile. The most recent among them is "Mario Benedetti's 'Corazonada': Silence That Reverses Power," in *Hispanófila* 121 (1997). She has also published works on Peruvian contemporary literature, the most recent being "Edgardo Rivera Martínez y la evocación de lo apacible," in *De lo andino a lo universal: La obra de Edgardo Rivera Martínez,* ed. I. Márquez and C. Ferreira (Lima, 1999). "*Ximena de dos caminos:* Self-Representation and the Power of Language" is forthcoming in *Hispanic Review.*

SHERRY M. VELASCO is associate professor at the University of Kentucky. Her first book, *Demons, Nausea, and Resistance in the Autobiography of Isabel de Jesús (1611–1682)*, was published in 1996 (U of New Mexico P). Her most recent book is entitled *The Lieutenant Nun: Transgenderism, Lesbian Desire, and Catalina de Erauso* (U of Texas P, 2000). She has published various articles on early modern women writers and the representation of gender and sexuality in Golden Age Spain.

HARRY VÉLEZ QUIÑONES is associate professor of Spanish at the University of Puget Sound. He has published articles in such journals as *Revista de Estudios Hispánicos; Journal of Interdisciplinary Literary Studies; Revista Hispánica Moderna; La Torre Revista de la Universidad de Puerto Rico; Confluencia; and Celestinesca;* among others. He is the author of *Monstrous Displays: Representation and Perversion in Spanish Literature* (UP of the South, 1999). His research interests center on the theater of Lope de Vega, queer theory, and twentieth-century Spanish prose. He is also involved in projects exploring the application of web-based technologies to the teaching of foreign languages and literatures, and the dissemination of writing, music, and the visual arts.

YVONNE YARBRO-BEJARANO is professor of Spanish and chair of the Department of Spanish and Portuguese at Stanford University. She is the author of *Feminism and the Honor Plays of Lope de Vega* (Purdue UP, 1994); *The Tradition of the "Novela" in Spain from Pedro Mexía to Lope de Vega's "Novelas a Marcia Leonarda"* (Garland, 1991); and the coeditor of *Chicano Art: Resistance and Affirmation* (Wight Gallery, University of California, Los Angeles, 1991). *The Wounded Heart: Cherríe Moraga's Writings* is forthcoming (U of Texas P). Her research concentrates on interdisciplinary representations of race, sexuality, and gender, as well as on the ongoing development of a digital archive of Chicana/o art accessible on the Internet.

Index

"La abandonada" (Mistral), 167
"Abel Madac" attack: on Mistral, 150–52
abuse: in Arenas's works, 301, 302–3, 304
Acevedo, Rafael, 224
aesthetics, 12, 170, 171, 311–12
Aïda (film), 263–64
AIDS, 4, 9, 10, 14, 15–16, 208, 210, 270, 299, 305, 306
Alarcón, Norma, 186–87
All about Eve (film), 267
Alvarez, Julia, 182, 184, 187, 196
Amar sólo por vencer (Zayas), 7, 21, 24–29, 30, 31, 32, 35
ambiente, 3–4, 9, 15–16. See also specific writer
"Amor imposible" (Mistral), 149
Andermahr, Sonya, 35
"Anillo de Moebius" (Cortázar), 239, 249, 250
Antes que anochezca (Arenas), 14–15, 299–315
Anzaldúa, Gloria, 6, 186, 194, 196
Arenas, Reinaldo: abuse in works of, 301, 302–3, 304; ambiente in works of, 5–6; authority/power in works of, 15, 306, 308, 311; autobiography of, 299–315; coming out in works of, 306–7; and distancing/marginalization, 307, 310–11, 312; eroticism in works of, 302–3, 304; family background/childhood of, 300, 301, 302–3, 304; fathers in works of, 15, 307, 308, 311; literary output of, 299–300; and machista, 301, 303, 307, 311; and modernism, 15; oppression/repression in works of, 305, 307; rural/urban opposition in works of, 301–5; and sexuality/sexual

identity, 300, 302, 304, 305, 307–8; and suicide, 299, 305, 310; and truth, 5, 312; and utopianism, 15
—works of: Antes que anochezca, 14–15, 299–315; Arturo, la estrella más brillante, 5–6
Argentina: feminism in, 221–22; homosexuality in, 233–34. See also Perón, Evita
Ariosto, Ludovico, 23
Arlt, Roberto, 226
"El arte" series (Mistral), 166–67, 170
Arte Público Press, 182
Arturo, la estrella más brillante (Arenas), 5–6
assimilation: and sexual identity, 211
Asunción Silva, José, 170
authority. See power/authority
autobiographies, 14, 15, 308, 309. See also specific person
Azevedo, Olga, 164

"Bad Faith" (Gaspar de Alba), 188, 191–92, 193, 195
Bal, Mieke, 108
Balderston, Daniel, 125–26
Barnes, Djuna, 167, 170
Barrin, Jean, 33
Barrios, Eduardo, 164
Barthes, Roland, 99
Bartky, Sandra Lee, 107
Baudelaire, Charles-Pierre, 161
"Bay Poem from Berkeley" (Cisneros), 196
Beauvoir, Simone de, 80, 226, 291, 292
Beggar on the Córdoba Bridge (Gaspar de Alba), 11–12, 188–96
Bejel, Emilio, 14–15, 299–315

323

Bellver, Catherine, 278, 292
Belsey, Catherine, 105, 181, 193
Benedetti, Mario: body in works of, 95, 96,
97, 98–99, 107; closet in works of,
110–11; clothing in works of, 10, 103–5;
gaze in works of, 10, 106, 107, 111; ideology in works of, 105–6, 108, 111; language in works of, 99, 108, 110; oppres-
sion/repression in works of, 10, 93, 94,
95, 98, 108, 111–12; and readers, 10,
107–8, 109–10; silence in works of, 9–10,
93–113; and suicide, 10, 107–8, 111
—works of: *Montevideanos,* 93; *La muerte y
otras sorpresas,* 93–94; "Para objetos solamente," 9–10, 94–112
Ben-Hur (film), 264–65, 267
Bergman, Ingmar, 270
Bergmann, Emilie L., 14, 259–98
Berlant, Lauren, 4
Besant, Annie, 163, 170
El beso de Peter Pan (Moix), 13–14, 257,
260–70
Bianchi, Soledad, 154
blacks: as lesbians, 182
Blanco, José Joaquín, 114–15, 116, 121,
125, 131, 133–34
Blavatsky, Helene P., 163, 164, 170
body: in Benedetti's works, 95, 96, 97, 98–
99, 107; fragmentary parts of, 10, 122;
and intergenerational relationships, 279,
281–82, 283; in Mistral's works, 11,
167–69; of mothers, 167–69, 279, 281–82;
of Perón, 219, 220–21; in Roig's works,
279, 283, 286; in Villaurrutia's works, 10,
122
"Bohemio" (Mistral), 149–50
Bomcrioulo (Caminha), 6
Borges, Jorge Luis, 226, 228
Bradbury, Gail, 55
Bradu, Fabienne, 115, 121
Brantôme, Pierre, 22, 27, 29, 34
Bravo-Villasante, Carmen, 55
Brecht, Bertolt, 202
Bredbeck, Gregory D., 4
Brontë, Charlotte, 292
Brown, Judith, 23, 33
La burlada Aminta y venganza del honor
(Zayas), 7, 21, 29–31, 32, 35
Burston, Paul, 94
Butler, Judith, 99–100, 104, 105, 201–2, 220

Byron, George Gordon (Lord), 80, 83,
84–85

"El cadáver de la nación" (Perlongher), 219
Califia, Pat, 250
"Calles" (Villaurrutia), 133
Caminha, Adolfo, 6
camp behavior/attitude, 12, 262
Campbell, Bruce F., 161
"Cántaros de greda" (Mistral), 170
Capote, Truman, 246
Cárdenas, Lázaro, 118
Cardoza y Aragón, Luis, 115
Carlini, Benedetta, 33
Carmelita Tropicana: Your Kunst *Is Your*
Waffen (film), 12, 200–201, 202, 208–10,
215
Carrasco, Rafael, 9
Carroll, Lewis, 190
Cartas inéditas (Gómez de Avellaneda), 63,
64
Castellanos, Rosario, 182, 242
Castillo, Ana, 182, 184, 186–87, 196
Castillo, Debra, 242
Castillo Solórzano, Alonso de, 24
Castro, Fidel, 305, 307
Castro-Klarén, Sara, 241, 249
Els catalans als camps nazis (Roig), 291
Cavafy, Constantine, 246
La Celestina (Rojas), 23, 43
celibacy, 35, 162
Céspedes, Elena de, 23–24
Chacón, Iris, 202
Chávez, Denise, 182, 196
Chávez-Silverman, Susana, 11–12, 181–99
Cheung, King-kok, 97–98, 107
Chicanas: stereotypical images of, 183–84,
186, 196; as writers, 6, 11–12. *See also*
Cisneros, Sandra; Gaspar de Alba, Alicia
Chile. *See* Mistral, Gabriela
chora theory, 282–83
El cine de las sábados (Moix), 257, 260–61
Ciria, Alberto, 233
Cisneros, Sandra, 6, 11–12, 182–88, 196
—works of: "Bay Poem from Berkeley,"
196; *The House on Mango Street,* 182;
Loose Woman, 11–12, 182, 184–86, 196;
My Wicked Wicked Ways, 182, 184; *Third
Woman,* 186–87; "With Lorenzo at the
Center of the Universe, el Zócalo, Mex-

ico City," 196; *Woman Hollering Creek,*
182; *Women Singing in the Snow,* 183–84;
"You Bring Out the Mexican in Me,"
184–85, 187
Clarke, Cheryl, 188
Clément, Catherine, 284
closet, 10, 110–11, 116, 119–20, 121, 137,
306–7. *See also* "coming out"
clothing: in Benedetti's works, 10, 103–5; in
Golden Age, 8–9; in Gómez's works,
211–12, 213; and Perón persona, 220; in
Lope de Vega's works, 9, 43–60. *See also*
cross-dressing; drag; transvestism
Cocteau, Jean, 123
Cohan, Steven, 259
colonization, 6
"coming out," 4, 110–11, 119–20, 121, 137,
190–92, 306–7. *See also* closet
"Conserva tu risa" (Gómez de Avellaneda),
80, 83–85
Contemporáneos, 118
"Continuidad de los parques" (Cortázar),
241–42
convents, 33–34, 35
Copi, 13, 219, 224–25
El Coquimbo: Diario Radical (newspaper),
148–49
Coronado, Carolina, 66, 68
Cortázar, Julio: distancing/marginalization
in works of, 13; gaze in works of, 248;
language in works of, 243, 246; power in
works of, 249–50; and readers, 13, 241–
42, 249; sadomasochism in works of, 13,
239, 240, 241, 242, 249–50; and sexuality,
239–53; victims in works of, 249–50
—works of: "Anillo de Moebius," 239, 249,
250; "Continuidad de los parques,"
241–42; "Historia con migalas," 243–47,
249; *Los relatos,* 241–47; *Rayuela,* 239,
242; "Reunión con un círculo rojo," 249;
"El río," 239; "La señorita Cora," 250
Cotarelo y Mori, Emilio, 72, 73
Cox Stueven, Mariana, 152
Craddock, Catherine, 183
Crompton, Louis, 22, 33
cross-dressing, 7–8, 9, 43–60, 200, 201,
221, 275. *See also* clothing; drag;
transvestism
Cuba: ambivalence toward, 201; homosexuality in, 307; journeys of daughters of ex-

iles back to, 200; nationality in, 311;
queering of revolution in, 208; romanti-
cizing nostalgia for, 209. *See also* Arenas,
Reinaldo; Gómez, Marga; Tropicana,
Carmelita
cubanidad, 12, 200–217. *See also* Gómez,
Marga; Tropicana, Carmelita
Cubillo de Aragón, Álvaro, 23, 26–27
"Cuentos: Oyendo los de kindergarten"
(Mistral), 160
Cuesta, Jorge, 118
Culler, Jonathan, 249, 250
cultural identity, 200–217

Dama de corazones (Villaurrutia), 122
D'Annunzio, Gabriele, 153
Darío, Rubén, 158, 159
"Dark Morning Husband" (Gaspar de
Alba), 188–90, 191, 193
Daston, Lorraine, 55
Dauster, Frank, 114, 125, 130, 132–33, 135
Davies, Catherine, 292
Davis, Vaginal, 208
death, 10, 161–62, 222, 269–70, 305, 306; in
Benedetti's works, 95, 96, 97, 98–99, 107.
See also suicide
"Décimas de nuestro amor" (Villaurrutia),
136–37
DeJean, Joan, 66, 67
Dekker, Rudolf M., 23, 46, 47, 48
del Río, Dolores, 187
de Man, Paul, 15, 305
Denning, Michael, 13, 257–58
Derrida, Jacques, 248–49, 250
"La desasida" (Mistral), 167
Desengaños amorosos (Zayas), 7, 21, 24, 25,
26, 27, 28, 29, 32, 34, 35–36
Los deseos imaginarios (Sebreli), 226–27,
232, 233
Desolación (Mistral), 154, 162, 165, 166,
167–68, 169, 172–73
"Despedida a la señora Da D G C de V"
(Gómez de Avellaneda), 75–80, 82–83
Diamond, Elin, 202, 215
Díaz Arciniega, Víctor, 117, 118
dissidence. *See* Arenas, Reinaldo
distancing/marginalization: and Arenas's
works, 307, 310–11, 312; in Cortázar's
work, 13; in Gómez's work, 211–12, 213,

distancing/marginalization (*continued*)
214; in Mistral's works, 167, 170, 171; in
Roig's works, 14. *See also* outsiders
Dolz-Blackburn, Inés, 24
domesticity, 64, 67–68, 78. *See also*
femininity
Domingo Silva, Víctor, 172
Donoghue, Emma, 23
Dos mujeres (Gómez de Avellaneda), 63
Doty, Alexander, 233
drag, 13, 103–5, 224. *See also* cross-
dressing; transvestism
drawings: of Villaurrutia, 122
Drukman, Steven, 258, 262
Dubois, Page, 67
Dujovne Ortiz, Alicia, 219–20
Dupláa, Christina, 290, 291
DuPlessis, Rachel Blau, 276
Dyer, Richard, 259, 260, 262, 263

Echeverría de Larraín, Inés, 152, 164
"Ecos" (Mistral), 149
Edelman, Lee, 10, 98, 106, 136, 258–59
"Electra en la niebla" (Mistral), 169
Eliot, T. S., 284
Ellis, Havelock, 68
Ellis, Robert R., 3–18, 13–14, 257–74
Eloy Martínez, Tomás, 219
El Saffar, Ruth, 35
En batalla (Mistral), 163, 164
Encinar, Angeles, 293
Enrique Carrera, Luis, 164
Epps, Brad, 282
Erauso, Catalina de, 7, 23–24, 46–47
Estrada, Genaro, 119
Estridentistas, 117, 118
ethnicity. *See* race/ethnicity
Eva (Guevara opera), 222
Evans, Caroline, 96, 97, 105, 106–7, 258
Eva Perón (Copi play), 13, 224–25
Eva Perón: ¿Aventurera or militante?
(Sebreli), 12–13, 225–34
Evita (rock opera), 222, 227
Examen magazine, 118
"Extasis" (Mistral), 165

Faderman, Lillian, 63, 68, 71
family, 194–95, 202–3. *See also* fathers;
mother–daughter/child relationship;
mothers/motherhood
Farwell, Marilyn, 276

fathers: and Arenas's works, 15, 307, 308,
311; in Gómez's work, 12, 200, 201,
212–15; in Tropicana's works, 12, 200–
201; in Zayas's works, 7
Félix de Jesús María, Fray, 34
Felman, Shoshana, 250
feminine/masculine binary, 5, 6, 11
femininity, 168, 211–12, 221. *See also*
domesticity
feminism: in Argentina, 221–22; in Cata-
lonia, 284; and Cisneros's works, 182–83,
186; in France, 277–78; and Gaspar de
Alba's works, 192; and Gómez de Avellaneda, 63; and lesbianism, 277; and Mistral's works, 147; and mother–daughter/
child relationship, 291–92; and Perón,
218, 220, 221–22, 226, 233; and Roig's
works, 277–78, 284, 290, 291, 292,
293–94; and Sandoval's proposal for new
order, 182; and Spanish women writers in
nineteenth century, 64
Fernández, Sebastián, 44
Fernández Guerra, Luis, 72
Figueroa, Virgilio, 155
"El final de la vida" (Mistral), 152
Fink, Agustín, 126
Finley, Karen, 215
Fiol-Matta, Licia, 126, 153, 156
"Flores negras" (Mistral), 150
Forster, Merlin, 114, 115, 119, 123, 125,
126, 131, 133, 135–36
Foster, David William, 12–13, 218–38
Foucault, Michel, 10, 15, 62, 67, 106–7,
258, 301
Franco, Francisco, 14
Franco, Jean, 148
Franco Calvo, Enrique, 126
Frankfurt School, 13
Freud, Sigmund, 15, 131, 241, 242–43, 249,
258, 301
Friedman, Susan, 98
friendships between women, 64, 68, 70–71,
82, 85, 86, 169. *See also* lesbian/
lesbianism
"La frontera" (Gaspar de Alba), 12,
195–96
Fusco, Coco, 200, 201

Galasso, Norberto, 223
Gamboa, Harry, Jr., 204
Gannan, Lorraine, 96, 97, 105, 106–7, 258

Garber, Marjorie, 44, 54, 56, 201
García, Cristina, 184
García-Moreno, Laura, 5
Gasalla, Antonio, 222
Gaslight (film), 13
Gaspar de Alba, Alicia, 6, 11–12, 182,
    188–96
—works of: "Bad Faith," 188, 191–92, 193,
    195; *Beggar on the Córdoba Bridge,* 11–
    12, 188–96; "Dark Morning Husband,"
    188–90, 191, 193; "La frontera," 12,
    195–96; "Gitanerías," 192–93, 195; "Giv-
    ing Back the World," 11–12, 194–96;
    "Leaving 'The Killing Fields,'" 190–91
Gastélum, Bernardo, 119
gaze: in Benedetti's works, 10, 106, 107,
    111; and camp, 262; in Cortázar's works,
    248; gay sexuality as, 258; in Gómez de
    Avellaneda's works, 84; and Hollywood
    films, 258–60; in Moix's works, 13–14; in
    Roig's works, 288
Geisdorfer Feal, Rosemary, 13, 239–53
Geltman, Pedro, 223
gender: in Benedetti's works, 104–5; in nine-
    teenth century, 67–68
"gender fuck," 250
Genet, Jean, 227
Genette, Gerard, 9, 97
Gide, André, 115, 119–20, 121–22, 130,
    133, 312
Gilbert, Sandra, 292
Gil de Biedma, Jaime, 270
"Gitanerías" (Gaspar de Alba), 192–93,
    195
"Giving Back the World" (Gaspar de
    Alba), 11–12, 194–96
Godoy, Emelina, 159
Godoy, Lucila. *See* Mistral, Gabriela
Goldar, Ernesto, 223
Gómez, Antonio, 33
Gómez, Marga: clothing in works of, 211–
    12, 213; distancing/marginalization, 211–
    12, 213, 214; and family life, 202–3; fa-
    thers in works of, 12, 200, 201, 212–15;
    femininity in works of, 211–12; humor in
    works of, 12, 202, 212, 215; identity in works
    of, 12, 211, 213–14; mother–daughter in
    works of, 211–12, 213, 214; in New York
    City, 212–13; and performance of Cuban
    men, 203; and performance theory,
    201–2, 215; in San Francisco, 213, 214;

    sexuality in works of, 211–12; and vio-
    lence, 213
—works of: *A Line around the Block,* 200,
    201, 202, 203, 210–15; *Marga Gómez Is
    Pretty, Witty and Gay,* 202–3, 211; *Mem-
    ory Tricks,* 201, 210–12, 213
Gómez de Avellaneda, Gertrudis: and avoid-
    ance of physical love, 64; dedications in
    works of, 75, 83; friendships in works of,
    64, 68, 70–71, 82, 85, 86; gaze in works
    of, 84; language in works of, 71, 75–78,
    80–81, 82; male reactions to, 72, 85; phys-
    ical landscape in works of, 78–79; Ro-
    mero Ortiz's relationship with, 64; and
    Sapphic tradition, 9, 66–86; and sexual
    identity, 9, 62–64, 65–66, 68–69, 72–74,
    82–85; silence in works of, 9, 77–78, 83,
    86; translation of male poets by, 70; and
    transvestism, 73, 74, 80; transvoicing in
    works of, 6–7, 83, 85, 86
—works of: *Cartas inéditas,* 63, 64; "Con-
    serva tu risa," 80, 83–85; "Despedida a la
    señora Da D G C de V," 75–80, 82–83;
    Dos mujeres, 63; "La mujer," 73–74; "Pro-
    testa de una 'individua' que solicitó serlo
    de la Academia Española y fué desai-
    rada," 72; "Soneto imitando una oda de
    Safo," 80, 81–83; *Tres amores,* 63; "El úl-
    timo acento de mi arpa," 80–81, 82; "Ver-
    sos que acompañaron a los anteriores
    cuando fueron enviados a la persona a
    quien están dedicados," 84–85
Gómez de Toledo, Gáspar, 44
Góngora, Mario, 149
González Vera, José Santos, 164–65
Gorfkle, Laura J., 28, 35
Gorostiza, Celestino, 121
Gorostiza, José, 121
Gorsz, Elizabeth, 240
Goytisolo, Juan, 6, 16
Greer, Margaret R., 31–32, 35
Griggers, Cathy, 188
Gubar, Susan, 292
Guevara, Che, 227, 231–32
Guevara, Nacha, 222
Guillén de Nicolau, Palma, 155, 160

Hall, Radclyffe, 167
Hall, Stuart, 186
Hammonds, Evelynn, 181, 182, 188
Harjo, Joy, 184

Hark, Ina Rae, 259
Harter, Hugh, 64, 69
Hasson, Liliane, 309
H. D. (poet), 167
Heidegger, Martin, 121–22, 130
Heise, Ursula K., 55
Hernández, Librada, 6–7, 9, 62–89
heterosexist panic, 172
Hirsch, Marianne, 283, 290–91
"Historia con migalas" (Cortázar), 243–47, 249
Hitchcock, Alfred, 97
Hocquenghem, Guy, 118
Hodges, Donald C., 218
Hollywood films: and Moix, 13, 14, 257–58, 260–66, 267; and queer gaze, 258–60; and utopia, 263
homosexuality: in Argentina, 233–34; in Cuba, 307–8; as death, 10; invention of term, 62; meanings of, 116
"homosexual panic," 10, 115–16, 119–20, 123, 126
honor: in Mistral's works, 156–60
Horan, Elizabeth Rosa, 11, 147–77, 245
L'hora violeta (Roig), 14, 275–94
The House on Mango Street (Cisneros), 182
Howard, Jane E., 55
Hughes, Langston, 120
humor, 202, 212, 215

identity: American, 206; Cuban, 204–17; cultural, 200–217; national, 5; racial, 12; transnational, 204–7. *See also* sexuality/sexual identity; *specific writer or work*
ideology: in Benedetti's works, 105–6, 108, 111
Iglesias, Augusto, 166
"La instrucción de la mujer" (Mistral), 152
intergenerational relationships, 281–82. *See also* mother–daughter/child relationship
internationalism, 161, 163, 204–7
"Intima" (Mistral), 165
Irwin, Robert McKee, 10–11, 15, 114–46

Jacobus, Mary, 277
Jagose, Annamarie, 188, 194, 196
Jiménez Rueda, Julio, 117
Los Juegos Florales (contest), 172
El juez de su causa (Zayas), 24

Kaminsky, Amy, 35, 66, 73, 74
Katra, William H., 226, 233
King, John, 226
Kirkpatrick, Gwen, 114
Kirkpatrick, Susan, 67, 68, 69, 70, 73, 74, 79
kiss: in Gómez de Avellaneda's works, 9, 75–78; Judas, 170; in Mistral's works, 170
Koch, Dolores, 303
Krafft-Ebing, Richard, 68
Kristeva, Julia, 277, 282–83

Labarca, Eugenio, 163, 164
Lacan, Jacques, 15, 258, 259, 308
Lagar (Mistral), 167
language: in Benedetti's works, 99, 108, 110; in Cortázar's works, 243, 246; in Gómez's works, 203–4; in Gómez de Avellaneda's works, 71, 75–78, 80–81, 82; in Mistral's works, 148, 165, 166, 168–69, 170, 171–72; in Villaurrutia's poetry, 136
Latina wiggle, 183
Lauretis, Teresa de, 63, 245, 277
Lavrin, Asunción, 34
Lazo, Agustín, 126
Leal, Luis, 117
"Leaving 'The Killing Fields'" (Gaspar de Alba), 190–91
lectora macho, 13, 242–49
lector cómplice, 242
lector/lectora hembra, 241–42, 243, 249
Left: and Perón, 225–34
legal system: and lesbianism in early modern Spain, 33
lesbian/lesbianism: aggressiveness of, 193; -as-exit model, 192; black, 182; cultural image of "butch," 185–86; definitions of, 168; difficulty in characterizing, 188; early appearance of term, 7; in early modern Spain, 21–36; and feminism, 277; as misunderstood outsiders, 167; as monsters, 69; and political oppression, 99; and silence, 99; as "silent sin," 7, 23. *See also specific person or literary work*
"lesbian panic," 276
Lessing, Doris, 286, 292
Lezama Lima, José, 312
A Line around the Block (Gómez), 200, 201, 202, 203, 210–15
literary criticism: as closet, 116; Latin

American, 116; sexual identity as aim of lesbian/gay, 4. *See also* male critics/writers
literature: as instrument of survival, 14
Lloyd Webber, Andrew, 222, 227
"Locas mujeres" series (Mistral), 167
Loose Woman (Cisneros), 11–12, 182, 184–86, 196
López, Gregorio, 22, 23
Los Angeles, California: Villaurrutia's views about, 123
love–hate relationship, 307
Lucey, Michael, 115, 130

machismo, 307, 311
machista: in Arenas's works, 301, 303, 307, 311
madness, 67, 75
Magallanes Moure, Manuel, 158, 170
male critics/writers: and Cisneros's works, 186; and Gómez de Avellaneda's works, 72, 85; and Mistral's work, 154–56; and Sapphic tradition, 68, 72–73, 75; and women writers as threats, 68, 73
Mal presagio casarse lejos (Zayas), 31–36
mambo craze, 205
Maples Arce, Manuel, 118–19
Marga Gómez Is Pretty, Witty and Gay (Gómez), 202–3, 211
Margarita (woman soldier), 46
marginalization. *See* distancing/marginalization
María de Jesús, 34
Mark, Rebecca, 110
Marks, Elaine, 181
marriage: Mistral's views about, 148
Martin, Biddy, 240
Martínez, Elena M., 148
Martínez, José Luis, 121
Martínez, María Isabel (Isabelita), 223
Martín-Rodríguez, Manuel, 125, 134
masculine/feminine binary, 5, 6, 11
masculinity: natural, 259
Masiello, Francine, 163
Massey, Kenneth, 125, 130
masturbation, 33
maternal imaginary: in Roig's works, 275–94. *See also* mother–daughter/child relationship; mothers/motherhood
Mayne, Judith, 260

Mayoral, Marina, 70–71, 74
McCormick, Ian, 23, 33
McKendrick, Melveena, 27
Meese, Elizabeth, 188, 282
Meléndez, Claudia, 183
Memory Tricks (Gómez), 201, 210–12, 213
men: acting performances of Cuban, 203
Menéndez Pelayo, Marcelino, 69–70
El Mercurio de Antofagasta (newspaper), 149
Mexico: feminization of literature in, 117; literature of revolution in, 117; meaning of homosexuality in, 116; virility debates of 1920s in, 117–18. *See also* Villaurrutia, Xavier
Meyer, Moe, 262
Michelet, Jules, 284
Milk of Amnesia (Tropicana), 200–201, 203, 204–8, 210
Miller, D. A., 97
Miller, Francesca, 233
Miller, Nancy K., 291
Millett, Kate, 99
Miranda, Carmen, 187
miscegenation, 5
El mismo mar de todos los veranos (Roig), 14
Mistral, Frederic, 153
Mistral, Gabriela: and "Abel Madac" attack, 150–52; aesthetics of, 170, 171; alternative identities of, 147–77; *ambiente* in, 11, 154, 159–60; and body, 11, 167–69; as celebrity, 172; death in works of, 161–62; distancing of, 167, 170, 171; as "la Divina Gabriela," 154; early works of, 148–53, 158–59, 172; eroticism of, 171–72; and homosexual panic, 126; honor in works of, 156–60; as innocent country girl betrayed by young man, 154–56; language of, 148, 165, 166, 168–69, 170, 171–72; letters of, 156–58, 160, 163–64; and mothers/motherhood, 11, 155–56, 168–69, 170, 171, 172; national mythology about, 153; and outsiders, 169–71; passion of, 156–60; and postsexuality, 171, 172; private life of, 153–54; as pseudonym, 152–53; reception of works of, 153, 156; as school teacher, 159–60, 245; self-censorship of, 171; sexual identity in works of, 167, 168, 170; sexuality

Mistral, Gabriela (*continued*)
  as hidden and obvious of, 11, 126; and si-
    lence, 156, 172; and smoking vibrator
    hunt, 154–55; and theosophy, 11, 160,
    161–66, 167–68, 170; utopianism of,
    167–69; and Videla Pineda's letters,
    156–58; violence in works of, 167, 168,
    169, 172; woundedness of, 166–67, 171
  —works of: "La abandonada," 167; "Amor
    imposible," 149; "El arte" series, 166–67,
    170; "Bohemio," 149–50; "Cántaros de
    greda," 170; "Cuentos: Oyendo los de
    kindergarten," 160; "La desasida," 167;
    Desolación, 154, 162, 165, 166, 167–68,
    169, 172–73; "Ecos," 149; "Electra en la
    niebla," 169; *En batalla,* 163, 164; "Ex-
    tasis," 165; "El final de la vida," 152;
    "Flores negras," 150; "La instrucción de
    la mujer," 152; "Intima," 165; *Lagar,* 167;
    "Locas mujeres" series, 167; "Motivos
    del barro," 169–71; "Poemas del hogar,"
    170; "Poesías de la Madre más triste,"
    156; "Poesías de las madres," 167–68,
    170; "Que no sé del amor," 172–73; "Re-
    cuerdo de la madre ausente," 168–69;
    "El rival," 161–62, 163; "Sonetos de la
    muerte," 162, 172–73; "El suplicio," 165;
    "Voces," 150
modernism, 11, 15, 148, 166, 167, 308–9, 312
Moix, Terenci: childhood of, 266; gaze in
  works of, 13–14; influence of Hollywood
  films on, 13, 14, 257–58, 260–66, 267;
  and popular culture, 13–14, 257–58
  —works of: *El beso de Peter Pan,* 13–14,
    257, 260–70; *El cine de los sábados,* 257,
    260–61
Molloy, Sylvia, 10, 115–16, 119, 136, 169
La monja alferez (Pérez de Montalbán), 23,
  24, 47
Monsiváis, Carlos, 119
Montemayor, Jorge de, 23
Montesa Peydro, Salvador, 24
Montevideanos (Benedetti), 93
Montoneros (radical movement), 225
Moraga, Cherríe, 6, 186–87
Moreiras, Alberto, 306
Moretta, Eugene, 119, 130
"motherbook," 291
mother–daughter/child relationship: and
  body, 279, 281–82, 283; and *chora* theory,
  282–83; and feminist memoirs, 291–92;

in Gómez's works, 211–12, 213, 214; in
  Riera's works, 281–82; in Roig's works,
  277–79, 283, 288, 292–93; in Tusquets's
  works, 281–82
mothers/motherhood: body of, 167–69, 279,
  281–82; and Mistral, 11, 155–56, 168–69,
  170, 171, 172
"Motivos del barro" (Mistral), 169–71
Mozart, Wolfgang Amadeus, 292
La muerte y otras sorpresas (Benedetti), 93–
  94. *See also* "Para objetos solamente"
  (Benedetti)
"La mujer" (Gómez de Avellaneda), 73–74
Mulvey, Laura, 258
Muñón, Sancho de, 44
Muñoz, José, 206, 208
Murray, Jacqueline, 33
music, 192–93, 205, 207–8
My Wicked Wicked Ways (Cisneros), 182,
  184

Naipaul, V. S., 219
narcissism, 133
Neoplatonism, 24–25
Nervo, Amado, 164, 170
newspapers: Mistral's work on, 148–49, 156
New York City: Gómez in, 212–13; Villau-
  rrutia's views about, 123
"Nocturno" (Villaurrutia), 128–30, 131
"Nocturno amor" (Villaurrutia), 126
"Nocturno de la alcoba" (Villaurrutia), 133
"Nocturno de la estatua" (Villaurrutia), 11,
  126, 131–34
"Nocturno de los ángeles" (Villaurrutia),
  123–24, 126, 133
"Nocturno en que nada se oye" (Villau-
  rrutia), 133
"Nocturno eterno" (Villaurrutia), 134–36
"Nocturno mar" (Villaurrutia), 114, 126
Nómez, Nain, 152
Norma (Bellini opera), 283–84
Nostalgia de la muerte (Villaurrutia), 115,
  128, 131–34, 136
Novelas amorosas y ejemplares (Zayas), 21,
  29–31
Novo, Salvador, 118, 119, 120–21, 124, 125,
  126, 130
nuns, 33–34

Ocampo, Victoria, 225–26
Ochoa, Marcia, 187

Olea, Raquel, 156

L'òpera quotidiana (Roig), 283–84

oppression/repression: in Arenas's works, 305, 307; in Benedetti's works, 10, 93, 94, 95, 98, 108, 111–12; closet as force of, 116; and consent of oppressed, 100; cultural, 98; political, 93, 94, 99, 111–12, 118, 121; and silence, 93–94, 95, 98, 99, 100, 108, 111–12; social, 95, 98, 108, 111–12; victims of, 95; of women, 6–7

Ordóñez, Elizabeth J., 35

Ortega, [Gregorio], 120

Otero, C., 121

otherness, 96, 98–99, 156, 169–71

outsiders, 167, 169–71. *See also* distancing/ marginalization

Owen, Gilberto, 119

Owens, Craig, 183

Pagán, Irma, 213–14

painters: and Villaurrutia, 118

panopticon, 106–7, 112

"Para objetos solamente" (Benedetti), 9–10; closet/"coming out" in, 10, 110–11; clothing in, 10, 103–5; Fernando's dead body in, 95, 96, 97, 98–99, 107; gaze in, 10, 106, 107, 111; gender in, 104–5; ideology in, 105–6, 108, 111; inventory in, 95–97, 98, 100–101, 103, 109, 111; language in, 99, 108, 110; letter in, 101–3; narrator in, 95–97, 107; reader in, 10, 107–8, 109–10; silence in, 9–10, 93–113; suicide in, 10, 107–8, 111

Park, Katharine, 55

La pasión según Evita (Posse), 222–24

passion: in Mistral's works, 156–60

patriarchy: and Cisneros's works, 185, 186; in Fusco's work, 201; in Gaspar de Alba's works, 193; and lesbianism in early modern Spain, 23, 35–36; in Mistral's works, 11, 168; and Perón, 224–25; in Roig's works, 14; and Sapphic tradition, 67; in Lope de Vega's works, 7–8, 9; and Villaurrutia, 116; and women in love, 181–82; and women as victims, 107; in Zayas's works, 7

Paz, Octavio, 114, 115, 118, 119, 120–21, 125, 131, 137, 186

Pellicer, Carlos, 123

Pelly, Laurent, 224

Pérez, Kathy A., 202, 203, 211, 214

Pérez de Montalbán, Juan, 23, 47

Pérez Firmat, Gustavo, 205

Pérez Prado, Dámaso, 205

performance theories, 201–2, 215

Perlongher, Néstor, 219

Perón, Evita: body of, 219, 220–21; books/ poems about, 219–34; Copi play about, 13, 219, 224–25; death of, 222; dress of, 220, 221; and femininity, 221; and feminism, 218, 220, 221–22, 226, 233; as gay symbol, 12–13, 218–19, 221, 233–34; and Left, 225–34; as martyr, 224; mythicization of, 224; as name, 229–30; as operatic heroine, 13, 227–28, 230–31, 233, 234; and patriarchy, 224–25; and popular culture, 233–34; Posse novel about, 222–24, 229; and power, 220, 221, 222, 224, 229, 231; as revolutionary figure, 12–13, 226–27; as saint or whore, 220; Sebreli's works about, 12–13, 225–34; and sexual identity, 220–21; as social liberation symbol, 218; as survivor, 224

Peronismo, 223–24, 225–26, 228–29, 230–34

Perry, Mary Elizabeth, 47, 48

Peter Pan: myth of, 13, 14, 282. *See also El beso de Peter Pan* (Moix)

Picón Garfield, Evelyn, 63, 64, 68, 69–70, 73, 80, 250

The Picture of Dorian Gray (film), 106

Piedra, José, 6

pimping: in *El rufián Castrucho* (Lope de Vega), 43–60

Piñera, Virgilio, 15, 308–9

Pinti, Enrique, 222

Pizarro, Ana Mistral, 148

Poe, Edgar Allen, 161, 170

"Poemas del hogar" (Mistral), 170

"Poesía" (Villaurrutia), 122–23

"Poesías de la Madre más triste" (Mistral), 156

"Poesías de las madres" (Mistral), 167–68, 170

politics: in Arenas's works, 299–315; in Benedetti's works, 93, 94; and lesbianism, 99; and Perón, 13; of sexuality, 277; and silence, 93, 94, 99, 111–12; split between rhetoric and, 5–6; and Villaurrutia, 118, 121

Ponç, Joan, 285

popular culture: and Moix, 13–14, 257–58; and Perón, 233–34

pornography, 240
Posse, Abel, 218, 222–24, 229
postmemory, 290–91
postmodernism, 5, 181, 195, 309, 311, 312
postsexuality: and Mistral, 171, 172
poststructuralism: and Villaurrutia's work, 122, 137
power/authority: and Arenas's works, 15, 299–315; in Cisneros's works, 184–85, in Cortázar's works, 249–50; and feminine/masculine binary, 6; and Gaspar de Alba, 6; *machista,* 307; and Perón, 220, 221, 222, 224, 229, 231; in Spain, 6; surrender of, 6
Prado, Pedro, 164, 170
Prado, Valeria Maino, 163
Pratt, Mary Louise, 153
pregnancy, 169
Prieto, Adolfo, 228
prosopopeia, 15, 305–6, 312–13
prostitution: in *La Celestina* (Rojas), 43; and cross-dressing, 43; Mistral's views about, 148; in Lope de Vega's works, 9, 43–68
"Protesta de una 'individua' que solicitó serlo de la Academia Española y fué desairada" (Gómez de Avellaneda), 72
Proust, Marcel, 120
Puerto Rican Traveling Theater Company, 206
Puig, Manuel, 6, 14, 258

queers: "good" and "bad," 240
"Que no sé del amor" (Mistral), 172–73

race/ethnicity: and Cisneros's works, 184; in Gómez's work, 12, 212; and sexual difference in Latino and Hispanic writing, 6; in Tropicana's works, 12, 206; in U.S. culture, 206
Ramona adéu (Roig), 278
Rayor, Diane, 75, 77
Rayuela (Cortázar), 239, 242
readers: aggressiveness toward, 307; and Arenas's works, 307; and Benedetti's works, 10, 107–8, 109–10; and Cortázar's works, 13, 241–42, 249; and Villaurrutia's works, 10
Real Academia, Spanish, 69, 72
Rebolledo, Tey Diana, 183, 184

Rechy, John, 125
"Recuerdo de la madre ausente" (Mistral), 168–69
Los relatos (Cortázar), 241–47
religion: and lesbianism in early modern Spain, 33
repression. *See* oppression/repression
"Reunión con un círculo rojo" (Cortázar), 249
Reynolds, Juli, 209
Rice, Tim, 222, 227
Rich, Adrienne, 63, 168
Richard, Nelly, 5
Richardson, Colin, 94
Riera, Carme, 281–82
Rimbaud, Arthur, 247–48
"El río" (Cortázar), 239
"El rival" (Mistral), 161–62, 163
Rodig, Laura, 153, 160, 167
Rodoreda, Mercé, 292
Rodríguez Lozano, Manuel, 126
Roig, Montserrat: body in works of, 279, 283, 286; distancing/marginalization in works of, 14; and feminism, 277–78, 284, 290, 291, 292, 293–94; and mother–daughter relationship, 277–79, 283, 288, 292–93; and patriarchy, 14; and Peter Pan myth, 14; women writers testimonial of, 292
—works of: *Els catalans als camps nazis,* 291; *L'hora violeta,* 14, 275–98; *El mismo mar de todos los veranos,* 14; *L'òpera quotidiana,* 283–84; *Ramona adéu,* 278; *El temps de les cireres,* 275, 278, 283, 287–88; *La veu melodiosa,* 283
Rojas, Fernando de. *See La Celestina* (Rojas)
Rojas, Marcial, 120
Rokha, Winnet de (pseud), 152
Román, David, 203, 204
Romanticism, 64, 66, 67, 74–75, 167, 311
Romera Navarro, M., 55
Romero Ortiz, Antonio, 64
Rope (film), 97
Rose, Jacqueline, 262, 270
Rose, Mary Beth, 55
Rubin, Gayle, 240
Rubio, Patricia, 154
Ruffinelli, Jorge, 117
El rufián Castrucho (Lope de Vega), 7–8, 9, 43–60

rural/urban opposition: in Arenas's works, 301–5

sadomasochism: in Cortázar's works, 13, 239, 240, 241, 242, 249–50; in Roig's works, 275
Salá, Coco, 310
Sand, Georges, 63, 67, 86
Sandoval, Chela, 182
Sandoval-Sánchez, Alberto, 169
San Francisco, California: Gómez in, 213, 214; Villaurrutia's views about, 123
San Luis, Conde de, 72
Santa Cruz, Lucía, 149
Santa Teresa, 66
Santiago, Silviano, 212
Sapphic tradition: and Gómez de Avellaneda, 9, 66–86; and male critics/writers, 68, 72–73, 75; and ridiculing of women writers, 72–73; and Romanticism, 74–75; and sexual identity, 62–69, 72–74, 82–85
Sappho: suicide of, 9, 78
Sarduy, Severo, 16, 312
Sartre, Jean-Paul, 13, 226, 227, 232, 233, 234
Schechner, Richard, 201
Schneider, Luis Mario, 122
school teachers, 159–60, 245, 281–82
Schwartz, Jorge, 117
Sebreli, Juan José, 12–13, 225–34
Sedgwick, Eve Kosofsky, 10, 62, 110–11, 116, 137
self-destruction: and silence, 112. *See also* suicide
"La señorita Cora" (Cortázar), 250
separatism: and lesbianism in early modern Spain, 34–36
The Seventh Seal (film), 270
sexuality/sexual identity: and aim of lesbian/gay criticism, 4; in Arenas's works, 300, 302, 304, 305, 307–8; and assimilation, 211; Chicana, 11–12; and Cisneros's works, 184–85, 186–87, 196; and coming out, 4; and Cortázar's works, 239–53; as gaze, 258; in Gómez's works, 211–12, 213–14; and Gómez de Avellaneda, 9, 62–64, 65–66, 68–69, 72–74, 82–85; in Mistral's works, 11, 167, 168, 170; and Perón, 220–21; politicization of, 277; and Sapphic tradition, 62–69, 72–74, 82–85; and Spanish women writers in nineteenth

century, 64, 72–74; in Villaurrutia's works, 10–11
sexual relations: in Arenas's works, 307–8; in Gaspar de Alba's works, 191; Gómez de Avellaneda's avoidance of, 64; Latino male, 6
Shakespeare, William, 55, 200
Sheridan, Guillermo, 115, 117, 118, 119, 126, 131, 135
Shohat, Ella, 210
silence: in Benedetti's works, 9–10, 93–113; and Cisneros's works, 196; and connotation, 97; as externally imposed, 106; in Gómez de Avellaneda's works, 9, 77–78, 83, 86; and lesbianism, 99; in Mistral's works, 156, 172; and oppression/repression, 93–94, 95, 98, 99, 100, 108, 111–12; and otherness, 96, 98–99; suicide as, 107–8, 111; of Villaurrutia, 11, 136, 137; of women in 1920s, 152
"silent sin," 7, 23
Silverman, Kaja, 282–83
Simons, Patricia, 27
sin, 7, 9, 23, 33, 52
Smith, Patricia Juliana, 276, 284, 286
Smith, Paul Julian, 260–61
smoking vibrator hunt, 154–55
social change: and Mistral, 149, 152
sodomites: in *El rufián Castrucho* (Lope de Vega), 43–60
Sommer, Doris, 243
"Soneto imitando una oda de Safo" (Gómez de Avellaneda), 80, 81–83
"Sonetos de la muerte" (Mistral), 162, 172–73
Soto Ayala, Luis, 158–59
Spain: national identity in, 5; nineteenth-century lesbianism in, 6, 21–36; power in, 6; sexuality and ethnicity in, 6
Spanish Inquisition, 8–9
Staël, Anne Louise Germaine Necker (Madame de), 63, 67, 86
Stam, Robert, 210
Stigers, Eva Stehle, 71, 89
Stimpson, Catherine, 168
Straub, Kristina, 50
suicide: and Arenas, 299, 305, 310; in Benedetti's works, 10, 107–8, 111; in Roig's works, 283; of Sappho, 9, 78; as silence, 107–8, 111; of Villaurrutia, 118
Suleiman, Susan, 291

"El suplicio" (Mistral), 165
Sur (intellectual review), 225–26
Susskind, David, 203
symbolism: and Mistral, 148
symbolist poets, 167
syphilis, 48–49

Tagore, Rabindranath, 170
Taylor, Julie, 220, 223
Tellado, Corín, 158
The Tempest (Shakespeare), 200
El temps de les cireres (Roig), 275, 278, 283, 287–88
Teresa de Jesús, 34
theology, 8–9
theosophy: and Mistral, 11, 148, 160, 161–66, 167–68, 170; and women as brothers, 162–66
Third Woman (Cisneros), 186–87
Third Woman Presses, 182
"30–30" group of painters, 118
Tisnado, Carmen, 9–10, 93–113
Tittler, Jonathan, 242
Tootsie (film), 29
Torres Bodet, Jaime, 118
transvestism: and Gómez de Avellaneda's works, 73, 74, 80; and lesbianism in early modern Spain, 23, 34; male, 275; as male in usage, 201; in Roig's works, 275; in *El rufián Castrucho* (Lope de Vega), 43–60; in Zayas's works, 7
transvoicing: in Gómez de Avellaneda's works, 6–7, 83, 85, 86
Tres amores (Gómez de Avellaneda), 63
tribades: in nineteenth-century Spain, 67; in *El rufián Castrucho* (Lope de Vega), 43–60
Tropicana, Carmelita: *Carmelita Tropicana: Your* Kunst *Is Your* Waffen (film), 12, 200–201, 202, 208–10, 215; creation of persona of, 203; and fathers, 12, 200–201; humor in works of, 202, 215; identity in works of, 12, 200–201, 202, 204–6, 208–10, 215; *Milk of Amnesia,* 200–201, 203, 204–8; music in works of, 205, 207–8; and performance of Cuban men, 203; and performance theory, 201–2, 215; racism in works of, 206
Troyano, Alina. *See* Tropicana, Carmelita
Troyano, Ela, 201, 209–10

truth: and Arenas's works, 5, 312
Turner, Victor, 201
Tusquets, Esther, 14, 281–82
Twelfth Night (Shakespeare), 55

"El último acento de mi arpa" (Gómez de Avellaneda), 80–81, 82
Uno, Roberta, 202, 203, 211, 214
Ureña, Pedro Henríquez, 118
Uruguay, 93, 94
utopianism: in Arenas's works, 15, 301; in Gaspar de Alba's works, 193–94, 196; and Hollywood films, 263; and lesbianism in early modern Spain, 35; in Mistral's works, 167–69; in Zayas's works, 7

Valdés Pereira, Fidelia, 159, 160
Valera, Juan, 82, 86
Valis, Noel, 73
van de Pol, Lotte C., 23, 46, 47, 48
Vargas, Chabela, 209
Vargas Vila, José María, 158
Vasconcelos, José, 118, 119
Vega, Lope de. See *El rufián Castrucho* (Lope de Vega)
Velasco, Sherry, 7, 9, 21–36
Vélez Quiñones, Harry, 7–8, 43–61
venereal disease, 48–49
"Versos que acompañaron a los anteriores cuando fueron enviados a la persona a quien están dedicados" (Gómez de Avellaneda), 84–85
La veu melodiosa (Roig), 283
"El viaje sin retorno" (Villaurrutia), 126–27
Vicinus, Martha, 63, 67
victims: in Benedetti's works, 10, 107; in Cortázar's works, 249–50; of oppression, 95; women as, 107
Videla Pineda, Alfredo, 156–58
Villalón, Cristóbal de, 23
Villaurrutia, Xavier: body in works of, 10, 122; and "coming out," 10, 119–20, 121, 137; dedications of, 126; drawings of, 122; and fragmentary body parts, 122; and homosexual panic, 115–16, 119–20, 123; language in poetry of, 136; and painters, 118; and politics, 118, 121; public and private split in, 121–22; and reader, 10; and sexuality/sexual identity,

10–11; silence of, 11, 136, 137; suicide of, 118
—works of: "Calles," 133; *Dama de corazones,* 122; "Décimas de nuestro amor," 136–37; "Nocturno," 128–30, 131; "Nocturno amor," 126; "Nocturno de la alcoba," 133; "Nocturno de la estatua," 11, 126, 131–34; "Nocturno de los ángeles," 123–24, 126, 133; "Nocturno en que nada se oye," 133; "Nocturno eterno," 134–36; "Nocturno mar," 114, 126; *Nostalgia de la muerte,* 115, 128, 131–34, 136; "Poesía," 122–23; "El viaje sin retorno," 126–27
Violante del Cielo, Sor, 23
violence: and Gómez, 213; in Mistral's works, 167, 168, 169, 172
virility debates (Mexico, 1920s), 117–18
"Voces" (Mistral), 150
"Voyelles" (Rimbaud), 247–48
La Voz de Elqui (newspaper), 148–52

Warner, Michael, 4
Waste Land (Eliot), 284
Welles, Marcia L., 35
West, Cornel, 186
Wetsel, David, 224
Whitman, Walt, 120
Wilde, Oscar, 120, 312
Winkler, Jack, 78, 79
"With Lorenzo at the Center of the Universe, el Zócalo, Mexico City" (Cisneros), 196
Wittig, Monique, 11, 188
Woman Hollering Creek (Cisneros), 182
women: as asexual, 68; as brothers among fraternal theosophists, 162–66; communities of only, 33–34; madness of, 67, 75; oppression of, 6–7; as victims, 107. *See also* friendships between women; lesbian/lesbianism; women in love; women writers; *specific person*

women in love: in Cisneros's works, 182–88; in Gaspar de Alba's works, 188–96
Women Singing in the Snow (Cisneros), 183–84
women writers: Chicana, 6, 11–12; defeminization of, 72–73; male reactions to, 68, 72–74; Mistral's defense of, 150–52; in nineteenth-century Spain, 64, 68, 72–74; pseudonyms of, 152–53; ridiculing of, 72–73; Roig's views about, 292. *See also specific person*
Wood, Elizabeth, 284
Woolf, Virginia, 226, 292
woundedness: in Mistral's works, 166–67, 171
writers: Semiticized, 5; in Spain, 6. *See also* male critics/writers; women writers; *specific writer*
writing: writing about process of, 309
Wyers, Frances, 14, 258

Yamamoto, Hisaye, 97–98
Yarbro-Bejarano, Yvonne, 12, 187, 200–217
Yingling, Thomas, 15
Yllera, Alicia, 24
"You Bring Out the Mexican in Me" (Cisneros), 184–85, 187

Zamora, Leocadia de, 80
Zayas, María de, 7, 21–36
—works of: *Amar sólo por vencer,* 7, 21, 24–29, 30, 31, 32, 35; *La burlada Aminta y venganza del honor,* 7, 21, 29–31, 32, 35; *Desengaños amorosos,* 7, 21, 24, 25, 26, 27, 28, 29, 32, 34, 35–36; *El juez de su causa,* 24; *Mal presagio casarse lejos,* 31–36; *Novelas amorosas y ejemplares,* 21, 29–31
Zimmerman, Bonnie, 63, 188, 192